Life with Lloyd George

SYLVESTER, Albert James. Life with Lloyd George; the diary of A. J. Sylvester, 1931–45, ed. by Colin Cross. Barnes & Noble, a div. of Harper & Row, 1975. 351p il 74-26182. 23.50 ISBN 0-06-496251-2

CHOICE   DEC. '75

History. Geography & Travel

Europe

Sylvester was a special sort of companion-valet-counselor, and a paid whipping boy who knew Lloyd George (nearly always referred to as LG) for 30 years and was his principal private secretary for 22. From 1931 to 1945, when LG died at the age of 82, Sylvester kept a secret shorthand diary running to well over one million words from which this book, about one-tenth the length, is culled, splendidly introduced, annotated, and indexed by the British author-journalist Colin Cross. The cumulative result is a vivid portrait of LG and an important source for political, social, and family life in the turbulent '30s. Sylvester, certainly not without admiration and loyalty for the George family, can be ruthlessly candid and acidic. He scores LG's dirty eating habits, his obsession with sex as long as he lived, the hypocritical and self-serving piety and lack of genuine moral principle, the sadistic, often cruel, treatment of his long-suffering wife. Sylvester admired the personal magnetism and perspicuity of the Prime Minister (he was no ordinary man and cannot be wholly judged by the usual standards). He also shows how flawed LG's judgment was about Hitler (a genius, LG believed)

and other dictators and how deeply defeatist he was about the chances of British victory well into the war. The book teems with anecdotage and Sylvester caught most of it. Cross is a wonderful collaborator and we owe them both our thanks for a most successful effort. For graduate, upper-class, and selective general readership.

Europe

Life with Lloyd George

The Diary of A. J. Sylvester

1931–45

Edited by

Colin Cross

BARNES & NOBLE

BOOKS

10 East 53d St., New York 10022

(a division of Harper & Row Publishers, Inc.)

Text © A. J. Sylvester 1975
Introduction and editorial matter © Colin Cross
1975

ISBN: 0–06–496251–2

LC: 74–26182

Published in the U.S.A. 1975 by
HARPER & ROW PUBLISHERS, INC.
BARNES & NOBLE IMPORT DIVISION

Printed in Great Britain

Dedicated by A. J. Sylvester
to the memory of
his parents
and to his sisters
Eva and May

Contents

List of Illustrations

Between pages 160 and 161

Acknowledgements are due to the following for permission to reproduce illustrations: Associated Newspapers, 2, 8a, 8b; F. Biondo, Antibes, 6a; Central Press, 6b; J. Feneyrol, Cannes, 7b; Hoffmann Archiv, 5a; Kurt Huhle, 5b; London News Agency, 1a; Photopress, 7a; A. J. Sylvester, 3b; *Yorkshire Observer*, 4a

Introduction

A. J. SYLVESTER has had a remarkable life. He was born in 1889 into a Staffordshire tenant farming family. In the agricultural depression of the time his father lost his independence and became a brewery farm worker at Burton-on-Trent. However, through visits to his grandparents' farms Sylvester grew up close to agriculture, to which it was long his ambition one day to return. The family's means were narrow, but the best possible was done for him, including the provision of the small fees required for his attending secondary school where one of the subjects he studied was Pitman's shorthand. He left school at fourteen to become a clerk at Charrington's brewery at a starting salary of six shillings a week. For the remainder of his teens he gave up most of his leisure to perfect his shorthand and typing, working often by oil-lamp and much aided by his sisters. He attained champion speeds of 210 words a minute in shorthand and 80 in typing, and also qualified as a teacher of these subjects. At the age of twenty he left his parents' home in Burton to seek his fortune in London, where he did a variety of jobs including the official record of House of Lords debates. In 1910 and 1911 he was a member of the British international 'speedwriting' (fast typewriting) team which competed at the Business Efficiency Exhibition at Olympia and came second to the Americans. In 1912–13 he went to India and Burma as assistant reporter for the Royal Commission on the Public Services. On his return he set up as a freelance shorthand-writer in Chancery Lane and soon acquired clients. Had there been no First World War, he would doubtless have built up a substantial business in this field.

When Britain declared war in August 1914, Sylvester was asked to do some temporary work for the Admiralty, at a salary of three gold sovereigns a week. From there, owing to another having been taken ill, he moved, as a stenographer, to the office of Colonel M. P. A. (later Lord) Hankey, and this was the start of his real career. Hankey was Secretary to the Committee of Imperial Defence and so at the heart of the conduct of the war. In 1915 Sylvester was the first shorthand writer ever to take a note of a cabinet committee. In 1916 Lloyd George became Prime Minister and one of his first acts was to make the Committee of Imperial Defence secretariat also the War Cabinet secretariat. (Previously the Cabinet had had no secretariat at all.) The champion note-taker Sylvester was promoted to be Hankey's private secretary. (He had attested for military service but was not called up on account of his job.) At the end of the war he became an established higher-grade civil servant with the status of those who had entered as university graduates after competitive examination. Lloyd George, of course, had come to know him well and to rely upon him. In 1918 Sylvester became O.B.E. and in 1920 C.B.E. In 1921 he left Hankey to become a private secretary to Lloyd George at 10 Downing Street. On Lloyd George's fall in 1922, Sylvester remained at 10 Downing Street as a private secretary to Lloyd George's Tory successors Bonar Law and Baldwin: he was the only member of Lloyd George's entourage to do so. However, he had an unorthodox background for a higher civil servant, and with the return of peacetime conditions and with the conventional 'Oxbridge' Whitehall establishment resuming its authority he began to feel to some extent out of place. Therefore in 1923 he accepted an invitation to rejoin Lloyd George, now in opposition, as his principal private secretary. (He stipulated for the word 'principal' owing to the existence of Miss Frances Stevenson, who was Lloyd George's mistress as well as a private secretary.) Lloyd George paid him a lump sum of £4500 to compensate him for the loss of his civil-service pension rights and a salary of £1000 a year, which was a considerable sum for the time. It was increased to £1500 in 1926 and reduced by ten per cent in the 1931 economic crisis. For the purposes of comparison it can be noted that in 1923 a civil servant of the grade of assistant secretary was on a salary scale of £1000–£1200 a year: the salary for the same grade in 1974 was £5550–£7476.

Sylvester's main function was to run Lloyd George's private office in London, which at its peak had a staff of over twenty, including research staff, shorthand typists and messengers. Lloyd George had the biggest postbag of any politician in Britain, and Sylvester dealt with most of it on his own initiative. He had other functions too. He was Lloyd George's press officer. He carried out most of Lloyd George's duties as a constituency M.P. in dealing with individual cases. When Lloyd George travelled to a public function, Sylvester usually accompanied him to see to the practical arrangements. As the years passed, Lloyd George became irregular in his attendance at the House of Commons; but Sylvester was there on his behalf, with his own seat in the officials' box under the gallery. At times of political and diplomatic crisis, he furnished Lloyd George with detailed reports of what was going on; these, now filed with Lloyd George's papers, are proving to be a significant source for scholars of the period. Sylvester did all the research in the Whitehall archives for Lloyd George's *War Memoirs* and interviewed former ministers.

With his fluent shorthand, Sylvester was a compulsive note-taker. From early in his career he wrote notes on the events in which he was concerned and at various periods he kept a diary. The bulk of what he recorded is now well known to historians, although there are a few lacunae which his papers may help to fill when they are open to researchers. (In particular, he has recorded his participation in the events which led to the appointment of Baldwin rather than Curzon as Prime Minister in 1923 and he kept a continuous diary in 1924, the year of the first Labour government.) For long, however, his diary-keeping was spasmodic. Then it was impressed upon him by the newspaper proprietor Lord Riddell and others that he should make continuous notes of everything Lloyd George did or said. The reasoning was that Lloyd George was such an extraordinary human being that everything about him was of interest. From 1931 until Lloyd George's death in 1945, therefore, Sylvester did keep a more or less continuous diary, and the result is the basis of this book.

He wrote up his diary, in shorthand, usually last thing at night before retiring. He used shorthand partly for speed and also to provide a degree of security. (His shorthand outlines are so beautifully formed that any Pitman expert could decipher them, but at least the diary was not legible to anyone who happened to pick it up.) All substantial passages in direct quotes were taken down in shorthand while the words were actually being spoken. It was (and is) automatic with Sylvester that whenever he conducts a telephone conversation he takes a shorthand note of it. Sometimes, too, when Lloyd George and others were talking at table, Sylvester was able to take an unobtrusive note. Unconsciously, he reveals in his diary some of his own attributes as a prince among private secretaries – his careful noting of who was present on any occasion, his care to record exact times. His meticulousness extends to what people ate, drank and smoked.

Some sections of the diary contain highly personal material. Discretion is one of the marks of the good private secretary, and Sylvester certainly had, and has, this. For long he regarded his diary as merely his own private record with no possibility open of his publishing it. In 1947 his book *The Real Lloyd George* was published, based upon his diaries but with much matter toned down or omitted. It was the nearest he felt able at that time to giving the whole truth. In fact, at that time the fashion in political biography was for hagiography and, even with his discretion, Sylvester was

criticised for showing one or two warts on Lloyd George, in addition
to virtues. The diary is a completely frank record, and Sylvester's
only request to the reader is to take it as a whole. It is a day-by-day
record, reflecting moods of particular moments and particular situa-
tions. Lloyd George could be a difficult man to work for, and in one
aspect the diary was Sylvester's safety-valve in which he worked off
momentary exasperations. But underlying it all is a deep sense of
his loyalty to, and almost unbounded admiration of, Lloyd George.
He takes the view that Lloyd George was the greatest man he has
ever known and the man with the widest vision. If proof is needed
for this, it can be seen simply in the fact that he remained with
Lloyd George until the very end, long after it was to his personal
advantage to do so. Indeed, at Lloyd George's death Sylvester found
himself unemployed at the awkward age of fifty-five. He joined the
staff of Lord Beaverbrook on a three-year contract and parted from
him amicably, there not really being very much that he could do.
Then for a year he worked, unpaid, as assistant to the current Liberal
Party leader Clement Davies.   .

During the Second World War Sylvester had fulfilled his life-
long ambition by becoming the owner of agricultural land in Wiltshire. (He never informed Lloyd George of this because there could
well have been a jealous reaction.) In 1949 he made the decision
to leave the political scene and go to the land. He now lets off his
major farm to a tenant, but he still runs his own smallholding. His
wife, whom he married in 1917, went with him but, after a long
period as an invalid, died in 1962, since when he has soldiered on
alone. In 1953 he was appointed a Justice of the Peace for Wiltshire;
and in 1962 his fellow-magistrates elected him to be their chairman,
and he served in this capacity until he reached the mandatory
retirement-age of seventy-five.

Sylvester's original diary consists of a dozen or so smallish notebooks, with black covers and crammed with shorthand. While he
was careful to inform members of his own family of the nature of
the material these notebooks contained, he regarded them as otherwise totally confidential. He began to think twice about this when
Lloyd George's elder son Richard published his book *Lloyd George*
in 1960 and for the first time made generally known certain irregulari-
ties in Lloyd George's private life. Then in 1967 Lloyd George's
second wife, Frances, Countess Lloyd-George (the former Miss Frances
Stevenson), published her autobiography *The Years that Are Past*,
and this dealt with some aspects of her long relationship with Lloyd
George. Sylvester considered it to be an over-romanticised account,
giving an incomplete story, and on some matters factually incorrect.
For example, the Countess stated that in 1926 Lloyd George's wife

and children sent him a letter demanding that he dismiss her from his secretariat and that he replied with 'a terrible letter' offering his wife a divorce. It is Sylvester's firm belief that no such correspondence ever took place, although he allows that Lloyd George might have caused Miss Stevenson, as she was, to think it had. Despite his disquiet, Sylvester still held his peace. The last straw for him was the publication in 1971 of the Countess's diary, edited by Mr A. J. P. Taylor, together with an interview given by the Countess to the *Liverpool Daily Post* of Friday, 13 August 1971. If only to safeguard the memory of Lloyd George's first wife, Dame Margaret, Sylvester decided at last to publish, although he first informed Lady Olwen Carey Evans, D.B.E., Lloyd George's surviving child, and Owen, the third Earl Lloyd-George of Dwyfor, the senior grandson, of his intention. He opened his notebooks and transcribed his material, some of which he had not looked at for forty years or more and the content of which he had entirely forgotten.

It is something of a tragedy that this, probably the most intimate study ever made of a world statesman, covers only the last thirteen years of Lloyd George's long career, and, moreover, years when he was out of office. However, it provides something of a corrective for more conventional studies of him which, naturally, treat his tremendous years as Prime Minister as the most significant part of his career and treat the events after his fall from power in 1922 as an aftermath rapidly to be dismissed. Yet in the 1920s and 1930s he was still a statesman of world rank. In British public life he occupied a very special position: he was not just an opposition politician but also a national hero, over and above party. He was 'the man who won the war', and there was at least partial truth behind this slogan. His public standing was akin to that of royalty. Moreover, for most of this period he was politically very active; he had achieved in terms of personal ambition all that a politician could ever hope to achieve, and what interested him now was not office at any cost but the opportunity to put ideas into action. In 1922 he had been quite relieved to quit office. He had served seventeen years continuously in the British Cabinet – the longest record of anyone so far this century – and they had included four years of war. Even he could do with a rest. Moreover, he had found himself the prisoner of the Tories, and opposition enabled him to return to his natural position as a radical reformer. He was fifty-nine years old, which politically, especially then, counted as still quite young. Well within living memory Gladstone had been Prime Minister at eighty-four. He had his political fund, derived originally from his share of political donations to his coalition government and augmented by the profitable purchase and sale of the *Daily Chronicle*, and he used this to finance investigations into, and campaigns on, economic problems which had become endemic in Britain. He wanted to eliminate chronic unemployment, which was a continuing social evil in Britain between the wars, and to revive the depressed British agriculture. He produced detailed policies for coal and power, for urban land and for agricultural land. In 1929 he produced his 'yellow-book' programme, summarised as *We Can Conquer Unemployment*, which was Keynesian almost before Keynes and, against the economic orthodoxy of the time, proposed to match unused resources with unused labour. He was at it again in 1935 with his 'new deal' and his Council of Action for Peace and Reconstruction, on which he spent £400,000. Yet for all his fame, his oratory, his energy and his vision the political impact was slight. This is an amazing fact and shows much about the British mentality in the 1920s and 1930s when 'safety first' was generally preferred to adventure. The Labour Party, run on highly conservative lines, had become the second party in the State and Lloyd George's own Liberals were crumbling to pieces. Yet it was said that the Labour leader, Ramsay MacDonald, was so afraid of him that he had his picture removed from the wall of Chequers so as not to be reminded of him. The Tory leaders Baldwin and, more particularly, Neville Chamberlain also feared his influence.

The major problem in editing Sylvester's diary for publication has been that of length. The transcripts from the original shorthand add up to something like a million words, which would be enough for half a dozen printed volumes. Therefore the original has had to be cut most drastically. Fortunately a certain amount of the material is repetitive, particularly in such matters as Lloyd George telling anecdotes about Welsh preachers; and eliminating such repetitions was the first stage in reducing the length. Secondly, a good deal of the material is a general political diary and also a diary of Sylvester's own private life with his family: the great bulk of this I have eliminated, although I have retained just one or two short passages to try to maintain a hint of the flavour of the original. Thirdly, Sylvester was meticulous in recording even trivialities, and I have cut out a lot of these: however, some are retained both to give the reader the flavour of the original and also on the principle that it is often from apparent trivialities that one can learn of the character of such a man as Lloyd George. The annotation of the text is mine save that certain footnotes are Sylvester's own comments (1974) on the text, and these are followed by his initials.

As a preliminary to reading the diary, it is necessary to know something of the arrangements of Lloyd George's life in this period. He lived virtually as a bigamist, with continuing relationships with both his wife and his mistress. This was in flat contrast to his public role as a spokesman for Welsh nonconformity and British nonconformity in general, and as a family man. Sylvester was the only person who spanned both sides of Lloyd George's life. Lloyd George's main home was Bron-y-de, Churt, Surrey, which he had built for himself, on the design of the architect Philip Tilden, in 1921 on luxurious but not stately lines. With the house went originally some sixty acres of land, and as time passed he extended the estate, by purchase, to some 700 acres. It was sandy soil, and he took a passionate interest in reclaiming and cultivating it, particularly for fruit farming. With him at Churt for much of the time lived Miss Stevenson, and she also had her own flat in London. In 1931 she bought a house at Worplesdon, not far from Churt, and later she had her own house and farm, Avalon, immediately adjoining the Lloyd George estate. Lloyd George's wife, Dame Margaret Lloyd George, had her house, Brynawelon, which she owned, in her home town of Criccieth, Caernarvonshire. She took a leading part in the local life at Criccieth and served as a Justice of the Peace and a rural district councillor. Dame Margaret and Lloyd George frequently visited each other's home. When Dame Margaret, or any of the Lloyd George children, came to Churt, Miss Stevenson had to leave, sometimes in a hurry. Sylvester recollects that there were occasions on which Dame Margaret was entering by the front door virtually while Miss Stevenson was leaving at the back. Dame Margaret had her own bedroom at Churt, which was not the same as that occupied by Miss Stevenson. Common ground for husband and wife was their London house, which for the period of this diary up to the end of 1937 was 2 Addison Road, off Kensington High Street. Subsequently they moved to 8 Victoria Road, behind the big stores in Kensington High Street, but in fact, owing to the war, they used this house very little. For a time it was used by Sylvester's office staff. Sylvester's own home was at Putney.

I acknowledge with special gratitude the courtesy with which I have been received by the former Miss Jennifer Stevenson, who was kind enough to read through the whole typescript: at her request one short passage of only marginal significance has been deleted. (In it, the diary quotes certain rather offensive words spoken by a third party who could not possibly have been fully acquainted with what he was discussing.) I am most grateful, too, for the interest and courtesy shown by the third Earl Lloyd-George of Dwyfor. I thank Mr A. J. P. Taylor for conversations which have been most valuable and am grateful for the permission he gave us, on behalf of the First Beaverbrook Foundation, to use material which is their copyright. I thank Mr David Jenkins, Librarian of the National Library of Wales, for his kind assistance. I acknowledge C. & T. Publications Ltd, for the Churchill copyright material. I owe a great debt to my wife, Pat, for her constant interest and encouragement. Above all, I thank A. J. Sylvester himself, both for giving me the project in the first place and for his warm hospitality on so many occasions in Wiltshire. His active assistance has greatly lightened my task. I feel I have been helped as Lloyd George was helped and this has been an experience of a lifetime.

COLIN CROSS

David Lloyd George's Family

THIS note is given to assist the reader in identifying the various members of the Lloyd George family whose names crop up in the text of the diary. It does not extend to the grandchildren's marriages or to the great-grandchildren.

DAVID LLOYD GEORGE (1863–1945) was the son of a schoolteacher, William George, and Elizabeth Lloyd. His father died while David was in his infancy, and his mother went to live with her brother, Richard Lloyd ('Uncle Lloyd'), a master-bootmaker and an unpaid minister of the Disciples of Christ at Llanystumdwy, Caernarvonshire. Richard Lloyd, a bachelor, acted as foster-father to his sister's children. As a young man Lloyd George qualified as a solicitor and set up his own practice in Caernarvonshire, in which he was later joined by his younger brother William George. Lloyd George was Liberal M.P. for Caernarvonshire Boroughs 1890–1945 (from 1931 as Independent Liberal), President of the Board of Trade 1905–8, Chancellor of the Exchequer 1908–15, Minister of Munitions 1915–16, Secretary of State for War 1916, Prime Minister 1916–22, and Chairman of the Liberal Party in the House of Commons 1926–31. Shortly before his death in 1945 he was created Earl Lloyd-George of Dwyfor.

Lloyd George's *first marriage* (1888) was to MARGARET OWEN (1866–1941), a farmer's daughter from Criccieth, Caernarvonshire. In 1920 she was created a Dame Grand Cross of the British Empire.

The children of this marriage were:

1. RICHARD (1889–1968), usually referred to in the diary as 'Dick'. He qualified as an engineer and saw military service in both world wars. In his business life he was a failure and became bankrupt. However, he was a man of generosity and charm, and Sylvester remembers him with considerable affection. Lloyd George came to lose patience with him, and there was an estrangement between them in Lloyd George's last years. Richard, despite the fact that he was to become the second Earl Lloyd-George, was left nothing in his father's will. Richard married first (1917) ROBERTA McALPINE (1898–1966), a daughter of Sir Robert McAlpine the building contractor. They separated in 1931, and in 1933 Richard provided grounds for divorce. Richard married second (1935) MRS WINIFRED

CALVE, and this too came to grief : she is referred to in the diary as
'June'. Roberta married in 1933 David Eifion Evans (b.1902). By his
first marriage Richard Lloyd George had a daughter VALERIE (b.1918)
and a son OWEN (b.1924). The latter is now the third Earl Lloyd-
George.

    2. MAIR (1890–1907).

    3. OLWEN (b.1892), who married in 1917 SIR THOMAS CAREY
EVANS (1884–1947), who was for many years in the Indian Medical
Service and became Surgeon to the Viceroy. Later he became a
leading genito-urinary specialist in Britain. Their children are
MARGARET (b.1918), ELUNED (b.1921), ROBERT (b.1923) and DAVID
(b.1925). In 1969 Lady Olwen was created a Dame of the British
Empire.

    4. GWILYM (1894–1967), who was Liberal M.P. for Pembrokeshire
1922–4 and 1929–50 (from 1931 as Independent Liberal) and was
Parliamentary Secretary to the Board of Trade 1931 and 1939–41,
Parliamentary Secretary to the Ministry of Food 1941–2 and Minister
of Fuel and Power 1942–5. After his father's death he definitely
joined forces with the Tories and he was Liberal and Conservative
M.P. for Newcastle-upon-Tyne North 1951–7, and was in the Cabinet
during the same period. In 1957 he was created Viscount Tenby.
He married in 1921 EDNA JONES (1900–1971) and their children are
DAVID (b.1922), the second Viscount Tenby, and WILLIAM (b.1927).

    5. MEGAN (1902–66) who, in Sylvester's recollection, inherited
more of Lloyd George's characteristics than any of his other children.
She was Liberal M.P. for Anglesey 1929–50 (from 1931 to 1942 as
Independent Liberal). She joined the Labour Party in 1955 and was
Labour M.P. for Carmarthen 1957–66. She was created Dame of the
British Empire shortly before her death. Sylvester wishes to stress
that his diary does not give a rounded portrayal of her. Towards the
end it records her in a particular situation of emotional strain. But
there was far more to her than that. She was a gifted politician,
dedicated to social reform, and could be a delightful companion.

    Lloyd George's *second marriage* (1943) was to FRANCES LOUISE
STEVENSON (1888–1972) whose daughter JENNIFER MARY (b.1929),
now a married woman, takes the view that she has never been
supposed to exist as Lloyd George's daughter and does not propose
to start to exist in that capacity now.

    Among the wider family, GORONWY OWEN (1881–1963), whose
wife Gladwyn was the sister of Gwilym's wife Edna, had a political
significance as a member of the 'Lloyd George family group' of
Independent Liberal M.P.s 1931–45. He was M.P. for Caernarvonshire 1923–45, Liberal Chief Whip 1931 and knighted 1944.

Life with Lloyd George

The Diary of A. J. Sylvester 1931-45

Chapter 1

'Who killed Cock Robin?'

1931

At the start of the diary, Lloyd George, aged sixty-eight, was Liberal leader in the Commons and having to steer a difficult course. The 1929 general election had returned 288 Labour M.P.s, 260 Tories and 59 Liberals, so the Liberals held the balance of power. Labour, under James Ramsay MacDonald, had taken office, dependent upon Liberal support. The bargain was that, in return, Labour should introduce legislation to reform the electoral system to give the Liberals fairer representation. In fact, in the session of 1930–1 a measure was introduced which was supposed to bring this about but it disappeared in the political maelstrom of the autumn of 1931. It was an unhappy time for almost all politicians. Large-scale unemployment had become endemic in Britain owing to the breakdown of some traditional industries in the 1920s. Now, under the effects of the world economic depression, unemployment was rising month by month towards a peak of three million. Wages and prices were steadily falling. The Labour Party was bitterly divided, with its left wing furious at the failure of the Government to introduce 'socialist' measures. The Tories, led by Stanley Baldwin, were split over India and other matters, and Baldwin's leadership had come under strong challenge. The Liberal Party was in the worst state of all and was falling apart. Nearly half the Liberal M.P.s were restive about keeping Labour in power and were challenging the most sacred of the Party's traditional doctrines — free trade. During the summer of 1931 this group was to break away altogether and become the Liberal Nationals, in such intimate alliance with the Tories as rapidly to become indistinguishable from them. Publicly Lloyd George held to the free-trade position but privately he was capable of being pragmatic about it.

1 *January*
L.G. got alarmed about the financial position [in his political organisation] and decided we must just cut down rigorously. He talked to me this morning and asked me to help.

2 January

I got rid of nearly a dozen of my own people, who have been with me a long time. A very miserable business.

3 February

Philip Sassoon[1] brought Charlie Chaplin to see L.G. in his room at the House and they had tea together. Frances[2] and Roberta[3] were there, as well as Charlie's male secretary. L.G. talked of London Bridge. He showed such intimate knowledge of the subject that it surprised Charlie.[4] Later Philip Sassoon telephoned me to retrieve a rough sketch L.G. had made of London Bridge, which I was asked to get him to autograph and send to Charlie, which I did.

Sylvester recorded in his diary a remarkable letter, dated 13 February, from George Lansbury, leader of the left within the Government, appealing to Lloyd George to join the Labour Party, with the clear implication that he could soon become leader of it. He said Lloyd George should take his 'place once more as a pioneer among pioneers' and concluded: 'Not a soul has seen this but my wife and I send it as one man to another in the hope that very soon we may appear actually side by side fighting on behalf of those unable to fight for themselves.' Sylvester also recorded Lloyd George's reply, dated 16 February, in which he said he had already pledged parliamentary support for constructive measures by the Government. For him to join the Labour Party would not aid the forces of progress. It would antagonise millions of hereditary Liberals. Personally, he had had enough of office and believed he could be of most help to the Government from an independent position. He ended: 'At present I am genuinely perplexed and disappointed by the stickiness of some of your colleagues. They are always finding reasons for not doing things. They are too easily scared by obstacles and interests. Unless you can innoculate them with some of your own faith and courage your party and ours will be landed in an overwhelming catastrophe.' The exchange of letters had followed a speech by Lloyd George on a Liberal resolution in the Commons calling for more-vigorous action

1. Sir Philip Sassoon, Bt (1888–1939). Millionaire, bachelor, art connoisseur, noted as a lavish host. Tory M.P. 1912–39. Lloyd George's Parliamentary Private Secretary in the closing stages of the Coalition Government and later a Tory minister.
2. Frances Stevenson.
3. First wife of Lloyd George's elder son Richard.
4. This in all probability was Tower Bridge, which came under Lloyd George's jurisdiction when he was President of the Board of Trade 1905–8, and not London Bridge.

to deal with unemployment. MacDonald had accepted the resolution, on the basis that it entailed merely the speeding-up of existing programmes. The Sylvester diary relates, in detail, that before making his speech on this resolution MacDonald had consulted with Lloyd George and with Liberal experts.

The following relates to a by-election in the constituency of Scarborough and Whitby, in which the Tories retained the seat against a strong Liberal challenge.

1 May

I arrived at Addison Road[5] at 9 a.m. and sat at table whilst L.G., Dame Margaret, Megan[6] and Eluned[7] breakfasted. We left King's Cross at 10 a.m. Chief worked at his speech in the train and slept. We arrived at York at 1.43 p.m. to an enthusiastic reception. We left immediately and L.G. addressed an enthusiastic crowd of 5000 from the car at Pickering. Thence we went to Whitby, where he had another very successful meeting of some 8000 people. He spoke from one of our vans before the Metropole Hotel. All along, the men working on road repairs and farm workers stopped their work in order to cheer him and, so reverently, took off their hats to salute him. There was a procession of 17 cars.

On arrival at the Pavilion Hotel, Scarborough, L.G. went to sleep. I went to inspect the place of meeting, which was the excursion platform at the station, which was first class. Some 10,000 people greeted L.G. at 7.30 p.m. He made a first-class speech, dealing with free trade and its importance to a seaside resort such as Scarborough. Everybody was delighted.

Seebohm Rowntree[8] and his son Peter joined L.G. for supper, at which conversation was brilliant. Peter Rowntree was doubtful what to do. He was interested in politics but immersed in business. His boss thought he had even been wrong to take up time to get married this year. L.G. said it was a decision about which he would have to make up his own mind. You can go into business and make wealth. That is one thing. Or you can concentrate on politics. You cannot do both. If you try, you will do neither. Even such an able man as Beaverbrook has found that out. Politics is a game of patience, not like making a successful issue. That was how Beaver-

5. 2 Addison Road, Kensington, then Lloyd George's London house.
6. Megan Lloyd George.
7. Eluned Carey Evans, younger daughter of Lloyd George's daughter Olwen.
8. B. Seebohm Rowntree (1871–1954). Chocolate manufacturer and pioneer sociologist. Colleague of Lloyd George in his 1913–14 land campaign.

brook had looked at the empire free-trade crusade. He had not sufficient patience to wait. Mosley[9] was very much like that, too. Chief said that he himself had stayed in politics all his life. He had to make up his mind, and he could not have done it had it not been for his brother, who carried on the practice, for the heroic help of his wife and for the inspiration of his old uncle. For the first five years of his parliamentary life, Chief said he had not been a success. His success had come by resistance to the will of the House of Commons rather than bowing to it. One of Rowntree's relatives had once issued a mild rebuke to Chief, which he had never forgotten. Chief had one day produced a newspaper which said he had made a good speech. Rowntree's relative had told him never to take notice of such statements. They did more than anything to ruin a young man.

13 May

Yesterday I arranged for Ann Parry,[10] who had written to me, to see L.G. at 2 Addison Road at 8.45 this morning. Last night, Frances told me that L.G. had informed her that he was thinking of putting Churt under Ann Parry and that she, Frances, had told him that if he did she would not go near the place.

14 May

Roberta came at 12.30 and we all went to lunch at Sovrani's in Jermyn Street. A conversation started about Ann Parry and the propriety of her becoming his Welsh secretary and of her being placed in charge at Churt. A chance remark by Frances made L.G. switch off immediately. It was no use, he said, discussing it, as she had prejudged the case, which was to be decided by Roberta. L.G. told Frances that she reminded him of the couple who always religiously quarrelled every Christmas Day. At the end of one Christmas, however, as they were retiring for the night, the wife said to the husband how nice it was to have gone through the festive season without having quarrelled, but, she added, of course it was always your fault, and there followed the biggest row they had ever had, as to whose fault it really was that they had ever quarrelled.

9. Sir Oswald Mosley (b.1896) had resigned office in the Labour government in 1930 and had just launched the New Party, forerunner of his later British Union of Fascists.

10. Ann Parry (b.1889). Welsh secretary to Lloyd George 1931–45. Also acted as librarian at Churt and was in charge of the bees there, with great success. All letters addressed to Lloyd George in Welsh were answered in Welsh. Miss Parry was curator of the Lloyd George Museum, Llanystumdwy 1951–65.

The following relates to the 1931 Liberal Party annual conference at Buxton, the last which Lloyd George ever attended. The reference in his speech to some having already made arrangements to be 'picked up' in the event of the Liberal Party being wrecked was to the group which a few months later became the Liberal Nationals and allied itself with the Tories. The speech lasted one and a half hours and was mainly a justification of the Liberals keeping Labour in office. Lloyd George gave three reasons for this – free trade, economic reconstruction and electoral reform.

15 May

I was awake early. The birds were singing but it was raining. As soon as I was dressed, I went in to L.G., in answer to his calling 'Maggie !',[11] who answered later. I found his stiff white shirt, put in the studs and links, got out his morning coat and vest and grey trousers, his collar, his bunch of ties, from which he carefully chose one, put his boots on, etc. Then, as he so often does, he asked me whether his tie suited. It was blue with a bluey-grey pattern on it. Meantime he was questioning and cross-examining me about the feeling in regard to today's proceedings. He said it would be very bad if the recalcitrants got a big vote. L.G. was worked up, as he usually is before a big meeting. He said : 'I feel like a prisoner who is to be executed, but it won't be long before it is all over.'

His speech will be long remembered. Hore-Belisha,[12] Rothschild,[13] Ernest Brown[14] and Shakespeare[15] had tabled a resolution on the independence of the Parliamentary Liberal Party, which amounted to a vote of censure on L.G. L.G.'s speech was devastating to his opponents. He drew a picture of Baldwin saying to the Liberals : 'Walk into my parlour said the spider to the fly – both wings

11. Lloyd George's pet name for his wife.
12. Leslie Hore-Belisha (1893–1957). One of the most flamboyant political figures of the time. He became a Liberal M.P. in 1923, went off with the Liberal Nationals in 1931 and lost his seat in 1945. He served as a minister in the 1930s but was eclipsed after his abrupt dismissal from the War Office in 1940.
13. James de Rothschild (1878–1957). Anglicised member of the French branch of his family. Liberal M.P. 1929–45 He was regarded, among other things, as the spokesman for British Jewry in the Commons. He owned the racehorse Tishy, who 'crossed her legs' in the Cesarewitch and became a famous cartoon-figure.
14. Ernest Brown (1881–1962) was reckoned to have the loudest voice in the Commons. He was Liberal M.P. 1927–45, from 1931 as Liberal National. He was continuously a minister 1931–45.
15. Geoffrey Shakespeare (b.1893) was a private secretary to Lloyd George 1921–3. Liberal M.P. 1923–4 and 1929–45 (from 1931 as Liberal National). Junior minister 1931–42. Baronet 1942.

please.' No one living has such platform arts as L.G. He was only waiting to create the right atmosphere. At last he got his chance and took it like a flash. He said: 'I am going to ask you to say today that the course we took was right.' Then he said: 'There are those who say: "Never mind that, we should have gone straight."' A woman's voice cried: 'Hear, hear.' L.G. at once turned in that direction and, pointing his finger at the speaker, said earnestly and with great meaning: 'Some time before the war, a liner was going full speed ahead on a defined course when a wire came through the ether that icebergs were ahead. The captain defied the warning. He went straight ahead. He did not slow down, and one of the most terrible catastrophies occurred in the history of the world. Let me say this here and now. I am opposed to Titanic seamanship. (Loud applause.) I would advise my friends to put on their lifejackets and put their deckchairs near the boats. Unless, of course, any of them have already made arrangements to be picked up.' In his deadly manner he just *rolled* this out. He told me afterwards that he knew from this moment that Hore-Belisha and company were definitely beaten.

At the end of the meeting, Arthur Brampton, the chairman, put the amendment moved by George Thorne,[16] and only some 20 persons stood up against. It was a great result.

We left Buxton for St Pancras and dined on the train. When we walked down the corridor to the dining-saloon, L.G. put his head in the doorway of the compartment where some of the recalcitrants were assembled, and where Hore-Belisha was going strong, and said: 'Who killed Cock Robin?' Then he ate every blessed thing that was put before him and regaled himself with Margaux, which he insisted should be divided evenly between him, Megan and myself. He said he was sure that the 'old gel'[17] had got whisky in her ginger ale.

16 May

Chief said that some years ago Bishop Gore[18] had either said in a speech or wrote in a paper about the 'professional politician'. Chief had written asking what he meant. Did not he, as a bishop, regard

16. Arthur Brampton (1865–1955). Birmingham brassfounder and bicycle manufacturer. Long a stalwart of Midlands Liberalism. President of the National Liberal Federation (the Liberal Party extra-parliamentary organisation) 1930–3.

George Rennie Thorne (1853–1934). Solicitor. Liberal M.P. 1908–29.

17. The 'old gel' was how Lloyd George frequently referred to his wife, in and out of her presence. She was a teetotaller.

18. Charles Gore (1853–1932). Leading Anglican scholar and bishop, successively, of Worcester, Birmingham and Oxford.

himself as a professional Christian? Bishop Gore had replied that he had never thought of it in that light and wrote to Chief that he could not disagree.

L.G.'s idea is that woman was made to look after man and that is why no one else could do that work so well. He hates the very idea of a manservant or valet.

A great annual event for the London Welsh community was the 'flower service' at Castle Street Baptist Church in the West End. For many years it was the tradition that Lloyd George presided at this service, which attracted a packed congregation.

28 June
I took Evelyn,[19] Winnie[20] and Bubbles[21] to hear L.G. at the Castle Street flower service. There was a great mass of flowers of all kinds around the pulpit and it seemed that L.G. was in the middle of them. He had come up from Churt with Dame Margaret and Dr Macnamara.[22] Sometimes he spoke in Welsh and sometimes in English. He said that a climber up Snowdon did not always keep his eyes glued on the summit. He was more immediately concerned how to get up this difficult bit and how to get around that corner. Then, when he was tired, he would look up to get direction.

3 July
Whenever L.G. speaks in the House, I always get a ticket for the ladies' gallery for Frances. After he has spoken, she always sends a note to congratulate him, signed 'P'.[23]

7 July
L.G. presided at Castle Street chapel for Miss Christabel Pankhurst,[24] who spoke on 'The Troubles of the World Today and the Way

19. Late wife of Sylvester.
20. Sister-in-law of Sylvester.
21. Nickname of Sylvester's daughter Maureen, now Mrs Maureen Sylvester-Evans.
22. T. J. Macnamara (1861–1931). Canadian-born son of an army sergeant. He became an elementary schoolteacher and then a Liberal politician. He was M.P. 1900–24 and a minister 1907–22. Always a fervent and loyal supporter of Lloyd George. His doctorate was honorary. He died in December 1931.
23. Short for 'Pussy', Lloyd George's pet name for Frances Stevenson. It was originally her nickname when she was a schoolteacher.
24. Christabel Pankhurst (1880–1958), with her mother Emmeline and sister Sylvia, led the violent 'suffragette' movement 1905–14 to try to secure votes for women.

Out'. She spoke of the advance of science. When we saw airmen in the sky, how could we doubt the Bible saying that He should come in the clouds. We were informed that someone would one day go to the moon, and she would not be surprised if it were a woman. L.G., speaking as chairman, said that there was every encouragement to a woman to be the first to go to the moon, seeing that there was a man there already.

The following refers to a Labour–Tory–Liberal agreement on British policy towards international disarmament. The League of Nations disarmament conference took place the following year but achieved little.

13 *July*

The disarmament conference met again tonight in the Prime Minister's room at the House. There was agreement, which means that L.G.'s draft has gone through. He has absolutely given this conference a new horizon.

Frances is busily sending photographs of Jennifer[25] to her friends. L.G. has a big book full of them, which he carries about in his special bag containing disarmament papers.

After the disarmament meeting and a party meeting, L.G. invited my wife to join him and Frances at dinner at Simpson's in the Strand. He spoke of the Boer War and reiterated the story I have heard several times of how he went to Nevin to address a meeting, and even his best and stoutest supporters were not very enthusiastic. On the appointed night he arrived at the hall, but no one would go inside. They just stood at the back. Then he started playing upon them, talking about the landlords and the clergy and, little by little, they came nearer the front, and when he had got the hall well filled he said: 'Now then, this is not what I came here to talk about. When you returned me to Parliament, you gave me a piece of blue paper. I return it to you now without one stain of blood upon it.' That speech won fame for L.G. in Nevin and rallied the whole Boroughs[26] behind him.

'Ah,' said L.G., laughing heartily, 'my one weakness is small nationalities. Some people think it is something else. If Germany had not invaded Belgium, I would have been against the war.' L.G. recalled the time when he first came to Simpson's, during a strike

25. Jennifer Stevenson.
26. Caernarvon Boroughs, Lloyd George's constituency.

when Asquith was Prime Minister. L.G. had been sitting late at a
strike meeting and had to see Asquith. Asquith was so tight that he
was inarticulate. 'Yesh, a very good . . . (long pause) . . . idea,' he
would say.

22 July

I accompanied L.G., Frances and Tweed[27] to Simpson's for dinner.
L.G. said that last night he went to dine with Archie Sinclair[28]
at Robin Hood Farm. There had been present Winston,[29] Bracken,[30]
Oswald Mosley and the womenfolk. All the talk had been about a
new coalition between Ramsay MacDonald and Baldwin. The story
seems fantastic, but there were those present last night who took
it very seriously. L.G. said that those two [i.e., MacDonald and
Baldwin] were very friendly. It was likely that it would please
both of them for L.G. to be out of it. He did not know, but Henderson[31] might be in it. It hardly seemed possible, if it were true, that
Henderson would be outside. J. H. Thomas[32] was in it up to his
eyes. He doubted if Snowden[33] would be in it, and would probably
be glad to be out of it altogether. L.G. said he would certainly
not oppose it, if it should mature. He would sit quiet, otherwise it
would be said that he was crabbing a national government. L.G.
said there were ugly rumours about the present economic situation:

27. Thomas Frederick Tweed (1890–1940) was educated at Liverpool
Institute and Liverpool University, and became a Liberal Party official.
By 1914 he was Liberal agent at Beccles and left there for the Army. He
had a distinguished First World War record, rising to lieutenant-colonel
and winning the Military Cross. He was secretary of the Manchester
Liberal Federation 1918–26 and prominent in organising Liberal summer-
schools. In 1926 he joined Lloyd George to organise the latter's land
campaign, and 1927–31 he was chief organiser of the Liberal Party. From
1931 he was termed 'chief of staff and political adviser' to Lloyd George,
although he had no jurisdiction over his private office, headed by Sylvester.
He wrote several novels, and became an underwriting member of Lloyd's.
He married Louise Anne Hatton in 1912, and they had a son and
daughter.
    28. Sir Archibald Sinclair (1890–1970). Liberal M.P. 1922–45, Liberal
leader in the Commons 1935–45, Secretary of State for Air 1940–5 and
created Viscount Thurso 1952.
    29. Churchill.
    30. Brendan Bracken (1901–58), Tory M.P. and strong supporter of
Churchill.
    31. Arthur Henderson (1863–1935) was currently Foreign Secretary and
also general secretary of the Labour Party. In fact he did not go with
MacDonald into the National Government.
    32. J. H. Thomas (1874–1949) was currently Dominions Secretary and
did go into the National Government.
    33. Philip Snowden (1864–1937) was the current Chancellor of the
Exchequer and did go into the National Government.

£13 million of gold was sent abroad yesterday, and more today. If there should be a flight from the pound, there might be a crash and things might mature very quickly.

Next follows Lloyd George's sudden illness and operation which knocked him right out of the political scene at the moment when the Labour Prime Minister, MacDonald, joined forces with the Tories to form the 1931 National Government. It has been argued that the illness was used by MacDonald and Baldwin as the opportunity to act while Lloyd George was out of the way but this cannot really be sustained. Sylvester's recollection (1974) is that Frances Stevenson was with Lloyd George at the first onset of the illness. But Lloyd George's wife Dame Margaret came very rapidly from Wales to take charge of the household, and Miss Stevenson had to leave.

26 July

Sarah[34] phoned me that L.G. was ill. I went at once to Addison Road to see L.G. He had developed prostate gland. Probably more than anyone else, Sir Thomas Carey Evans[35] saved his life. Having satisfied himself that the heart, kidneys and other organs were sound, Sir Thomas advised that there should be one operation, instead of dividing the operation into two separate ones. L.G. could stand a big operation but two smaller ones, necessitating a lot of attention, would irritate and fret him to death. His physical condition was wonderful. Lord Dawson[36] has been called in, and also Dr Swift Joly, who is the biggest expert in this disease. They agreed that they should operate on Wednesday morning. It was particularly desirable that no mention should be made to the Press about an operation. L.G.'s anxiety was not to give the idea to his enemies that he might be done for. Carey said that if the operation were successful L.G. would probably be an even better and stronger man.

27 July

I went to Addison Road and got a bulletin from the doctors which read as follows: 'Mr Lloyd George is suffering from an attack of haematurea,[37] which necessitates him being confined in bed.' My

34. Sarah Jones. For many years the Lloyd George family housekeeper. An outspoken, unsubservient 'character'.
35. Lloyd George's son-in-law.
36. Lord Dawson of Penn (1864–1945). Famous consultant physician of the day. His patients included Edward VII and George V.
37. Blood in the urine.

instructions were not to send this out until I got the word. The Press had no knowledge of L.G.'s condition, so it was quite easy to deal with it. When it was released, I was on the phone until midnight answering questions from the Press.

28 July

I was at Addison Road with L.G.'s family. The doctors were in consultation. I issued a bulletin as follows: 'Mr Lloyd George passed a somewhat disturbed night, although his general condition is satisfactory. The haematurea is diminishing, but until this subsides there will be cause for some anxiety.' L.G. was greatly touched that the King and Queen had sent a message to him, which I had received from Sir Clive Wigram,[38] that he was in their thoughts; he said I was to make sure that the King was the first person to receive the news after the operation.

29 July

I was up at 6.30 a.m. and at Addison Road at 7.30. Cars belonging to the doctors were assembled in the courtyard and an ambulance full of medical equipment and supplies stood nearest to the door. Everybody was busy. Dame Margaret along with Edna[39] sat in the study: she handed me charming letters to read from Austen Chamberlain,[40] Philip Snowden, Lord Devonport[41] and other people. Then she was joined by Olwen and Gwilym. She started working on another cover for the chairs in the dining-room. She has done three already. L.G. himself was awake at 6.30 a.m., and Megan read a Wild West story to him. Later he talked about the Eisteddfod and said he would like Megan and her mother to go to it. Then he dictated a message to Megan for the summer school, where she is going. When five minutes past seven arrived, he started calculating how much longer it would be before they were prepared. He calculated that it would be 7.30. Soon Sir Francis Shipway[42] administered something which caused him to sleep.

No more was heard until 8.40 when, as Gwilym and I were talk-

38. Sir Clive Wigram (1873–1960). Private secretary to George V.
39. Wife of Lloyd George's son Gwilym.
40. Austen Chamberlain (1863–1937), elder son of Joseph Chamberlain and elder brother of Neville. In his forty-five-year political career he held many offices, and as Tory leader 1921–2 supported the continuance of the Lloyd George coalition.
41. H. E. Kearley, Viscount Devonport (1856–1934), was a Liberal M.P. 1892–1909 and Lloyd George's Parliamentary Secretary at the Board of Trade 1905–8. He was the first chairman of Lloyd George's creation the Port of London Authority 1909–25 and Food Controller 1916–17.
42. Sir Francis Shipway (1875–1968). Leading anaesthetist of the day, knighted after attending George V 1928.

ing in the hall, we heard Lord Dawson's voice saying: 'It will soon
be over now.' Then we went upstairs. Carey came to us with Sir
Francis Shipway to say that it was over, and very successfully over.
A beautiful clean job had been made of it, and it was very necessary
as his muscles in that quarter were amazing. Then Lord Dawson and
Mr Swift Joly appeared in their white operating-attire and sweating
like bulls. They confirmed that it had been a most successful operation and they were both obviously very pleased. When Dick[43]
arrived, Dame Margaret just fell into his arms and wept. Megan
soon after came on the scene; she had been praying in her room.
After consulting Lord Dawson, I telephoned to Sir Clive Wigram
on the royal yacht. Lord Dawson spoke to him personally and said:
'Tell the King that the operation has gone very well, but it has been
a severe one and L.G. has some rough weather still to go through.'

Then I went to the adjoining room to talk to Dame Margaret and
immediately afterwards I telephoned to Frances to tell her that the
operation had been successful. Lord Dawson then drafted the Press
communiqué, which was agreed by the other doctors and which I
issued to the Press as follows: 'An operation was performed on Mr
Lloyd George this morning and the cause of the haematurea was
completely removed. Considering its severity, the patient's condition is so far satisfactory.'

Then the telephone started and never ceased during the rest of
the day. Telegrams, letters and messages of all kinds came in shoals.
Ambassadors left their cards. Sir John Simon called, having written
on his card: 'Good luck.' When L.G. came round, he said to the
nurse: 'Aren't they ready? Why don't they come?', thinking that
they had not yet begun the operation. Then he asked Carey if the
message had been sent to the King before anyone else, and he was
told this had been done. Then he said: 'Give the King and Queen
my respects and my loyalty from my sick bed.'

When the doctors had gone this morning, some time after
11 o'clock, I went to bring my car from the road into the yard.
A group of some 20 persons stood at the gate, including one poor
but respectable elderly woman. She timidly asked me about L.G.
I told her: 'Yes, he has had his operation, and I am very pleased
to say that it has been a complete success.' She put her face in her
hands and wept. Then she ran across the road, saying: 'He is the
greatest man in England. I feel I could go mad with joy.'

The only thing L.G. did not want to see this morning, before the
operation, was anything in the way of preparation or instruments.

After a very heavy day, but a day full of thankfulness, I left

43. Richard Lloyd George, Lloyd George's elder son.

Addison Road at 9 p.m. Sarah said to me: 'If he ever gets over this, I'll never quarrel with him again.'

30 July

When I arrived at Addison Road, Dame Margaret told me she had seen L.G., who had had a good night. He had said to her: 'You are not going to get rid of me so easily, after all.' Megan went in to see him later and he winked both eyes together, in his accustomed fashion. Carey told me tonight that L.G.'s brain is as clear as a bell.

31 July

L.G. is always highly suspicious. Dame Margaret said it had suddenly occurred to him, when she saw him this morning, that there might be something the matter about which he had been told nothing. Dame Margaret said he had looked at her straight in the face and asked if she were really telling the truth. She had replied that Dr Swift Joly had told her that he was not only right there, but everywhere else. L.G. had been trying to read Dame Margaret's face, but, she told me, he had never been able to. But one could always read his face.

Only one or two members of the family have so far been allowed to see L.G. since his operation, so I had a wonderful surprise this afternoon when Carey suddenly said to me: 'Would you like to help me take L.G.'s painting in to show him? We quickly got the new portrait of him by Laszlo[44] from the drawing-room and carried it up to L.G.'s bedroom. There he was, propped up in bed. He nodded his head and I smiled and gave him a little salute. We put the picture on one side of the bed and he said, in a voice that was a little husky: 'A wonderful painting.' I gave him another smile and a little salute, and we took the picture out. I was literally thrilled. It was the most wonderful cocktail I have had. Just to see him was sufficient to generate new life and vigour. I thanked Carey most warmly.

1 August

As Dr Swift Joly arrived this morning, he said L.G. was a model patient. Dame Margaret told me afterwards that the wound was healing beautifully. L.G.'s blood was in such good order and he had always been known to heal quickly.

2 August

Dame Margaret said that he was always very suspicious and that she always had to go to see him the moment the doctors have gone.

44. Philip Alexius Laszlo de Lombos (1869–1937).

L.G. listened on the wireless to Handel's music, his favourite. This is the first time he has been allowed to have the wireless. I went to see Frances at her flat. There are many complications, which are being ironed out.

4 August

L.G. always has something to say which is very apt. When Carey put new bandages on his stomach today, he said he was a fit member for the round-table India conference[45] and ought to sit next to Gandhi[46] in *his* loincloth. Frances came to Addison Road this afternoon and saw L.G. I was at the office. When I got back at about 6 o'clock, I received a message from her saying how fit he looked and that he wanted to see her again on Wednesday. Would I ask Sir Thomas Carey Evans. I asked him. He said very definitely he was not going to be brought into this kind of thing. He was already in great trouble with the family because Dame Margaret was saying that he had taken her out of the way in order that Frances Stevenson could come. Dame Margaret had been for a drive. He would not do it again. Dame Margaret had said to him that if she found her there she would turn her out of the house. I told Frances this. She naturally did not like it, but she said it was for L.G. to put his foot down.[47]

The daily bulletins on Lloyd George stopped on 7 August, and his recovery continued. Sylvester went off on holiday. Meanwhile the political and economic crisis deepened. The report of the May Committee on 31 July had recommended £96 million of economies in government expenditure, the bulk of it to come from reductions in unemployment benefit. (There were at that moment over two and a half million registered unemployed.) The May Report, with its implication that Britain was on the verge of bankruptcy, actually worsened the economic situation, and wholesale selling of overvalued sterling followed. However, the Tories accepted the validity of the May conclusions, as did the acting Liberal leader, Herbert

45. The first round-table conference on the constitutional future of India sat in London in 1930.

46. M. K. Gandhi (1869–1948). Leader of the non-violent movement against British rule in India. He was an ascetic who dressed with extreme simplicity.

47. I later learned that Dame Margaret had her way and Frances did not go again. When she came, Frances made the mistake of bringing flowers. Dame Margaret asked who the flowers were from and the nurse, not knowing anything about the subtleties, just let the cat out of the bag. A.J.S.

Samuel,[48] and the bulk of the Labour Cabinet. Or rather, in the case of about half of the Cabinet, they accepted the validity of the conclusion that public expenditure must be reduced but baulked at doing it at the expense of the unemployed. From 20 to 23 August the Cabinet discussed the issue, failed to reach agreement and reached the verge of dissolution.

23 August

The political situation during the past fortnight has undergone a tremendous change. Last week there were conferences on account of the dangerous position in the financial situation. If L.G. had been well, I should certainly have returned from holiday at once. He had one conference in his bedroom the other day. Frances told me on the phone that L.G. had taken the line that he was ill and could not take an active part. The reason, really, is that he does not agree with Samuel and Donald Maclean.[49] They are in agreement with the May Report; L.G. is not.

On 24 August Ramsay MacDonald resigned as Labour Prime Minister and was reappointed Prime Minister to form the National Government, with the Tory leader Baldwin and the acting Liberal leader Samuel serving under him. The bulk of the former Labour Cabinet and parliamentary party went into opposition. Of the Lloyd George 'family group', Gwilym became Parliamentary Secretary of the Board of Trade and Goronwy Owen a government whip.

24 August

I went to Addison Road. L.G. had just gone to bed. I was taken by Dame Margaret to his bedroom and found him sitting up in bed, awaiting the arrival of his supper. We talked on the political situation. I asked him: 'Are you in or out of this?' He replied: 'I am keeping outside. I would not take office under MacDonald and yet it would have been impossible to have refused. I am glad, therefore, that it has happened thus.'

9 September

Megan, Gwilym and Tweed went to Churt, the first time Tweed has seen L.G. since his operation. The one thing of importance which

48. Herbert Samuel (1870–1963). A former Asquith Liberal.
49. Sir Donald Maclean (1864–1932), currently a member of the Liberal 'shadow cabinet'. He joined the National Government.

transpired was that L.G. said that if there were a general election
in November, then he would be out of it.

10 September

L.G.'s voice on the telephone today was full of vigour and life.

*On 16 September MacDonald visited Lloyd George at Churt. The
original intention behind the National Government was that it was
to be an emergency operation only and that when the 'crisis' was
over there should be a reversion to normal party conflict. However,
and particularly after the devaluation of sterling when Snowden took
it off the gold standard on 21 September, the idea grew up that the
Government should remain in power indefinitely and obtain a
mandate in a general election. The great problem, however, was that
the Tories wanted to introduce taxes on imports whereas the
Liberals, and also Snowden, strongly upheld free trade.*

17 September

At 1.15 p.m. Tweed told me that he had just come from a meeting
at the Home Office, which was attended by Sinclair, Ramsey Muir,
Stanmore,[50] himself and others at which Samuel had informed them
that the Cabinet, late on the previous evening, had decided upon a
general election, which was to be finished and over by 20 October.
Tweed telephoned to Frances at Churt. L.G. was very upset at the
news and could hardly believe it was true. Tweed said that there
was to be an arrangement about seats with the Tories on the basis
that wherever either a Tory or a Liberal ran in danger of being
ousted by a socialist, then either the Liberal or Tory should stand
down. Samuel had instructed Tweed to get busy with Topping,[51] the
chief agent of the Tory Central Office.

This evening the Liberal Parliamentary Party met. I telephoned
a report to L.G. on the following lines: 'The chief topic was the
general election. Sir Herbert Samuel made a general statement that
no decision had been taken by the Government. Strictly speaking,
this was not true. But his opinion was that a general election was
not likely to be long postponed. Conservative leaders were resolved

50. Ramsay Muir (1872–1941). An academic who turned to Liberal
politics in the 1920s. He fought as a candidate in many elections from
1922–35 but served as an M.P. only 1923–4.
    Lord Stanmore (1871–1957). Liberal Chief Whip in the Lords 1923–44.
    51. Robert Topping (1877–1952) was director of the Tory Central Office
1927–45.

to go to the country on a full tariff programme. They would not consider any compromise. The one thing which was considered of vital importance was that the socialist opposition should not be returned to power. A statement was issued to the Press that "the Liberal Party declined to accept any responsibility for a general election until the object for which the National Government had been formed had been achieved".'

18 September

Frances told me that L.G. was definitely against a general election and, furthermore, that he was definitely against the Liberals having any sort of arrangement with the Tories. Tweed was instructed, therefore, not to meet Topping. L.G. had also said that any Liberal who remained in this National Government during the general election would receive no assistance from Liberal funds. L.G. had said that he would sooner have half the present number of Liberal M.P.s than have an arrangement with the Tories.

26 September

There has been considerable activity at Churt. L.G. saw Reading,[52] Herbert Samuel, Sinclair and H. A. L. Fisher.[53] He sent a strong message to the Prime Minister asking him to stand firm against a general election.

30 September

At 2.30 I motored to Churt. I found L.G. in the library, remarkably fit and well and looking ten years younger. Then Sir Herbert Samuel, Sir Donald Maclean and Sir Archibald Sinclair arrived. They stayed until 6.45 p.m. and only went when the nurse said it was time for L.G. to go to bed. Peels of laughter came from the library. L.G. was telling them that there was nothing left for him to do but to join the Liberal Council.[54] L.G. is absolutely implacable. He is dead against a general election. He says there is no need for it. He is also very insistent that the Liberal members of the Government should threaten to resign in a body if Ramsay and the Tories

52. Rufus Isaacs, 1st Marquess of Reading (1860–1935). Close political friend of Lloyd George of long standing and implicated with him in the Marconi scandal of 1913. His remarkable career included being a Liberal M.P. 1904–13, Attorney-General 1910–13, Lord Chief Justice 1913–21, Viceroy of India 1921–6 and Foreign Secretary in the 1931 National Government.
53. H. A. L. Fisher (1865–1940). Historian and also an active Liberal politician, M.P. and minister.
54. A largely honorific body

insist on an election. He says that would prevent them, even now. Samuel was disappointed, because he had got the Tories so far along the road towards agreeing a formula[55] and he probably thought L.G. would have been pleased. L.G., describing Samuel, said : 'One day he is as firm as Mount Zion; the next he is floating about like the ark.'

1 October

At 5.30 p.m. the Liberal ministers in the Government met to consider whether they should stay in the Government or resign according to L.G.'s advice. They decided to stay in, against his advice. Tweed went to Churt. L.G. told him that as a consequence of his advice not being followed there would be financial help only for certain candidates, and that after the election he intended to resign the chairmanship of the parliamentary party.

2 October

The Liberal Parliamentary Party meeting was in favour of ministers remaining in, for the present, which is against L.G.'s advice.

On 6 October Ramsay MacDonald announced that there would be a general election, with polling on 27 October. The National Government was to ask for a 'doctor's mandate' or, in other words, for a free hand to legislate how it considered best. Really, of course, it was a formula to help the Liberals: it avoided their being in the position of supporting the Tory policy of abolishing free trade. In fact, tariffs were introduced the following year, following the National Government's landslide election-victory. Lloyd George and his family group fought the election as Independent Liberals, opposing the National Government. Gwilym Lloyd George and Goronwy Owen resigned their offices in it before the election. Lloyd George was now isolated politically and was to remain so for the rest of his life.

8 October

Nobody knows quite what to do or what to work for. Many have said to me : 'It is a good thing L.G. is out of it.' L.G. has remarked to Megan : 'To think of a fight and me not in it.' Tweed announced that there would be no money for Liberal candidates. He resigned the position of organising secretary of the Party.[56]

55. i.e., a formula for an election programme.
56. On resigning his official position with the Liberal Party organisation, Tweed moved into Lloyd George's direct employment.

9 October

L.G. had a manifesto to be issued tonight and to go to his adoption meeting tomorrow. Dictation of this [from Churt] started at 5.45 p.m. I had a team of girls to take this over the phone in relays, whilst on another phone I took a check note. At 6 o'clock we were suddenly cut off. I had a dreadful row with the exchange and wrote a strong letter to the Postmaster-General. I had to insert some Welsh sentences at the end and send it by registered express post [to Caernarvon].

In his manifesto, Lloyd George said he would not be able to campaign personally owing to his illness but that he hoped soon to be fit again. He described the election as 'unnecessary': the National Government already had an ample majority in the Commons to legislate as it wanted. The Tories were exploiting the crisis for party advantage. Lloyd George said the Tories were out to smash the power of organised labour. This could lead to great mischief in the future. The right policy, as during the war, should be to draw labour into discussions on how to solve the country's difficulties, not to antagonise it. He affirmed support for free trade, although in relatively lukewarm terms.

10 October

I phoned Caernarvon. A number of local meetings have been held throughout the Boroughs to adopt L.G. One particularly good meeting was held at the Liberal Club, Caernarvon, where 'the old blind man' was present and gave very interesting reminiscences of every one of L.G.'s previous adoption meetings. L.G. was much touched when I told him and said that 'the old blind man' was one of the few friends whom he now had. L.G. has definitely set his mind on being isolated, and then intends to support Labour, but not definitely and deliberately, but by speeches in the House which will make them come over to him, rather than him to them.

Sylvester goes to Churt to help with Lloyd George's election broadcast.

16 October

I was up at six o'clock and was tramping across the ploughed fields with my gun as the sun rose at 6.40 a.m., in the hope of getting a shot, but no luck. I was back at Bron-y-de soon after 9 a.m. I

breakfasted and then was busy with the broadcast speech. I made
arrangements in London for its release. Photographers came to take
L.G.'s picture at the broadcasting machine. An official of the B.B.C.
came to tea. L.G. talked to him rather frankly. He said that Baldwin
was an impulsive man. He had proved that in the General Strike.
He first of all said definitely that he would give no subsidy. Suddenly, without any warning, he gave in and gave £23 million.
That was why A. J. Cook[57] said in a later strike that if you stick to
it long enough he may give in. Then there was the flapper vote.[58]
It definitely had not been agreed to in Cabinet. But Joynson-Hicks[59]
stood up in the House of Commons and suddenly promised the
flapper vote at 21. Baldwin did not even try to get out of it. Not one
member of the Cabinet remembered any decision. This had been
told to L.G., long afterwards, by Winston. L.G. himself would have
defended the franchise at 25 for men and women. The franchise had
been given to men of 21 in the war, because many men were at
the Front long before that age, and that was the special circumstance.

Sir John Reith[60] came to dinner with L.G. L.G. said that the
trouble of the present day was that if some politician or statesman
or public man says something which is frightfully commonplace it
is heralded as good, plain common sense. Anybody who has an
inventive mind is 'not safe'. Winston, for instance, had an inventive
mind but he was regarded as dangerous.

At the appointed hour, L.G. proceeded to the library. Across the
corner had been arranged a table on which had been laid a thick
cloth. L.G. took his seat in an easy chair. Each page of his speech
was turned up at the corner, so that he could turn the pages over
without making a noise. He delivered it in fine style and finished
with a phrase in Welsh which, translated, means: 'Good night to
my friends in my beloved Wales.' Sir John Reith, Dr Nicoll,
Thomson[61] and I were with L.G. Frances listened in from the
portable set in the studio.

57. A. J. Cook (1885–1931), the miners' leader.
58. The full enfranchisement of women on the same terms as men,
1928. From 1918 to 1928 women had the vote from the age of thirty.
59. William Joynson-Hicks, 1st Viscount Brentford (1865–1932). He
was a Tory M.P. 1908–10 and 1911–29. He became a junior minister in
1922 and entered the Cabinet 1923. He was at his most famous as a
puritanical Home Secretary 1924–9.
60. Sir John, later Lord, Reith (1889–1971). First director-general of
the British Broadcasting Corporation 1922–38.
61. Dr C. Vere Nicoll was Lloyd George's local doctor at Churt.
Malcolm Thomson (b.1885). A Baptist army chaplain 1917–20 and
a research assistant to Lloyd George 1925–40. He wrote a biography of
Lloyd George (1948) with the endorsement of Frances, Countess Lloyd-
George. He became an Anglican clergyman in 1958.

In his broadcast, Lloyd George said the election was a political ramp by the Tories. There was only the remotest possibility that socialism would come as a result of the election, whereas protectionism was an imminent danger. Therefore all Liberals and free traders should vote against the National Government.

17 October

I arranged for the film companies to go to Churt to film L.G. and make a talkie of his speech. They evidently expected to find a decrepit old man, but were utterly surprised when he stepped out of the house very briskly, looking his old self, his hair flowing in picturesque fashion and his shoulders covered with his Tyrolean cape.

19 October

Tweed has been to Churt. L.G. asked him why so many of the Liberals had gone Simonite,[62] and he had told him that it was because of the money, and because nearly all of them had at one time or another had their backsides kicked by L.G. L.G. had forgotten, but they hadn't. L.G. rang up to see whether I had seen the film. I said 'No' and that I wanted to see it not in the studio but in a proper theatre to see the reaction, and was seeing it in London tonight. He asked me to go to one of the poorest parts of London. I went to Southwark. It was the only film which got a cheer. It was most successful, and such a contrast to some of the others, particularly Henderson. I felt very proud. L.G. had come out life-like and looking so fit and well.

On 23 October Sylvester, with his wife Evelyn, went up to the Caernarvon Boroughs to help in the final stages of Lloyd George's election campaign. In Lloyd George's absence, Dame Margaret was playing a crucial role in standing in for him.

24 October

I went early to the central office, Caernarvon, with Belcher.[63] Then we toured along the northern part of the constituency, calling at

62. Nickname of the Liberal National group, after its leader Sir John Simon.
63. Walter Belcher (1883–1965). Originally a statistician, he became a highly competent member of L.G.'s political staff. He went to the United States with me in 1928 to examine, on L.G.'s behalf, American election methods. For some time he supervised L.G.'s estate. A.J.S.

Bangor, Llanfairfechan, Penmaenmawr, Conway, Deganwy, Llandudno Junction and Llandudno. I spoke to L.G. at Churt, giving
him an appreciation of the situation. I told him that the situation
was very difficult, especially in the northern part. People could not
understand why L.G. was not for the National Government. It is
difficult in some places to get people to canvass.

25 October

It is no use trying to do any political work in Caernarvon Boroughs
on a Sunday. It is holy day and would do harm. Belcher, my wife
and I had tea with Dame Margaret at Brynawelon and discussed
the political situation and our programme. Dame Margaret has been
working very hard both in the Boroughs and for Megan in Anglesey.
Here she is loved, admired and is the uncrowned queen. I have been
working until 2 a.m. on a speech I have decided to make at
Llandudno the following night. Everybody is afraid to criticise
Captain Gourlay[64] but I am going for him.

27 October

Polling day. Belcher and I, with Evelyn, again toured the northern
part, visiting every polling station. The more we inquired, the more
was it plain that the position was difficult. Some of L.G.'s staunchest
friends were not sure about the stand he is taking and are upset.
Belcher and I, working in the closest collaboration, were of the
opinion that L.G. should make up some of his losses, or most of
them, by the number of Labour people who would vote for him.
Things are not too easy in Anglesey for Megan, but she has the
Labour people voting for her there, where she is strong, whereas
Labour in the Boroughs is only about 3–4000.

Polling was on 27 October and the count was on the twenty-eighth.

28 October

Soon after seven o'clock this morning, the telephone bell rang. It was
a call from L.G. at Churt. I had just shaved one side of my face and
was about to start on the other. I ran downstairs in my dressing-
gown. L.G. wanted to know how I accounted for the differences
between the figures of the canvass and those of the estimated poll.
That shows how cute he is. Belcher and I noticed the same thing
last night, and that was what was worrying us. We first noticed
it in the figures for Penmaenmawr. There were 1900 promises for

64. Francis Page Gourlay, Lloyd George's Tory opponent in 1931.

Liberal on the canvass. Yet in the estimate of the poll there were only 1400. That showed that large numbers had promised support for L.G. They would not vote *against* him, but when it came to the voting they would not vote *for* him, and abstained. I explained all this to L.G. Nevertheless, I said, Belcher and I were convinced that his majority would be somewhere between 5000 and 7000. There was no doubt that he was 'in'.

Belcher, Evelyn and I went to the count. As we walked around the tables, it was clear that Gourlay had polled heavily, surprisingly so to my mind. When I saw his line of thousands of votes growing, and at one time neck and neck with L.G., I said to Belcher that I should be glad to see L.G. in with anything. I had made arrangements with the returning officer and the head of the police that I should be allowed out immediately the figures were known, in order to telephone L.G. at Churt. I ran like a rabbit back to the central committee room and mounted three flights of steps, only to find the door locked and the caretaker away. I fled to the post office and ran in to the postmaster, who kindly helped me. I got a priority call to L.G. and told him that he was in with 5000-odd votes. He said nothing then. He was too overcome.

Later I phoned L.G. again. He said he thought we had done very well. He was well pleased. He gave me the following message to be given as a wire to Nath Roberts,[65] secretary of the association, and Caradog Evans, chairman of the executive : 'Thankful the peaks of Snowdonia remain above the deluge. Lloyd George.' This was dictated to me in Welsh by Frances. Then L.G. gave me the above translation.

Deluge it was. The National Government was returned with the biggest turnover of seats in British electoral history. At the dissolution the National Government had 336 seats and Labour had 256. In the new parliament the National Government had 554 seats and the Labour opposition was down to 52. Lloyd George's 'family group' of Independent Liberals, also in opposition, did well. However, three of them had no Labour opposition and one of them no official Tory opposition. Their 1929 and 1931 results were as follows:

Caernarvon Boroughs

1929		1931	
D. Lloyd George (Lib.)	16,647	D. Lloyd George	
J. B. Davies (Tory)	7514	(Ind. Lib.)	17,101
T. ap Rhys (Lab.)	4536	F. P. Gourlay (Tory)	11,714
Lib. majority	9133	Ind. Lib. majority	5387

65. L.G.'s constituency agent. He was a solicitor and was bossed by Polly his wife. A.J.S.

Pembroke

1929		1931	
G. Lloyd George (Lib.)	19,050	G. Lloyd George	
C. W. M. Price (Tory)	14,235	(Ind. Lib.)	24,606
J. W. Jenkins (Lab.)	12,235	C. W. M. Price (Tory)	19,560
Lib. majority	4815	Ind. Lib. majority	5046

Anglesey

1929		1931	
Megan Lloyd George		Megan Lloyd George	
(Lib.)	13,181	(Ind. Lib.)	14,839
W. Edwards (Lab.)	7563	A. Hughes (Tory)	10,612
A. Hughes (Tory)	5917		
Lib. majority	5618	Ind. Lib. majority	4227

Caernarvonshire

1929		1931	
Goronwy Owen (Lib.)	18,507	Goronwy Owen	
R. T. Jones (Lab.)	14,867	(Ind. Lib.)	14,993
D. F. Jones (Tory)	4669	W. E. E. Jones (Lab.)	14,299
L. E. Valentine		W. P. O. Evans (Nat.)	7990
(Welsh Nat.)	609	J. E. Daniel (Welsh	
		Nat.)	1136
Lib. majority	3460	Ind. Lib. majority	694

In the new parliament Lloyd George did not at first attend, owing to his illness, and in any event was at odds with the rest of his party. So there was no question of his resuming the leadership. Herbert Samuel became leader of the group of 33 Liberal M.P.s and John Simon leader of the 35 Liberal Nationals. The Samuelite group continued to support the National Government until September 1932, when it broke away over the issue of protection and went into opposition. Lloyd George, however, never officially rejoined it, although Megan did so in 1942. Gwilym, too, never rejoined it and became a member of the Tory (still termed National) Government at the start of the Second World War: for the whole of his career he continued to style himself Liberal, although latterly as Liberal and Conservative. The Liberal Nationals carried on with their own organisation into the 1960s (changing their name to National Liberal in 1948) but from 1931 onwards they were completely tied to the Tories.

Lloyd George's next step, after the 1931 election, was to go on a convalescence voyage.

2 *November*
I am at Churt, with all the information about the various trips abroad. L.G. talked about the political situation and reckoned that he would have thirteen,[66] his lucky number, on whom he could depend when the time arrived. He said he might now be only half a man, but he was a bloody sight better than two Jews.[67]

The Indian nationalist leader M. K. Gandhi was in London for the second round-table conference on India, which ended in failure. During his time in London, Sylvester escorted him to visit Lloyd George at Churt.

18 *November*
I went to Morley's College, where I was introduced to Gandhi. He is a great personality and I got on well with him. I know the Indians, am sympathetic to them and have travelled in India. It was a teeming wet night. Gandhi was clad in his native dress, but as he went out he drew a thick garment around him, covering his head and body; only his bare legs could be seen. In the car had been placed some goat's milk and one or two dates. This comprised his dinner, which he ate on the journey.

Later L.G. told me that Gandhi was a most remarkable man, and they had a most interesting discussion. L.G. described how Gandhi curled himself up on the settee and how a stray cat, which arrived at Bron-y-de only a few days ago, took a great fancy to Gandhi. It got up on his knee and made itself thoroughly at home. Gandhi would not hear of it being taken away. L.G. has named this cat Gandhi. Gandhi had insisted on shaking hands with all the domestic staff. L.G. thought he showed a good deal of dignity, even though he wore few clothes, and that he was the cleverest of all the Indians he had seen. Although he might be called a mystic, he knew precisely what he wanted and was fighting stubbornly for it. L.G. said he spoke to Gandhi as one politician to another. Gandhi wanted the best of both worlds: that was why he was such a good politician.

66. Presumably, thirteen M.P.s on whom he could rely.
67. This refers to Samuel and Simon, the leaders of the two wings of the Liberal Party. Simon, in fact, was not Jewish, although there was a quite widely held belief that he was.

Chapter 2

With Lloyd George to Ceylon

NOVEMBER 1931–JANUARY 1932

As the final stage of convalescence from his prostate operation of July 1931, Lloyd George went on a cruise to Ceylon. With him were his wife Dame Margaret, his son Gwilym and his wife Edna, his daughter Megan, Dr C. Vere Nicoll, his local general practitioner from Churt, and Sylvester, who kept a detailed diary in shorthand of practically everything that transpired during the cruise. The full transcript of this diary runs to some 60,000 words and it is possible to give only extracts here.

19 November

We were seen off from Victoria by heaps of friends. L.G. and Dr Nicoll, accompanied by Tweed and Miss Stevenson, motored from Churt. The family were already on the train.

The party went by train to Marseilles, where they joined their ship.

20 November

We arrived at Marseilles at midday. L.G. was received on the platform by the agent of the P. & O., and numerous other people, including a battery of cameras and journalists. We lunched on board, at the captain's table.

At coffee and old brandy in the drawing-room, L.G. talked of old Sir Thomas Sutherland[1] who was in the House of Commons when L.G. first entered, at about the same age as Megan. L.G. explained how old Sir Thomas sat in the House with a trumpet to his ear because he was so deaf. It reminded him of Disraeli's saying

1. Sir Thomas Sutherland (1834–1922) made his career with the P. & O. line and rose to be its chairman. Liberal Unionist M.P. 1894–1900, so in fact he was not in the Commons when Lloyd George first entered in 1889.

of a similar case: 'Fancy throwing away his natural advantages in such a fashion.'

When he arrived on the boat there were masses of wires and letters of congratulation and good wishes for L.G.'s restoration to health. Someone had sent him a number of leaflets and booklets from some mission. The one which sent him into fits of laughter was entitled: 'Safety, security, certainty'. He showed this to Edna and then to Gwilym and there was great hilarity and laughter. He said it might have been about sexual relations and birth control.

I posted letters home and from L.G. to Miss Stevenson and Jennifer.

We bought a magnificent basket of fruit, which Gwilym and Edna labelled: 'Bon voyage: hoping you will soon return feeling quite well. John Simon: Herbert Samuel.'[2] This was brought to L.G.'s cabin while he was lying down. He shrieked with laughter, his old laugh, and thoroughly enjoyed the joke.

At dinner L.G. talked about Loewenstein,[3] the millionaire who fell out of an aeroplane. Everybody thought he had committed suicide but Sir Eric Geddes[4] had told L.G. that Loewenstein suffered from blood pressure. At times he had to undo his collar and open the door to get air. It was thought he was doing this when the aeroplane suddenly turned another way and he fell out. This brought up the incident of Deschanel[5] falling out of a train. The train went on and Deschanel was left behind – in his pyjamas. He went to a small farmhouse and said he was President of the French Republic. Not unnaturally the farmer regarded him as a mental case, appearing as he did in his pyjamas. Clemenceau[6] hated him. Years previously they had fought a tremendous duel. Every time Clemenceau made a thrust at him, Deschanel retreated, until at last Clemenceau put his sword under his arm and, with a shrug, said: 'Monsieur is leaving us.' But in this presidential election Deschanel had his

2. i.e., the leaders of the two wings of the Liberal Party, both opposed by Lloyd George.

3. Alfred Loewenstein (1879–1928) was a Belgian multi-millionaire of flamboyant habits. He fell into the English Channel from his private aeroplane, and there was much speculation about whether this was an accident, suicide or murder.

4. Sir Eric Geddes (1875–1937). A railway administrator brought into Whitehall by Lloyd George as Deputy Director of Munitions Supply 1915–16. He was later in the Cabinet.

5. Paul Deschanel (1856–1922). Defeated Clemenceau to become President of France in January 1920 and resigned in September of the same year owing to neurotic troubles.

6. Georges Clemenceau (1841–1929), nicknamed 'Tiger', was Prime Minister of France 1917–20.

revenge. Clemenceau felt he had been fooled. He did not want to
stand for the presidency but was pressed by his friends.

21 November

We walked on the deck where L.G. met a little girl of two years of
age and lifted her up, and she kissed him. He asked all about her
and discovered that she was born in Singapore. At breakfast he was
full of this child, saying that he had found *his* little friend on board.
Dame Margaret said at breakfast that if she owned a boat she would
have all British sailors and none of these Goan waiters. L.G.
remarked that he would not mind betting that they would all be
Welshmen, and that most of them would come from Caernarvonshire and mostly from Criccieth. We were on deck after breakfast.
There was a considerable sea and it was a little cold. L.G. said:
'Why I ever left Churt to come on a bloody ship with all this
discomfort I do not know. I was perfectly happy where I was, but
everybody insisted that I must make a trip.'

At tea L.G. did himself well, with toasted teacakes and melon and
lemon jam. He said that the most destructive thing to a man was
jealousy.

After dinner, we assembled in the writing-room. L.G. talked of
the Boer War and of his pacifist opposition towards it, and how at
the relief of Mafeking he got home to find that Dick and Gwilym
had put out all sorts of flags in celebration. Everybody else had
flags at the windows and they did not mean to be left behind. His
boys had a bad time at school during those days. Speaking of the
relief of Mafeking reminded L.G. that Gladstone had said of Buller[7]
that he was the greatest general since Joshua. L.G. said that he went
to see Balfour just before he died. Balfour, speaking of death, had
said: 'It will be a great experience.' This was a true Balfourism.
L.G. said that when Lord Reading came to see him after his operation he was only allowed to stay a certain length of time. When the
time was up, L.G. suggested to Dr Nicoll another ten minutes.
Before Dr Nicoll went in again, he said to someone he did not
know: 'I think they ought to break off now, don't you? In any
case, Lord Reading is not very exciting, is he?' To this the reply
came: 'Well, he is my husband, and I have only been married to
him for a fortnight.'[8] L.G. gave another instance of a *faux pas*. At

7. General Sir Redvers Buller (1839–1908). Distinguished himself in
colonial campaigns and became Adjutant-General at the War Office. But
as Commander-in-Chief in South Africa 1899–1900 he sustained severe
reverses at the hands of the Boers.

8. Stella, Marchioness of Reading (1894–1971). Married Lord Reading
in August 1931, his first wife having died the previous year. As Miss

one time the most unpopular Member was St John Brodrick.[9] Why he was so unpopular was not quite clear. L.G. related how, on one occasion, Lady Brodrick was talking about one of their children, who had red hair. Brodrick said: 'You see I have not red hair, neither have you, and none of our respective relations have.' Whereupon Lady Brodrick said: 'Ah, but then we had a red-haired footman.'

22 November

I went into L.G.'s cabin early this morning and found him sitting on the edge of the bed in his pyjama jacket and his pants, and Dame Margaret helping him with his clothes. I asked him if I could help and he said: 'You certainly can. I am no good at this job, and particularly now.' I put the studs and links in his shirt, found the suit he wanted and his boots, helped him on with them, and then we went to see Miss Roberts, the maid, who was seasick. Before he left the cabin he pulled out of his pocket a photograph of Jennifer in the garden at Churt. He is tremendously proud of her.

Mr Lister Harrison[10] brought Sir Owen Seaman[11] to see L.G. He had had a similar operation to that of L.G., at about the same time. L.G. suggested to him that they should run a race.

At lunch, talking of seasickness, L.G. gave a saying of Balfour. They had crossed to France in a torpedo boat destroyer and it was a very bad crossing. Kitchener was there and Asquith and McKenna[12] and others. When they reached Boulogne, all went off leaving Balfour to come along behind. When he boarded the train, L.G. said to Balfour: 'This is the kind of weather when one might get hit by a submarine torpedo', to which Balfour replied: 'I have been praying all the time that one *would* hit us'. Speaking of Austen Chamberlain, L.G. related how Bismarck had been asked what he thought of Austen. Austen had been to Germany and dined with Bismarck. 'Oh,' said Bismarck, 'he is a very nice fellow, but rather weak *here*', tapping his head, meaning that he could not drink much.

Stella Charnaud she had been private secretary to the first Lady Reading when they were in India. On their return home she became secretary to Lord Reading himself. At the time of the marriage she was thirty-seven and he was seventy. The new Lady Reading went on to make a considerable public career in her own right, notably in the Women's Voluntary Service, and in 1958 became one of the first women to be created members of the House of Lords.

9. W. St John Brodrick (1856–1942) was a Tory M.P. 1885–1906 and in the Cabinet 1900–5. He succeeded as 9th Viscount Midleton 1907.

10. Lister Harrison, a fellow-passenger.

11. Owen Seaman (1861–1936), editor of *Punch* 1906–32.

12. Reginald McKenna (1863–1943). In the Liberal Cabinet 1907–16.

Sir Owen Seaman said he was going to Egypt. L.G. said that Sidky Pasha[13] seemed to be doing quite well, but he himself was never in favour of giving democratic control to the Egyptians so soon.[14] Oddly enough, Milner[15] and Curzon[16] were in favour of it. L.G. could not say how it was, but some time after 1918 something snapped in Milner and he was not the same fellow. Up to that time he was wonderful. He died of a kind of sleepy sickness. . . .

At 7 p.m. we all assembled in L.G.'s cabin and there enjoyed a bottle of Veuve Clicquot and some of Aimée McPherson's[17] sermons and negro spirituals on the Decca gramophone. I was called out and when I returned Dame Margaret said: 'Do sit down.' I sat on a chair, in which she had concealed a bag of wind under the cushion. It made a terribly vulgar sound and there were shrieks of laughter.

After dinner we assembled in the writing-room, as usual, for coffee and a smoke. Dame Margaret talked about Sunday schools in Wales. L.G. said it was the custom for each pupil to read a verse of the Scriptures and then for the clergyman or minister to ask questions as to what was each pupil's version of this particular point. One was about the tower in the vineyard and why it was built there. One bright lad replied that he expected it was to enable the foreman to see what time the workmen came to work. L.G. said that Thomas Charles Williams[18] was one of the last great Welsh preachers. He was very good, especially on the spur of the moment. One day he arrived at Bangor and the fellow who was a porter on the station went up to him and said: 'Well, Mr Williams, I wanted to shake hands with you. I am the son of ginger beer Williams of Holyhead.' 'Ah,' said T. C. Williams, 'you are the son of ginger beer Williams, and what did you say you were?' 'A porter, sir.' 'Well,' said T.C., 'I have heard of water being made into wine, but I have never heard of ginger beer being made into porter.' . . .

13. Ismail Sidky Pasha (1875–1950). Prime Minister of Egypt 1930–3.
14. Here, presumably, Lloyd George is referring to the agreement of 1922 in which the British relinquished their protectorate over Egypt, although continuing to keep an army of occupation and to control Egyptian foreign relations.
15. Alfred Milner (1854–1925). War Cabinet colleague of Lloyd George. He had been a British proconsul in Egypt and South Africa.
16. Marquess Curzon of Kedleston (1859–1925). One of the leading Tories who served under Lloyd George.
17. Aimée Semple McPherson (c. 1893–1944), founder of the Angelus Temple, Los Angeles, famous for her spectacular evangelistic methods.
18. T. C. Williams (1868–1927) preached elegantly in both Welsh and English. His only pastorate, in which he spent his whole career, was at the Calvinistic Methodist church at Menai Bridge.

23 November

I helped L.G. dress and we walked on deck. At breakfast L.G. started a conversation about the convoy system, with which he had great difficulty with the sailors, the Admiralty people. In the end, L.G. had to decide the matter himself, and he did it by asking Lord Carson, who was then First Lord of the Admiralty, and Jellicoe[19] to come to breakfast with him at 10 Downing Street. He listened to Jellicoe and then said: 'Well, you must try it. If it fails, it cannot be worse than it is at present.' At that time we were losing 700,000 tons of shipping a month. It was tried, and it was a success.[20] The worst thing Kitchener ever did, said L.G., was after the battle of Neuve Chapelle.[21] He came to the Cabinet for a discussion on the situation and there was talk about wastage. Someone drew his attention to the casualties and Kitchener said: 'It is not that; it is the wastage of shells that I complain about.'

At 4.20 p.m. there was boat drill. I went to inform him. He was reading Winston's first book.[22] He said he would rather drown. All the same, a very few moments afterwards he came up for tea and enjoyed his jam and hot toasted teacakes. He remarked the two things that made life worth living these days were 'this jam' and 'the thing which A.J. sat on last night'. At 7 p.m. we assembled as usual in his cabin. Great amusement was caused by Gwilym, who sat on the article which makes rude noises. L.G. laughed himself almost to death. L.G. said Criccieth, especially when he was a young man, contained families nearly every one of which had lost someone at sea, for they were a seafaring community. One day a great orator and preacher visited the town, and everyone was carried away by his appeal. He described how on the last day Christ would call out for certain men to answer the roll, and as every family had lost some loved one they were all deeply affected. The preacher said that Christ would first of all describe how Evan Williams went down in

19. Edward Carson (1854–1936). Tory M.P. 1892–1921 and leader of the Ulster Unionist resistance to Irish Home Rule 1911–14. Attorney-General 1915, in the War Cabinet 1917–18, Lord of Appeal 1921.

J. R. Jellicoe (1859–1935) commanded the Grand Fleet 1914–16 and was First Sea Lord 1916–17.

20. Lloyd George's insistence upon the Navy adopting convoys to beat the German submarines was probably the most significant single act in his war leadership, without which Britain might have lost the war.

21. The battle of Neuve Chapelle, 10–13 March 1915, was a British attempt to break through the German lines.

22. This must have been the first volume of Churchill's autobiographical account of the First World War, *The World Crisis*, published in six volumes between 1923 and 1931. Lloyd George was reading it in anticipation of writing his own *War Memoirs*.

a ship off the Spanish coast. Then Jesus would say to one of his angels: 'Go and fetch him here.' Then Jesus would say: 'Where is William Jones, I do not see him here, either. Ah, he was dashed on the rocks of the Welsh coast.' Christ would send another angel to fetch him. Then he would call for Robert Roberts, who was buried under the rock at Blaina, and another angel would be dispatched to fetch him. And so he went on and on, until the whole congregation was weeping and under the preacher's spell.

L.G. recalled a rather devout religionist, who was also a railway official at Chwilog, was in the habit of shouting out on the arrival of every train: 'All change for Caernarvon.' One particularly hot summer's evening he was in his chapel at Chwilog, and the sermon was very long, and he fell asleep. He did not wake up until all the people were on the move. Waking up in a half-asleep condition, and thinking that he was still on the station platform, with all the people moving about, he cried out: 'All change for Caernarvon.'

In L.G.'s cabin tonight he read part of Winston's book and said that he had got some of the things he wanted to put in his own book. Winston related how Kitchener had come to see him – he was then at the Admiralty – and told him what a serious situation had developed as a result of the retreat from Mons. Winston had gone immediately to the Treasury. He never asked anyone if he could see L.G. He used just to open the door. On this occasion, L.G. had a number of important bankers with him, so Winston beckoned him out with his finger. L.G. came out and they went into a small place, like a cupboard, and there Winston told L.G. the position. L.G. said it was like Winston to come to him when he, Winston, was in trouble. When things were going well he would always walk about with his head in the air. Consequently, when Winston wanted to see him he knew it was because he wanted his help.

As the foregoing shows, Lloyd George was reading Churchill's war memoirs with a view to getting on with his own. It has often been suggested that in view of the parliament that had been elected in 1931 there was little real role for him to play and so he got on with his memoirs as an alternative activity. However, as the following shows, he had by no means lost interest in current politics. On 20 November 1931, having been rushed through Parliament, the Abnormal Importations Act became law. This breached free trade by empowering the Board of Trade by order to levy duties on goods it reckoned were being 'dumped' in Britain at below their true value, owing to the international economic depression.

24 November

L.G. is panicking for news about the reaction of the Liberal Members to the emergency orders. I have wired Tweed. Having pressed Gwilym like hell to come out, L.G. is now mad keen to get him back in time to make a speech against the quotas. Gwilym is fed up to the teeth with it. He told me he could not stand it any longer. All he wanted to do was to keep out of the old man's way because every time he saw him he brought up the question of how he was going to get back. Edna has had such a bad time at sea that he wants to give her a little time in Egypt.

Gwilym and Edna left the ship at Port Said.

25 November

We arrived at Port Said at 9.30 this morning. The Chief of Police was the first to greet us, followed by the British Consul. L.G. did not get off the boat, and the doctor stayed with him. Dame Margaret, Megan and I went off with Gwilym and Edna. We went to Simon Artz, the general emporium, and bought topis and had some samples sent on board for L.G. to choose from. Then we saw Gwilym and Edna off safely on the train.

At lunch L.G. talked about the lives of the kings of England and how short-lived they were, principally as a result of high living. He went through the lives of the kings of England, one by one, with amazing knowledge of the details. He then talked about the unveiling of the war memorial at Cardiff, when he was present at the command of the King, and went down in the same train as the Prince of Wales. Presently, he said, someone peeped round the door of his compartment – it was the Prince himself, who had come to ask L.G. if he would give him some suitable Welsh phrase with which he could conclude his speech. The rest of the journey was occupied by L.G. giving him the Welsh version of : 'They will never be forgotten as long as the breeze blows over their graves.' I remember so well hearing the Prince learning this. He pronounced it very well at the ceremony and it produced a tumult of cheering. That was the occasion on which, at the psychological moment, the wreath which he was to have laid did not turn up. He was very angry and, as L.G. said, rightly so, because it was letting him down. Megan said that Olwen's remark on that incident had been : 'It is a good thing for Sylvester it was not father's wreath that was missing.'

At dinner L.G. was very talkative. He said the dominions had behaved very well, and some fine men had been sent over to England from time to time, especially Laurier,[23] Botha,[24] and Smuts.[25] He related having breakfast with Botha. He explained to him that what they were giving South Africa was a government with the same rights as Canada or Australia, which meant that they could pass what laws they liked and we should not interfere with them. Botha simply answered : 'I will do it.'[26] Botha was the biggest man of the lot. Botha had been accustomed to an open-air life. When that ceased, he still lived in the same way, eating the same kind of food. As a consequence, his system got clogged and that was what probably did for him. The first time Botha spoke in London was in Dutch. It was at the time of the suffrage movement. Women were not admitted, but they had carefully arranged to have men present who would create an uproar![27] There had been some commotion. Botha spoke in Dutch and suddenly a little fellow got up at his side on the platform to interpret. This apparently had not been arranged for, or the chairman had not been acquainted with this part of the procedure. The next moment, someone at the back of the platform took the interpreter by the scruff of the neck, and pitched him headlong outside. When Botha saw what had happened, he shrieked with laughter. L.G. said it was a great disaster when Botha died. . . .

26 November

We have passed by the spot where Pharaoh and his chariots passed through the Red Sea. L.G. said he could not believe that the Jews could have crossed Egypt into *that* country and lived there for 40 years. The whole range of mountains was just as barren as it was possible to be. There was not a single tree and not a piece of vegetation of any kind. L.G. said that the Jew was what he thought he was and that, in this particular case, he was a liar. Lady Elliot[28]

23. Wilfrid Laurier (1841–1919). Liberal Prime Minister of Canada 1896–1911.

24. Louis Botha (1863–1919). Commander-in-chief of the Transvaal forces 1900–2 and Prime Minister of the Union of South Africa 1910–15.

25. Jan Christiaan Smuts (1870–1950). Close colleague of Lloyd George in the later stages of the First World War.

26. This must have been in 1907, when Lloyd George was President of the Board of Trade. Botha visited Britain in 1902, 1907 and 1911. The conquered South African republics of the Transvaal and the Orange Free State were given internal white self-government in 1906, and united with Cape Colony and Natal in 1910 to form the Union of South Africa with dominion status.

27. i.e., the violent suffragette movement of 1905–14, aimed at forcing votes for women. It became quite customary to exclude women from public meetings, because of suffragette interruptions. The suffragettes enlisted male sympathisers to interrupt on their behalf.

28. Lady (Rachel) Elliot, fellow-passenger, wife of Sir George Elliot. See note on p. 57.

said they were fed on manna and water descended from heaven, but
L.G. said they could not live on that for forty years.

We assembled in L.G.'s cabin as usual at 7 p.m. for a bottle of
the best. L.G. talked of Winston and his book, which today he had
been reading. He said he had never been in favour of the Dardanelles
operation. L.G. talked of the political situation. When he talked of
Samuel there was fire in his eyes. He said the Tories would have been
fools if they had not introduced these tariffs, because tariffs had been
their policy for years. Now was their opportunity. He would not
bother attacking them. They would have been damned fools not to
have done it. But the man he was waiting for was Samuel. He would
rub his nose in it when the time came. Sir George Elliot[29] reminded
L.G. that Ludendorff[30] said that if Germany had had L.G. they would
have won the war.

27 November

L.G. is intensely interested in the second volume of Winston's
memoirs, which he is now reading. It deals with 1915 and the
Dardanelles. I am particularly interested because I dealt with the
whole of the records of that committee, formerly the War Committee,
then developed into the Dardanelles Committee, and later became the
War Council. Through the whole of these stages I was the one who
kept the record for Hankey.[31] He dictated them to me, and I typed
and circulated them and all the associated memoranda. L.G. reminded
me that he was not a member of this committee and that things
happened of which he knew nothing. He was too busy with munitions. One thing transpires in this book, said L.G., and that is that
Winston does not say I was against the Dardanelles operations. L.G.
said it was a crime to send such a man as Ian Hamilton[32] in command
of the troops at Gallipoli. He was a fine journalist but what was
required was a young fellow with dash and courage. This will provide any amount of material for his own book, I can see. . . .

29. Sir George Elliot (1868–1956). Chairman of the Bank of New Zea-
land 1922–31, 1936–7.

30. General Erich Ludendorff (1865–1937) was *de facto* dictator of
Germany 1916–18.

31. Maurice Hankey (1877–1963). The man through whom Sylvester
first came to the notice of Lloyd George. Sylvester was Hankey's confidential shorthand-writer, and later private secretary 1914–21. Hankey was
a Royal Marine officer who in 1908 became Assistant Secretary of the
Committee of Imperial Defence. He was Secretary of the Committee of
Imperial Defence 1912–38 and of the Cabinet 1916–38.

32. General Sir Ian Hamilton (1853–1947). Commander-in-chief of the
army which assaulted the Gallipoli peninsula in the Dardanelles. He had
a literary reputation resulting from his *A Staff Officer's Scrap Book*,
2 vols (1905–7).

L.G. talked about Northcliffe, a remarkable man. L.G. said Northcliffe used to come to see him at 10 Downing Street. It was quite
clear that Northcliffe was not thinking of L.G.'s answers to his
questions. He was merely thinking what other questions he could
put. He said Northcliffe started life as a journalist and then, with his
wife, they started *Answers*. Then somebody called Kennedy Jones[33]
had a paper, the *Evening News*. He invited Northcliffe to join him
and made it a gigantic success. Kennedy Jones was in the House of
Commons. He was a tremendous drinker. L.G. said he had seen him
drink a bottle of green Chartreuse in one evening. He came to the
House one night very drunk. His arm slipped down as though useless,
and suddenly there was an awful thud. It was old Kennedy Jones,
who had slipped off his seat in the House and could not get up. The
House was a wonderful place and very considerate of all these
things. The Press never said a word of these things.

28 November

L.G. related how all the soldiers [in the First World War] had
nicknames. Henry Wilson[34] would, for instance, talk about 'Tit
Willow' when he meant Sackville-West. He would call General
Maurice[35] 'Putty Nose'. Henry Wilson used to take the role of the
Boche in his military talks at the Cabinet. When he went to Ver-

33. Kennedy Jones (1865–1921). Editor of the London *Evening News*
1894–1900 and associate of Northcliffe in other enterprises. Tory M.P.
1916–21.
    34. Henry Wilson (1864–1922). Commandant of the Staff College,
Camberley, 1906–10, Director of Military Operations 1910–14, Deputy
Chief of Staff in France 1914–17, British Representative on the Supreme
War Council 1917–18 and Chief of the Imperial General Staff 1918–22,
being promoted to field-marshal in 1919. On leaving the Army he began
a political career as an Ulster Unionist M.P. and was assassinated by
Sinn Fein.
    35. Charles Sackville-West (1870–1962) held various field commands
on the Western Front in the First World War and became a major-
general. He became chief staff officer to Wilson at the Supreme War
Council 1917. Succeeded as 4th Baron Sackville 1928.
    Frederick Maurice (1871–1951). A key figure in Lloyd George's
career. From 1915 to 1918 he was Director of Military Operations at the
War Office. On his removal from this post in April 1918, he wrote to
The Times alleging that Lloyd George had misled the Commons over
British strength in France. This led to the 'Maurice debate' the following
month, which definitively split the Liberal Party: M.P.s who had voted
against Lloyd George in this debate were refused the coalition 'coupon'
in the 1918 general election. Maurice was discharged from the Army,
without the court martial or court of inquiry he demanded, and became
a journalist, university teacher and military historian. His nose was flat,
as if he had been punched.

sailles he also took this role, and used to turn his cap around. He was styled 'Henry von Vilson'.

A telegram arrived from Frances this afternoon, saying that she had bought a house at Worplesdon. L.G. told me he would not have bought it.

L.G. talked about a misstatement that Winston has made in his book. He states that L.G. went to Asquith and said if he did not agree to Bonar [Law] and the Tories coming in he would resign.[36] L.G. did no such thing. L.G. said the difficulties he had when he started the Ministry of Munitions were terrific. He started in 6 Whitehall Gardens with only J.T.[37] and a box. He did not think he even had a chair. Nobody would help him and everybody was against him. He had given up the next most important post to that of Prime Minister to take on a job which all his so-called friends were saying was either useless or at which he would fail. The War Office were absolutely against him. . . . McKenna, who took his position as Chancellor of the Exchequer, was tremendously jealous. L.G. said he did not go to Cabinet but concentrated absolutely on his munitions job. He was in a difficult position because Asquith at that time was very much prejudiced in favour of Mrs McKenna. L.G. said that even his old uncle was against him taking on the munitions. . . .

29 November

At coffee, L.G. talked of Winston falling in the stream near Llany-stumdwy. He said he was merely trying to dam it. Tonight, before dinner, we had a bottle of Bollinger and Megan put on the gramo-phone. We had the 'Volga Boat Song', *Tannhäuser* and Handel's 'Largo'. L.G. said that *Tannhäuser* was the finest music ever written. He was also passionately fond of Handel's 'Largo'. Then we had 'For all the Saints', sung by the choir of the Temple Church, with that boy's beautiful voice. L.G. said it was the finest piece ever sung by any choir. The choir was built up by Walford Davies.

L.G. said that Gandhi was by far the cleverest man he had ever come across.

30 November

L.G. said Winston had said that the Dardanelles were the hope of the world. He spoke of it, said L.G., as if it were Calvary.

36. This would have been at the time of the formation of the coalition government of May 1916, when Tories joined Asquith's administration and Lloyd George became Minister of Munitions. Churchill's statement comes in *The World Crisis*, vol. II (1923), p. 365.

37. J. T. (Sir John) Davies (1881–1936) was a private secretary to Lloyd George 1912–22.

1 *December*
L.G. walked round the deck for his usual quarter of a mile before
breakfast, the doctor and I accompanying him. He was particularly
brilliant at breakfast this morning. He is now reading Winston's
third volume. He said how tremendously conceited Winston was
regarding his own efforts in the war. He gave the book the title
The World Crisis and, under this heading, he simply and solely
explained his own case and defended himself. He devoted two pages
to showing what great efforts the Russians made to make munitions,
yet he dismissed the whole of the British effort – which was, of
course, L.G. – in two lines. Talking of casualties in the war, L.G.
said the Belgians had had the lowest of all. He said they opened
their mouths pretty wide at the peace conference, until they had to
be told. One day, when they had been pressing their case very hard,
Clemenceau sent for the Belgian Foreign Secretary, M. Hymans.[38]
He said: 'Monsieur Hymans, do you love your country?' 'Ah,' he
said, putting his hand on his heart, 'I love my country very dearly.'
'And are you a great patriot?' said Clemenceau. Moving his hands
in the air, he said: 'Indeed I am.' 'And are you willing to do anything for your country, by giving it any service?' continued Clemenceau. 'Indeed, there is nothing in the world I would not do to serve
my country.' 'Then', roared Clemenceau, 'go and drown yourself.'

2 *December*
. . . I received a wire from Colombo asking whether L.G. would
receive a deputation on board and afterwards receive the Reception
Committee of Welcome, when the Speaker of the House would
garland him. L.G. said that this was the kind of thing that spoiled a
holiday but he supposed he would have to do it.

L.G. said Wilson[39] was a man full of personal hatred. He remembered his attitude when Roosevelt[40] died. It was very ungenerous.
L.G. was reminded of what an American senator said when he read
of the death of a man whom he loathed. He said: 'Speak not ill of
the dead – but all the same he was an awful skunk.'

L.G. said that when Megan arrived at the [ship's] fancy-dress
party last night looking like Queen Victoria he was glad that he had
never had anything to do with her, for he would have quarrelled
terribly with her [i.e., with Queen Victoria].

38. Paul Hymans (1865–1941). Belgian Minister in London 1915–17,
Foreign Minister 1918–20. In 1920 he presided over the first Assembly
of the League of Nations.
39. Woodrow Wilson (1856–1924). President of the United States
1913–21.
40. Theodore Roosevelt (1858–1919). President of the United States
1901–9.

The ship arrives at Bombay.

4 December

This has been a most successful day. I was up early and wrote letters
home and posted L.G.'s private one to Frances. We could see Bombay
and were soon alongside at 9 a.m. A huge crowd assembled at the
quay and alongside the road from the docks to the town hall, shouting and cheering and clapping 'God bless Lloyd George'. The town
hall was beflagged and looking very gay. The Mayor made a very
good speech, and L.G. replied in splendid fashion. He was just his
old self, and it did my heart good to see him. This was the first public
appearance he has made since his operation. His voice was good; there
was his usual vigour and fire. After the meeting, we all went to
Government House. We were very kindly welcomed by the Governor[41] and Lady Sykes.[42] He is not very popular but she is extremely
so. It was a very interesting lunch. On our way back to the ship,
Dame Margaret stopped at an optician's and bought a pair of
spectacles on the spot, by selection, and not by testing.

At four o'clock the ship heaved her anchor and we left Bombay
behind. We assembled in Dame Margaret's cabin in the evening as
usual at 7 p.m. L.G. was again on about Winston and said that he
was an obstinate fellow and that had been his ruin. The captain [of
the ship] said that Keir Hardie was said to have done a great deal
of harm in India by spreading bolshevism or communism. L.G. said
he had been rather fanatical on subjects like tobacco and drink, but
he had not been a bad fellow. Over our champagne, L.G. usually
speaks his mind freely. We gave him a toast, in the middle of which
Megan said: 'Here's to Liberalism.' L.G. said: 'Liberalism be damned.'
He said he had been thinking a good deal about it. Smuts had told
him that one of the best things he could have done was to break
away from it. L.G. said he would drink to radicalism, but be damned
to Liberalism as it is now practised – Liberalism which mixed itself
with rancid oil. Liberalism was oleaginous.

41. Frederick Sykes (1877–1954). He joined the Army during the Boer
War and stayed on as a regular. He was briefly in 1914 commander of
the Royal Flying Corps and he commanded the Royal Naval Air Service
at Gallipoli. He was Chief of Air Staff 1918–19 and Controller of Civil
Aviation in the Air Ministry 1919–22. He was a Tory M.P. 1920–8 and
1940–5, and Governor of Bombay 1928–33. Knight Grand Cross of the
Bath 1919.
42. Lady (Isabel) Sykes was a daughter of Bonar Law. When she told
her father of her engagement, he replied: 'Oh, Isabel, how could you
when you knew I was so worried about Ireland?'

5 December

At breakfast L.G. said there was once a Member of Parliament who had a farm and milk business at Maidstone. Wheeler was his name. One day he was summoned for having water in his milk. The poor old boy died soon afterwards, probably because of the worry of the case about which, of course, he knew nothing. L.G. said he used to sell milk but he had suddenly thought of this case and he had decided that, before he was summoned for allegedly watering his milk – for it would be easy for any spiteful person to water his milk – he would get rid of his cows, and he had done so.

Over the usual bottle, Megan and I put on the gramophone, which played selections from Gracie Fields, including 'The Five-barred Gate', and Aimée McPherson and her sermon 'Come unto Me'. L.G. said it was a good thing for Megan to have a difficult time. She had been spoiled in the last parliament. There was nothing like the comradeship of a small, despised band.

6 December

The doctor and I started in good style this morning: in the swimming-tank at 6.30 a.m. and at Holy Communion at 7.30 a.m., the service being conducted by Bishop Green[43] of Melbourne, Australia. At breakfast L.G. said he often thought how much he would like to lead the opposition in Heaven: what fine material there would be for him to make an attack. Look, said L.G., how much water there is in the sea. Look how much rain falls in one part of the world and practically none in another, where everybody was suffering from drought. L.G. and Dame Margaret invited the Elliots to take coffee with them tonight. L.G. sat with Lady Elliot on his right and I sat on his left. He talked to her for the first part of the time and then, as usual, got the ear of all. Talking of aeroplanes, he said he had never been in the air, but that if he did so he would prefer to go in an airship rather than aeroplane. Lady Elliot talked of the strains through which he must have gone in the war. L.G. said it was terrible, of course. The great thing was to be able to throw off difficulties. He thought that temperament played a very important part, more so than physical fitness. One of his greatest blessings in time of difficulty, L.G. said, was that he was able to sleep. In the middle of the day a sleep enabled one's organism to relax and broke the tautness and the strain imposed upon the body and brain. Fortunately, he could sleep at will. That was brought about largely by temperament but also by practice. The terrible thing in the war, L.G. said, was to

43. Rt Rev. A. V. Green (1857–1944), Bishop of Grafton and Armidale, Australia, 1894–1900 and of Ballaret 1900–15.

wake up in the morning and think that here we had about 5 millions of men faced by many more millions, and that his job was to devise means of killing more men. It was an awful subject to contemplate and the only thing to do was to put it out of one's mind.

We arrived at Colombo at 11.15 p.m. I wrote up my journal and retired at 2 a.m.

7 December

At the jetty L.G. was received by the Speaker and a distinguished reception committee. In reply, L.G. said how delighted he was to visit this wonderful island.

Talking at dinner about people being mollycoddled, L.G. gave the instance of Sir Herbert Lewis.[44] When L.G. was a young man he went to speak at Liverpool. He was taken to the house of Herbert Lewis. L.G. was warned beforehand that Herbert was very ill, dying of tuberculosis. He might just be able to sit up sufficiently to welcome him, but he could not remain up until L.G. returned from the meeting. There he was, coddled and muffled up by his wife. Then L.G. described how the wife died, although she had been a very strong young woman. He married again and forty years later he was under-secretary in the Ministry of Education.[45] L.G. always said that Herbert would live to see all his contemporaries die, and write a letter of condolence to their relatives. Only two were left now – L.G. and Sir Vincent Evans.[46] Some five years ago Herbert met with an accident. He fell down a quarry, breaking his spine. Everybody said he would die. But L.G. said: 'No, he won't', and he was still alive. He read every new book that was published. He kept a list of all his friends who died and he wrote as firm a hand as ever he did. Last time L.G. went to see him, he was discussing the latest book on Russia which, fortunately, L.G. had read.

The following relates to the visit paid by Ramsay MacDonald to Lloyd George at Churt on 16 September 1931, just after he had formed the National Government.

44. Sir Herbert Lewis (1858–1933). Liverpool solicitor. He was a Liberal M.P. 1892–1922 and a junior minister 1905–22. His first wife died 1895 after nine years of marriage and he married again 1897. He became bedridden after an accident in a disused quarry 1925.

45. Strictly, the post was Parliamentary Secretary to the Board of Education, which Lewis held 1916–22.

46. Sir Vincent Evans (1846–1934). Leading member of the London Welsh community who did much to revive cultural traditions back in Wales. Knighted 1909 and made Companion of Honour 1922.

L.G. described that Ramsay MacDonald was precisely the same. From the earliest days L.G. remembered this. He would say to him: 'Ramsay, you are looking very well.' Ramsay would reply: 'Ah, but I am not really. I have got such a pain in my heart.' Another time it would be his kidneys, another time it would be his stomach and another time his head. When he came to see L.G. at Churt, L.G. said he was glad he was looking so well, after having been through so much. 'Ah,' said Ramsay, 'but I have terrible pains in my head.' L.G. said: 'Yes, I know how you feel. I remember that towards the end of my premiership how I suffered from neuralgia.' 'Ah,' said Ramsay, 'but *these* pains are like red-hot irons in my head.' L.G. said he made out that he had a noise like a whistle in his head.

8 December
After breakfast we all went shopping. L.G. wanted to buy something for Frances and Jennifer. Megan watched me like a cat watching a mouse. First there was an elephant that he liked. I had to bargain for that. Megan came up to me and said: 'Well, A.J., what are you getting?' So I said, 'Oh, much too dear,' and walked away to look at something less noticeable. The same with the silver bull. I went back later and bought both for L.G. at reduced prices. We went to lunch at the Governor's.[47] L.G. talked about Kitchener and said he was like a lighthouse. He flashed now and then with brilliance, but was not otherwise so.

11 December
L.G. is worked up about getting his mail from Frances. He keeps counting the hours when we should have it.

12 December
At about tea time, when L.G. wanted to go out, it started to rain, and he was decidedly difficult and very uneasy. If it rained, he said, he would go. Where, I do not know. It was quite clear what was on his mind. The next moment he was excited about his mail. When would it arrive? What arrangements had I made?

When at dinner we got to the stage of eating ginger, Megan asked L.G. if he had some. He replied: 'No, old Swift Joly has cut all the ginger out of me.'

13 December
. . . It was decided tonight that tomorrow we leave for the hotel at Banderawela. If the letters do not arrive, I shall have to stop here

47. Sir Graeme Thomson (1875–1933). Governor of Ceylon 1931–3.

and bring them on. L.G. is all worked up at the mere prospect of getting a letter from Frances. He is just like a bundle of electricity. He said today: 'Do you realise that when we leave here we shall have our noses for the first time towards home?'

14 December

All is well. A letter has arrived, addressed to me, from Frances for L.G. We had a lovely sit-out after dinner. L.G. said apropos of our going to lunch with the Suez Canal authorities that he was definitely against these kind of things now. Ramsay MacDonald would revel in them, but he had reached the stage where he disliked them and preferred not to have them. Bonar was the same. L.G. said that he loathed courts and he liked now to cut out all such engagements.

15 December

L.G. thought it would be nice to send a wire to Mrs Churchill to see how Winston was. So I immediately dispatched a cable saying that L.G. was sorry to hear of Winston's accident[48] and hoped that he was progressing favourably. At dinner, talking of Winston, L.G. said that Labby[49] once said that one could rat but not re-rat. Winston had re-re-ratted.[50]

There was a discussion over dinner on the question of two women shooting a judge in Bengal. L.G. said they [the British] would have to make up their minds whether they were going to give the Indians what they wanted, or handle the situation. The trouble was that, although the Englishman talked about handling things, when the Government tackled the question the nation got up in arms about the methods, which would have to be like the Black and Tans in Ireland. In that case anyone could come along and shoot a defenceless officer in bed, or his wife, but immediately the assassin was hounded out there was a hue and cry from some of our own people. There was a curious sentiment in the English, said L.G.

48. On 13 December 1931 Churchill was knocked over by a taxi on Fifth Avenue, New York, where he had been due to lecture. He suffered shock, concussion and bruising, and later developed pleurisy. He was on his feet again by the end of the month. He exonerated the taxi driver from blame and said he had momentarily forgotten that traffic in the United States goes on the right side of the road.

49. Henry Du Pré Labouchere (1831–1912). Liberal M.P. 1867–8, 1880–1906. Founder and editor of *Truth*, a radical, campaigning weekly paper.

50. Churchill was elected as a Tory M.P. in 1900 and crossed the floor to join the Liberals in 1904. He rejoined the Tories in 1924 but by 1931 was at odds with most of the party over India.

C

16 December

After breakfast I went with L.G. to the fort. He asked me to buy an ivory tiger. They wanted £20; I got it for £15. I also got a Turkish carpet, which I had packed in a zinc-lined box. It is not going to be easy to get these things home without the family knowing.[51] I went by launch to the *Rajputana*[52] to see our accommodation and returned for lunch. L.G. was talking about the League of Nations. He said it was a factory for manufacturing flapdoodle. Speaking of Winston's accident L.G. said: 'How like him.' It was because of his impulsiveness and going against all traffic signals. He saw the traffic signals and paid no heed to them, and in consequence was knocked flying. It is not the only time he has paid no heed to signals.

The party is now back aboard ship on the homeward voyage.

17 December

We assembled in L.G.'s cabin and drank a bottle of Bollinger, which was grand. L.G. related how, when he went to Germany in 1908 to inquire about national health-insurance in that country, he had an interview with Bethmann-Hollweg,[53] who talked very tactlessly. He said that East Prussia would always stand loyally by the Kaiser, but Bavaria and some other parts 'ach, ach'. L.G. said: 'Fancy my saying that England would remain loyally by the King but Wales and Scotland, never, never.' Bethmann-Hollweg also said: 'What are England and France becoming so friendly for? Ach, merely to strangle Germany, of course.'

L.G. said he was glad he had sent that wire to Mrs Churchill because he was a nice creature and he liked him. Winston was exceedingly funny when he related the story of the Mayor of Sheffield who said: 'We are in a clinical position, the scene is dark and obscene, and the prospect buggers description.' L.G. said he must get that story properly from Winston.

22 December

It seems extraordinary, but Megan has not been up one day before eleven o'clock. She spends the whole of the morning saying her

51. These were presents for Frances and Jennifer.
52. The ship in which they were to return home.
53. Theobald von Bethmann-Hollweg (1856–1921). Chancellor of Germany 1909–17. At the time of this meeting with Lloyd George he was State Secretary in the Imperial Office of the Interior.

prayers. Then she seems to sit up half the night. I like Megan, and she is attractive, but she is a very difficult person to manage. She is clever in a certain kind of a way, but so self-centred that I wonder how far she will get when she is left to herself, and has not the reflex action of her father. He, too, is terribly self-centred. At the table he is sometimes most funny. How it is that he has any digestion left, I cannot understand for the life of me. He must have an inside like a horse. He sits down and says 'Now' and, in quick succession, demands this, that and the other, and complains if it is not produced *now*. He bolts his food and then says: 'Now, Maggie, are you ready?' and although she had only just got her fruit on the plate she is expected to leave it and follow him.

I sent a wire to Frances, saying: 'Happy Christmas for all at Bognor Carmel.'

25 December

We all went to divine service and the Rev. Sandys, a minister from China, who had been captured by bandits, preached a short sermon which was very effective, and which L.G. much enjoyed. He sent him a message through me to this effect. Tonight the second-class passengers came to dine in the first-class saloon. L.G. and his party had been invited to a party of sixteen, but did not go. He said to me afterwards that the king should never be seen with his crown at a slant. That is what he thought of the captain when he saw him wearing a little toy hat and a paper nose.

When the ship arrived at Port Said, Lloyd George and his party travelled to Cairo and to see the pyramids.

27 December

We went to pay our respects to the Coptic Patriarch. He is a remarkable old man of eighty-six, with a long, grey beard and such a keen black eye. I have met three men who have attracted me by their eyes. L.G. is the first and most outstanding one; King Feisal[54] is the second; and this old man is the third. The two latter have identical black eyes whilst L.G.'s are bluey grey or greyish blue. The Minister of Communications had placed his own special coach at L.G.'s disposal and we had a very comfortable journey back to Port

54. King Feisal I (1885–1933) was the son of the Emir or Mecca and rose in revolt against the Turks 1916–18, in alliance with Britain. Feisal visited Britain in 1918–19 and 1921. He was King of Iraq 1921–33.

Said, dining on the train. At the ship my cabin was full of mail.
I found two letters from Frances for L.G. and that kept him quiet.

29 December

At coffee there was talk of L.G.'s visit to Sandringham with Dame
Margaret. He was making his way to the bedroom, wearing his
frock coat, when a big door was opened by the butler and there
were the King and Queen waiting for L.G. and Dame Margaret. Tea
was laid for four and they all sat down. Dame Margaret said the
Queen was knitting. The gramophone in the lounge of the ship is a
very good one. L.G. said that the King had one somewhat similar, in
which he took great pride. He himself [i.e., the King] put on a piece
which he said was the best of all : 'In a Monastery Garden'. He was
as pleased as a boy. L.G. said he had come to the conclusion that
there was more suffering in the world from boredom than from pain.
Jokingly, he said : 'Look what I have to suffer', and pointed at Dame
Margaret.

30 December

We did our usual round the deck. L.G. was musing about Ramsay.
He said he was the most conceited prime minister there ever was.
I showed L.G. a letter which has come from J.T. [Davies] in which
he said he would even yet win his bet that L.G. would be Prime
Minister at eighty. He also said he had seen St Davids[55] who was
concerned at our expenses and that we would have to tighten our
belts. The investments were down badly, but the hope was that
Runciman[56] would introduce protection on paper and that would
send up Inveresk shares.

The doctor and I went to tea and were joined by L.G. and Dame
Margaret. Megan was very late. L.G. left soon after she arrived and
I joined him. He said to me as we sat down in the drawing-room
what a peculiar girl she was. He had seen scarcely anything of her
on this boat. He said she was just the same at Churt. Although he
often begged her to be up early, she was never up before eleven
o'clock to go for a walk with him, even though he was probably
absolutely alone and dependent upon her. I said to L.G. that this
selfishness was having a great effect on her whole career. No one
would want to marry her. L.G. remarked that she had made up her

55. John Winford Philipps, 1st Viscount St Davids (1860–1938). He was
a Liberal M.P. 1888–94 and 1898–1908. Made a baron 1908 and a viscount
1918. Landed proprietor and businessman. He, Sir John Davies and Gwilym
Lloyd George were the trustees of the Lloyd George Political Fund.
56. Walter Runciman (1870–1949), the current President of the Board
of Trade.

mind to celibacy when she took up a political career. She liked the company of men and wanted to be the centre of attraction. . . .

1932

2 January

We left our moorings in Marseilles harbour at 7.45 and sailed into the Gulf of Lions, and immediately ran into bad weather with very high seas. L.G., Dame Margaret and I were the only ones of our party who went to the dining-saloon for lunch. L.G. said he would not lose any time, and it was almost agony to eat with him. He had Scotch pie, which was made of minced beef and macaroni. He woofed this up almost before I had started on my curry. He gobbled up an orange and sat looking at Dame Margaret and said 'Now' in his characteristic fashion, meaning 'Come on!' He ought by every rule to be a chronic dyspeptic. It is damned miserable to eat with him, that is all I know about it, especially on occasions like this. We nearly lost all the things off the table once or twice, so great was the roll. After a cognac which L.G. had, we went to sit outside again and he went to sleep. It was all beginning to quieten down at tea time, and we all five had a walk on the deck. Dame Margaret then practised with deck quoits and L.G., observing her, said : 'The old gel is very game, isn't she?'

Rothermere sent L.G. a new year's message tonight, which is very kind of him. L.G. said he would trust him far more than Beaverbrook. The doctor said he thought Beaverbrook was a friend. 'Yes,' said L.G., 'he likes me and I like him, but that would not prevent him doing me in.'

3 January

I went with L.G. and Dame Margaret to the barber's shop where, despite it being Sunday, he had his hair cut. We all went to divine service at which the Rev. Sandys officiated. He gave a splendid sermon of five minutes' duration. Before dinner, L.G. said that he and Curzon used to have a good many discussions on the Bible. Curzon was probably actually better than L.G. on the Bible, and L.G. is remarkably good. But Curzon was never at fault. He knew his Bible from beginning to end. At divine service this morning we had the hymn 'Thy Kingdom Come, O God', which L.G. said he had first heard sung at Walton Heath during the war. He was so struck by it that he got Megan to sing it to him when they got home. This morning he got Megan to write it out, so that he could translate it into Welsh. He has already translated the first verse. His idea is to get William George[57] to have it sung in his little chapel of Berea, Criccieth.

4 January

This morning I was called at 5.30 by the steward and informed that we were passing Gibraltar. I got up at once and called Miss Roberts,[58] who in turn called Dame Margaret and Megan. I just looked through the porthole on the starboard side of the ship, but could see only a few lights and nothing of the rock. So I quickly got back to bed. Dame Margaret went in to L.G., who was fast asleep. L.G. has never ceased to tease Dame Margaret about it since. He relates how Dame Margaret woke him up in the middle of the night to say it was impossible to see the rock of Gibraltar. He roars with laughter. . . .

At dinner L.G. said that the ablest industrialists, economists and financiers in the world would be found in America, Germany and England, and yet it was there that things were worse than elsewhere. [He is referring to the world economic depression.] Businessmen, financiers and economists had been fools. They had not seen the depression coming and they had not any remedy for the troubles which were now upon us. Capitalism had broken down. The communists had a very good case. They said that it is not that you have not good men – you have plenty; it is your system that is wrong. The plan they were now working on in Russia was one of the most wonderful experiments the world had ever seen. They were now in their third year. They said they wanted five. Well, even if it took ten years, it would be a wonderful thing. They were a hard-working people, though they were not practical.

5 January

The doctor gave L.G. a thorough examination this evening. He told me afterwards : 'He is a bloody marvel. He has got the heart of a young man of thirty-five, and the blood pressure, too; and he has the chest and expansion of a prize fighter.'

Lloyd George disembarked at Plymouth and finished his journey to Churt by train and car. The rest of the party sailed on to London.

6 January

The Deputy Mayor and Mayoress greeted L.G. at Plymouth. Photographs were taken and there were crowds of press to see him. I got

57. Lloyd George's younger brother.
58. Maid to Dame Margaret and Megan.

all L.G.'s things to the Friary station, including the special trunk[59]
I had bought for him without the rest of the family knowing. I saw
L.G. on to the train. He said : 'Goodbye Sylvester, God bless you', a
thing he has not said before.

59. Containing presents for Miss Stevenson and Jennifer.

Chapter 3

'I have not the slightest intention of retiring'

1932

On his return from Ceylon, Lloyd George rented a suite of offices in Thames House, Millbank, adjacent to the Houses of Parliament. Here T. F. Tweed was the director of such central political organisation as the Lloyd George family group of four Independent Liberal M.P.s had. Here, too, Sylvester ran Lloyd George's private office.

20 January

We are now installed in Thames House. The other day Tweed told L.G. of the up-to-dateness of the office and chutes for letters and chutes for rubbish – the latter went down to the furnace. L.G. thought that was brilliant and asked who would be the first Liberal to be put down the chute.

2 March

I was amazed when Megan suddenly walked into my room in the House. I thought she was at Criccieth. I was further surprised when she said she was going to speak, and she spoke very well. She said that the Liberals on the front bench who were friends of Sir Herbert Samuel seemed to be a marriage of convenience, not a love-match; they did not even try to keep up appearances. It was well received. I had to promise that I would not tell her father that she had spoken. I did tell L.G., privately, and he asked me to get a paragraph in the *Evening Standard*. Whenever Megan has a good remark it is always said to be from her father. It always upsets her. She is more effective when she works out her speech on her own. (It is difficult to tell L.G. that, however.)

8 March

I left Paddington for Shrewsbury with L.G., breakfasting in the train. We were joined by Sir John Reith at High Wycombe. . . .

Reith asked L.G. if he was in favour of all this national feeling which was showing itself in Scotland and Wales. L.G. said he did not mind what happened as long as something would get men's minds away from the terribly mercenary and materialist attitude which had prevailed in the last few years. This was an age of commonplace things, of mediocrity. It was because Baldwin had the happy knack of saying commonplace things in an emphatic way that he was heralded as a safe man and was popular.

L.G. said that Garvin[1] wanted him to write on democracy for the *Encyclopaedia Britannica* but he had declined. We were only just in the middle of democracy.

9 March

Tom Clarke of the *News Chronicle* gave a lunch to L.G. at the Hotel Metropole. I introduced L.G. to a number of the new Liberal Members of Parliament, whom he had not yet met. One of them said: 'How are you, Mr Lloyd George?' He replied: 'I am very much better than the Liberal Party.' In his speech L.G. said: 'I have not the slightest idea of trying to form a party. I have not the slightest intention of trying to lead the Liberal Party. Nor have I the slightest intention of retiring.'

21 March

I accompanied L.G. last night to Emery's[2] presentation. He has been a lobby journalist for fifty-two years. Practically the whole of the Government was present. Mr Baldwin said he hoped that Mr Emery would write a book of reminiscences. 'I wish you would write a book on "The Truth about Lloyd George".' I did not think L.G. was very comfortable about this.

Sylvester was on a visit to Churt.

4 April

L.G., Frances and I breakfasted at 9.15. L.G. asked whether Aristotle was an Athenian. He thought he was not. He said how much he had learned by looking up things like this. When he was a boy, his uncle insisted on getting the book at once, and not waiting until after

1. J. L. Garvin (1868–1947). Editor of the *Observer* 1908–42 and one of the most influential Tory journalists of his day. He was editor-in-chief of the fourteenth edition of the *Encyclopaedia Britannica* 1926–9.
2. R. J. Emery (1860–1940). Political correspondent of the *Morning Post*. This occasion marked his retirement.

breakfast. Frances got the book, but it did not contain the information. So I got John Gillie's *Aristotle* and there we found that L.G. was right, for Aristotle was born on the shores of Thrace, at a place called Stagira.

L.G., Nurse Neal,[3] Jennifer and I walked through the orchards. It was delightful to see the young buds springing forth. We visited the duck pond. L.G. turned on the water and 'made rain for Jennifer'. She turned the hosepipe on Taid[4] and Taid got wet. I could not help asking myself who was the bigger baby.

Later, I accompanied him to Green Farm, which L.G. has given to Megan, which is still vacant. I asked him why Megan did not let it. He said that she was like his old uncle in many respects. His uncle's mother left him with a first-rate boot-business. It was her money which paid his fees to become an articled clerk and pass his law examinations. When machine-made boots came in, instead of stocking them and saying to his customers: 'If you want the cheaper ones, here they are', he just did not bother. He was unpractical. L.G. implied that Megan was the same. He could not remember his uncle ever talking to him about religion with a view to influencing him. He gave up a lot of time to prayers. Megan takes after L.G.'s uncle, yet one never hears her talking of religion. L.G. said she had no business instincts, yet she had more of his own flair than the rest.

I said it was a pity that she had not a husband who was a good businessman. He suddenly stopped, as is his habit, and said: 'She would never allow anybody to dominate her now.' As we walked across a ploughed field, L.G. wondered whether Megan would be any good as a minister. He thought she might, if she had a good private secretary and officials, who would be responsible for the administrative side. The important thing was to know which was the bright idea when brought forward: in other words, judgement.

Later he went to see Jennifer put to bed. Presently there was a call to me from her nurse saying that 'Uncle Vester' was requested by Jennifer to say goodnight. There I found her in her little cot. L.G. worships that kid.

12 April

At lunch at the Metropole with L.G., Frances and Tweed, we were joined by Sir William Sutherland.[5] L.G. said he was one of the best

3. Jennifer's nurse.
4. Welsh for 'grandpa'; used by Jennifer of Lloyd George.
5. Sir William Sutherland (1880–1949). A journalist who was press secretary to Lloyd George 1915–18 and then a joint parliamentary private secretary to him 1918–20.

and cutest politicians of the day. McCurdy[6] was the other. Frances reminded L.G. of what Keynes[7] had said in his letter to L.G. about his book on reparations.[8] He had reminded L.G. of Cunliffe's[9] remark when asked how he had arrived at such and such a figure. He had said: 'I thought about it in church.' L.G. said that Cunliffe probably never put his nose inside a church. He then related how in 1914 he took Cunliffe to Paris to a meeting of the Russians, the French and ourselves, and how he, L.G., made a speech on the general situation and then called upon Cunliffe to give the policy of the Bank of England. Cunliffe rose with several sniffs, as was his habit, and said: 'We do not intend to part with our *gold*.' Then he sat down.

Sylvester refers here to various petty rivalries and quarrels in Lloyd George's office and among him and his entourage.

27 April

The atmosphere which surrounds me is the most unpleasant and distasteful that I have experienced for some years. In addition, there is a great shortage of money. J.T. [Davies] has again mentioned that it may be necessary for me to ask for a reduction of salaries. Tweed says he will agree if L.G. will get rid of certain persons. J.T. says that L.G. is afraid of Tweed and that is why he will not get rid of him.

13 May

L.G. asked me to get Beaverbrook's latest book about politicians during the war.[10] Then he turned to a particular page, which contained a photograph of three persons. On the left was Sir Herbert Samuel, on the right Lord Curzon and in the middle Lord Robert Cecil.[11] He asked Dame Margaret and me whether we saw anything particular in the photograph. We both noticed an extraordinary expression on Lord Robert Cecil's face and said so. L.G. then told us

6. Charles McCurdy (1870–1941) was Lloyd George's Chief Whip 1921–2.
   7. John Maynard Keynes (1883–1946), the economist.
   8. *The Truth about Reparations and War-debts* (1932).
   9. Walter Cunliffe (1855–1920). Governor of the Bank of England 1913–20.
   10. This is *Politicians and the War* (1928).
   11. Lord Robert Cecil (1864–1958). Third son of the third Marquess of Salisbury. Tory M.P. 1906–10 and 1911–23. Foreign Under-Secretary 1915–16 and Minister of Blockade 1916–18.

it was taken at a time when they were all three against him. They had just left a conference. There was Cecil, his whole being animated by hatred, which was photographed on his face. Meantime he was wearing the cross of the Church of England on his heart.[12] L.G. said he [i.e., Lord Robert Cecil] would sacrifice anything on the altar of high principle. He said it was Cecil who had come to him when he was Prime Minister and suggested that his own cousin, Balfour, was not well fitted for the post of Foreign Secretary, and suggested that Balfour ought to be sacked and that he, Cecil, should succeed him. Balfour had told L.G. that, with all the difficulties those boys – the Cecils – had caused him, they had not prevented him getting where he had got, or doing what he wanted. His gardener admirably described such people when he said: 'Ah, sir, the trouble with them there trees is that they are too 'igh-minded to be any good.'

On our way to Criccieth we went via Sutton Courtney to see Asquith's grave. I remarked how remarkable it was that Lady Oxford[13] had had him moved. L.G. said that she never could let him rest at any time.

Sylvester is now with Lloyd George at Criccieth.

16 May
L.G., William George and I went fishing. L.G. caught a small trout. William George soon followed and later I got one, all very small. I got a big bough from a tree. On this we tied the three fishes in the middle. On arriving at Brynawelon, L.G. took one end, his brother the middle and I the other end, and, as though stooping under the immense weight of these small fishes, we walked in, much to the amusement of Dame Margaret and Megan.

23 May
L.G. said that when de Valera came to see him at 10 Downing Street he made a point of the Irish language. So L.G. brought down to the Cabinet Room two biographies in the Welsh language. One was of John Jones, Talsarn, which L.G. said was the finest biography in any language. 'Have you anything like that?' L.G. had inquired. De Valera had not.

L.G.'s attitude to religion is remarkable. He goes to chapel when

12. The picture is entitled 'The Three Cs' and shows Austen Chamberlain, Cecil and Curzon (not Samuel). There certainly is a peculiar look on Cecil's face.
13. Asquith had been ennobled as Earl of Oxford and Asquith.

in Wales. He loves good sermons. He delights in good singing. But he himself does not pray. He has told me so himself.

27 May
At mealtimes, L.G. staggers me by the rate at which he eats. If only members of the family are present, he will disappear as soon as he has finished, and does not wait for the rest. If there is company, then he will get them on to the cigar and coffee stage as soon as he can.

At dinner, speaking of his stay with Judge Bingham[14] in Kentucky, he said he had inquired who those white men were in the choir which came to sing, and was informed that they were of black parents. In time it was quite possible that if these particular people married nothing but white that all trace of black would completely go. For instance, Winston undoubtedly had nigger blood in him. Look at his build and slouch. The Marlboroughs were a poor type physically, but Winston was strong. Another characteristic of Winston is that when he gets excited he shrieks: again the nigger comes out.

7 June
L.G. comes to the House so seldom these days that a number of new M.P.s have not even seen him, let alone heard him speak. Today was an occasion. He went to the ladies' gallery entrance and waited behind the Speaker's chair until prayers were over. Then, on the call 'Speaker in the chair', he entered. I was in my front seat under the gallery. When he walked to the corner seat of the front opposition-bench, members leaned forward, nudged one another and pointed, and this process went on as more members entered the chamber. The sun streamed in through the stained-glass windows and fell on L.G. He looked a fine picture, dressed in a blue suit, with his white hair and russet-coloured face. Professor Morgan Jones[15] was the first speaker, and he greeted L.G., and the House applauded that welcome. When he came to his room, Megan said that one felt one would like to wet one's finger and rub it on his face to see it was not painted, he looked so well.

4 July
Aneurin Bevan[16] was dining at the next table at the House and there was a running conversation with our table. Aneurin did most

14. R. W. Bingham (1871–1937), American Ambassador in London 1933–7.
15. Morgan Jones (1885–1939). Labour M.P. 1921–39. He was not an academic but was a member of the Court of the University of Wales.
16. In the 1929–31 parliament Bevan made a speech attacking Lloyd George and it was written at the time that Lloyd George looked as if he

of the talking. When he had ventilated one of his themes, L.G. warned him to be careful on that. 'One day', said L.G., 'you may have responsibility and you may find yourself in difficulty if you do that.'

4 August

At dinner, L.G. said that he had been very much interested in seeing what kind of books some of his colleagues were reading during the war. On one occasion there were gathered together Asquith, as Prime Minister, Balfour, Bonar Law, Beaverbrook and Kitchener, although Kitchener did not read much. All of them were reading detective stories to get their minds from the war. He much preferred reading Wild West stories because there was always the feeling that the fellow with the pistol would make good and do the other in.

Speaking of the war, L.G. thought that the Kaiser did not deliberately engineer the Great War. He was not a sufficiently good horseman. He galloped on and on and could not pull up in time. He thought that the Germans made a first-class mistake in 1918. They should have withdrawn to the Rhine. England would never have risked another life after Belgium had been cleared. France would have obtained Alsace-Lorraine; she had already lost one and a half million men and she would not have continued either. Pershing[17] was the only man at the time of the Armistice who was willing to go on.

L.G. said that before the war 40 per cent of our trade was with foreign countries: hence our present difficulties. We were the only country which had had persistent unemployment for twelve years. We could not have weathered the storm of unemployment if we had not had unemployment insurance. We should have suffered rebellion. This unemployment insurance was a fire-insurance premium. One could not say that on the platform because it would be said that we were afraid of communism, but it was a fact.

The following reflects political eddies of the moment. The position was that Ramsay MacDonald, whose physical and mental powers

were facing the ghost of his own youth. In fact, not too close a parallel should be made of the two men. Lloyd George came from the lower middle class in rural north Wales. Bevan came from the working class in industrial south Wales and could not speak Welsh. Bevan had less opportunity than Lloyd George to prove himself in office. However, both went straight from the back benches into the Cabinet.

17. John Joseph Pershing (1860–1948). Commander-in-Chief of the American Expeditionary Force in France 1917–19.

were beginning visibly to wane, remained Prime Minister in the National Government until just before the general election of 1935. Baldwin, the Tory leader, was Lord President of the Council and, since the overwhelming majority of the M.P.s supporting the Government were Tories, the real power. In 1935, just before the general election of that year, Baldwin became Prime Minister and MacDonald went down to Lord Privy Seal. Whereas in the 1931 election there was some shade of reality in the idea of the Government being 'National', by 1935, although it kept the name 'National', it had become almost wholly Tory.

6 August

I told L.G. of J.T.'s[18] talk with Lord Bridgeman[19] outside the Ford Motors headquarters. Bridgeman told J.T. that Baldwin was not against L.G., as has been suggested. Bridgeman said that Baldwin did not want the premiership. He was sick of it. If L.G. came in [to the Government] there was the absolute succession to the premiership for him.

This is Lloyd George limbering up towards writing his War Memoirs.

24 September

Captain Liddell Hart[20] and his wife came for lunch at Brynawelon. He is the world's great military historian. Liddell Hart said that a short time ago he was in France and the attitude of the military authorities on the frontier was that they were ready to march into Germany, in respect of reparations. L.G. asked if he thought the French Army would march on Berlin. Liddell Hart was doubtful and thought it would be very difficult. This interested L.G. very much. L.G. said he could see from his book[21] that Liddell Hart was generally against Foch.[22] The effect it had had on L.G., after reading the book, was to strengthen his belief in Foch. Liddell Hart replied that he, along with other generals, was responsible for the policy of offensives,

18. J. T. Davies. (He was a director of Ford.)
19. W. C. Bridgeman (1864–1935). Tory M.P. 1906–29 and in the Cabinet 1922–4 and 1924–9.
20. Basil Liddell Hart (1895–1970) wrote some thirty books which deeply influenced military thinking.
21. Presumably his A History of the World War, 1914–18 (1930).
22. Ferdinand Foch (1851–1929). Allied Commander-in-Chief in France 1918.

which had been so disastrous. L.G., like lightning, pointed out that Foch was the only man who learned from his mistakes, which showed how much bigger he was than any of the other soldiers. 'Ah,' said L.G. in his characteristic fashion, 'Foch was a big man, the biggest of the lot. It is no use trying to carry three hundredweight on a 100-ton lorry. It rattles all over the place.' Then he added: 'There are men who I would make cabinet ministers who I would not think of making under-secretaries.' He went on to describe how some men had a big flair for a thing, but no executive or administrative ability, and vice versa. 'Foch was a man who was at his best when he had full responsibility. I fought and obtained it for him at Beauvais.[23] Clemenceau was against Foch because of his religious tendencies.' Liddell Hart said the whole trouble was that the soldier had a traditional distrust of politicians.

L.G. asked Liddell Hart what he thought of Robertson,[24] to which he replied: 'He is a one-eyed man.' Lloyd George said: 'He is a one-eyed fellow in blinkers.' He was a man with no historical background, but who, in a pompous sort of way, grunted out a few commonplace statements. He was merely the echo of 'aig,[25] as Robertson used to call him. Yet Asquith had thought him the greatest military strategist in the world.

L.G. said he sent Smuts and Hankey right round the whole of the generals to see whether they could find anyone sufficiently good to supersede Haig. They had only one suggestion to make. 'Who do you think it was?' he said. 'Jacob.'[26] He had asked them: 'Jacob? To make a change I shall have a tremendous fight in the Cabinet and with the soldiers. It will mean a lot of trouble. Is a change worth while for Jacob? The answer was "No".'

L.G. said he had recently seen documents which he had never seen before, even when he was Prime Minister, and which he most certainly ought to have seen. Here came in that distrust by soldiers of politicians. In the light of what he now knew, it was a question

23. At an Anglo-French Conference on 3 April 1918 in Beauvais, attended by Lloyd George, Foch was placed in strategic command of the whole Western Front. This was in face of the extensive breakthroughs secured by the Germans in the spring of 1918.

24. Field-Marshal Sir William Robertson (1860–1933), the only man in the history of the British Army to have risen from private to field-marshal. Chief of the Imperial General Staff from 1915 until February 1918, when Lloyd George removed him.

25. Field-Marshal Sir Douglas Haig (1861–1928). British Commander in France 1915–19. Lloyd George had a low opinion of his capabilities.

26. Sir Claud Jacob (1863–1948) made his career in the Indian Army but became a divisional commander on the Western Front 1915 and was a corps commander 1915–19. Then he returned to India where he rose to be Commander-in-Chief. He was made a field-marshal 1926.

whether he ought not to have interfered more. For instance, even as Prime Minister the news of the mutiny in the French Army was absolutely kept away from him.

Liddell Hart said that, unless one had a profound knowledge of war, it was utterly impossible to oppose the soldiers. L.G. said that he now knew that Pétain had been against the attack at Passchendaele.[27] 'They never told me that,' said L.G. and he went on: 'Here is a thing that most people would laugh at, when I say politicians do not lie, as a rule. I dare say one reason is that once they are caught they are done. Therefore a politician is much more careful. I have never known a prominent politician who tells an absolute lie. That is a curious thing to say, and I know every soldier would laugh when I say it, but it is true. By a lie I mean a man who knows it is a misstatement of fact and still makes it. These fellows (he meant the soldiers) absolutely lied to me.'

The Ottawa Conference of July–August 1932 agreed to a permanent system of tariffs for Britain, with dominion preference. This was the end of free trade, and the Liberal ministers resigned from the National Government in the September.

28 September
The Liberal ministers have resigned from the Government. I have been very busy on the phone.

L.G. was on the point of going for a walk with Gwilym and Megan when he suddenly rushed in to see me, and suddenly dictated the very first words of his war memoirs, amounting to some 400 words. In the evening he dictated just under 3000. He then wrote an envelope to Frances. It is funny how he forgets whether her name is spelled with a *v* or a *ph* and today he put *ph* and I posted it.[28]

3 October
When I arrived at Brynawelon this morning, Dame Margaret and L.G. were at breakfast alone. 'What do you think of this?' he said and proceeded to read out a letter from Ramsay Muir, which invited

---

27. Henri Philippe Pétain (1856–1951). Commanded the fortress of Verdun 1916 and became French Commander-in-Chief 1917.
    Passchendaele, more accurately the third battle of Ypres, was the British offensive 1917 which got bogged down in the mud with 324,000 casualties.
28. This, of course, refers to her surname, Stevenson.

him to the Queen's Hall meeting on 12 October to celebrate the Liberal ministers leaving the Government. But he was not asked to speak. In fact, it was made plain that he was just to sit on the platform. I said it was a preposterous position. L.G. said: 'I will give him a snorter.' Dame Margaret said, laughing: 'The best thing would be to go and sit in the body of the hall and then listen to what happened. There would be pandemonium if you were not asked to speak.'

Gwilym Lloyd George makes a speech in the Commons, attacking the Ottawa agreements, saying that they would further dislocate world trade to Britain's detriment and were likely to contribute to the ultimate disruption of the British Empire.

26 October
Gwilym made one of the best speeches I have heard him make. Dame Margaret was in Mrs Speaker's gallery and Megan was on the bench behind the front opposition-bench. Baldwin entered the chamber when Gwilym spoke, and soon the House filled, members standing at the bar. L.G. did not remain to hear Gwilym, although I had kept him informed in detail. Afterwards I phoned my impressions to him. He asked me to congratulate Gwilym and say he was sorry he had to go away.

28 October
The family are very upset about L.G. not staying for Gwilym's speech. Dame Margaret told me that it was a disgrace, and people were talking about it in the House. Gwilym is very sick; he told us that his father had not listened to him speaking for three years. They are giving him a bad time, and he deserves it.

10 November
My wife and I are at Churt. At dinner L.G. told how, when he met Taft[29] at the White House when Coolidge[30] was President, Taft had related that Mrs Lincoln was a most cantankerous woman, so much so that Abraham[31] never went home until he was obliged to do so.

29. W. H. Taft (1857–1930). President of the United States 1909–13.
30. J. C. Coolidge (1872–1933). President of the United States 1923–9.
31. Abraham Lincoln (1809–65). President of the United States 1861–5. From an early age Lloyd George had regarded Lincoln as his hero and, to some extent, his model.

When Lincoln was about to be chosen candidate, an important delegation came from New York to see him in Springfield. Lincoln talked about the different characters in families. He said : 'For instance, there is my wife's family. There are two distinct characters, one of which is cantankerous, difficult and always quarrelling; and the other is amiable, loving and broad-minded. My wife', said Lincoln, 'belongs to the latter.' The last remark was made to the accompaniment of a cup and saucer whizzing through the air towards Lincoln's head. It had been thrown by his wife.

Another story by Taft was that Lincoln was asked one day to receive a man from Tennessee. He did. He asked the President a large number of questions. In the end the visitor said : 'Well, Mr President, you have answered all my questions very clearly, and I am well pleased. I shall be able to go back to my home town and explain everything very satisfactorily. But there is one further question I should like to ask. I apologise for asking it. I am told that you are very fond of the ladies and I should like to know if that is true, Mr President.'

When L.G. got thus far, he laughed heartily and said, 'No, I cannot tell that story.' But, with a little persuasion, he proceeded.

'Lincoln said : "Well, Mr Phillips, when I was a boy in Kentucky, I used to have to walk four miles to school, and as I could not come home to lunch my mother packed my lunch in a wallet. One day she made some gingerbread and packed it up for my lunch. Now one of my playmates was a little boy, and when he saw my gingerbread he said : 'I like gingerbread.' My mother was poor and Joe's mother was poor, so I said : 'Yes, you can take some of my gingerbread', but I was surprised to see that he took it all. So I said to Joey : 'Joey, do you like gingerbread?' 'Yes, Abe,' he replied. 'I like it very much, but I never get any.' That's my answer to you, Mr Phillips," said Lincoln. "I like it very much, but I never get any." '

12 November

Major and Mrs Nathan[32] came to dinner. L.G. said there was one thing that he would not say in his book. Winston had come up to him at Walton Heath and said : 'I shall be the biggest man in Europe if this comes off' – the Dardenelles. That was Winston's trouble, said L.G., personal ambition. If soldiers had been sent, it would have been Kitchener's success. Winston and Kitchener put in Hamilton. Both made the same mistake, through having no judgement of men. Nathan asked : 'Supposing anything had happened to

32. H. L. Nathan (1889–1963). Liberal M.P. 1929–34, then joined the Labour Party. Defeated in the 1935 election but was a Labour M.P. 1937–40. A neighbour of Lloyd George at Churt.

Haig, who would you have made head of the Army?' L.G. said:
'It did not happen, and the reason why was because there was no
one to put in his place, at least sufficiently good to make it worth
while making a change. There was no one with intellect except
Foch.'

22 November

L.G. said that he had discussed with Winston on one occasion
whether he would like to have another go at life. Winston had said
'No', and so had McCurdy. L.G. said he would like another chance
if he could go on from where he now was.

24 November

Today is my 43rd anniversary. Everybody worked hard today to get
off to Norman Collins,[33] literary editor of the *News Chronicle*, 40,000-
odd words. L.G. has an arrangement with him to advise as to whether
the material is good reading-matter for the public. For dinner we
had soup and sausages and mashed potatoes. L.G. said that if he had
known it was my anniversary he would have had something better.
I said it was good enough for me.

*Sylvester visits Sir Eric Geddes to obtain material for Lloyd George's
memoirs.*

2 December

I saw Sir Eric Geddes to question him on L.G.'s behalf about
munitions in the war. I made shorthand notes of everything he said.
He told me how in an empty building in Whitehall Gardens he
first met L.G. in those early days when he was first made Minister
of Munitions. His methods were strange to everybody. He interviewed applicants with a crowd of secretaries and hangers-on around
him. He considered you much as a casual labourer at the docks
would be treated. 'He asked me if I knew anything about munitions.
I did not. He asked me what I could do. I said I had a faculty for
getting things done. "Very well," said he, "I will make you head
of the department." '

Sir Eric said: 'How this ministry ever succeeded, God only knows.
It was the craziest department ever organised by mortal man. There
was a whiskey salesman organising ammunition factories, and a ship
owner and a boot-factory owner combined buying gun ammunition.'

33. Norman Collins (b.1907). Novelist and broadcasting executive.
Assistant literary editor of the *News Chronicle* 1929–33.

Sir Eric said that millions of shell cases had accumulated at Woolwich, but there was nothing to put in them because of no decision on filling. What shells were being filled were laid out in rows on tables and were filled by pouring the filling, like treacle, by hand with a ladle and spilling it on the ground. He said that that was where L.G. nearly got his biggest toss. If he, Sir Eric, had not put the filling situation straight, L.G. would have been held up to execration by the Army and the nation because he had millions of shell bodies and no means of filling them. It was because of this that L.G. had had such faith in Sir Eric. L.G. had been on the edge of catastrophe.

Sir Eric said that in the last quarter of 1915, owing to the extraordinary driving power of Mr Lloyd George, we could see the results for ourselves. 'Yet the War Office jeered at us.'

Sir Eric went to Kitchener and told him he wanted to know the proportions of rifles to machine guns that would be required nine months hence, so that he could make his plans. Kitchener's reply had been: 'Do you think I am God Almighty that I can tell you what is wanted nine months ahead?' 'No, sir,' Sir Eric had replied, 'and I do not think that I am either, but we have to work it out between us and try to get it right.' Then Kitchener had given the old War Office answer: 'I want as much of both as you can produce.' Eventually Kitchener had said that the proportion was to be two machine guns per battalion as a minimum and four as a maximum. Anything above four was a luxury.

'That', said Sir Eric, 'was the opinion of the Secretary of State for War and our supposedly greatest soldier on 26 July 1915.' Sir Eric went on: 'I took a sheet of notepaper from the desk and wrote this down. I was so elated at my success at having at last got something on which I could work, I spelled "luxury" wrong. I asked Kitchener to sign it. He always had a reluctance to sign documents, and said that he gave orders and expected them to be obeyed, and threw it on the floor.' Eventually Kitchener had agreed to initial it with a 'K'.

'I took it to L.G.,' said Sir Eric. 'He read it and burst out laughing. He said: "Multiply that by four, double that for luck, and double that again for contingencies. The sum is four, multiplied by four, multiplied by two, multiplied by two, equals sixty-four, and provide that per battalion."' Sir Eric had said that he disputed this and pointed out that their constitution was that they got their indents from the military; that we did not frame estimates ourselves. L.G.'s reply had been: 'Never mind the constitution. I will take responsibility. You plan for 64.'

Sir Eric said to me: 'In the later years of the war, without that provision we would not have won.' My report to L.G. on what Sir Eric told me covers some sixty pages of foolscap.

11 December

Yesterday evening L.G. phoned me personally, saying: 'Come down to Churt early in the morning.' When I arrived, Carey[34] met me at the door and said: 'Look out.' I found L.G. in the library with Dame Margaret, Megan, Carey and Olwen. Presently he said: 'Put a match to the fire in my bedroom and let us have a talk about Geddes.' After saying what further information he wanted me to get from Geddes, he suddenly said: 'Now you owe your first duty to me.' I said: 'There has never been any doubt about that on my part, ever.' He then said: 'Do you know about Frances and Tweed?' This was indeed a poser. I told him what I knew. He was terribly upset. I have never seen him so weighed down with grief in my life. Then I discovered that my information supported that brought to him by the family.[35] A photographer from the *Daily Sketch* took a picture of the whole of the family. L.G. explained to the photographer that he never worked at a desk, but always sitting in his chair or in bed.

14 December

The domestic situation has produced strained relationships and a peculiar atmosphere. It will pass. Meantime more work than ever falls on me. Tonight L.G. asked me to dine with Dame Margaret and Megan at the [name of restaurant illegible]. He was exceedingly tired, doubtless with all this anxiety on his mind.

Megan related an incident when Lord and Lady Lee[36] invited L.G.

34. Sir Thomas Carey Evans.
35. So far as possible, Sylvester's diary, as he made it at the time, is being left to speak for itself. However, an explanation is called for here. That Miss Stevenson and Colonel Tweed were for a time in love has long been known within a restricted circle. Sylvester did not feel it his duty to inform Lloyd George until he was asked direct. What happened was that Dame Margaret came to know of the matter from a Welsh maid employed by Miss Stevenson in her flat at Morpeth Mansions, Westminster. Dame Margaret, with members of her family, went to Churt for the weekend and informed Lloyd George. Sylvester was summoned to Churt on 11 December, a Sunday, to provide confirmation. He already knew about the matter, and subsequently Tweed discussed it with him in considerable detail.
36. A. H. Lee (1868–1947). Tory M.P. 1900–18 and created Lord Lee of Fareham 1918. Closely associated with Lloyd George in various departments during the war and was in the Cabinet 1919–22. In 1922 he donated his stately home, Chequers, as the country residence for the prime minister of the day.

and Dame Margaret to spend a weekend with them at Chequers at the time L.G. was Minister of Munitions. They had a wonderful time. Everybody was most happy. L.G. and Lord Lee travelled back to London in the same car and, as they entered Whitehall Gardens, which was the office of the Ministry, there did not appear two better friends in the whole world.

No sooner had Lee got to his room than he received an urgent message that L.G. wanted to see him. L.G. stormed and blustered away at him for ten minutes, in the most furious temper; he wanted to know why this had not been done and why that had not been done. Lee said afterwards that he had never been so spoken to in his life and it had been the worst ten minutes he had ever had. We all laughed heartily, and L.G. turned to me and said: 'Have you ever experienced anything like that, A.J.?' I replied: 'Yes, sir, on a good many occasions. It is very characteristic of you.'

16 December

Sir John Davies, secretary of the Fund, asked me whether, in view of the very bad financial position, I would consent to a ten per cent cut in my salary. If I would consent, it would make it easier for him to deal with other members of the staff. If the situation should improve, then he would repay this deduction. I agreed.[37]

Evelyn and I joined L.G. and Frances for dinner at Churt, during which he told us of the difficulty with which he was faced when Minister of Munitions when there was an acute shortage of acetone. He said that one day he was talking to C. P. Scott, editor of the *Manchester Guardian*, and confided in him his deep concern and how vital it was that we should find a solution. C. P. Scott told him that he knew a distinguished professor of chemistry at Manchester University. He did not know whether he was Russian or Polish by birth, but he did know that he was heart and soul devoted to this country and wanted to help.

L.G. sent for Professor Weizmann[38] and told him what he wanted, that it was a matter of the greatest secrecy, importance and urgency. Weizmann promised to try. L.G. told him that he could have whatever he wanted to assist him; a battleship or a cruiser, a factory, anything. Weizmann worked night and day and in a few weeks he returned to tell L.G. that he had solved the problem, and that it was to be found in the chemical treatment of maize – Indian corn – on a

37. It was never repaid. A.J.S.
38. Chaim Weizmann (1872–1952) was born in Russian Poland and became a distinguished research-chemist. He was a leading Zionist and was chairman of the Jewish Agency for Palestine 1929–31 and 1935–46. He was the first president of Israel.

massive scale. L.G. was amazed. It was also found possible to produce acetone from horse chestnuts – conkers – and potatoes, but these were less satisfactory.

Then L.G. asked Weizmann what we could do in recognition of the immense service he had rendered this country. He could have an earldom, or whatever he wanted, and L.G. would recommend him to Mr Asquith, the Prime Minister. Weizmann replied : 'I want nothing for myself, but I would like something for my people.'

When L.G. became Prime Minister, he said, he sent for Weizmann and discussed what could be done. The outcome was the now famous Balfour Declaration for the establishment of a national home for the Jews.[39] I have got to know Dr Weizmann well and admire him greatly. He always speaks to me of L.G. as 'the Boss'.

17 December

At dinner, L.G. said that he remembered Winston making his maiden speech. By that time, L.G. had established himself in the House. He was to speak before him. He threw down his notes and made only a short speech, in order to give way to Winston. Afterwards, when Winston was standing at the bar of the House, someone asked L.G. whether he would like to be introduced to him. L.G. said to Winston : 'You are sinning against the light.' Winston replied : 'You take a very detached view of the British Empire.' L.G. said that Grey[40] and he were the only feminists[41] in the Cabinet. Winston had been attacked by the women and was definitely against them.

L.G. said that old Joe Chamberlain was a great fellow. He understood British psychology. He remembered how they all scoffed at him when he started a scientific research section in Birmingham University into beer. They all forgot what an important part beer played in the life of the nation. The great mistake which Joe Chamberlain made was that when he left the Liberal Party he moved to the right instead of to the left.

30 December

I lunched with Sir William Sutherland in Grosvenor House. He said it was Boswell who made Johnson live.

39. The Balfour Declaration of 1917 pledged Britain to establish a 'Jewish national home' in Palestine. It was named after A. J. Balfour, Foreign Secretary at the time. Of course, Lloyd George is here telling the story of it in the form of a dinner-table anecdote. It is true that Weizmann did vital work on acetone and asked for British support for Zionism as his reward and this was of some influence. However, there were also broader implications in what the British were to do with Palestine, which they conquered from Turkey in 1917–18.

40. Edward (later Earl) Grey (1862–1933) was Foreign Secretary 1905–16.

41. Supporters of votes for women, before 1914.

Chapter 4

'Why should the King be against my book?'

1933

Sylvester is at Criccieth.

17 January
L.G.'s seventieth birthday. The post office made a special delivery of letters. I have never seen such a post, even when he was Prime Minister. I went early to L.G., who was in bed working on his message to the films, and gave him my affectionate greetings and wished him many happy returns of the day. Miss Parry and I presented him after breakfast with the present from the office in the form of a cigar box, which he obviously liked. Gwilym presented him with a Welsh sheepdog puppy. The disappointment was that Dame Margaret is laid up with a cold. . . .

At night, L.G. went to a concert in his honour at the Memorial Hall, Criccieth; seventy brass candlesticks, each containing a lighted candle, burned brightly on the table.

18 January
Speaking in the Pavilion, Caernarvon, L.G. said 'The Government have been rummaging all the ancient precedents of reactionary governments in the early decades of the nineteenth century to find out expedients for meeting the emergency. They are like a dog digging up old bones, and the older and rottener the bones the more tasty they find them.' He also talked in his speech about the death-watch beetle and, looking up to the ceiling, he demonstrated how decay started, and likened this to the national situation. 'Sometimes in old buildings, which have stood firm for centuries, a little insect enters the woodwork and gradually eats away its strength.' Here he moved his hand with fingers outstretched in and out, and looked up at the ceiling. He went on : 'To all outward appearances for a long time it seems as solid as ever, but the mischief is gradually reducing the core of the timber to dust.'

20 *January*

In his speech at the Guildhall, Caernarvon, L.G. said that it was no use selling a hen in a thunderstorm. The Liberal Party had been sold in a thunderstorm at the last election.

He remarked to me that he was fitter mentally and physically now than before the operation. Previously he could never have done what he was now doing in the way of writing his book.[1] He had started in August – incidentally, when everybody else had been about to go on holiday – and finished on 1 December. During that time he had written 230,000 words.

23 *January*

At dinner at the Metropole, L.G. said that when he was a boy he was never touched by his old uncle. It was always quite sufficient for his uncle to look at him and say something in Welsh. But his mother gave him severe whackings, one of which he never forgot. There was some talk about somebody's funeral. L.G. remarked: 'I want no moaning at my funeral. I always liked to have lots of people around me in life; so in death. I want to have plenty of my old pals and friends around me, with lots of quarrymen coming down from the mountains and lots of farmers flocking from the mountainside, all singing my favourite old Welsh tunes.'

5 *February*

At lunch, L.G. said that he was never worried about going to Hell, but was greatly troubled about going to Heaven. When a boy, he had to go to chapel three times on Sunday, but think of having to be in chapel always every day for all the time. It would be too much for him.

Talking about Dr Charles Williams,[2] he told the story of the deacon who left his wife the first night of the honeymoon. Dr Charles did not belong to that particular presbytery, but he happened to be preaching there. The deacons were terribly down on their fellow-deacon and threatened to excommunicate him. They asked Dr Charles to arbitrate, which he did. He heard the husband's case, which was that he had had no idea that his wife had a wooden leg until he had married her, and had only discovered it on the first night. Addressing the deacons, Dr Charles Williams said: 'There is not one of you present who would not have found that out long before.'

1. The first volume of his *War Memoirs*.
2. T. C. Williams. See note to p. 52.

L.G. said he belonged to a creed which did not believe in paying ministers. His old uncle tramped miles to preach without payment or expenses. He and his brother William were the only Baptists in their school.[3] That was why he developed such fighting instincts. He fought extremely hard in those days, for by his own creed he did then think he would get to Heaven. I am personally quite sure that the last thing that L.G. would desire is for anyone to write here-after that he was a pious man. He is much moved by emotions. His character is the most complex I have ever known. He is tender-hearted to a degree on occasions. Although I have never seen him cry, he is so affected that it takes hold of his throat. Yet he seems to have no conscience at all in other things. He never says his prayers. He never prays, although he goes through the form of praying in chapel. He is not deeply religious, as so many think he is. He is not religious at all. He is essentially a pagan.

6 *February*

Sir Herbert Samuel spoke at a dinner of Liberals on policy at the Metropole, which was confidential and from which we had been excluded. I gate-crashed and, secreting myself behind the stage curtain and looking through the cracks, I could look down on the assembly. I took a summary of Samuel's speech. I was nearly detected at one time, when someone opened a window, which caused the curtains to blow out from stage so that it touched the nearest chairs of those at dinner.

Immediately Samuel had finished, I telephoned my impressions and a summary to L.G. at Churt. There is a story circulating in the lobby that when L.G. heard that the policy of the Party must be left to Samuel's judgement he had remarked: 'By heavens, I am leaving for bed.'

28 *February*

L.G. dined at Schmidt's restaurant in Charlotte Street. Winston, Bracken, Gwilym and Edna and I were present. L.G. and Winston were brilliant. Winston said that at the very commencement of the Liberal Government in 1905 they had almost decided to throw up their hands. In fact, they had all but done so. For instance Grey, Haldane and McKenna all said that they did not see how we could

3. Lloyd George was in fact baptised by his uncle into the denomination known as the Disciples of Christ. This was very small in Wales and later united with the Welsh Baptists. It became, however, a considerable body in the United States. It distrusted emotionalism in religion, had an unpaid ministry and would baptise only people old enough to make a profession of faith.

go on. Winston then passed a note over to L.G. saying: 'If you are going to speak, now is the time, otherwise it will be too late.' L.G. spoke, with the result that they stayed in for eight years. Winston said he did not remember any of the arguments used by L.G. All he did remember was that L.G. could talk a bird off a tree.[4]

L.G. said that he did not use arguments. He simply talked the stuff that he knew was in the other fellows' minds. Winston said that persuasion was always L.G.'s great forte, never exposition. L.G. was at his best when trying to persuade ten or a dozen people. Winston made us all shriek with laughter when he said that Ramsay was like the fellow who said: 'I'ze eating very well indeed. I'ze drinking very well indeed. But it's when I'ze asked to do anything in the way of work that I feels all wrong.'

Talking of himself, Winston said he was only a caterpillar on a small twig, having to feel his way. L.G. said: 'Yes, I know, a caterpillar on a *tank*, you mean. Whenever you were going to be particularly truculent in Cabinet, you always prefaced your remarks by saying: "Of course, I am only a humble person." We knew then what was coming.'

7 March

R. T. Evans[5] and I dined with L.G. in the House. R.T. wanted to write a life of L.G. in Welsh, but L.G. discouraged it. R.T. asked whether there had been any doubts in L.G.'s mind during the war and, if so, whether he would mention them in his book. L.G. replied that he had had one great doubt. It was about Passchendaele. He wondered whether he ought not to have stopped that offensive. Had he done so, it would have been said by the soldiers that he unwarrantedly interfered with military matters, and that had it not been for such interference the war would have been won twelve months earlier. Who could have disproved such a statement? One of his difficulties at the time had been that Smuts, who was a very distinguished soldier, had been in favour of the operation.

30 March

I dined alone at Addison Road with L.G. He showed me his contracts he had just signed, one for £25,000 for the serial rights, and the other for £20,000 for the book rights.[6] He said that Winston had

4. The Liberals were in office from December 1905 until May 1915, when they formed a coalition with the Tories. Churchill's anecdote should be read as table talk. In 1905 he and McKenna were only junior ministers and Lloyd George was only a junior member of the Cabinet.
5. R. T. Evans (1890–1946). Liberal M.P. 1931–5.
6. For his *War Memoirs*.

told him that he made £5000 of his rights when things were good, and that in the view of the general depression if L.G. were fortunate he might make as much. L.G. said he had made nine times as much. America was in a difficult position at the moment, but he thought he ought to bring up the amount to something like £70,000. . . .

L.G. was in the chamber of the House for a considerable time. Later he told me he had run into Baldwin, who had given L.G. the impression that he would like to work with him.

4 April

L.G. asked me to see Hankey,[7] who said that this second lot of manuscript gave him the impression that L.G. had hurried it.

Hankey said he had an idea. We seated ourselves before his big Adam fireplace in the boardroom of the Committee of Imperial Defence, which was once Disraeli's drawing-room, and he unfolded his plan. In reading through L.G.'s casts of various people, such as Asquith, Carson, etc., it had occurred to him: 'Why not have one on the King?' L.G. was the only Prime Minister who had seen the King in action in the war, and it ought to be done. He had reason to know that the King did not like the idea of L.G.'s book. He imagined he would attack the soldiers, and the King had a great liking for Kitchener and Robertson. The idea of a cast of the King might have a twofold effect. It might in itself please the King and get over this difficulty of his dislike of the book. Nobody else could do it. L.G. could do it even better than Asquith could have done were he alive. The King had played a wonderful part and it ought to be recorded. He had remained in London during the air raids. He had never failed to encourage his people. He had encouraged tanks. His sons had all taken their part in the war. L.G. had got the King to go 'dry'. Hankey said he had heard the King's own account of that, which was not very flattering to L.G., as the King thought he had been spoofed.[8] Nevertheless, he stuck to it. A prominent place in the book would do the King a lot of good, and Hankey thought it ought to be done.

The question of approach was very important, however. It would never do for L.G. to be snubbed, yet it could not be done without the King previously having been approached. Hankey thought that he himself would not be the best intermediary. He thought Clive

7. As secretary to the Cabinet Hankey was involved in Lloyd George's use of government documents.
8. At Lloyd George's request, King George V announced in 1915 that no alcohol would be consumed in his household until the end of the war. Very few followed his example, and he became annoyed. (In fact, he obtained medical advice that he needed an occasional tot of whisky.)

Wigram would be the best. L.G. might, for instance, get him to lunch in his private room at Thames House and there sound him and take his advice. Wigram was a very sound, sensible and tactful fellow.

I was full of this. I thought it was a wonderful idea, the best I had heard for a long time. When I got back to the office, I immediately phoned L.G. and related it to him. L.G.'s reaction was that it was good, but that he had not come into contact with the King very much until he became Prime Minister at the end of 1916, and that would come in a later part of his book. He then flared up: 'Why should the King be against my book? Was he against Arthur's book on Kitchener,[9] or against the book on Haig?[10] No, he was not. He raised no objection to what was said about me, yet when I am about to defend myself he does not like it. He can go to Hell. I owe him nothing; he owes his throne to me. Ask Hankey to come to see me when he can spare time; find out when he can come.' And he put down the receiver.

8 April

Today I was received by M. Maisky, the Soviet Ambassador at twelve noon.[11] He was very helpful about the Russian edition of L.G.'s book. Publishing unions or co-operative unions deal with both serial and book rights and he promised that, if L.G. would write him a letter giving his intentions and suggested price, he would communicate with Moscow.

11 April

Frances left Churt in a huff. There is a domestic upheaval there.

18 April

At the office I found a letter from Sir Clive Wigram returning the proposed chapter about the King, with which His Majesty is delighted. He had made only one small alteration, in his own hand. Instead of saying: 'He picked out one worker at Sheffield whom he recognised as having served with him on H.M.S. *Bacchante*', His Majesty in black-lead pencil had inserted the word 'in' over the word 'on'. I immediately phoned this to L.G. at Churt and he was delighted, saying it was just the difference between the sailor and the land man.

9. Sir George Arthur, *The Life of Lord Kitchener* (1920).
10. Presumably J. Charteris, *Field-Marshal Earl Haig* (1929).
11. I. M. Maisky (b.1884). Ambassador of the Soviet Union to Great Britain 1932–43. He became a prominent figure on the British political scene and mixed extensively in opposition circles.

22 April

Gwilym and I went to Churt for the weekend. L.G. is tremendously pleased with a letter he has received from Baldwin about his book.[12] He says he wished he had started writing at fifty. He would then have written a real life of Gladstone. Gladstone had not realised the difficulties of the poor, but Disraeli had. Gladstone could not come down to the level of the common people; that had been his trouble.

L.G. made a strong defence of F. E. Smith. Somehow or other he always thrusted the worst side of his nature on to the public, whereas he was a man of sterling character and one of the finest he had ever known. L.G. thought he was the son of an auctioneer; consequently the swagger Tories did not like him. Asquith asked him to be his Attorney-General in the first coalition government. Birkenhead[13] never forgot that and when he became Lord Chancellor in L.G.'s government, although there were fierce attacks made on Asquith, Birkenhead never took any part. He always remembered the chance given him by Asquith.

When L.G. made him Lord Chancellor, there were a number of important people, including judges, who 'thought I made a great mistake'. But some time afterwards two judges, one of whom was Lord Dunedin,[14] came and said: 'When you made Birkenhead Lord Chancellor, we frankly thought you had made a great mistake. We now see you were right and we were wrong. He is the best Lord Chancellor we have ever had.' Yet, said L.G., the public only saw him at the Embassy Club with a lot of girls, when he was probably drunk, a most foolish thing to have done in his high office. At St Moritz he did likewise and thus got a terrible name abroad.

Again, his whole life had been given to the cause of Ulster, which made it very difficult for him when he came to deal with the Irish question. Although he had great difficulty with his own people, he never flinched. He rode right up to the fence with terrific courage. That was at a time when even Austen Chamberlain flinched. He was better than Winston.

27 April

On the train to Shrewsbury, L.G. said to me that once one had assured oneself of food and shelter, which meant security, the next thing that mattered was advertisement.

At High Wycombe L.G. was joined by Sir John Reith. They

12. Baldwin read Lloyd George's memoirs before publication.
13. F. E. Smith became Earl of Birkenhead.
14. A. G. Murray (1849–1942). Lord Justice General for Scotland 1905–13, Lord of Appeal in Ordinary 1913–32, created Baron Dunedin 1905.

talked on the effect of the climax of a speech, and Sir John remarked
how easily it could be upset by the use or misuse of the wrong
adjective, which immediately created an anticlimax. L.G. added:
'Yes, just like water. Just one drop of something added will take it
off the boil.'

5 May

At dinner, L.G. talked of Grey. He said he had always created difficulties; he had done so with Harcourt, with Gladstone, with
Campbell-Bannerman and with Asquith. He never came down into
the arena and therefore got a false reputation. He was absolutely
worthless. By the second year of the war Grey had completely
crumpled up. He was pure funk. Asquith was not a funk. If you
had had a Palmerston or Disraeli at the Foreign Office in 1914, there
would have been no war – not Gladstone, because Gladstone was a
bad foreign minister. We nearly had war over Agadir had L.G.
himself not stepped in and warned them to be careful. That caused
them to think and stopped them.[15]

15 May

I accompanied L.G. and Dame Margaret to Scarborough for the
National Women Liberals Conference. In responding for Dame
Margaret, L.G. paid tribute to her and said he could not have
accomplished what he had done without her assistance. He spoke
those words about her as if he felt deeply affected. Yet for the
greater part of the time she is either in Criccieth or London and
he is at Churt, living with Frances.

28 May

L.G. said he had heard an interesting story the other evening of
King Ferdinand of Bulgaria[16] and how he disliked the Kaiser. One
day, when the Kaiser was staying at Sofia, Ferdinand was leaning
on a wall, which overlooked a wonderful panoramic view. He had
a big posterior. The Kaiser went quietly behind him and gave him

15. In the Agadir crisis of 1911, Germany tentatively challenged
France's claim to paramountcy in Morocco. Lloyd George, then Chancellor
of the Exchequer and, because of his attitude to the Boer War, widely
regarded as a pacifist, made a speech in which he said that Britain's
interests, too, were affected in Morocco. If Britain were not listened to,
then 'peace at that price would be a humiliation intolerable for a great
country like ours to endure'.
16. Ferdinand of Saxe-Coburg-Gotha (1861–1948) was elected Prince of
Bulgaria under Turkish suzerainty 1887 and declared independence, with
himself as King of the Bulgarians, 1908. He abdicated 1918.

a big smack on his bottom. Ferdinand never forgave him for that action. All this showed how incredibly stupid was the action of Grey in not sending a really first-class man to Bulgaria and how he might easily have brought Bulgaria into the war on our side.[17] Instead he merely kept there a second-rate diplomat called Bax-Ironside, or, as they used to call him, 'Iron Backside'.[18]

20 June

L.G. came to town for the banquet at Buckingham Palace tonight in honour of King Feisal. Sarah[19] helped him on with his white silk breeches. When he was dressed, he looked splendid – his clear complexion was bronzed, his white hair was well groomed, his broad chest was covered with his big medals, and the Order of Merit was around his neck. He had his navy-blue coat, covered with masses of gold braid. A pair of well-shaped legs filled the white silk stockings; his patent-leather shoes, with gold buckles, fitted like a glove. As he walked, his sword rattled about him. Then he strolled into the boudoir to see his brother William and said : 'Here I am, and anybody is welcome to wear this. You can strike me off the list at once. I loathe it.'

26 July

At dinner in the House with L.G., Sir Henry Fildes[20] and Sir William Letts,[21] the latter said to L.G. : 'You know, sir, that there have been a good many rumours lately that it will not be long before you are in this government.'

'Ah,' said L.G., 'not this government. Baldwin has a good mind and a well-balanced mind. But he has no drive. Ramsay has neither. Simon has made a bad show at the Foreign Office.' Simon, said L.G., was a great advocate who made his case and then, having done that, he sat back and neatly tied up his papers. Here L.G. mimicked Simon tying up his wad of documents. He went on that it was not the advocate's business to make decisions. That was left to the judge. The advocate simply said : 'May it please your lordship.' A foreign minister not only had to act as an advocate but as a judge.

17. Bulgaria fought on the side of the Central Powers 1915–18.
18. Sir Henry Bax-Ironside, K.C.M.G. (1859–1929), joined the Diplomatic Service 1883 and was British minister to Chile 1907–9, to Switzerland 1909–10 and to Bulgaria 1910–15, after which he retired.
19. Sarah Jones.
20. Sir Henry Fildes (1870–1948). Liberal M.P. (pro-L.G.) 1920–3, Liberal National M.P. 1935–45. Sylvester remembers him most affectionately as a witty, warm-hearted man who looked just like 'Mr Punch'.
21. Sir William Letts (1873–1957), a pioneer of the British motor-car industry. Also manufactured aircraft during the First World War.

D

7 August
Turning to me suddenly, L.G. said: 'You are a young man. Let me warn you that hate is a two-edged weapon. It is like fighting with a haftless knife. You may do damage to someone else, but you are likely to do more harm to yourself.' Why the hell he should turn on me and say this I did not appreciate.

Lloyd George and his entourage set off for the Welsh National Eisteddfod at Wrexham. Of course, Miss Stevenson could not appear publicly with him, especially in Wales.

9 August
L.G., Frances, Evelyn[22] and I left Churt by car via Oxford, Stratford-on-Avon and Kidderminster to Bridgnorth, just outside of which we picnicked. It was the finest picnic lunch I have ever had – Sainsbury's pie and sausages. He spilled tomato all down him and Evelyn cleaned him. He said he was always like that as a child. He never could do anything for himself and he could never find anything. He always cried out to his mother for his socks and anything he wanted. We dropped Frances and Evelyn at Chester.

10 August
L.G. made a wonderful speech at the Eisteddfod at Wrexham. There was a great crowd; something like 15,000 people. In the evening I accompanied L.G. to the private dinner of a selected number of bards, to do honour to Vincent Evans on his having celebrated more than fifty years at Eisteddfodau. L.G. paid an eloquent tribute to Vincent, in the course of which he said: 'Emotion is a kind of mortar. A building cannot be all brick. You must have mortar. But if the mortar is simply hot lime, as soon as it cools and dries it crumbles and the building goes to pieces, and you must have someone who will put a little sand in the mortar, just to bind it together, just to bind it and harden it. That is what Vincent has done.'

A farewell party for Miss Stevenson and Jennifer before Lloyd George goes to see his family in Wales.

5 September
L.G. invited me to take lunch with him, Frances, Jennifer and her nurse at the Metropole, in a private room. We each had a partridge

22. Mrs A. J. Sylvester.

and Jennifer had some steamed fish. On the way up in the car, they had been talking about having a crow for lunch. 'Taid' was to have the head and Jennifer was to have the tail. L.G. said that his was a very nice crow, and would she like some of the tail. 'Yes, I would.' He corrected her to say 'please'. Then he picked up the choicest morsel from the breast of his partridge and put it in her mouth. 'I very much like tail,' she said, and L.G. shrieked with laughter. Life was full of new thrills for Jennifer today and L.G., who loves little children, was even more thrilled than the child. They came in the car to Euston to see us off to Criccieth.

7 September

L.G. and I returned on an early train from Bangor, when he gave lunch to Kerensky.[23] He asked me to accompany him and take notes of the conversation about the condition of Russia in 1916 and 1917. One of the most important things that Kerensky said was that the Russian high command had been dead opposed to Romania entering the war at the moment she came in.[24] L.G. was intensely interested. Nobody had been ready for her entry at that time. Our generals had not even thought of that.

The first of Lloyd George's six volumes of War Memoirs was published this September. The second followed in the next month.

22 September

Evelyn and I have spent the weekend at Churt, at L.G.'s invitation, during which time she asked him if he would inscribe something in my copy of his book (which, incidentally, I bought myself). He wrote: 'To: A.J.S. in recognition of loyal, arduous and valuable help and service in trying days. D. Lloyd George, September 21, 1933.' I was immensely proud of this and told him so. He said it was true.

23 September

We were up at 6.30 this morning at the Queen's Hotel, Aberystwyth. Whilst he was shaving, L.G. said he often thought of Richard Baxter's saying when he saw a fellow marched off to gaol: 'There but for the grace of God goes Richard Baxter.' He remarked that he was infinitely more interested in apples at the present time than

23. A. F. Kerensky (1881–1970). Head of the Russian provisional government of 1917 which was overthrown by Lenin.
24. Romania declared war upon Germany in 1916 and immediately went down in defeat.

he was in politics or, extraordinary as it might seem, even in his book.

We then went to see Professor Stapledon[25] . . . and proceeded to inspect his experiments up in the mountains. Professor Stapledon said that we could feed three sheep by his means to every one at present. L.G. showed me Plinlimmon and the point where the River Severn starts as a tiny stream, and where the River Wye starts. In his opinion, his best illustration he ever made was taken from the River Severn. He had been criticised for not taking a more active part in Welsh affairs, and how he had become absorbed in imperial affairs. He had related how the River Severn started as a tiny stream in Plinlimmon and how it grew as it proceeded, fertilising the valleys of Cardiganshire and Montgomeryshire, how it flowed through the fertile valley through Worcestershire, through the Vale of Evesham, then it turned back into Wales, and, again, onwards until at last it lost itself in the great ocean beyond. It was all an act of God. That was his answer to his critics.

He told me how disappointed he was that Megan took no practical interest in the farm he had given her at Churt. She left it all to him because it was a trouble, but, said L.G., 'It is the trouble which is the interest.'

31 September

I left with L.G. and Dame Margaret for the quarter sessions at Caernarvon.[26] I enjoy more and more the proceedings of that court. What impresses me so much is L.G. giving judgement. He makes no notes of the witnesses' statements, but misses not a single material point.

6 October

I went to Walton Heath to tea with Lord Riddell,[27] at what was formerly the dormy house of the golf club. I found him a shadow of his former self. He was physically not strong, but he was as mentally alert as ever.

'Why is it,' asked Lord Riddell, 'that L.G. has lost all his friends and today is absolutely deserted?' I replied that he was so busy that he neglected them, and gave some examples.

25. Sir George Stapledon (1882–1960). Professor of Agricultural Botany, University College, Aberystwyth, 1919–42.

26. Lloyd George was chairman of Caernarvonshire Quarter Sessions 1929–38.

27. G. A. Riddell (1865–1934). Owner of *News of the World*, old friend and golfing companion of Lloyd George. Made a baron 1920. An assiduous collector of details of people's private lives.

'What a remarkable man L.G. is,' he said. He then talked to me of the Frances–Tweed relationship, about which he knew practically everything. He remembered meeting L.G. for the first time. It was in a house at Fulham. John Rowland, who was at that time Welsh secretary to L.G., who was Chancellor of the Exchequer, went to Lord Riddell and said that L.G. would be very much obliged if he could come to see him. He wanted to get his advice about a libel case. Lord Riddell went. L.G. was lying on a settee, his brow being mopped by a lady who turned out to be Mrs Timothy Davies.[28] She was feeding him with beef tea out of a spoon. . . .

19 October
In the evening L.G., Frances and I went to the World's News Theatre in Shaftesbury Avenue to see the film which L.G. made yesterday on the international situation caused by Germany's withdrawal from the League of Nations. Afterwards he said : 'Surely that is not my voice.' He had heard his voice on the talkies for the first time.

I dined at Kettners with L.G., where Sir Henry Fildes joined us. He informed L.G. that he had been asked to stand for Dumfries. L.G. said it was no use unless one did take risks, whether in politics, in business or in love.[29]

7 November
Parliament reassembled after the summer recess with a full-dress debate on rearmament. J.T., Frances and I lunched with L.G. at Thames House.

J.T. told an amusing story about Chiozza Money.[30] When L.G. was made Prime Minister, Money had no post. He came to ask for one. There was only one possible vacancy and that was at the Ministry of Shipping. L.G. appointed him Parliamentary Secretary. Money went straight across to the Ministry and told Sir Joseph Maclay[31] that he had been appointed his Parliamentary Secretary. 'Who says so?' asked Sir Joseph in his high-pitched voice. 'The

28. Old flame of Lloyd George. Her husband, Timothy Davies (1857–1951), founded a prosperous drapery business in Fulham 1885. Her maiden name was Elizabeth Jenkins, and they married 1893.

29. Fildes did stand for Dumfries in 1935, and got in.

30. Sir Leo Chiozza Money (1870–1944) was an active radical journalist who was a Liberal M.P. 1906–18 and then joined the Labour Party. He was Lloyd George's Parliamentary Private Secretary 1915–16 and a junior minister 1916–18.

31. Sir Joseph Maclay (1857–1951). Self-made Glasgow shipowner whom, on Bonar Law's recommendation, Lloyd George made Minister of Shipping in 1916.

Prime Minister: he has just appointed me,' said Money. 'Well, what are you to do?' asked Maclay. 'I shall represent your Ministry in the House of Commons and answer questions.' 'When does the House of Commons meet?' asked Maclay. (It was now December.) 'February,' replied Money. 'Very well, then,' said Maclay, 'come and see me on 5 February and I will have the questions and answers ready for you.'[32]

21 December
At a family lunch in the House, L.G. said that he had been trying for a long time to find out what were Haig's objectives. He had now discovered that at Passchendaele Haig had been aiming at Bruges as the first of his objectives. In the end he did not get five miles towards it, which meant that he was still some eighteen miles away.

28 December
L.G. asked me to go to Churt as he wished to talk to me about the papers he wished to take with him on his trip to Estoril. George Lambert[33] and his daughter came to lunch. L.G. said that he had a great opinion of Lord Balfour. He liked office, which was a different thing to liking power. He said that there would never have been a Great War had Bismarck been alive.

32. Of course, customarily a parliamentary secretary expects to play a part in the work of his department and not be just a spokesman.
33. George Lambert (1866–1958). Liberal M.P. 1891–1924, 1929–45 (from 1931 as Liberal National). Junior minister 1905–13. Chairman of the ('Wee Free') Parliamentary Liberal Party 1919–21.

Chapter 5

'I planted Samuel on Sinai'

1934

6 January

We left Tilbury and sailed for Estoril on the *Andalusia Star*. The party consists of L.G., Dame Margaret, Megan, Gwilym and Edna, Miss Russell,[1] Miss Roberts[2] and myself. At coffee on the veranda, L.G. was asked whether he had ever doubted the outcome of the war. L.G. replied: 'No, though 21 March 1918[3] caused me to think deeply.' He remembered the words of Napoleon that the bravest of troops were at times seized with panic. It all depended then upon whether you could rally them. L.G. said they did this by pouring more and more troops into France. This was what Napoleon could not do, because he had exhausted his supplies. L.G. went to see Sir Joseph Maclay and said: 'We are sending 3000[4] troops a day to France. Will you arrange to send 30,000 a day?' and in his high-pitched voice Maclay had said: 'Yes, I can do that.' And he did.

Talking of the Tudors, L.G. said that Henry VII was the fellow who started taxing the landed aristocracy. He talked of Henry VIII and Elizabeth. He said the foundations of the British Empire had really been laid by the Welsh.

8 January

In our favourite haunt in the veranda café at night, Dame Margaret said that when she married her husband he had a beard. This was because he had a bad throat. She liked him better without it. But she did not like him without a moustache: it showed up his enormous lower lip. L.G. said that, when he went to Canada for the first time,[5] he went into the prairie and grew a beard. About to return, he went

1. Miss Winifred Russell, a shorthand-typist from the staff at Churt.
2. Miss Roberts, a maid.
3. This was when Germany's last offensive of the war achieved a breakthrough of the British lines on the Western Front. The assault was eventually contained, but it was a time of grave anxiety for the Allies. In this situation Lloyd George forced the appointment of Foch as supreme commander.
4. Lloyd George was speaking loosely: the correct figure was 8000.
5. In the autumn of 1899.

into a barber's shop and the barber used the clippers and, before he had realised it, he had cut off half his moustache, so the rest had to go. When he returned to the House of Commons, the Speaker, Gully, absolutely failed to recognise him, and when he rose time after time he did not call him. It was only when no one else rose that he got his chance to speak, and then the Speaker did not know him and pointed to him with his finger, without mentioning his name. It was under these circumstances that he made his first speech against the Boer War. He said that when he grew a beard he had a very gentle face, but when he shaved off his moustache and beard it was a most insolent face indeed.

10 *January*

In the evening, L.G. told us that Robson,[6] Attorney-General, had related to him how great men like Palmerston went before Queen Victoria to kiss hands on appointment as cabinet ministers. L.G. went down on his knees and went through the action of kissing the Bible. Then he rose, walked a few paces and then kissed an imaginary hand. That was the proper way. He then demonstrated to us how Queen Victoria had insisted on her ministers grovelling to her. Instead of rising after kissing the Bible and walking a few paces to the Queen, they were compelled to walk on their knees, the demonstration of which made us shriek with laughter. I asked L.G. what would have happened if he had been a cabinet minister in Queen Victoria's time. He shook his head ominously. The reason why Gladstone had stood her, he said, was that he had been a snob, which was the only thing L.G. did not like about him.

14 *January*

At lunch . . . L.G. said if he were a preacher he would like to preach on the subject of the thief on the cross.

At whiskey time,[7] L.G. said: 'Don't you think it is rather an achievement to have learned a new business at my time of life? Bernard Shaw said that he knew I was a good speaker, but he did not know that I could write.' He said that the war was by far the greatest event of modern times. Consequently it would be more and

6. Sir William Robson (1852–1918). Solicitor-General 1905–8, Attorney-General 1908–10, Lord of Appeal in Ordinary 1910–12.

7. Lloyd George enjoyed a glass of Irish whiskey. Sylvester's opinion (1974) is that, especially as he grew older, Lloyd George on occasion drank more than was good for him. The reason was not the quantity that he imbibed but the fact that as few as three or four whiskeys were enough to make him quite tipsy. Sylvester believes that this was because Lloyd George, as a young man, had been a near-teetotaller and so had never acquired a head for alcohol.

more read about as the years rolled by. That was where Gollancz[8] had made a miscalculation. He had said he was prepared to lose £2000. Yet Nicholson[9] had got practically all his money back on the first two volumes and there were two, if not three[10] more to come.

18 January

L.G. said he had liked Woolly Robertson[11] better than Woolly had liked him. But Woolly had been a 'stiff' man. L.G. got up from the tea-table and walked to the door. Buttoning up his coat, he demonstrated exactly Woolly's walk and gait. There had been no bend in him, he said. If there had been even a little, it would have been better.

21 January

The *Liverpool Post* and the *Caernarvon and Denbigh Herald* have some interesting observations by Dr Morris-Jones[12] about L.G. He has said: 'Mr Lloyd George possesses the most marvellous physical and mental machinery of any man of his age. His physical metabolism is unique. He walks the lobbies of the House of Commons with an agility which even his young secretary, Mr Sylvester, can scarcely cope with.' L.G. is very delighted with this report.

28 January

L.G. said the most important thing in life was to be able to concentrate. 'I tell you young people', he said, 'to concentrate on the thing you are doing at the time and be oblivious to everything else. That means training yourself.'

30 January

We are on the *Andalusia Star* on our way home. The Captain lent me an album which contained references to our trip from South America in 1928. The Chief Engineer, named Morris, has a mother who keeps the post office at Portmadoc. L.G. described how, when he had been an articled clerk there, it had been his duty to copy the letters and he described how he had done it in a letter-book, by means of a press which he screwed down. He then had to write the

8. Victor Gollancz (1893–1967), the publisher.
9. Ivor Nicholson (1891–1937). Chairman of Ivor Nicholson & Watson, Lloyd George's publishers.
10. In fact, there were four more to come, and also two on the peace treaties.
11. Sir William Robertson. See note to p. 80.
12. Sir Henry Morris-Jones (1884–1972), a medical practitioner who was a Liberal M.P. 1929–50 (from 1931 as Liberal National). He was a government whip 1932–7.

envelopes. Gwilym at once said he would have given quids to see Tada doing this work.

31 January
We left the boat at 2.30 p.m. During his stay at Estoril L.G. has revised 230,000 words of his third and fourth volumes and written a chapter on Italy, comprising many thousands of words.

12 February
Talking to Walter Jones[13] on Liberalism in Wales, L.G. said that, although he was very absorbed in his book, at the first sign of any really important political situation he was prepared to throw down his pen to take up the political cudgel once more.

25 March
At 11 a.m. we listened to a [broadcast] service from Cardiff. The preacher was a Rev. Roberts, whose father had lived at Portmadoc and whom L.G. has always especially remembered. He said:

'Why I opened an office at Portmadoc, I cannot say, because I had absolutely no prospects. It was opened on nothing. I always travelled by train each morning from Criccieth, which got me to Portmadoc about 8 a.m. This old minister lived in a house which I had to pass on my way to the office. He came into my office one morning and said: "You seem to be looking rather worried and anxious. Don't trouble, everything will come right." I have always remembered that kindness. It helped me enormously then, and since. This old boy was a Methodist, yet I was a Baptist.'

4 April
Sir John Davies advised that it would be better for me not to hurry talking to L.G. about my agreement,[14] which comes to an end next year. Choose the moment. As to what would happen to the Fund[15] when L.G. passed away, that raised another, very difficult question. His own attitude would be to treat generously everybody who, like myself, had served L.G. well, and then place, say, £50,000 in the hands of the court.

9 April
Tonight I received two letters from Hankey about L.G.'s manuscript. He thought that the chapter on the Tsar's future residence[16] should

13. A keen Lloyd George supporter from Neath.
14. Employment contract.
15. The Lloyd George Political Fund.
16. That is, after his deposition in 1917 and before his murder, with his family, in 1918.

be suppressed altogether. Some parts of it made him feel that it would be premature to publish – for instance, the reference to the anti-monarchical movement that was developing in England at the time. Hankey thought that the King would object to this and to the extract from the cabinet minutes on the subject. I sent these to L.G. at Churt and phoned him the gist. He said he did not want to do anything that was injurious to the monarchy and certainly not to the King and would discuss the matter with Hankey, alone or along with Baldwin before Hankey showed it to [the King's secretary] Wigram. The Court were very jumpy and nervy, and they might take the line that we must not publish anything.

10 April
I saw Hankey and fixed up with him to see L.G. for tea. As I walked through Whitehall Gardens with him on his way to see the C.I.G.S., he said he had spent a good deal of time 'to get the King right' as regards L.G.'s book. It had not been easy because the King was very suspicious, and Hankey thought it would be better in L.G.'s own interest to suppress the chapter on the Tsar's future residence. Hankey told me that Baldwin thought the book well written and that he was not the man to give advice in cases of this kind and was very much in Hankey's hands.

11 April
When I left the House at 11 p.m., I met Mr Baldwin behind the Speaker's chair. He said: 'You sent me a rare bundle of stuff to read.' I asked him how much he had read. He replied: 'I have read it all.' I was surprised. He said: 'I am a very quick reader.' He went on: 'It is wonderfully well written He (L.G.) fairly skins some of them. I cannot say that I agree with all of it, but then it is not my function to criticise. It is very well written and I can see what an enormous amount of work it has meant for you.'

24 April
I spoke to L.G. on the phone. He was in bed. He said he was suffering from the fact that he had written 400,000 words in eight months, whereas H. G. Wells only writes 100,000 in eighteen months.

25 April
Sir Clive Wigram called to see me at the office.[17] He brought with him the chapter on labour unrest. He thought that the part dealing with the King was admirable, but he hoped very much that the

17. Lloyd George's London office at Thames House.

reference to Ramsay and Snowden[18] might be deleted. These were
references to the part played by them in the war which were not
very creditable. Sir Clive said that L.G. was a big man and he did
not want him to make himself small. He could afford to be mag-
nanimous. Sir Clive did not like the idea of L.G. being vindictive
towards people like these, who were holding high office. I talked to
L.G. on the telephone immediately afterwards. He said he would
not alter it.

2 *May*

I dined at Kettners with Sir Henry Fildes and Sir William Letts.
Letts said he would give me £5000 straightaway for part of the
rights of any book I cared to write on my reminiscences.

12 *May*

Curtis Brown, L.G.'s literary agent, was here yesterday, and said he
would not have my job for anything.

19 *May*

I accompanied L.G. and Dame Margaret to Chwilog, where he spoke
at a memorial service in the congregational chapel to Eifion Wyn.[19]
I watched L.G.'s face as he read passages in Welsh from Eifion Wyn's
works; it wrinkled with delight. On the way home he gave me a
translation of two lines which, he said, would immortalise the name
of Eifion Wyn :

> O God, why didst thou make the Glen of Pennant so lovely
> And the life of an old shepherd so short?

20 *May (Sunday)*

At ten o'clock this morning I found L.G. reading in the library, full
of fun and humour. He talked to me about the horrors and tortures
of going to listen to Dai Williams[20] preach. Carey and Olwen entered.
L.G. said his waking thought this morning had suggested that some-

18. These were references to Ramsay MacDonald and Philip Snowden
having opposed the First World War. In 1931 they had been the leading
Labour influence in forming the National Government. MacDonald was
still Prime Minister, but Snowden had resigned.

19. Eliseus Williams (1867–1926) was for thirty years a clerk with the
North Wales Slate Co., Portmadoc, and was a leading poet in both the
free and classical Welsh forms. Eifion Wyn was his bardic name.

20. Dai Williams was the son of Mr Williams, the ironmonger at
Criccieth who had been a great friend of L.G.'s old Uncle Lloyd and one
of L.G.'s oldest supporters. Dai was very deaf. A.J.S.

thing unpleasant was to take place. Ah, then it had occurred to him – Dai Williams preaching. He remarked to Carey: 'At any rate, when you torture your patients you do first of all give them an anaesthetic.' He then said to me: 'You ought to come just to see what I have to suffer. Believe me, the fact that you won't understand what he says will be an advantage. Unfortunately, I never sleep through a sermon. I must listen, and continue to be tortured.'

As we walked up the hill to Brynawelon afterwards, he said he had found a new dodge. Stopping in the middle of the road, he explained that during the sermon he had been counting up to 300 and found that it occupied five minutes. He said to himself: 'Thank God, that is five minutes gone. Now I will have another. But I found that the more annoyed I became the quicker I counted. So I then counted in Welsh, which made me take longer. I counted right through the sermon.' Yet, looking at him during the sermon, one might have thought how closely he was following the arguments.

I asked him if he intended going to tonight's service. He stopped again and said: 'Christ was only crucified once. Even He would have jibbed a second time.'

13 June

I had a long conversation on the telephone with L.G. tonight at Churt. He said he was in bed suffering from exactly the same thing as he had when he was Prime Minister, a temperature and a run-down. Arnold Bennett had once told him that his greatest feat had been to write 275,000 words in a year, but he had written 400,000 in eight months. 'I shall have to go a little slower,' he said. 'I have been starting work at four o'clock in the morning.'

14 June

I talked to Sir John Davies about my position, that I was the only person who was not getting anything extra for work on the book. Frances and —— were getting a consideration, and L.G. said that the latter had let him down badly. Tweed was making money on the Stock Exchange whilst in the office, doing nothing for L.G. I felt sure that L.G. did not realise that he was doing an injustice to me, especially as my stock with him was never higher. I was the fellow who had unearthed from secret places vital information which had given him big scoops for his book, which he could never have had but for me and out of which L.G. was making a fortune. Sir John Davies said he would bear all this in mind and it would be put right.[21]

21. It never was. A.J.S.

26 June

L.G. has decided to write another chapter about the Tsar. The other one has been scrapped because of objections to it from Hankey, Baldwin and the Court. The new material is not to refer to the movements which were regarded as anti-monarchical in this country.

7 July

At breakfast, L.G. said Lord Dawson had told him to live on cheese and lettuce.

He said that Lord Devonport was 'a remarkable fellow'. He had asked L.G. if he thought there were a hereafter and L.G. had replied 'Yes'. Then Lord Devonport had asked: 'Do you think that I shall meet my wife again?' 'Yes,' L.G. had replied, 'but whether you would know her I cannot tell. You might meet her in a different form.'

12 July

At Brynawelon, L.G. unfolded a plan to Geoffrey Crawshay,[22] which he said he had had in his mind for a long time, that when the Eisteddfod is held at Neath, and L.G. is staying at St Donats Castle, there should be held a medieval display. It should be done in true medieval fashion, and he wanted Crawshay to take it in hand. William Hearst had agreed.[23]

30 July

L.G. lunched at the Metropole, accompanied by Frances, Evelyn and myself. He was full of the pageant to be held at St Donats Castle on 9 August. It was essential that no one should be present unless clothed in the dress of the fourteenth century. There would be a march of bards, and pikemen would be present. Sucking pig would be served. There would be just flagons of mead to drink. Evelyn asked what they would do about knives and forks. He said he had not thought of that. He was rather upset because Crawshay had cut out the hanging of a pirate. There would be ancient Welsh music.

2 August

At lunch, L.G. said the best thing he had ever said about Samuel had, on the advice of his friends, been cut out of his manuscript.

22. G. C. Crawshay (1892–1954) belonged to a Merthyr Tydfil ironmaster dynasty and held many public posts in Wales.
23. William Randolph Hearst (1863–1951), the American newspaper magnate who had bought St Donats Castle, Glamorganshire.

He had written: 'I planted Samuel on Mount Sinai as the lineal descendant of Pontius Pilate.'[24]

7 August
L.G. told me that when Winston was a minister he had remarked to L.G. that Baldwin was the craftiest man in politics. He had repeated this to J. H. Thomas, who had replied: 'What about you and me?'

9 August
I slept in the ghost room at St Donats. At 8 a.m., dressed in my garb as a Norman nobleman, I asked L.G. what he thought of it. He came out of his bathroom stark naked and told me to stand in the middle of the bedroom. He was pleased with it.

The pageant in the evening was wonderful and carried out with great dignity. The march of the bards to the castle was led by Geoffrey Crawshay on horseback. His call in Welsh to the officer in charge at the entrance and the response in Norman French were striking. Then came the reception of the bards by L.G. inside the castle grounds. The banqueting-hall presented a striking scene. I sat at the end of the high table. On my card was 'Yr Arglwydd Sylvester' – the Lord Sylvester.

L.G. had obtained a fourteenth-century setting, but judging by his impetuosity he had not got the spirit or the atmosphere. No sooner had we sat down than he signalled me to find out why we were waiting for the soup, then in turn the sucking pig, then why the music had stopped, and then that the singing of the choir was not loud enough. I had a very busy time, and got little food. I felt smothered in this nobleman's garb, which was very heavy. With a mop of artificial hair all over my face, I tried to eat with sweat pouring all over me on this hot night.

9 September
L.G. left [Brynawelon] for Churt. My wife and I have remained at Criccieth for a few days' holiday. I am finding a peace and contentment at Brynawelon which I have not known before. No rush. When L.G. is here, it is turmoil.

3 October
L.G., Frances and I dined together. He said he was very sick that Haig and Robertson were not alive. He intended to blow their ashes to smithereens in his fifth volume. Unfortunately, he could not get

24. This refers to Lloyd George's appointment of Samuel to be the first British High Commissioner in Palestine in 1920.

at them personally. He could not even *send* them a book and, he added, Sylvester cannot even telephone to them.

In the autumn of 1934, Lloyd George's mind moved back to current politics and he began to prepare his plan for the fundamental reorganisation of the British economy to eliminate unemployment, which was still running at over two million. This plan was to become his 'New Deal'. During the weekend 12–14 October Lloyd George held a conference of experts at Churt as a step towards drawing up his plan. Sylvester attended to take notes.

15 October
Early this morning I found L.G. having breakfast in bed. Frances was with him. I told him that everybody was delighted with the progress made at the talks and they wanted to know if he was satisfied. He wanted an organised movement to secure a parliament of the left, pledged to an advanced, progressive policy of peace, liberty and reconstruction. The transcript of my notes of these talks runs into 500 folios. Multiply that by seventy-two, and you have the number of words.

16 November
Evelyn and I went to Churt. After dinner the question was, he said, whether he would go to bed or hear Winston on the wireless at 10 p.m. He decided to go to bed, and asked me to take a shorthand note of what Winston said, and let him have it before seven in the morning. I put the transcript outside his bedroom door at midnight.

17 November
I was out with my gun at 7 a.m. When I returned for breakfast, L.G. said not a word about my having done the transcript, but that he had a good mind to speak in the House of Commons and say that had he not known the Rt Hon. Gentleman he would have said it was the speech of an unbalanced mind. Winston had talked as if Germany would come over here with her aeroplanes and blow us to pieces and as if France, Italy and everybody would meantime just wait and do nothing.[25]

25. In fact, Churchill made no actual mention of Germany. His broadcast advocated that Britain should build up the strongest air force in Europe, thus recovering the security which had formerly been provided by the Navy.

Then he put on his clogs, his latest fancy. Dame Margaret put on hers, and we walked round the farm.

10 December

I accompanied L.G. to Lord Riddell's memorial service at St Bride's Church. I have lost a great friend. Lord Rothermere travelled to Charing Cross in L.G.'s car and promised to back his 'New Deal' policy. (Beaverbrook has also promised, and L.G. says that if he could get the News Chronicle he would be pleased.) As I took L.G. and Frances down in the lift[26] to go to Churt, L.G. took out of his overcoat pocket a little notebook. He said it was curious what ran through one's mind, but that during the memorial service he was thinking what a handy little notebook that was.

22 December

Tonight a delicious ham arrived from Harrods, sent by L.G. This is the first time he has ever sent us a Christmas present.

26. At Thames House.

Chapter 6

'I am not going to be tricked into a sham'

1935

Election year. Lloyd George launched his last great political pro-gramme, his 'New Deal', in a speech at the Drill Hall, Bangor, one of his Caernarvon boroughs, on his seventy-second birthday. Special trains brought people from all parts of Wales to hear him. The hall was jammed with 7000 people, and a further 5000 heard the speech through loudspeakers outside. Lloyd George spoke for the first half-minute in Welsh and then switched to English for the rest of the speech. He said he was now 'entirely non-party' and that 'I am neither a party leader nor have I the desire to become one. I have had enough of that misery.' He said he was merely making an appeal to the British nation to tackle the problems of economic dislocation which resulted mainly from the war. 'In 1914 the God of War sent the world reeling through the gates of hell. The God of Money has since been completing the tragedy.' There should be an all-party approach to the problem, but not on the basis of the present National Government, with which many even of the younger Conservatives in the Commons were dissatisfied. There should be a national Development Council, with representatives of industry, commerce, finance, the workers and economic thinkers, with independent power to plan bold schemes. Over them there should be a small cabinet of only five, largely non-departmental ministers, on the lines of his own war cabinet. The schemes should cover housing, roads, land and the reconstruction of depressed industries. It was not just a question of rectifying unemployment but of abolishing social evils. In housing it was not just a matter of slum clearance but of replac-ing all inadequate housing. There should be two budgets a year, one for ordinary revenue and the other for capital expenditure. Capital should be raised by a Prosperity Loan to which, as with the War Loan, the public would subscribe enthusiastically. It was a question of making use of capital that now lay idle.

11 *January*

For days I have been busy with arrangements for a massive meeting at Bangor, where L.G. is to unfold his grand proposals for a 'New Deal'. Two photographers came from Berlin today to take photos of L.G., which shows that the vast public interest in the proposals has spread to the Continent.

16 *January*

I breakfasted at Brynawelon. L.G. had been at work on his speech since 5 a.m. I spent all day working on alterations, and finally issued forty copies to the Press Association at 5.30 p.m.

At 5.45 p.m. came news from the Press Association to me privately that Lord Riddell had left £1000 to L.G., and also to Winston. L.G. was in the library with his family. I said: 'I have a nice birthday present for you. Lord Riddell has left you £1000.' He gave another pull at his cigar and his face lit up when I said 'and Winston £1000 also'. An hour later, Miss Smithers, my secretary, phoned me that Lord Riddell had left Miss Stevenson £1000 and Sir John Davies and me £500 each.

17 *January*

I was at Brynawelon early. L.G. was the only one up. 'Come along,' he said. 'We'll start our breakfast. This is what is wrong with the post-war generation.'

This is his seventy-second anniversary. I shook hands with him and wished him many happy returns, and presented him with a signed message from the office staff, together with a grey silk hand-kerchief, with his initials worked in the corner, with the request that he should wear it at today's great meeting, initiating his 'New Deal' proposals. After breakfast, I presented him with a beautiful gold cigar-cutter from my wife and myself. He said: 'This is just what I wanted. Look how I spoil my thumbnail by pinching off the end of the cigar.' He was obviously delighted.

At 5 p.m., at the Castle Hotel, Bangor, I interviewed the Press and distributed advance copies of L.G.'s speech. There were some seventy Press representatives, including not only the cream of journalism from the lobby of the House of Commons, but also representatives from Germany, France, Poland and America.

L.G. spoke to an amazing gathering of some 7000 in the drill hall and got them in the right mood at once by saying: 'I am not here', and then suddenly paused, to roars of loud laughter. Then he un-folded his proposals, introducing some very good phrases here and there, as when he said: 'There was too much corn in Egypt and the Egyptians were starving.' 'There was so much flood there was a drought.' When someone dared to interpolate a question, L.G. flashed out in an instant: 'I came here to answer questions – when I put them to myself.' He spoke for one hour and fifty-five minutes.

18 January

The Press is the most wonderful I have known. L.G. is very pleased.

21 January

I left with L.G. from Caernarvon by train for Euston, after he had received a deputation from the local council on the King's jubilee celebrations. In the train he said that he was very pleased with the situation. The fact that the Labour people were critical made it clear to the Tories that there was no stunt and made them give him more support. . . . In an interview which he gave to Guy Eden of the *Daily Express*, who asked him what he thought was the best life of himself, he said: 'I have never read one of my biographies.'

25 January

Correspondence on L.G.'s 'New Deal' proposals is amazing and takes me all my time to read, let alone deal with it. . . .

I accompanied him to the Birmingham jewellers' dinner, where he spoke on his 'New Deal' proposals. Afterwards he talked about his visit to Birmingham during the Boer War. L.G. said he had then delivered every word of his speech, but only to the reporters. He had then retired, not run away, to the anteroom, until he escaped in the disguise of a policeman. Stones and other missiles had flown in all directions.[1]

9 February

At lunch I passed on a suggestion from Tweed. L.G. replied: 'He thinks I want to go into this government. I don't. I want my proposals accepted. That is all I want.'

Thelma Cazalet[2] asked if L.G. would be satisfied if he got 80 per cent of his proposals accepted. He replied that everything depended upon whether it spanned the gulf. If you only got within an inch of the span, then that was just as bad as if you were only halfway across.

1. This was the occasion on 18 December 1901, on which Lloyd George faced a hostile crowd of 30,000, many of them armed with sticks and missiles and intent upon lynching him. He had been lucky to survive.

2. Thelma Cazalet-Keir (b.1899) was a Tory M.P. 1931–45, a junior minister 1937–40 and 1945, and holder of many other public positions. For long she was a close friend of Megan Lloyd George. Her surname was originally Cazalet but she changed it to Cazalet-Keir on her marriage in 1939 to David Keir, then political correspondent of the *News Chronicle*.

At dinner, L.G. said he always thought this country was not a place to live in all the year round. He thought we might eventually arrive at the stage when we should have produced all our requirements in a certain number of months. Then for the rest of the year, leaving a sufficient number of people at home just to look after things, we should go to places like Africa where there was plenty of sun.

22 *February*
I accompanied L.G. to Manchester for a grand meeting in the Free Trade Hall. Cummings[3] in the *News Chronicle* says: 'He is still the mightiest personality, the grandest orator of them all.'. . .

Hopes rise for Lloyd George's campaign.

5 *March*
L.G. is getting under the skin of the Government, by trying to split it. Hore-Belisha[4] is with L.G. He knows he can smash the Minister of Health.[5] He can smash the Minister of Agriculture[6] to bits, and Oliver Stanley[7] and Lady Maureen Stanley[8] are going down to lunch at Churt on Sunday. That is not a bad wedge into the Government.

8 *March*
At lunch today,[9] when Megan and I were with him, Arthur Henderson came to speak. He has been ill. L.G. said to him : 'It is no use my wishing you good luck. You won't have any whilst you have this government.' (Henderson is chairman of the disarmament conference.) 'It reminds me of the saying of the Duke of Cambridge when asked to pray for rain : "It is no use praying for rain when the wind is in the east." This government is like the east wind.'

3. A. J. Cummings (1882–1957) wrote a column in the *News Chronicle*, of major significance in political journalism, from 1932 to 1955.
   4. Currently Minister of Transport and one of the members of the Government most prominent in the public eye.
   5. This was Edward Hilton Young (1879–1960). The scope of this ministry was at this time wider than its title would suggest and included housing, slum clearance and supervision of local government.
   6. Currently Walter Elliot.
   7. Oliver Stanley (1896–1950). A man who might have become Prime Minister had he not died so young. Tory M.P. 1924–50, a junior minister 1931–3 and in the Cabinet or of cabinet rank 1933–45.
   8. Wife of Oliver Stanley, daughter of the 7th Marquess of Londonderry.
   9. At the House of Commons.

9 March

For several days, L.G. has had a conference of all his experts sitting at 2 Addison Road, going through the report on the 'New Deal' word by word.

L.G. said that he had recently seen the Chinese Minister. Transport was the keynote to progress in China. L.G. was in favour of making a loan to China of, say, £100 million. We might provide half and America the other, the money we advanced being spent in this country. Russia, too, should be invited to join in. He had also seen the Soviet Ambassador, M. Maisky, who had welcomed the idea. Japan should be told that she would not be allowed to encroach upon Chinese rights but that she might have equal rights with the western powers and might also come in on the loan. There was an enormous amount of trade awaiting us there, if only that vast Chinese territory could be opened up by transport.

11 March

I delivered a copy of the report[10] privately to Tom Jones[11] at 83 Vincent Square. L.G. does not want to deliver the proposals to the Prime Minister on Friday, he being superstitious to that extent. He is keen on their being delivered on Thursday night. Tom Jones told me he remembered how Winston, when he appeared as No. 13 on the distribution list for cabinet papers, asked for his number to be altered. Thereafter, there appeared no No. 13 on the lists.

25 March

I accompanied L.G. and Megan to Newcastle. In the train he told me that he now knew what this lot was after. 'They simply want to get me to join the Government, on the promise that they will adopt my plans. They will immediately have an election and then, having been returned for five years with my assistance, they will politely tell me to go to Hell. But they must remember they are not dealing with Herbert Samuel. They will find that I have conditions. I do not want to go into the Government. I am like Joe Chamberlain: all I am concerned about is to get my proposals adopted and put into practice. If this necessitates my taking office, I will take office, but I am not going to be tricked into a sham affair. If they won't accept my proposals I will smash them.'

10. Lloyd George's detailed proposals.
11. Intermediary for MacDonald. Thomas Jones (1870–1955) had a finger in many pies. He was a Welsh university teacher who became deputy secretary to the Cabinet 1916–30 and was secretary of the Pilgrim Trust 1930–45. He kept up his relations with Lloyd George but was also close to MacDonald and Baldwin.

27 March

As I strolled into L.G.'s bedroom at eight o'clock this morning, he was in bed, working on his speech. His hair was all over his face. He was using the flat of his hand as a backing sheet to the flimsy paper upon which he was writing. He was writing almost madly in his microscopical characters, with a huge yellow pencil, the point of which was blunt, thereby adding materially to the illegibility of his hieroglyphics. Presently he got up and proceeded to shave. He handed me the speech and said: 'Read it aloud.' I started to read his speech. To read it straight off and incorporate all his numerous corrections is not an easy task. When I could not decipher a word, he snatched it out of my hands very impatiently. When he returned from the bathroom, he asked me to proceed with the reading and to incorporate the still further corrections he had thought of in the bathroom. Between sentences, he cried out for some article of clothing, and when I had handed it to him he said: 'Now go on.' I read a sentence. I buttoned up his collar. I read another sentence and then put on his socks. I read another sentence and then helped him with his boots. I was damned glad to come to the end of it. All the time, he was terribly worked up, like a ball of energy. When he is in these moods, energy seems to ooze from him.

All the mayors from Berwick-on-Tweed to Middlesbrough were present at the dinner given by the Lord Mayor of Newcastle to L.G., after which we went to the meeting. It was a wonderful gathering. His peroration was one of his finest. He said: 'I saw springing up beyond those ruins. . . .' Then he repeated: 'I saw.' Then he said 'despair and squalor had been dispelled by the dawn'. He repeated slowly: 'by the dawn'.

A cabinet committee was appointed to confer with Lloyd George on his proposals. It comprised Ramsay MacDonald, Baldwin, Hailsham (War),[12] J. H. Thomas (Dominions), Runciman (Trade), Neville Chamberlain (Exchequer), Simon (Foreign Office), Cunliffe-Lister (Colonies),[13] Kingsley Wood (Postmaster-General),[14] Collins (Scot-

12. Douglas Hogg, 1st Viscount Hailsham (1872–1950).
13. Philip Cunliffe-Lister (1884–1972), whose career as a Tory politician spanned the period 1918–55. He originally had the surname Lloyd-Greame and changed it in 1924. A further change came in 1935 when he was made Viscount Swinton.
14. Kingsley Wood (1881–1943) was a Tory M.P. 1918–43 and his career culminated when he was Chancellor of the Exchequer in the Second World War.

land),[15] Elliot (Agriculture),[16] and Ernest Brown (Mines). *Various civil servants also attended. It had six meetings with Lloyd George between 18 April and 15 May 1935.*

18 April

Parliament adjourned today, and L.G. appeared before the Cabinet Committee and presented his proposals on reconstruction and development. L.G. arrived at the House at 10.45 a.m. He is always very nervous before a speech, but he told me that he was not a bit nervous before facing this committee, which was composed of the Prime Minister, Mr Baldwin and seven other members of the Cabinet. At a few minutes to 11 a.m., L.G. asked me to go down to the Prime Minister's room and say that he would come down when they were all assembled. *They* must wait for him.

He returned at 12.45 p.m., looking radiant and slightly flushed. He told me that he had had a kindly reception and the atmosphere had been friendly, though he did not know quite what it all meant, as they had not got sufficiently far. I do not think there was ever an occasion before when the Cabinet had allowed ministers to come and take instructions from a leader of the opposition.

9 May

Sir Godfrey Thomas, the Prince of Wales's secretary, came to see L.G. and handed him the draft of a speech for the Prince to make at Cardiff on Saturday.[17] Thomas said that the Prince was very much upset because L.G. was not going to be present on this occasion. L.G. and Dame Margaret went to the state banquet at Buckingham Palace tonight.[18]

10 May

L.G. phoned me at 7 a.m. this morning to tell me that he was going with the Prince of Wales to Cardiff in his special train at midnight tonight and wanted me to go with him. I was to make all the arrangements and breakfast with him at Addison Road, which I did.

15. Sir Godfrey Collins (1875–1936). Liberal M.P. 1910–36 (from 1931 as Liberal National) and, after holding various positions as a whip, was in the Cabinet 1932–6.
16. Walter Elliot (1888–1958). Tory M.P. 1918–58 (with some short gaps). He was in the Cabinet from 1932 to 1940, but thereafter his major career languished.
17. The Prince was visiting Cardiff in connection with the silver jubilee celebrations of the twenty-fifth anniversary of George V's accession.
18. This was a dinner given by the King for the silver jubilee.

He then told me how, immediately after the King had received the Prime Minister, His Majesty had sent for L.G. and had taken him off to see his pipers. The Prince had then put in an appearance and had told the King that L.G. was not going to Cardiff and what was the use of his going to speak to a Welsh audience without L.G. being present. The King had expressed the hope that L.G. would go. That being a royal command, L.G. had said he would go.

Ever since the Prince of Wales had been invested at Caernarvon Castle in 1911, he had been on good terms with Lloyd George, who had played a prominent part in the ceremony and coached him to say a few words in Welsh.

11 *May*

At breakfast on the train, the Prince of Wales entered the dining-saloon. His hair was all over his head and he was wearing a red-and-white check dressing-gown. In a very cheery voice he said: 'Good morning.' He then turned over the pages of a newspaper and read a headline about a court case for breach of promise between a peer and a girl who had been a beauty queen. L.G. recalled an incident from his legal experience when, as solicitor representing a lady, he had deemed it advisable to consult counsel in respect of a breach-of-promise case. L.G. said he had always remembered the question put to him by this K.C. 'What does she look like?' L.G. had replied that she was good-looking. The K.C. had replied: 'Then you have a case.' . . .

The Prince said it must be very interesting for L.G. to look back upon events since the peace conference. L.G. said that the mistake they had made had been to give the Austrian Tyrol to the Italians.

The Prince reminded him that he had served at the Italian head-quarters. L.G. made the Prince roar with laughter, as he ate his breakfast, by relating how Orlando[19] had said: 'We will fight, even if we have to make a stand in Sicily.' L.G. said he had told Orlando that he thought they had better make a stand before that. . . .

As the train moved into the station at Cardiff, the Prince came into the saloon dressed in the uniform of Colonel of the Welsh Guards. Adjusting his busby, he suggested that L.G. should ride in the second carriage, which he did. He had a tumultuous reception from the great crowds. I rode in a car with several lords lieutenant

19. Vittorio Orlando (1860–1952). Prime Minister of Italy 1916–19.

to the City Hall for lunch. The Prince spoke in clear tones and well, the main theme being that written by L.G., which delighted the hearts of those in distressed areas in south Wales. It was a great misfortune that the B.B.C. did not broadcast it. After the lunch, hundreds of thousands swung round L.G. and he was in danger of being 'killed by kindness'. Police rushed to the scene and formed a cordon round him until he was safely in the car. They had come in thousands from the valleys of south Wales, and L.G. had his own procession to the station.

13 May

Gwilym, Dick and I accompanied L.G. to lunch at Thames House. Arthur Henderson and his son Willie[20] joined us for coffee and cigars. In reply to a question by Willie as to whether he would go into the Government, L.G. said he would support any party, even Beelzebub's, that promised to put through his proposals.

23 May

This morning, Wilson Black[21] breakfasted with L.G. and invited him to address a meeting of free church ministers, at a luncheon, to explain his proposals from the moral and spiritual point of view. L.G. now wants to bring them into a big scheme and have a great drive throughout the country. He is willing to finance such a movement.

25 May

Evelyn and I are at Churt for the weekend. We found L.G. alone in the sun parlour. He invited us to have a sherry. I remarked that this was an anxious time for him, whereupon he rapped out: 'Not at all. I am only anxious when I have not made up my mind. But now I have made it up, and I am going to *fight.*'

With his hands in the top of his trousers, he paced from one end of the sunlit room to the other in a blue-grey suit, with his white flowing hair and the fresh complexion of a country girl. There is a little roll in his walk because he throws all his weight on his right leg and does not walk evenly. He is what they call in Wales 'k-legged'. 'I should not be happy working with men like Neville Chamberlain and that crowd,' he said. 'When I was in the presence of men like Balfour, Birkenhead and Bonar, at any rate I felt I was

20. William Henderson (b.1891). Labour M.P. 1923–4 and 1929–31. Publicity Secretary of the Labour Party 1921–45, made a baron 1945, junior minister 1947–8.
21. Robert Wilson Black (1871–1951) was a prominent Baptist layman and had been on friendly terms with Lloyd George since the latter's early days in London as a young M.P.

fighting on equal terms. But these fellows – pooh. Yet despite that they would be in a majority against me. Once they got back, they would overrule me, saying that the majority was theirs.

On 1 and 2 July 1935 a 'convention' of some 2500 members met under Lloyd George's auspices at the Central Hall, Westminster. It voted to set up the Council of Action for Peace and Reconstruction which was to be Lloyd George's new political instrument. The idea was that it should cut across ordinary party ties in advancing his proposals. He also tried to enlist religious opinion, especially in the free churches, on his side but, although the 'convention' included some 440 clergymen and ministers, this turned out to be a flop. It was difficult to present his campaign other than as being in opposition to the National Government, and the churches inevitably saw this as party politics. Among those who attended the convention were George Lansbury, leader of the Labour Party, Sir Herbert Samuel, the Liberal leader, Lord Cecil of Chelwood, Lord Lothian, Isaac Foot, M.P.,[22] and Harold Macmillan, a leading light among a group of Tory M.P.s who with their 'The Next Five Years' policy were working on lines akin to those of Lloyd George.

The first day was devoted to 'peace', and there was much discussion of the League of Nations, to which Abyssinia (Ethiopia) had just appealed in the face of threats from Italy. There was a general consensus that the League should maintain collective security against any aggressor and that Britain should not increase her armaments. The main resolution was moved by Dr J. Scott Lidgett, a leading Methodist minister, who stated in the course of his speech that in the main he supported the National Government. Lloyd George did not speak on this day.

On the second day came the subject of 'reconstruction'. Among the speakers were Harold Macmillan, Hugh Molson and W. J. Brown.[23] Lloyd George's speech contained an eloquent attack on armaments expenditure – the money should be devoted to social purposes. He said he 'wanted to see a genuine non-party govern-

22. Philip Kerr, 11th Marquess of Lothian (1882–1940) was a private secretary to Lloyd George 1916–21, inherited his peerage 1930, was a junior minister 1931–2, secretary of the Rhodes Trust 1925–39 and British ambassador to Washington 1939–40.
Isaac Foot (1880–1960) became the doyen of West Country Liberalism. Liberal M.P. 1922–4 and 1929–35.
23. Hugh (later Lord) Molson (b.1903). Tory politician.
W. J. Brown (1894–1960). General Secretary of Civil Service Clerical Association 1919–42. Became a well-known broadcaster and writer. He was a Labour M.P. 1929–31 (resigning from the Labour Party 1931 to become an Independent) and an Independent M.P. 1942–50.

ment' dedicated to reform. He wanted M.P.s who would place this cause above their party obligations.

The Council of Action was duly voted into existence, and a network of provincial councils followed. However, the organisation was from the start a fragile one. Lloyd George hoped to get a House of Commons in which a majority, drawn from all parties, would support his principles. It was possible, if this were achieved, that he would become Prime Minister, but this was not particularly his aim. What he wanted was to overthrow the National Government. He got nowhere near his objective. There were 1348 candidates in the general election which came in November 1935, and of these 362 received, after answering a questionnaire, Council of Action endorsement. Of these latter 67 were returned – 11 Tory, 17 Liberal, 34 Labour and one Independent: they did not in any real sense act as a group.

17 June

L.G. invited me to accompany him to the Reform Club, where he had asked Dr Addison[24] to dine with him. He said that the leadership of the Labour Party was about as bad as that of the generals in the war. Addison demurred. Both he and George Lansbury have accepted invitations to the convention. L.G. was delighted.

20 June

Dr Scott Lidgett phoned me to say that the Bishop of Rochester had written to say that he was sorry he could not move the resolution at the convention. He had been to Lambeth Palace and the Archbishop had practically instructed him not to take part in the convention. The attitude of the Archbishop had been that no Anglican could do anything.[25]

Scott Lidgett told me that he was nervous about the publication of L.G.'s proposals, which he had sent to the Cabinet. He wanted to avoid the publication of these around the date of the convention. Otherwise free churchmen who were now supporting L.G. would be put in the position of attacking the National Government on these proposals. This he wanted to avoid, otherwise they would be split from top to bottom.

Walter Layton[26] called to see L.G. Afterwards L.G. told me that he had given him a piece of his mind. He said: 'I told him that I

24. Christopher (later Lord) Addison (1869–1951). Liberal minister 1914–21 and later in his long career prominent in the Labour Party.
25. i.e., in support of Lloyd George's claim.
26. Walter Layton (1884–1966). Chairman of the *News Chronicle* 1930–50. He was an economist who held various university and public posts.

would not go rat-catching with the *News Chronicle*, let alone tiger-hunting.'

28 *June*
Today I lunched with Tweed at Le Bon Viveur. He told me in detail of his personal position and his thoughts with regard to L.G. and the future, about which he made no bones.[27] He said he had told J.T. that if anything happened to L.G. the trustees would not be allowed to divide up the fund between the family. Tweed intended to see that he got his share.

1 *July*
The first session of the convention, with Lord Lothian in the chair, was a success, though there is a whispering campaign in the smoke-room of the House of Commons that it is a flop. Lord Cecil spoke, also Dr Scott Lidgett and George Lansbury. L.G. was satisfied.

2 *July*
Angus Watson[28] was chairman of the second session of the convention. At the end of the morning meeting, I received a message from Frances asking me to make arrangements for Jennifer to be present at the afternoon meeting. What a mad idea. It is a delegate meeting of churchmen and here is a child of five. I have never known such audacity as that of L.G. After his sleep in the House, I asked him if he realised the position. He knew about it all right, and passed it off. I accompanied L.G. to the convention. He spoke for one hour and five minutes and did brilliantly. In the course of his speech he said :

'They had some idea of dressing me up as a statesman who had achieved great things in the past, and putting me in the window for sale, the proceeds to be given to the National Government. That was in February and March of this year. Since then there has been a change in the weather. The electoral weather has become more congenial to the Government, and they have come to the conclusion that they would prefer flimsier material.'

4 *July*
Tweed, Finney[29] and Scanlan[30] were summoned to Churt. Tweed told

27. These were the actual words used by Tweed. It is a good old North Country and Midland expression. A.J.S.
28. Angus Watson (1874–1961). Self-made millionaire and prominent Congregationalist.
29. Victor Finney (1897–1970). Liberal M.P. 1923–4 and later an official in the Liberal organisation. He became secretary of the Council of Action 1935. In 1941 he left politics and went into the film industry.
30. Press officer of the Council of Action.

me that L.G. just regarded him in a matter-of-fact way, which Tweed felt. When L.G. asked Tweed what his objection was to a luncheon at the Metropole, Tweed told him that it would be a bad thing to start off the Council of Action with a big lunch at a millionaires' hotel. L.G. said it was not a millionaires' hotel. Tweed said it was not a fish-and-chip shop. Tweed said that L.G. had had a double dose of brandy before dinner; later they had music. In future, Tweed told me, the slogan would be 'say it with music'. I have a feeling that Tweed is carefully noting all these points in case he writes a book attacking L.G.

19 July
This morning L.G. received the official reply from Mr Baldwin, the Prime Minister, to his 'New Deal' proposals. This, generally, turns down the proposals.

22 July
I have spent a very busy weekend on a memorandum by L.G. in answer to the Government, to be issued to the Press today. He phoned me at 7.30 a.m. giving me additions, one of which was: 'Most of their document is taken up, not with an examination of my scheme, but with a torchlight procession of their own achievements in every sphere of activity.'

At 11.15 a.m. I accompanied L.G. to the large committee room at the House of Commons, where there was a big gathering of journalists, to whom I distributed the relevant documents. For the next hour, he reeled off answers to the questions which poured in on him. Afterwards I lunched with L.G., Dick and Gwilym at the Harcourt Room at the House. L.G. said as he was leaving the meeting one of the lobby correspondents had come up and said: 'Would you mind telling me what is the lotion you use which keeps you so fit?' L.G. said: 'I answered John Power.' (Sir Henry Fildes has just brought him a bottle of John Power Irish whiskey for him to try.)

8 August
L.G. presided at the Royal Welsh National Eisteddfod at Caernarvon. It was a marvellous occasion. He spoke entirely in Welsh for the longest time on record, twenty-one minutes. For many years he has taken just seventeen minutes: I always time him. He asked me to get a number of the bards and arrange a picnic for tomorrow in Cwm Pennant, where Eifion Wyn, who had been the greatest bard and whose works would be immortal, had tended his sheep in the mountains.

Sir William Jenkins, M.P.,[31] with his son and daughter, came to dinner at Brynawelon. There was talk about hymn tunes. Sir William sang a number. L.G. thought Parry[32] was the greatest hymn-tune writer the Welsh had thrown up. William Ambrose[33] was a wonderful man. L.G. then talked of Cynan,[34] a Methodist minister, who has just been appointed Recorder of the Gorsedd.[35] L.G. caused fits of laughter by reading Cynan's verses.

L.G. said that the greatest artists in Wales were Goscombe John[36] and Brangwyn.[37] Two of the greatest architects were Sir Owen Williams[38] and Lutyens[39] and he thought Sir Owen Williams was the greater. It was true that we had no great prose writers – that was where we were undoubtedly short – but the poets we had today were splendid.

Lloyd George describes what happened when he was called to the Foreign Office to discuss the threatening attitude of Italy towards Ethiopia. He saw Samuel Hoare,[40] Foreign Secretary, and Anthony

31. William Jenkins (1871–1944). Former miner from Glamorgan who was a Labour M.P. 1922–44.

32. C. H. H. Parry (1848–1918). Noted composer of choral music, although his instrumental music, including five symphonies, was not so successful. He composed a setting for William Blake's 'Jerusalem' in 1916, largely under war inspiration.

33. William Ambrose (1813–73). Congregationalist minister at Portmadoc 1837–73 and leading Welsh poet and hymn-writer.

34. Rev. Albert Evans-Jones (1895–1970). Welsh Calvinistic Methodist minister who was extra-mural lecturer in literature and drama at University College, Bangor, 1931–60 and for many years a leading figure at eisteddfodau. He won silver crowns for poetry 1921, 1923 and 1931, and a chair 1924. He was Archdruid of Wales 1949–52 and 1962–5. His bardic name was Cynan.

35. Gorsedd y Beirrd – Bardic Institute, the corporation of poets closely linked with the Welsh National Eisteddfod.

36. Goscombe John (1860–1952), the sculptor who, among many other things, executed the statue of Lloyd George at Caernarvon. He was knighted 1911.

37. Frank Brangwyn (1867–1956).

38. Owen Williams (1890–1969), civil engineer and architect whose works include the Dorchester Hotel, the *Daily Express* offices and the Empire Pool, Wembley.

39. Edwin Lutyens (1869–1944), architect, among other things, of the Cenotaph in Whitehall, New Delhi and the British Embassy in Washington.

40. Samuel Hoare (1880–1959) was a Tory M.P. 1920–44 and, after holding other ministerial appointments, became Foreign Secretary 1935 but was forced temporarily out of office at the end of the same year because he attempted to negotiate with France a compromise settlement to the Italian–Ethiopian war.

Eden, Minister for League of Nations Affairs. The war, in which Italy was to conquer Ethiopia, did not start until 3 October 1935. Churchill adopted a neutral, or even pro-Italian, stance on the matter but Lloyd George was on the side of Ethiopia.

23 August

Dame Margaret and I met L.G. at Bangor station tonight. During the evening L.G. gave an account of what had been said when he was called to the Foreign Office on Tuesday, 20 August, and received by Hoare, with Eden. He asked them whether the French knew what was in their minds. Eden said: 'Well, yes.' But L.G. insisted on knowing whether they had been told bluntly, to which Hoare and Eden replied 'No.' L.G. told them he considered it vital that the French should be told plainly.

He then asked if they intended to raise the embargo on munitions and was informed that this would be lifted. He told them that if, as seemed certain, Mussolini was going to fight we ought to see that Abyssinia was supplied with munitions. He told them not to be frightened by our fighting services. They would be sure to say that they had not a sufficient force and that there was a shortage of ships. He had had all that in the Great War.

Eden related that during the Paris talks it was alleged that Laval[41] had said that he did not know that there was a Covenant.[42] This seemed to be an incredible story, but this is what Eden disclosed. L.G. said he wondered whether Laval was too clever for Eden. He said that Mussolini ought to be told what would be the consequence of war. It was no use waiting to tell him this when the Council of the League met. L.G. said he had come away with the impression that, of the two, Hoare had the better brain, even allowing for his greater age and experience.

Megan asked her father what he would do. He replied that he had answered that point in the House by saying he would not have allowed the situation to develop as it had. The Tories had laughed, but it had been true. If you got a cart into deep ruts, he could not tell you how to get it out, but he knew how to prevent it getting there. He would remind the French of the sanctions agreed upon at Stresa.[43] Those were for general application, and not to be applied

41. Pierre Laval (1883–1945) was currently French Prime Minister.
42. The Covenant of the League of Nations, which among other things obliged members to respect each other's integrity and to submit disputes to arbitration.
43. Ramsay MacDonald, Laval and the Italian dictator Benito Mussolini had met at Stresa, Italy, in April 1935 and agreed to work together against breaches of international order.

only to Germany. If the French did not act in the present situation, then we would know that we ourselves could never rely on them. He would talk bluntly to the French and make them think.

5 September

L.G. invited my wife, Evelyn, and me, along with Frances, Mrs Morris[44] and Dr Thomas Jones to dinner at Prunier's. All the talk was about preachers and hymns. L.G. said that the greatest hymnologist was Pantycelyn.[45] He said that whenever he was worried he flew to Pantycelyn. Whenever Sylvester acquainted him with difficulties ahead, he consoled himself with some of those old hymn tunes or verses. He said that Pantycelyn was so human. He was so good because he understood all the human passions. One line he interpreted was : 'Hide my sins from God; let not my sins be known to the people.'

L.G. said the Roman Catholics knew how to make saints and where to put them. Saints were not people to live with. He had never felt that he would have liked to have lived with John Elias.[46] He might have been all right in his day, but he was all hell-fire and very severe. . . .

L.G. told stories of Herber Evans,[47] the finest of which, said L.G., was about the little lamp. It was at the time when it was fashionable for young men in the universities and colleges to criticise the Bible. Speaking at Portmadoc, Herber Evans dealt with the higher criticism. He told of a visit to a little chapel in the Pennant Valley. At the end of the service an old lady came to him and said : 'Mr Evans, you are staying with us tonight. But the night is very dark and stormy, and the way is long and very difficult. There are several precipices in the way, but here is a little lamp. It has many holes in it, and there are rents in it, but it will light you home.' Then, turning on the critics of the Bible, who were trying to pick it to pieces, Herber Evans said : 'It is full of holes. There are even rents in it. The five books of Moses may be said to be all wrong, the dates may be wrong, the geography may be wrong, I myself may even have doubts about it, but, although they pick it to pieces, the little

44. Wife of Lloyd George's solicitor, John Morris.

45. William Williams of Pantycelyn (1717–91) was an itinerant preacher in Wales for nearly fifty years, published ninety-two books and wrote some 800 hymns.

46. John Elias (1774–1841) was ordained a Calvinistic Methodist minister 1811 and became noted for his extreme fundamentalist views.

47. Evan Herber Evans (1839–96) was ordained as a Congregationalist minister 1862 and he was reckoned to be the most eloquent Welsh preacher of his generation.

light still burns on. "Thy word is a lamp unto my feet, and a light unto my path" – Psalm 119, verse 105.'

As we said goodnight, Tom Jones said that he felt that he had had a religious bath.[48]

Lloyd George returns with Sylvester to the bosom of his family, from Churt.

9 September

Dame Margaret met us at Bangor. At Brynawelon we were greeted by Gwilym dressed up as the Emperor of Abyssinia and Thorpey[49] dressed up as the Empress. Gwilym wore a great black beard and whiskers, which he had pulled out of his mother's hearth rug and stuck on his chin and cheeks, and his face had been sallowed by the pollen from the flowers in the garden. His flowing robes consisted of one of Dame Margaret's nightdresses, which showed off to full advantage his big, bare legs. A huge bath towel formed his turban, and the big lid of a Cadbury's chocolate box formed a great medal. He carried a long shepherd's crook. Thorpey wore one of Dame Margaret's best dresses, with a cushion underneath to form a more than adequate bust, with pollen on his face, two beautiful plaits of Edna's own hair and a set of beads which were given to Dame Margaret by the Ecumenical Patriarch when we were in Cairo. Olwen, Megan, Mrs Thorpe and the grandchildren, carrying a huge flag of the Welsh dragon, stood behind.

As L.G. alighted from the car, the Emperor welcomed him in broken English to Addis Ababa, while the Empress, with a delightful charm and attractive shyness, made two graceful bobs. Those behind shouted lustily.

L.G. was thrilled.

At dinner L.G. said he felt anxious about the attitude of the Government towards the Italo-Abyssinian question. The nigger in the woodpile was Neville,[50] so Max[51] had told him, who would not allow the Government to commit themselves to sanctions.

48. In the original, full text of Sylvester's diary there are many passages of this type, running into tens of thousands of words. It is possible to publish only a few of them here, as samples. Welsh preachers was one of Lloyd George's favourite conversational topics.

49. J. H. Thorpe, K.C. (1887–1944), father of Mr Jeremy Thorpe, who was elected leader of the Liberal Party 1967. He was a Tory M.P. 1919–23 and he and his wife were friends of the Lloyd George family.

50. Neville Chamberlain, currently Chancellor of the Exchequer.

51. Lord Beaverbrook.

10 *September*

After L.G. had spoken tonight to 6000 Methodist delegates from
all parts of Wales, he and I had a picnic dinner in the car overlooking the Menai Straits. We motored to Bangor and went thence
by train to Chester. L.G. told me that this was the train on which
he had used to travel regularly, second class, with three changes.
One change had been at Crewe where he had got the worst coffee
imaginable. On arriving in London, he had taken a growler to the
National Liberal Club. Few members realised what it meant in
those days, and few even remembered that it was he who had got
them their parliamentary pay.[52]

*The following relates to a conference which set up the Welsh Council
of Action.*

11 *September*

We arrived at the Gwalia Hotel, Llandrindod Wells. I spent much
time obtaining information on the Italo-Abyssinian situation in an
old-fashioned telephone-box, with an old-fashioned instrument, writing on a small ledge with no electric light and aided only by a torch.

Whilst awaiting the arrival of Dame Margaret and Megan, L.G.
decided to change. When I went into his bedroom, I found that he
had got out his black boots, of which he had two pairs. He had
put on the right boot, and he was now struggling with the right
boot of the other pair to get it on the left foot and could not understand what was wrong.

He told me a story about old Dr Parker. Parker's niece lived with
him. One day she heard her uncle in his study calling out: 'Statistics,
STATISTICS, STATISTICS'. She opened the door and inquired what
was the matter, thinking the old boy had gone dotty. He replied:
'My dear, it is all right. I am just experimenting with a new plate.'

He had a grand meeting with a crowded hall, and an overflow
meeting downstairs.

Afterwards he was in a reminiscent mood, which is a delight. He
told me how he first came before public notice. It originated, he said,
through old Dr Evans, Carey's[53] father, at Festiniog. Michael Davitt,[54]
the Irish Nationalist, was to speak at Blaenau Festiniog before Gladstone proclaimed for home rule in 1885. None of the strait-laced
Liberals would speak or help. An old quarryman, with a great gift

52. Lloyd George, as Chancellor of the Exchequer, introduced payment
of M.P.s with effect from the beginning of 1912. The rate was £400 a
year.
53. Sir Thomas Carey Evans.
54. Michael Davitt (1846–1906). Extreme Irish-home-ruler.

of speech, took the chair. Dr Evans invited L.G. to propose a vote
of thanks to Michael Davitt. He made the speech of the evening.
It was then that Michael Davitt said publicly, and later privately
at Dr Evans's house: 'You must get this young fellow into Parliament. He is saying in Wales what we are saying in Ireland.'

It had really been the Congregationalists who had put him in
Parliament. Michael Jones of Bala had agreed on this particular
night with Michael Davitt that L.G. should be in the House.

The second meeting which brought him before the public was at
Portmadoc, in connection with the church question. A man named
Helm, a paid speaker of the Established Church, was speaking. L.G.
had not long been married and was living with his father-in-law
and mother-in-law at Mynyddednyfed Farm, Criccieth. He was suffering from a sore throat. When he heard of this meeting, he said to
his wife: 'I am off to this meeting.'

Helm was a very pompous fellow who spoke with great authority
on church matters. L.G. sat in the audience. Presently L.G. ejacula-
ted: 'That is not true.' Helm looked over his glasses as much as
to say: 'How dare you interrupt me!' Presently, L.G. interrupted
him again, saying: 'That statement is not true.' Whereupon Helm
said: 'If that gentleman has anything to say, let him come on the
platform and say it.'

L.G. grasped the opportunity. He was very cheeky, but was
absolutely right on his facts. The result was a complete failure for
Helm and a great success for L.G. He had forgotten his bad throat.

I said that one of my regrets was that I had never known his old
uncle.[55] L.G. said that he was a very generous man. He never had a
penny piece in his pocket. He lived a very spartan life. He liked a
simple meal of bread and cheese and butter, and had no enjoyments
outside his work as a cobbler, except reading and preparing his
sermons. He was very sociable. 'I never had his passion for mystic
religion, praying and that sort of thing,' said L.G. 'He was very
broad-minded, very friendly with the village curate, who lent him
books of reference. Thus, I myself was brought up very broadly and
that is why I have never been a good party man. My uncle did not
drink or smoke and never had a woman. He was freer from the
passions than any man I know. He had an instinct for discerning
a decent fellow.'

19 *September*
On our return journey by train from a Council of Action convention at Bradford, L.G. talked of Winston. He said he remembered

55. Uncle (Richard) Lloyd, who had brought Lloyd George up after
the early death of his father.

a discussion between Winston, who was then Home Secretary, Reading, who was then Solicitor-General, and Riddell on whether they had expected to be where they were then. All of them said 'No', except Winston who was Home Secretary at the age of thirty-five. His answer had been 'Yes' and he had added: 'Napoleon won Austerlitz at my age.'

4 October

In the car today, referring to the forthcoming general election, L.G. said that this was the last fight he would make.

Polling day in the 1935 general election was on 14 November. It was a quiet campaign with almost no doubt that the Government would win. Lloyd George led his little 'family group' of Independent Liberals and, again, had a Tory but no Labour opponent in his constituency, Caernarvon Boroughs. This was his fourteenth and last contest there.

24 October

I left with L.G. by train for Bangor. He said that if the Government got a big majority he wondered whether he would continue. I said I did not think he would be happy outside the House. We are now in Caernarvon Boroughs for the general election. He discussed his itinerary with some of his principal officers, a draft of which I had worked out. He inserted extra meetings in his own handwriting.

31 October

L.G. had a magnificent meeting in the Pavilion, Llandudno, tonight. After a meal tonight, he said: 'I know my people.' He was talking at Belcher and me because we had told him the truth about feeling against him in the Boroughs. Smoking his cigar, L.G. said that Welsh people loved to listen to a speech. That was the real reason why always, before an election, they [i.e., his constituency organisation] spoke pessimistically, for the one purpose of getting him down to hear him speak. 'That is a thing you English do not understand at all,' said L.G. Don't we?

4 November

Thomson and I accompanied L.G. to Bangor drill hall, where he addressed a crowd of 5500. I had circulated an advance copy of his speech to the Press in the afternoon, as it was a reply to Neville

Chamberlain's broadcast.[56] L.G. described him as a man with a retail mind in a wholesale business, and the only thing they had in common was a cold.

5 November
It was discovered tonight that Megan has a slight temperature, and her engagements were cancelled. L.G. and Megan fuss each other terribly; it is mostly humbug, too.

6 November
Last night someone telephoned Dame Margaret that the meeting of the Council of Action in Llangefni had not been very good. Dame Margaret told this to Megan. L.G. delivered a devil of a lecture to Dame Margaret and me this morning, saying that as a consequence of the pessimistic information given to her last night Megan had not slept at all. He went on: 'It is no good telling the little girl (she is thirty-four) of the difficulties in Anglesey when she is ill. Tell her the things which will help her in the fight. It is like one of his seconds telling the prize-fighter: "The other fellow is beating you." You ought to tell him, even if it is obvious that he is losing, that he is getting in some good blows and doing well.'

8 November
Edna phoned me today from Tenby. L.G. was annoyed with her when I gave him Edna's news that the result would be very close in Pembrokeshire. Later L.G. spoke to Gwilym personally. Gwilym confirmed what Edna had told me: things were not too good. L.G. literally pumped optimism into him over the telephone.

9 November
L.G. telephoned Max Beaverbrook, and they agreed that the Government was going back.

13 November
When I went to see L.G. in his bedroom this morning at 8 a.m., he asked me to call a special meeting of workers at Llandudno Club. I gave an advance copy of his speech to the Press, for the evening papers. He is moving heaven and earth to get electors to vote Labour where there is no Liberal. He had two magnificent eve-of-poll meetings, one at Caernarvon in the Pavilion and the second at

56. Neville Chamberlain, Chancellor of the Exchequer, had devoted almost an entire election broadcast to an attack on Lloyd George, both over Ethiopia and unemployment. He was suffering from a cold and was heard to ask for water during the broadcast.

Bangor in the drill hall. The Caernarvon speech was relayed to Denbigh. During his speech a one-armed man walked right across the huge platform to say to L.G.: 'Someone wants Mr Sylvester on the telephone.'

Polling day.

14 November

When I greeted L.G. in his bedroom at 6.45 this morning, he wanted me to telephone for news to people who could not be found because they were asleep.

In drowning rain, we started our visits to all the committee rooms. He asked me for my copy of the itinerary, which contained all my personal notes as to the precise places where we were to meet our guides. When he arrived at Bangor, despite the fact that loyal workers were all along the line waiting for him in committee rooms in such inclement weather, he suddenly decided to go to Llangefni to see how Megan was progressing. There was only one responsible person there, who told him that Labour was doing exceptionally well, which caused him much concern. He showed little concern for Gwilym, who is the one in difficulty. He had said earlier that he would like to see Megan with a majority of only eighteen, which was his first majority.

The National Government, now with Baldwin as Prime Minister, won the election comfortably but with a reduced majority, and with Ramsay MacDonald himself, until recently Prime Minister, losing his seat. (He was soon found another.) The Labour strength went up from the 52 seats it had managed to hold in 1931 to 154. The Liberal strength dropped from 33 to 17. Lloyd George's Independent Liberal group held all its 4 seats. The Government won 431 seats, of which 387 were Tory, 33 were National Liberal, 8 were National Labour and 3 were plain 'National'.

15 November

When the Mayor declared the result that L.G. had been returned, there was great applause. Meantime someone put a piece of paper in my hand which I took to L.G. and John Williams, the Returning Officer, who read it out. It was Megan's result, which was loudly applauded. I shall never forget L.G.'s emotion. Tears stood in his eyes and he made a big swallow.[57]

In a Press interview on 19 November in London, Lloyd George said it was obvious that the country had preferred even the National Government to another Labour one. He himself was to take a holiday in the Mediterranean. For the next six months he would do nothing in Parliament but would devote himself to writing his memoirs and building up the Council of Action.

20 November

A Press attack on L.G., saying that he is going abroad for six months to write his book. They had misinterpreted his statement about going abroad and being away from politics for six months to write his book to mean that he will be abroad for six months. Even his constituency is up in arms against him.

Yesterday he asked me to arrange his seat in the House and try to keep his rooms. When I went to the House and talked to my Labour friends and others concerned, they laughingly asked what L.G. wanted rooms for, seeing that he was going away for six months.

Yesterday I looked up precedents as to whether the Father of the House spoke at the election of the Speaker. In every case, T. P. O'Connor, as Father of the House, took part. L.G., however, does not want to speak. He did not like my telling him on the phone that everybody was expecting him to speak. In these matters, he makes mistakes.[58] The House is jealous of its tradition, and members like

57. Results for the Lloyd George 'family group' were:

Caernarvon Boroughs		Anglesey	
D. Lloyd George (Ind. Lib.)	19,242	Megan Lloyd George (Ind. Lib.)	11,227
A. R. du Cros (Tory)	9633	F. J. W. Williams (Tory)	7045
		H. Jones (Lab.)	6959
Majority	9609	Majority	4182
Pembroke		Caernarvonshire	
Gwilym Lloyd George (Ind. Lib.)	16,734	Goronwy Owen (Ind. Lib.)	17,947
G. E. Allison (Tory)	15,660	W. E. Jones (Lab.)	16,450
W. J. Jenkins (Lab.)	12,341	J. E. Daniel (Welsh Nat.)	2534
Majority	1074	Majority	1497

58. Lloyd George succeeded T. P. O'Connor as 'father' of the Commons on the latter's death in 1929. Lloyd George, as Liberal leader, had spoken

to see the tradition observed. Baldwin always observes these niceties.

Lloyd George sets off from London for a working holiday in Tangiers.

29 November

As L.G. got into the car for Tangiers, Megan said: 'We shall be coming out with our equerry' (referring to me). I then drove off with him.

There had been a situation. Megan had intimated that she would go to the station with her father. L.G. therefore told her that he was motoring to Tilbury. He did no such thing. At the very last moment only, I had arranged the train journey so that there would be no clashing of the family and Frances.[59]

on the election of the Speaker in 1929. In 1931 he had been absent owing to his illness. In 1935 he did, as it turned out, speak on the election of the Speaker (A. E. Fitzroy), saying he was the sixth one he had known and what a good fellow he was.

59. The point was that Miss Stevenson was accompanying Lloyd George to Tangiers and he did not want his family to know this. The programme was that later on Miss Stevenson should return home and then some of his family, accompanied by Sylvester, would join him.

Chapter 7

'Germany has trained up a leader'

1936

*At the beginning of the year Lloyd George, with Miss Stevenson,
was in Morocco, working on his memoirs. They were staying at the
same hotel as Winston Churchill. Then Miss Stevenson returned
home and Dame Margaret Lloyd George and Megan Lloyd George,
accompanied by Sylvester, came out to join Lloyd George.*

10 January
L.G. met us at Marrakesh in blazing sunshine, looking the picture
of health. At lunch, L.G. said that a few days ago a fellow started
practising on a ukulele. Winston was painting in his room above
and L.G. was writing his memoirs and finding it very difficult to
concentrate because of the noise. Presently, he heard a terrific yell
from Winston, which was long and continuous. The ukulele stopped.
After a pause, it started again. Winston repeated his yell. This
process went on for some time, until the ukulele was stopped by the
management of the hotel. L.G. said that the irritation caused by the
noise of the ukulele was quite wiped out by Winston's performance.

Whilst we were enjoying our apéritif this evening with L.G.,
there was a knock at the door and in walked Winston, with a picture
which he had painted. He said it was done in an hour. It was a
little gem, depicting a Marrakesh building, coloured in ochre, and
with the red setting sun on it, tall palms, a Moor in the middle of
the road and a native woman at the well. L.G. said it was an inspiration. Winston was as pleased as a child. He wore a blue suit, with
paint smeared all over his sleeve.

15 January
On our way to golf today, L.G. said that he realised that his Russian
chapter would be longer than he had expected. It [the Russian
Revolution] was a development which had an enormous influence
on the rest of the world. He intended to make that very plain. 'It
was the greatest development in the world since the Crucifixion.'

He said he wished he could say that publicly, but it would shock people too much.

17 January
L.G. gave a dinner to celebrate his seventy-third birthday. Present were L.G., Dame Margaret, Megan, Thomson and myself, together with Winston, Duncan Sandys[1] and his wife.

There is no doubt that Winston and L.G. stimulate each other. I was immensely interested watching the facial expressions of these two brilliant men.

A cake was brought in, which bore an inscription in Welsh, meaning 'To Tada. Many happy returns'. Around it were seventy-three small candles. I put out the electric light. . . .

Immediately afterwards, Winston rose and said: 'This is a memorable occasion, although it is an informal one. I am going to add to the many thousands of speeches which I have inflicted upon people by asking you to join with me in drinking to the health of our illustrious friend. Ours is a very long political friendship. It is now forty years or more since we began to be friends in the House of Commons. There have been many vicissitudes in public life during that period, and all the time I have thanked God that he has been born to work for our country, for the masses of those poor people in times of peace, and for our strength and security in the great days of the war. I ask you to join with me in drinking his health on his seventy-third birthday, and let us hope that another decade, at least, of vigour lies before him for, I can assure you, we shall need his counsel and his efforts in the years that lie before us.'

L.G. replied: 'If I may be allowed to add to the scores of thousands of speeches I have delivered in the course of my life, I do so thank you very warmly for drinking my health on an occasion when I have attained years of which I am not proud, and of which I am not very pleased to remind myself too often. What has added to the pleasure of my seventy-third birthday is that I have the good fortune to have present with me today, on this occasion, my oldest political friend. It is the longest political friendship in the life of Great Britain. It is a friendship which has not depended in the least upon agreement, even on fundamentals. I doubt very much whether there is any other country where it would be possible for men to fight, and fight very hard, as we have done, more particularly during the last ten or fifteen years, without for one moment impairing the good feeling and the warmth and, if I may be allowed to say so, no one knows better than my family the affection, with which I return my friendship. It is to me a very great delight that he should have been

1. Duncan Sandys (b.1908). Tory politician.

here today to propose this toast. I thank you from the bottom of my heart.'

King George V had contracted a chill which had now turned serious. He died on 20 January.

18 January

L.G. discussed the whole position with Winston and I worked out various alternatives. Winston takes the view that there is no hurry. Winston came in to listen to the wireless at 9.30 p.m., when L.G. had gone to bed. I listened in at 10 p.m. and at midnight. Still nothing further, and I put a note under L.G.'s door, and one under Winston's.

Lloyd George decides to return to London, in view of the King's illness.

19 January

I worked through the night and by eight o'clock this morning I had made arrangements for L.G. and his party to leave today at 4 p.m.[2]

20 January

We boarded the *Maloja* at 3.15 p.m.

21 January

At 12.30 this morning, the nightwatchman brought me a message from the chief officer that 'The King died at two minutes to twelve'. At 5.30 a.m. I went in to L.G. He was still asleep with the lights on, having gone to sleep while reading a novel. I put a note on a chair.

At 7.30 a.m., I went in again. 'Good morning, sir,' I said. 'Have you seen the note I left?' He replied: 'Well, he has gone.' I suggested he should send a message of condolence to the Queen, which he did. During the morning a reply was received, very much appreciating the message of sympathy and signed 'Mary'.

2. The Dowager Countess stated in her autobiography, *The Years That Are Past*: 'We returned from Marrakesh earlier than we had intended, owing to the death of King George V.' Here her memory must have been at fault. As my diary shows, she had left Morocco before Dame Margaret's arrival on 10 January. A.J.S.

Lloyd George attends at Buckingham Palace with a Commons deputation, which presented an address to the new king, Edward VIII, on his accession. With him, among others, were Baldwin, Eden, Churchill, Attlee, Samuel and Simon.

27 January

When L.G. returned from Buckingham Palace, he said the King had told him that he was pleased with his article in the *Sunday Express* on his father.

I told L.G. that, as I had not been able to get any instructions from him, I had ordered a wreath to be sent to Windsor for the late King's funeral from Dame Margaret and himself. Turning peculiar at once, he said: 'I am not going to send a wreath.' I replied: 'Mr and Mrs Baldwin are sending one.' He said: 'Baldwin is Prime Minister.' I pointed out that he had been Prime Minister during the war, in the greatest days through which King George had lived, and that even the humblest persons were sending flowers. He said he would not pay for a wreath. Who else was sending one? I said: 'I have just spoken to Winston personally. He and his wife have already sent one.' That did it. I told him it would cost £10 and produced a black-edged card. This he inscribed: 'Deep grief from loyal servants, D. Lloyd George: Margaret Lloyd George.'

5 February

Mr Baldwin asked me behind the Speaker's chair how L.G. was getting on with the next volume of his *War Memoirs*. I told him he had worked tremendously hard in Marrakesh. He had written 160,000 words in six weeks. He asked me what that worked out a day. I replied that in round figures 4000 on the average. On one or two days, however, he had done nothing, because he had been travelling, so that on other days he had written, in his own hand, as many as 10,000 words. Mr Baldwin said it was a great achievement; he thought L.G. should write a volume on the peace to round it off.

26 April

L.G. said that he definitely would never ever trust the Tories again. He did, at any rate, write to Asquith his views, when he had a disagreement with him, but the Tories sat round a cabinet table when he knew they had already made up their minds to do him in. Yet they said not a word to him of their intentions.[3] *They* were supposed

3. Presumably Lloyd George is here referring to the events of 1922 when the majority of his cabinet and parliamentary support were Tory and he was ejected from Downing Street.

to be the gentlemen of England. He repeated that he would never trust them again.

At dinner Edna said that David[4] wanted to go into politics when he was old enough. He is now thirteen. L.G. said that when he had been that age he had wanted to be either the skipper of a three-masted schooner or a missionary in Africa, at which remark there were shrieks of laughter. What he had wanted, he said, was adventure.

5 May

At dinner at Churt talk was about Winston. L.G. said that his whole attitude was summed up in a remark he had once made: 'Success in politics depends upon whether you can control your conscience.' Thomson asked: 'Has that been published?' L.G.: 'Good Lord, no.'

20 May

When I met Dame Margaret and Megan they both asked if L.G. had got over his temper of the other night. As I had not been present, I frankly did not know what they meant. Then Dame Margaret explained what had happened. Edna had asked him if he would stay with them at Tenby in August, in connection with the eisteddfod at Fishguard. She had pulled his leg by saying that she had another guest, Sir John Simon. At this, L.G. had gone off at half-cock. When Dame Margaret had intervened to say that it was all fun, he had said that she was siding with the rest.

Dame Margaret said that as she had gone home with L.G. that night he had said that his family were disloyal to him. She had told him not to talk to her about *disloyalty*. No family was more loyal. He then said that Megan had been talking about his morals, and this had spread through Wales. Dame Margaret had vigorously denied this and asked who had told him such a thing. When pressed as to who had told him, he had replied: 'Sylvester.' Dame Margaret said at once, before I answered, that she knew it was not me. She said: 'He always says: "It is Sylvester." ' She knew that L.G. had been lying and so I do not worry. But it shows that someone is jealous of my good relations with the family and wants to break them. They won't succeed.

2 June

Jennifer has whooping cough. L.G. is so upset that he stayed in bed today.

4. Son of Gwilym and Edna.

*In the Derby by-election of July 1936 Lloyd George supports the
Labour candidate, Philip Noel-Baker, who had a straight fight
against a National Labour – that is, pro-government – candidate,
A. G. Church.[5] The election was caused by the resignation of J. H.
Thomas, the National Labour minister, who had been forced to quit
public life because he had been involved in a budget leak. Noel-
Baker won the seat.*

6 July

Tweed and I left St Pancras with L.G. for the Derby by-election.
The main point about L.G.'s intervention in this by-election is the
beginning of the popular front.

The drill hall was packed with 3000 people, and thousands stood
outside in the pouring rain. He spoke for fifty minutes to this magnificent meeting on behalf of Noel-Baker, the Labour candidate. When
he returned to the hotel I helped him change, for he was wet
through with perspiration. Then we had supper in his sitting-room.
Amongst others, Randolph Churchill and A. J. Cummings were
present. Then Harold Nicolson,[6] who had been speaking for Major
Church, came into our room by mistake. L.G. invited him to stay
and have supper, which he did.

L.G. said that Asquith had had a first-class mind, but he had not
been a man of action. He had left the war to Kitchener. Asquith
had always stood by his word. In the 1909 budget, L.G. had not
cared very much personally about land values, but he had known
that it was the best question upon which to attack the Lords.

'At the first row in the Cabinet about land values, not a voice
was raised in favour of them except by Winston and me. After
Asquith had listened to all sorts of objections, he sniffed, in his
usual manner, and then, rubbing his hands over his face, he said :
"Well, I think the general sense of the Cabinet is in favour", and
he stuck to his guns.'

30 July

In the train at Chester, I got L.G. a good whiskey and water. Presently he talked. The worst thing Asquith had ever done, said L.G.,
had been to join the Church of England. He had been the son of a

5. Philip Noel-Baker (b.1889). Labour M.P. 1929–31, 1936–70, junior
minister 1942–5, minister 1945–51.
    A. G. Church (1886–1968). Labour M.P. 1923–4, 1929–31. He was
one of the minority of Labour M.P.s who had supported MacDonald in
forming the National Government 1931.
    6. Harold Nicolson (1886–1968) was a National Labour M.P. 1935–45.

nonconformist minister.[7] He had not joined because of principle but, L.G. could only suspect, because of society. He thought this had been one of the meanest things Asquith ever had done and had always held him in contempt for doing it. He himself had always belonged to the Church of Christ and had become associated with the Baptists. He held no great belief in their doctrines, but he had been brought up amongst them and, having progressed among them, he would never have it thought that, once he had made his position, he had let them down by transferring to some other faith.

In September 1936 Lloyd George spent almost a fortnight in Germany and had two meetings with Adolf Hitler, at one of which Sylvester was present. Hitler had then been in power for just over three and a half years and had acted vigorously and successfully (aided by improved world economic conditions) to eliminate mass unemployment in Germany. This was an achievement that greatly impressed Lloyd George, and he wanted to see something of it for himself. It was somewhat similar to the vigorous economic programmes he had advocated for Britain in the 1929 election and with his 1935 Council of Action. Hitler, on his side, was convinced that the German collapse of 1918 had been due to lack of effective political leadership of the Lloyd George type. Lloyd George had long agreed with this assessment. Thus the two men were fascinated to meet each other, and there can be little doubt that they saw themselves as two super-statesmen, with imaginations which soared far beyond those of ordinary politicians. After the meetings, Lloyd George described Hitler, in a newspaper article, as 'the George Washington of Germany'.

The position at the time of the Lloyd George–Hitler meetings was that Hitler had refused to accept the armaments restrictions placed upon Germany in the Versailles Treaty and had begun to build up a modern army, based upon universal military service, and supported by a new air force. In the 1935 Anglo-German Naval Treaty the British had tacitly admitted the right of Germany to ignore the Versailles restrictions

In March 1936 Hitler had put a garrison into the Rhineland, German territory which by international agreement was supposed to remain unmilitarised. He had been greatly relieved that the French had not marched against him. Then in July Francisco Franco had started the nationalist revolt against the republican government in Spain, and this led to the civil war which for three years was to have strong international reverberations. Mussolini from Italy was to give Franco strong military support and Hitler, too, was to help

7. Asquith's father was in fact a Congregationalist layman.

him to a limited extent. (In Britain, Churchill was at first a supporter of Franco.) Lloyd George firmly supported the republican
side. Hitler's overriding aim, in relation to Britain, was to secure
British acquiescence in German eastward expansion. To this end, he
had just appointed Ribbentrop, Nazi foreign-affairs specialist and a
non-professional diplomat (in fact a former wine-merchant), to be
his ambassador in London.

Sylvester kept a detailed diary of the visit to Germany, during
which Lloyd George was accompanied also by Gwilym Lloyd George,
Megan Lloyd George, Lord Dawson of Penn and Thomas Jones.
With them, as a kind of liaison officer, was T. P. Conwell Evans.[8]
At its full length the diary would make almost a book itself and
only brief extracts are given here. In his The Real Lloyd George
Sylvester included two chapters on the visit, based upon his diary,
and these remain the standard account, together with that given by
Jones in his A Diary with Letters (1954). Only limited extracts
from the Sylvester diary are given here.

26 August
L.G. wants me to get Tom Jones to come on the German trip. He is
at present abroad. Tom was connected with Baldwin and if he joined
the party it would take off any appearance of L.G. interfering. L.G.
was also anxious to see Ludendorff, and he wants me to find out
whether there would be any objection. He said he wanted to talk to
Ludendorff about the war.

On the phone, Conwell Evans had told L.G. that he was the only
man who understood Hitler and that, conversely, L.G. was the only
man for whom Hitler had any respect on this side. Nathan came to
dinner. Immediately we sat down I received a telephone call from
Dr Weizmann from Zürich saying that the High Commissioner in
Palestine had agreed with the Arabs to stop Jewish immigration and
asking what pressure L.G. could exert. In reply to Nathan as to
what he would do, L.G. said that he would like to see the Jew armed,
in order to defend his own rights in his own domain.

29 August
Ribbentrop has told Conwell Evans that he is not highly favourable
to L.G. seeing Ludendorff, as Ludendorff is regarded as mad.[9] It is
questionable what attitude Ludendorff would adopt towards L.G. But

8. T. Philip Conwell Evans (1891–1968) had been a visiting lecturer at
the University of Königsberg and was a joint secretary of the Anglo-
German Fellowship.
9. Ludendorff did in his later years become extremely eccentric.

L.G. could see him, if he chose. Tom Jones has accepted L.G.'s invitation to join the party.

Gwilym, Tweed, Finney and I dined with L.G. at the Savoy Hotel. L.G. said that last night he had been discussing with Conwell Evans that during the past forty years Germany had suffered through having a great many mediocre statesmen, including Bethmann-Hollweg. Germany had now trained up a leader in Hitler. We in this country were in the same position as Germany had found herself in during those forty years. We had no leader.

2 September

We had a smooth crossing and arrived at Flushing at 5.30 p.m. Baron Geyr, who has been attached to our party by Ribbentrop, met us. At dinner on the train, L.G. asked Conwell, if he were to be born again, what country he would choose as his native land. Conwell unhesitatingly answered: 'Germany.' L.G. thought Germany was too similar to our own country as regards weather. He would prefer a sunnier climate.

We arrived at Cologne after eleven o'clock at night. L.G. went to bed. Gwilym, Conwell, the Baron and I took a stroll to the cathedral. We met parties of men and women singing and enjoying themselves, and eating hot sausages they bought in the streets as they landed from boats on the Rhine.

3 September

We arrived at Munich at ten o'clock this morning. Here we were joined by Lord Dawson, who said he was interested in Germany from the angle of the health of the individual and the sterilisation of the unfit. We were joined at lunch by Tom Jones. L.G. told me afterwards that he was very disappointed with Tom, because of his attitude in hoping that the rebels would win in Spain. L.G. said how much he had altered from the radical he used to know. After lunch, we left for Berchtesgaden, where we dined at the Grand Hotel with the new German ambassador to London, Herr von Ribbentrop, and Frau Ribbentrop. Present also was Baron Geyr and Dr Schmidt, the official German Foreign Office translator from Berlin.

L.G. said it was most fortunate for Germany that she had found a leader in Hitler. He was much looking forward to seeing him. Ribbentrop replied that Hitler had been looking forward to this opportunity for years. There was no doubt a great fellow-sympathy. L.G. said there was no doubt that Hitler, as far as Germany was concerned, was the resurrection and the life.

Ribbentrop gave a wonderful appreciation of the present religious

situation in Germany. He said that he had explained the position to
a number of people in England, but the only man to understand
him had been the Archbishop of Canterbury. In pre-Hitler days,
Germany had become anti-Church. The communists were anti-God.
Had it not been for Hitler, the communists would have captured
the country, and the country would have become anti-God. The
Church had done nothing to save Germany from communism in
the way of stopping the anti-God movement. Today there was a
striving for a new faith. Hitler himself thought it would take many
years to reveal its true form. They were now waiting for the birth
of this new faith.

It was agreed that the great blunder on the German side had
been not to have taken advantage of Joe Chamberlain's offer of an
alliance in 1898. Ribbentrop said that Hitler absolutely agreed with
this view. L.G. suggested that Ribbentrop should try to get Winston.
The trouble with Winston was that he was fighting with everyone
in turn : one day it was Russia, now it was Germany. L.G. added :
'If you could get him into your new church, it would be worth
while.'

L.G. said that Russia would be far more dangerous as a military
nation when she became nationalist than when she was Bolshevik.
Ribbentrop talked of little else but Russia and is annoyed with the
Czechoslovaks because of disabilities they have inflicted on the
German population. L.G. said he did not trust Beneš[10] in his sight,
let alone out of it. He had behaved very badly at the peace conference.

4 September

Each morning at 7.30, I go in to see L.G. and later help him to
dress. He repeated this morning that he was astonished to find that
Tom Jones had changed so much. He did not like him sticking up
for the rebels in Spain.

Lord Dawson, T.J. and I talked in the drawing-room. Lord Dawson
said he had been very much impressed by Ribbentrop. Anyone more
unlike an ambassador he had never seen. If he spoke like he had
last night, even to the extent of 50 per cent, he would not be a
success. Lord Dawson was amused by the way Ribbentrop had said
that he and his wife were not married according to the Church.
Ribbentrop had said that rather warily, wondering how the com-

10. Eduard Beneš (1884–1948) was a university teacher who became
Foreign Minister of Czechoslovakia 1918–35 and President 1935–8 and
1945–8. At a number of points in the Sylvester diaries Lloyd George
talks disparagingly of him, on at least one occasion terming him 'the
jackal of Versailles'.

pany would take it. He had felt his way and sought to put himself right by saying he had mentioned the matter to the Archbishop of Canterbury.

L.G. returned at noon from a talk with Ribbentrop. He said that Ribbentrop wanted to go too far. He wanted to organise a great anti-Bolshevik front. We would not join that. We would not have anyone make a wanton attack on Germany, or France or anyone else.

The whole of our party lunched with Ribbentrop and his wife in the Grand Hotel. In addition there were several high officials from the Foreign Office in Berlin. L.G. said he could not understand why the Germans had signed the Armistice. That had certainly been a mistake on their part. Ribbentrop said that Hitler would not have signed it. During coffee L.G. talked about the war with terrific energy until I thought, at 3 p.m. it was high time he broke up the party and had a rest before seeing Hitler. But he would not do so and still went on, despite the fact that at 4 p.m. he was due for one of the greatest interviews of his life. Yet, if I had asked him for a little instruction, he would have said that I was working him to death.

L.G. returned from his interview with Hitler in great form, very delighted with his talk and obviously very much struck with Hitler. 'He is a very great man,' said L.G. ' "Führer" is the proper name for him, for he is a born leader, yes, and statesman.' He said that Hitler was not in favour of rearmament or conscription. They did not make him popular with his own people. He favoured productive measures, such as roads, in which he was very interested, and improved agriculture. What had struck L.G. very much was that Hitler had been much more enthusiastic when talking about these latter things. 'We talked about everything,' said L.G., 'including Spain. I talked with great bluntness and frankness and the Führer liked it.'

I produced a whiskey and water for L.G., and when he had taken this Lord Dawson said to him : 'If you want to get full benefit of that, go and rest for half an hour', which he did.

The whole of our party dined with the Ribbentrops and their entourage. Ribbentrop asked L.G. about Winston. L.G. replied that he was a rhetorician and not an orator. He thought only of how a phrase sounded and not how it might move or influence crowds. The question for every Prime Minister was whether Winston was more dangerous inside or outside the Cabinet.

Lloyd George's second meeting with Hitler, at which Sylvester was present, was more of a social occasion. Lloyd George took his entourage along for tea at the Berghof.

5 September

When I went to his bedroom early this morning, I found L.G. at work on the preface to the sixth volume of his War Memoirs. He said he had started this at 5.30 a.m. He said that he was very pleased with his interview with Hitler yesterday. Whilst I helped him to dress, I told him that he would be pressed to go to the German party meeting at Nuremberg.[11] Tom had suggested to me last night that L.G. should be put in the 2s 6d seats in order to avoid detection by the crowd. I had said it would be quite impossible – L.G. would be instantly recognised.

L.G., Gwilym and I started breakfast alone. L.G. said the best description of Hitler was: 'He is a leader; not a cabinet minister or a prime minister, but a leader.' In his conversation he had had the directness of a cannon ball and L.G. had liked this. Quite the reverse was the case with Ribbentrop.

After lunch we had coffee on the veranda, overlooking the lovely Bavarian Alps. L.G. said that the amazing thing was the casual way in which the greatest war the world had ever seen broke out, when nobody who had a right to decide wanted it. The German Foreign Secretary was away on his honeymoon. He did not want it, and we did not. Grey was away fishing in Wiltshire and there was no one of real authority at our Foreign Office.

We all accompanied L.G. to see the Führer in three cars. The Berghof is about 4000 feet up in the mountains and the gradient is very steep. On the arrival of L.G.'s car, Hitler walked down the steps to greet him and shake hands very warmly, first with L.G. and then with the rest of the party. I took a film as they entered the house.[12] We proceeded immediately through very wide corridors to the book room, where tea was set. It was an enormous room, with one enormous window which overlooks the Bavarian Alps, which can be seen for miles ahead. In the break in the mountains to the right, in the valley beyond lies Salzburg, which can be seen quite plainly.

I asked Ribbentrop if Hitler would mind my taking films for L.G. He told me that I had permission to do so, and Hitler nodded. I did not stop filming. My difficulty was that the films had to be taken indoors and the light outside had already gone, for it was already

11. i.e., the annual Nuremberg congress of the National Socialist Party, an occasion marked by spectacular parades and displays and by a speech from Hitler. Lloyd George could not attend as an official guest without seeming to give a degree of public endorsement to the Nazis – hence the idea that he should sit in the public seats.

12. Sylvester had a movie camera, with which he was shooting in colour.

5 p.m. Our interview had been fixed first for three, then four, and eventually five o'clock. Dr Schmidt acted as interpreter. He is marvellous. We first of all looked round the room and inspected some beautiful tapestries on the wall, then a large bust of Wagner, who produced Hitler's favourite music. After admiring the wonderful view from the enormous window, we all sat down for tea.

I was thrilled in watching the animation with which Hitler talked, with gestures, with great energy, enthusiastically, and without the least hesitation. His blue eyes were full of fire. He has a fairly large head, his dark hair dropping over the right side of his forehead. He wears a shaving-brush moustache. He is forty-six years of age and looks, perhaps, slightly older. He is about my height, 5 feet 10½ inches, and well built. He wore a light, pin-point coloured suit. L.G. told Hitler that he looked remarkably fit, to which he replied that the mountains were full of salt, and it was that that kept him young and gave him health. When L.G. repeated this later, Lord Dawson remarked: 'At any rate, he should cherish that idea.'

We all sat in easy chairs round a very low tea-table, on which candles were lit. It was a wonderful setting. It was a great moment when Hitler handed to L.G., a beautifully framed and autographed photograph of himself. L.G. immediately rose and shook Hitler very warmly by the hand. L.G. was immensely pleased with this. We had taken a number of photographs of Hitler with us and, after he had signed these, we took our leave.

A most remarkable experience.

6 September

On arrival in Munich L.G. had tea with Herr Hess, Hitler's Deputy Chancellor.[13] He is about Hitler's age, and with very dark hair. He does not speak English. Frau Hess is a blonde and speaks English well and is one of the most striking women I have seen in Germany. L.G. riddled Hess with questions about conditions in Germany, some of which completely nonplussed Hitler's Deputy Leader. One of the things they really wanted, said Hess, was to be able to draw on raw materials. For this purpose, the return of their colonies was vital. L.G. pointed out that these colonies did not supply many of the particular raw materials which they required. L.G. decided he would not go to see Göring, as this would mean an extra day in Munich.

At dinner in Munich, L.G. said to Ribbentrop he would give him a piece of advice. In the City of London they had a saying, 'Never job backwards.' That meant that it was no use, when you lost on the Stock Exchange, to say that if you had only done this you

13. The more correct title would be Deputy Führer.

would have made so-and-so. It was like that with countries. Be like
the English businessman. Just sit down and write it off as a bad debt,
and not job backwards.

L.G. asked Ribbentrop if he knew Blum personally, and he said
'No'.[14] They then discussed France generally. In jovial mood, L.G.
said to Ribbentrop: 'Here, don't swank because you've got a leader.
Remember that you have been without one for forty years, and they
(the French) are now in the position in which you were.'

Talking of Winston, L.G. said he had no judgement: he had
a brilliant mind and his obsession today was Germany. He was a
brilliant writer. Ribbentrop said it was what a man had done for
his country which would last more than a book. Tom Jones said
that books were deeds and mentioned *Mein Kampf*. 'Ah,' said L.G.,
'*Mein Kampf* is a Magna Charta.'

Lloyd George lays a wreath to the German war dead.

7 September

I went in to see L.G. at 7.30 to make sure he had his coffee and fruit.
I told him I was going to order a wreath as soon as the shops were
open and warned him about an inscription for it. He said he was
glad I had told him. At breakfast, he read to Gwilym, Conwell
Evans and me the proposed inscription, as follows: 'A respectful
and sincere tribute to the memory of very brave men who fell fighting for the Fatherland in the Great War. D. Lloyd George.' When
I showed the card to Lord Dawson which L.G. had written in his
own hand, he said 'the Fatherland' ought to be 'their Fatherland'.
L.G. wrote another card.

Conwell Evans read a translation from the German newspapers to
L.G. about trouble in Danzig.[15] L.G. said the sooner the Germans
cleared up that situation the better.

L.G. left for the War Memorial with Ribbentrop. It was a most
impressive sight. Terrific crowds lined the streets.

8 September

I helped L.G. to dress, as usual. He had written 1200 words for the
sixth volume of his *War Memoirs* before breakfast.

14. Léon Blum (1872–1950) had just formed his 'Popular Front' government in France.

15. Danzig (now Gdansk) was then a city with an almost wholly
German population. In 1919 the territory around it was allotted to
Poland and Danzig itself was under League of Nations control. There was
a vigorous and successful Nazi movement there, demanding reunion with
Germany.

This morning we visited a number of factories and saw how, under Hitler, a representative was there to look after the interests of the workers, and how an old factory had been rebuilt. L.G. returned to the hotel in a very bad mood. 'I am not interested in processes,' he said. 'I do not want to see how spectacles and cameras are made and how milk is made into powder. I want to see what Hitler has done.'

During luncheon, L.G. told of the part J. H. Thomas played in the great strike of 1919 when there was a threat of direct action. J.H. was the first to get into trouble. He sent for the miners and the others and laid his plan before them. But the miners did not think it was any good and would not help him.

Presently the miners' turn came, and they got into trouble. They sent for J.H. and asked him to help them. 'Certainly,' replied J.H., 'I will just put it before my executive.' The executive decided straightaway to turn the miners down.

J.H. went to his own room, in his own office, put his feet on the mantelpiece, lit the biggest cigar he could get and poured out a jolly good tumbler of whisky. Suddenly there came a knock at the door and his secretary announced that the miners had come to hear what was the railwaymen's decision. The cigar was hurriedly put away, likewise the whisky. When the miners' representatives were ushered into the room, there sat J.H., his head in his hands, sobbing like a child in evident distress, and muttering to himself, in tones which were calculated to be plainly audible: 'Mi bloody 'eart's broke.'

At dinner L.G. and Dawson talked to Conwell's best friend, who is the son of a bishop in Germany. L.G. said that he had never seen any situation in England where Parliament could not do what a dictator might do. He had got through a Bill in forty-eight hours.

9 September

During lunch, L.G. said that Germany had the advantage that she had had to start from the bottom. 'You must read John Bunyan,' he said, 'for you have to go through the Valley of Humiliation in our country before we are likely to get this. Germany is building up something which we have not got and which is better than ours. In our country you will do nothing until you get a slump. I put similar proposals to those now being carried out in Germany before our Cabinet, at their invitation. But they would not even sniff at them.' Looking at T.J., he said: 'You are the accredited representative of this incompetent government.'

L.G. is very excited about getting home. He keeps saying: 'Do you realise that we are only just halfway through?' Then he added:

'I do not like holidays. It is a bad thing to accustom yourself always to work hard; you can never stop.'

10 September

Before seven o'clock this morning, I went to L.G. in bed and got him to write an inscription on a photograph for Ribbentrop. In his own hand he wrote: 'With best wishes for success in his noble mission of reconciliation between two great nations. D. Lloyd George.'[16]. . .

Tonight I hired a powerful wireless set so that L.G. could listen to Rosenberg and Goebbels speaking at the party meeting at Nuremberg. Rosenberg was a dull speaker. L.G. was rather sick with both, because they talked so much about Bolshevism.

11 September

How L.G. can concentrate on writing new chapters of his War Memoirs so early in the morning, whilst he is soaking up information about Germany like a dry sponge soaks up water, beats me. He was at it again this morning when I went to see him.

12 September

. . . Experts from the Ministry of Agriculture in Berlin came to lunch. L.G. talked of the Great War. He thought that a country that could produce four-fifths of its food supplies ought not to have starved. We in England cut ourselves down in our supplies enormously and were producing only one-fifth of our food supplies. 'If I had had a proposition placed before me giving me four-fifths food supplies, I would not have worried,' he said.

L.G. said that when the earth passed through the tail of a comet it came in contact with a gas which, when it came into the atmosphere of the earth, made everybody doubly happy and feel more kindly and more well disposed. 'Upon my oath,' said L.G., 'I am not at all sure if Hitler has not been that comet in Germany.'

13 September

Baron von der Ropp and the Rev. Dr S. W. Simoleit, who are prominent Baptists, the former a distinguished layman and the latter a distinguished preacher, came to breakfast with L.G. They talked with great freedom. Both were favourable to Hitler, though not members of his party. They said the mistake that had been made was that the Nazis had interfered with religion in order that

16. Ribbentrop presented his letters of credence as ambassador in London the following month.

there should be no secret movement against them in the churches. They were not even allowed to collect money by means of boxes.

L.G. said he did not like Hitler's attack on the Jews. 'We put up with them in our country,' he said.[17] 'England would not tolerate interference in religion. We fought that battle in England many centuries ago and cut off a king's head for interfering. One reason why Foch was not made commander-in-chief earlier was because he was a Roman Catholic. Clemenceau was afraid that if they made Foch a hero of the French nation the next thing would be that the Roman Catholics would seize power and govern France.'

The pastor asked L.G. if he thought war was near with Russia. L.G. answered that he was more afraid of events developing into a war in Spain, with Germany and Italy equipping one side and France equipping the other. He was afraid of seeing a repetition of the old religious wars, which had prostrated Europe, and not between the two faiths of Bolshevism and anti-Bolshevism.

I was late for dinner, at which Baron von Ropp was present, as I had had to telephone to Churt to find out how many blackberries had been gathered, the position of the honey yield, progress of the building of the glasshouses and when the new manager was taking up his duties.

Lloyd George returned from Germany on 15 September.

23 September

L.G. and I travelled to north Wales last Monday. Before dinner tonight, I went with him into the drawing-room alone for a quiet whiskey and water. He talked of Jennifer, saying that the Bavarian dress, which I bought for him to give to her, fitted her perfectly. She had posed as the little Bavarian girl brought back by L.G. The belt gave it a real finish. 'She is an extraordinary kid,' said L.G. 'She has read through the whole four columns of my interview in the *News Chronicle*. She wanted to know the meaning of the Latin I quoted.' He then asked me if Frances had anything to do with Tweed now. I said: 'No.' He said: 'I look to you to tell me if you see anything.' He continued: 'Your loyalty is first of all to me. I cannot understand her. I do not know what to do with Tweed.

17. This remark should not be read as a full exposition of Lloyd George's views on Jews. He wrote in 1923: 'Of all the bigotries that savage the human temper there is none so stupid as the anti-Semitic. It has no basis in reason; it is not rooted in faith; it aspires to no ideal; it is just one of those dank, unwholesome weeds that grow in the morass of racial hatred.'

His agreement has expired. It would suit me if Tweed found another job. On the other hand, he is a good politician and useful in counsel.'. . .

29 September

I have been sizing up a row which has suddenly developed between L.G. and Frances. Yesterday morning he packed his bags and came up from Churt alone in the car. Frances has been on the telephone a number of times to me, and I am trying to straighten it out.

30 September

L.G. dictated his speech to Miss Lea[18] for the Honey Exhibition at the Crystal Palace this afternoon. The extraordinary thing is that, although he is preoccupied and his mind is obviously full of private worries, his power of concentration on other matters is immense. Accompanied by Miss Parry and myself, L.G. spoke at the Honey Exhibition. In the course of his speech he said :

'When I go to my hives, I regard myself as one of the greatest employers of the best workmen in this country. There is no looking at the clock to see whether it is lunch time. There are periods of enforced idleness even among bees. When they have no food, you must give them the dole, and not too much means test. They are just standing in the market waiting for the sun to tell them that there is a job waiting for them. . . . Honey is good for the old; it is very good for young children. . . . I know it. I feel it after I have taken a feed of honey. I am then ready for anything or anybody.'

We returned for tea in the office. When I asked for his instructions on some of my important papers, he brushed me aside, saying he would do them later, and called for Tweed, and merely to gossip. These days I am particularly interested in his handling of Tweed. What's the game?

7 October

Sir Thomas Artemus Jones has informed L.G. that, as he was laid up with laryngitis, he could not, as vice-chairman, preside at Caernarvonshire quarter sessions. I went by train to Shrewsbury. I was leaving the Raven Hotel, when I heard L.G. outside, asking the porter : 'Have you seen my secretary, Mr Sylvester?' He had motored from Churt with Frances. I told him of the ship accommodation I had obtained for our trip to Jamaica. Then I accompanied L.G. in his new Rolls-Royce, at eighty miles an hour, to Criccieth, and Frances returned to London.

18. A member of Sylvester's secretarial staff.

After dinner, Dame Margaret said she had met someone for whom
L.G. had acted in the Llanfrothen case, the burial case which first
made L.G.[19] This person had said that she had come to L.G. after
the case to inquire how much were his fees. 'But', Dame Margaret
added, 'you said you would not charge anything, because it was a
case that might do you a lot of good.' Dame Margaret said she had
met another person who at the same time had consulted L.G. Again,
he had refused to make any charge, because he knew the person
was very poor. L.G. said he had hated making any charges at all,
and it was a good thing that his brother William had come in to
look after the money, otherwise there might have been no practice.

L.G. said that he had dined with Sir Eric Geddes the other night.
They had talked about Baldwin. L.G. said the 'old woman' (referring
to Mrs Baldwin) meant her husband to remain Prime Minister at all
costs until after the coronation. She was so eager that, if anything
happened to him before the coronation, she would stuff him with
straw and have him stuck up in his chair in the Cabinet Room.
The fact that he could not speak would make no difference, because
he never did say anything in Cabinet.

*Lloyd George was planning, or rather Sylvester was planning for him,
a visit to Jamaica, where he was to write more of his memoirs. In
the first part of the visit, Miss Stevenson would be with him. Then
she was to return home and Dame Margaret would join him.*

9 October

L.G. and I motored to Churt. Whilst in Wales he was very happy.
He has successfully carried his family with him in his going to the
West Indies in advance of them. He has explained what a great
work the writing of his memoirs has been. Dawson had warned him
that he should go away. He had had before him the case of H. A. L.
Fisher, who had written only three volumes of the history of
England, and it broke him up almost completely. Dawson had
advised him to write something entirely different in character.
Dawson had written suggesting that he should write a book on his
stories of Welsh preachers. L.G. has explained to the family that
the difficulty about going to the West Indies was to get accommoda-

19. In this case, in 1888, an Anglican incumbent refused to permit the
burial of a quarryman with nonconformist rites in the parish graveyard.
Lloyd George, as a young solicitor, advised the mourners to break into
the graveyard and conduct the burial. The ensuing court action, which
Lloyd George won, brought him important publicity.

tion. He could only get a place on a *cargo* boat. (What a boat it sounded from his pronunciation of the word *cargo*.) With a roar of laughter, he said : 'Sylvester. Where do you think he is going? The only place he can get is in the crow's nest.' The family has taken it exceedingly well. L.G. said to Dame Margaret : 'Would you like to come out to the West Indies?' He was pleased when she said : 'Yes, of course.' Meantime, Megan and Edna watched closely. Would they be invited? He went no further. He has worked it very well.

12 October

I have now worked out a plan for the West Indies under which Dame Margaret and Megan will leave here on 31 December, arriving at Kingston, Jamaica, on 14 January. Frances will now leave Jamaica on 13 January.

13 October

Having said yesterday that he would not speak at Dinsdale Young's jubilee celebration, today L.G. said he would.[20] The truth is that he does not want to be on the same platform as Dr Scott Lidgett, who withdrew from the Council of Action executive some time ago. He just wanted to go late, make his speech and leave. Those were the arrangements I made.

Lady Carey Evans and I joined L.G. for a high tea of ham, eggs and coffee in his room and went thence to the Central Hall. He was received with tumultuous cheers. It was a great audience of 3000, with a big overflow-meeting downstairs. I give some of the most striking passages of his speech :

'I come from a country where, in the days of my youth, great preachers were held in reverence. When they came to our village, it was an event that was talked of for weeks, nay months, in advance. After, when they had left, what they had said was remembered and discussed for years. Men used to come to my uncle's workshop to tell what they had said. I was a young lad then and heard it all repeated. It made a deep impression on my mind and I have retained to this day a deep homage for the great preachers.'

Lloyd George speaks at the Free Trade Hall, Manchester. Before he started his speech, he received an address of welcome from the Manchester Jewish community. He devoted himself to international affairs and to an attack on the British rearmament programme. He

20. Dinsdale Young (1861–1938). Minister of the Methodist Central Hall, Westminster, 1914–38.

*said he was 'against dictatorships out and out, root and branch,
lock, stock and barrel'. He said there was no need for British
rearmament because the world's two most powerful armies were the
French and the Russian and the world's two most powerful fleets
were the British and the French. Air power in itself could not be
decisive, and Russia and France certainly had air preponderance
over Germany. It was not rearmament that was wanted but the
consolidation of the power of the League of Nations, collective
security and all-round disarmament.*

23 October

Tweed and I met L.G. at St Pancras. In the train to Manchester he
said: 'When I begin to make a speech, I always ask myself what
on earth I can say, and I always end up wondering what on earth
I can cut out.' I had warned him that I was not sure if Dame Margaret would be able to come, because of an attack of lumbago, but
that Megan would come if her mother did not. I had added: 'I bet
Dame Margaret will come.' When he arrived at Manchester Exchange
station tonight, my prophecy was fulfilled. He greeted her with
'Bravo', and was very delighted to see her.

He said that Megan was curiously mystic. She prayed regularly.
It was all private. There was no outward demonstration. She disliked gossip, just as Uncle Lloyd had done. She disliked any conversation about sex. She had once said she would never marry,
unless it was to someone who could dominate her.

L.G. said there was talk that the King would marry Mrs Simpson.
'If the little fellow marries her, I shall back him. The only people
who will be against it will be the aristocracy, and they are the
rottenest lot of people.'

L.G. said: 'If Ernest Bevin takes an honour in connection with
the coronation, that will be the end of him. Gladstone, Bright,
Cobden, Labby,[21] Joe Chamberlain never made the mistake of
taking an honour. They were old radicals. Dilke was a baronet by
birth.'

The Free Trade Hall was packed with some 3000 people, and the
hall could have been filled twice over. He gave them the best
argument I have ever heard against rearmament, favouring more
co-operation.

8 November

My wife and I arrived at Churt this evening. L.G. said he had had
a great luncheon party of his grandchildren. 'All my own,' he

21. Labouchere.

added, laughingly. He was in a rollicking mood, for tomorrow he is off with Frances.[22] He wanted to keep the family in good heart, particularly as they had decided to go back to town after dinner tonight.

'Who do you think came here today, Maggie?' asked L.G. of Dame Margaret, and without waiting for her answer he said: 'The Speaker. I was delighted to see him. He talked about the late King. An odd thing, the Speaker said, the King liked me but did not like Winston. The Speaker said: "The one man I hate in the House is Gallacher." '[23] L.G. went on: 'So do I. He affects me physically. The Speaker said: "Yes, but you can go out and I can't." '

L.G. said that some time ago he read a book which had opened his eyes concerning Spain. 'One principle I have is my Protestantism,' he said, and went on to show how the priests in Spain were on the side of Franco. They were wallowing in riches, expensive jewellery and fine vestments, all of which were obtained from grinding down the poor peasant and worker.

I got from Miss Parry a list of books L.G. was taking to the West Indies. They numbered 135, to say nothing of piles of documents, all selected by L.G.

22. To Jamaica.
23. William Gallacher (1881–1965). Communist M.P. 1935–50. On the whole, at the personal level, he was well liked

Chapter 8

With Lloyd George to Jamaica

NOVEMBER 1936–FEBRUARY 1937

9 November
L.G., accompanied by Frances, my wife and myself, boarded a cargo ship at Southampton docks for the West Indies.

12 November
For the last few days we have experienced terrible gales. The Captain said that they were blowing at seventy-five miles an hour. Frances and my wife were soon violently ill. I went to the topmost part of the ship to get a film of the great sea.

Last night L.G. and I had a pink gin. As he lay on his bed, he placed his on the dressing-table by his side. Presently a mighty wave hit the ship, and she gave a tremendous lurch. Away went his pink gin right across his face into his eyes. Climbing over luggage, I bathed his eyes, which smarted badly. Then, to my surprise, he ate goose, which he never normally eats because it does not agree with him – and in a seventy-five-mile-an-hour gale.

13 November
A wire to Jennifer was concocted by L.G. and Frances. Jennifer loves long words. It was dispatched by me: 'Halcyon seas after tempestuous billows. Love, Mummy, Taid.'

16 November
When my wife and I went into breakfast this morning, L.G. said: 'Do you know that on 27 December Frances has been with me twenty-five years.[1] It is a testimony to her patience and toleration in having put up with me for all those years.' Frances said: 'It has been reciprocal.' L.G. said: 'You have been very patient.' Frances, laughing, said: 'Why this unusual amount of humility?' L.G. said: 'I must be very difficult at times. Anyhow I am conscious of it,

1. Miss Stevenson entered the Lloyd George family household in July 1911 as a holiday tutor for Megan Lloyd George and afterwards resumed her work as a schoolteacher. She became a private secretary to Lloyd George at the Treasury in 1913.

Private secretaries at work and play. *Left*, A. J. Sylvester with Lloyd George at the door of 10 Downing Street, circa 1922.

Right, Sir Philip Sassoon 'tempts' with fruit Frances Stevenson who was a private secretary of Lloyd George, his long-term mistress and ultimately his second wife. Sassoon, a millionaire, a Tory MP and a life-long bachelor, was Parliamentary Private Secretary to Lloyd George 1920–22, during which period this picture was probably taken.

In the library at Churt. This picture was taken on Sunday, 11 December 1932, during the weekend in which Dame Margaret Lloyd George had brought remarkable information to her husband's attention. The picture shows, also, Sir Thomas and Lady (Olwen) Carey Evans seated side by side. Megan Lloyd George rested on the right while Lady Margaret

Above, Lloyd George with Dame Margaret and their daughter Megan on their arrival at Bombay 1932.
Below, Lloyd George's other family. Left to right, Frances Stevenson, Lloyd George, the nanny, Jennifer Stevenson, the Dutch captain of the ship in which they were travelling and Mrs A. J. Sylvester, circa 1935.

Left, Lloyd George speaking at Bradford in 1935 in his Council of Action campaign. Immediately behind him, seated with folded arms, is his chief political aide, Colonel T. F. Tweed.

Below, Lloyd George confers with Tweed through a train window.

Germany 1936. *Right*, Adolf Hitler welcomes Lloyd George to his mountain home, the Berghof. Joachim von Ribbentrop, ambassador-designate to London and later German Foreign Minister, is immediately to Lloyd George's left.

Left, Lloyd George lays a wreath at the Munich war memorial in honour of the German dead of 1914–1918.

Left, Lloyd George and Dame Margaret during their golden wedding celebration at Antibes in 1938.

Below, the forecourt and main entrance of Lloyd George's house at Churt, Bron-y-de. The house was built to Lloyd George's specifications during the last years of his prime ministership. It has since been destroyed by fire.

Left, two who detested each other – Lloyd George with Neville Chamberlain. They are at the Silver Jubilee celebration for George V at St Paul's: Lloyd George has turned up in incorrect uniform.

Right, political friends of nearly half a century, Lloyd George and Winston Churchill: they are at Antibes together, 1938, and Churchill had just given a lunch to celebrate the Lloyd George golden wedding.

The death of Dame Margaret Lloyd George, 1941. *Above*, Lloyd George at her funeral, supported by his sons Richard (in uniform) and Gwilym. A. J. Sylvester is on the left.

Below, the funeral procession through Criccieth, with members of the Home Guard pulling the farm cart on which the coffin rests.

and that helps me to check myself.' He laughed and went on: 'If only you are patient with me.'

Over coffee he talked about Clara Novello Davies.[2] He thought that Ivor Novello was a cleverer fellow than Noël Coward. 'Keep the Home Fires Burning' had made Novello. His mother had started to write it but he had had the bright idea which made it a success. L.G. remembered the first time he met Clara. He had gone to speak in south Wales and stayed with some Liberal friends. He expressed a wish to see a small chapel which had produced Islwyn, a great Welsh preacher.[3] So they had made a party and a picnic. There was an old harmonium in the chapel, and someone was playing it so divinely that the brethren present thought there was no tune like it. It was the tune of 'But, alas and alack, she came back with a naughty little twinkle in her eye'. Clara had turned it into a minor hymn melody.

After tea, L.G. dictated to me the following telegram to Geoffrey Crawshay, the Commissioner for the distressed areas of south Wales:

'Please convey my loyal apologies to His Majesty for not being able to join as a Liberal Member of Parliament and a member of your committee in welcoming him on his important errand of mercy to the desolated areas of south Wales. His visit is a message of hope....'[4]

17 November

L.G. said that when he was Prime Minister the Cecils and other high churchmen went to see him to protest about his appointing

2. Clara Novello Davies (1861–1943) was founder and conductor of the Royal Welsh Ladies' choir which toured Europe and the United States on several occasions and performed before Queen Victoria in 1894. Her maiden surname was Davies and she married James Davies, who died in 1931. Their only child was Ivor Novello (1893–1951).

3. William Thomas, bardic name Islwyn (1832–78), prolific poet who was ordained a Calvinistic Methodist minister 1859 at Babell chapel, Rhymney.

4. A visit by King Edward VIII to the distressed areas in Glamorgan and Monmouthshire on 18 and 19 November 1936 attracted much attention. Seeing with his own eyes the effects of mass unemployment – Merthyr Tydfil's rate at the time was 60 per cent – obviously shocked and moved him. He was well received: when he visited the Labour Exchange at Merthyr, the men lining up for the dole cheered him. The streets were hung with flags; at Brynmawr, among the patriotic colours, was a banner: 'We need your help.' When he visited the Dowlais steelworks, which had once employed 9000 men and was now derelict, the King said: 'These people were brought here by these works. Some kind of employment must be found for them.' It was reckoned that the Prime Minister, Stanley Baldwin, was irritated at such observations by the King, which could be taken to have a political connotation.

F

bishops. L.G. said: 'Would you like Bonar Law to make the appointments?' (Bonar Law was a Scottish Presbyterian.) 'No' was the answer. 'Then would you like your Chief Whip to make the bishops?' (Lord Edmund Talbot was a Roman Catholic.) Again 'No' was the answer. L.G. said that he had promised to set up a committee to advise him on such appointments, but he had never called it or consulted it.

He said that when he was a young man he went to London for his legal examination. He went with a friend to see O'Dell, the phrenologist. O'Dell had told him that when he started a thing he must always be very careful to see it through, as he was apt to take up a lot of things and leave them unfinished. From that moment, said L.G., he had made a point of reading a book through from start to finish, no matter how boring he might find it.

19 November
At breakfast, L.G. gave us an illustration of his Celtic imagination – brilliant, so exaggerated. 'Wait until you get to the tropics and you are off this ship,' he said. Then he talked about the Red Sea and quoted Kipling's verses about the worst and the best, and there ain't no Ten Commandments east of the Suez Canal. Then his imagination took flight. 'There', he said, 'everybody became naughty. Why, even respectable women had their beaus. The Red Sea is a hot place, I can tell you. Sylvester took four days leave from his position as private secretary. Where he went, I do not know. You could see everybody pairing off in the heat, in full view of Mount Sinai and the home of the Ten Commandments. No wonder Moses dropped the Ten Commandments and broke his tablets when he descended to the bottom of Mount Sinai into that heat.'

23 November
L.G. is most peculiar and behaves like a madman at times. Frances cannot be out of his sight for a moment, but that he is after her to see where she is and what she is doing.

29 November
At dinner, L.G. said Megan was very interesting when she was about eight years old. She used to tell people how hard she had to work. When the old Archbishop of Wales[5] called at 10 Downing

5. A. G. Edwards (1848–1937) became Bishop of St Asaph 1889. He and Lloyd George were at first opponents but became friends and helped to work out the compromises involved in creating the disestablished Church of Wales. He was the first archbishop of Wales 1920–34.

Street, Megan put on a little apron and rolled up her sleeves. She told him that she had to be up at six o'clock every morning to scrub the steps at 10 Downing Street, and that when she had finished she had to go to do those at No. 11.[6] On another occasion, she received someone saying she was Dame Margaret's secretary.

30 November
We drew alongside at Kingston, Jamaica, at noon and were met by Commander Rushbrooke, secretary to the Governor, and took up our quarters at the Constant Spring Hotel. With the mountains around, L.G. said it reminded him of Wales.

The crisis leading to the abdication of Edward VIII, through his desire to marry Mrs Simpson, took place at stunning speed. It first became known to the general British public on 2 December 1936 (although it had been discussed in the foreign Press for months beforehand) and the matter was first raised in Parliament on 3 December. A week later the King announced his decision to abdicate, owing to the refusal of the Baldwin government to accept his marriage plans, and the abdication came legally into force on 11 December.

1 December
During dinner the latest news bulletin arrived and L.G. opened it in such a fashion that he tore the contents in half.[7] He read out aloud the news that the Cabinet had decided to resign unless the King took their advice with regard to Mrs Simpson. Also that the Opposition had agreed that in such event they would not form an alternative government.

4 December
I have been flat out all hours of the day and night sending and receiving cables. Tweed and Finney have been given long and detailed instructions by L.G. to get the opinions of Gwilym, Megan, Winston, Beaverbrook, and of the reactions in Parliament and the Press. As news arrived his opinion began to take shape. He has talked of going home by the very next boat. He said: 'The nation has a right to choose its Queen. The King also has a right to choose

6. When Megan was eight, Lloyd George was Chancellor of the Exchequer and living at 11, not 10 Downing Street.
7. This would have been a private bulletin for Lloyd George, probably from Tweed in London.

his own wife.'[8] If Baldwin were against them, then he was against Baldwin. He said he was glad he had had that talk with Winston on the subject. Then he had said he would stand by the King, and they had both agreed.

Early this morning, L.G. asked me to send the following cable to Gwilym and Megan: 'Hope you are not going to join the Mrs Grundy harriers who are hunting the King from the throne. It is for the nation to choose its Queen, but the King cannot be denied right of humblest citizen to choose his own wife. Had he not decided to marry the lady not a word would have been said by the Scribes and Pharisees. Had King not as prince and sovereign exposed continued neglect by Government of chronic distress, poverty and bad housing conditions amongst his people in realm, convinced they would not have shown such alacrity to dethrone him. You may make any use you like of this telegram. Lloyd George.'[9]

8 December

I had made detailed arrangements for us to return to England this afternoon on the *Carare*, which sailed at 6 p.m. On receiving the latest cables from London that the crisis was virtually over, L.G. asked me to send a message to Tweed, saying: 'Delighted squalid crisis over. Cancelled departure.'

11 December

At 5 p.m., seated on L.G.'s balcony, we listened to the King's broadcast. L.G. was deeply affected. He said we had got rid of a king who was too progressive. The new one would give them no cause for anxiety. L.G. said if he had been at home he might have been able to influence the result, which would have been different.[10]

12 December

Last night the Governor invited L.G. to be present this morning to hear him read the proclamation in regard to the new king. L.G.

8. Presumably here Lloyd George is endorsing the King's own request that he should marry morganatically; that is, Mrs Simpson would become his wife but without the status of Queen.

9. Gwilym and Megan did not in fact make any public use of this telegram.

10. Of course, Lloyd George was out of touch with the feeling in the House of Commons at that moment. Churchill was howled down when he pleaded for delay before a final decision was reached and the episode did him substantial political damage. However, Lloyd George and Churchill working together for the King would have been a far more formidable proposition, and there were many on Baldwin's side who were relieved that Lloyd George was out of the way. (See Brian Inglis, *Abdication*, 1966.)

said to me: 'I am damned if I will be there.' I telephoned to say that he had a little digestive trouble and begged to be excused. Sipping his coconut milk on the balcony, he said he felt he could have advised the ex-king. Frances said that there might have been trouble. L.G. said: 'It is time there was a row in England.'

13 December

Frances told Evelyn and me that a doctor who had seen L.G. had said that he was double everything possessed by an ordinary man. That means, of course, that he has double an ordinary man's weaknesses. Frances said she could not be out of his sight a fraction of an instant without his calling out and looking slyly around for her. She said that he had held her down by force in an endeavour to get her to confess to things she had never done. But she now had her remedy. When she found herself at the end of her tether, whatever he said or did could not hurt her any more than she had already been hurt. He had been so cruel to her and had said such terrible things in the past.

Most mornings L.G. plays golf with Frances, starting at 7.30 o'clock. This morning she beat him: consequently he is very annoyed and critical. He is a bad sportsman.

20 December

L.G. is very pleased because he won his game of golf with Frances.

His observant eye had plenty to distract him this morning, for the swimming-pool under his veranda was full of almost naked females and little children. Oddly enough, he took grave exception to the scanty clothing worn by some of the women.

27 December

At 7.30 a.m. we played the first foursome between L.G. and I and Frances and Thomson. We beat them. L.G. was, however, dissatisfied with his driving. He said: 'Well, I feel like the bishop who, having arrived at a certain stage in this game and feeling terribly exasperated, said: "I must give it up." His caddie said to him, "What, give up golf, sir?" "No," said the bishop acidly, "the Church." '

L.G. has today brought the total of his book to 10,000 words.

1937

2 January

L.G. said he was a much shyer person than we imagined. The remark arose out of a discussion as to whether he should return via New York, and we had gone through the names of persons whom he could meet. He said he did not like meeting people really. It was all right when he just ran into them. Then he was not shy, but he was shy in the contemplation of meeting them. Shyness was a different thing to nervousness. Winston was nervous before a speech, but he was not shy. L.G. said he himself was both nervous and shy. Winston would go up to his Creator and say that he would very much like to meet His Son, about Whom he had heard a great deal and, if possible, would like to call on the Holy Ghost. Winston *loved* meeting people.

5 January

. . . Conversation fell on Hailsham and Majoribanks.[11] Frances said that the latter had shot himself because of overwork. 'Good heavens,' said L.G., 'he was a very young man and did not know what work was. I have had some different kinds of feelings during my writings, but I have never felt like shooting *myself*, though I know a good many people who I felt like shooting.'

He told us that John Burns once said to him : 'You know you are an acquired flavour, but, once acquired, people like you very much.' L.G. said that John Burns was Minister of the Local Government Board and was the fellow who should have put through National Health Insurance, but he would not do it, and that is why L.G., as Chancellor of the Exchequer, put it through. John Burns funked it. . . .

6 January

. . . After dinner, L.G. said there was one story which he had not really sufficiently told in his memoirs, and that was the munitions story. He took his decision to undertake that job in Newnes' restaurant in Putney.

'Things were going badly for us in the war,' he said. 'There were no munitions.' Everybody had thought L.G. was the man for the job and 'honestly, I thought so myself'. As Chancellor of the Exchequer he had occupied the second position in the country. He had been very troubled about the position, especially as his old uncle 'who was certainly the best friend I ever had, and certainly one of the wisest' had been against him taking it. 'I therefore thought that I would try to get the inspiration which sometimes comes through talking to a child. So I picked up Megan, who was at school, and took her to tea at Newnes'. It was whilst having tea in that restaurant that I decided definitely to take on the job.

11. Edward Marjoribanks (1900–32). Tory M.P. 1929–32. He was stepson to 1st Viscount Hailsham, in whose home he shot himself.

'McKenna became Chancellor of the Exchequer and from that moment the whole of the Cabinet thought: "Now we have got that little devil out." For the next six months I had the worst time of my life. Everybody was against me and, starting with no staff at all, and, when I did get a staff, having spies against me all over the place. It was a terrible time. There is no doubt that munitions saved us in the war, but it nearly finished me. All the Wee Frees[12] were against me, hoping to see me go under. All their papers and writers were against me. My heavens, no wonder I gave them hell in the 1918 election.'

7 *January*
L.G. reached 51,000 words by lunchtime.

8 *January*
Frances and my wife left us by car at 8.30 a.m. for the Myrtle Hotel, Kingston, prior to sailing to New York tomorrow homeward bound. There is a big gap now they have gone.

L.G. asked me to go for a walk with him. He told me that as soon as they left him this morning he started to write doubly hard and he had written 7000 words since then – a prodigious task. To console us, he called for planter's punches, but he is very sad.

He talked about the election of 1918 and described to me how Northcliffe came to him to ask that he might be one of the representatives of the British Government at the peace conference. L.G. said: 'No.' Then he pleaded that he might be put in charge of British propaganda at the peace conference. Again L.G. said 'No.' Northcliffe said in that case he would attack L.G. L.G.'s reply was: 'Then you go to Hell.' Relating what had happened to Bonar Law, L.G. said that, after listening to the whole story, Bonar remarked: 'And when you told him to go to Hell, he came straight to me.'

9 *January*
When we assembled in the evening for our whiskey, L.G. asked me to write a list of those of whom he could make character sketches. I suggested Philip Kerr, among others. L.G. agreed and said that Philip was no good unless he had a definite line to go upon. Then he made another remark and said, 'By Jove, that's a good thing to put down,' and I wrote it down. It was: 'His rudder is not equal to his horsepower.' Then L.G. added: 'Lots of us come in there,

12. The term 'Wee Free', strictly, covers the handful of Liberal M.P.s elected in 1918 who opposed the Lloyd George government. Here he is using it loosely to describe his opponents in the Liberal Party.

but to what extent God knows. Winston does and probably I do
too.'

This morning he asked me to go for a stroll. We walked up the
hill as far as he and Frances were in the habit of going. He said
that women were funny creatures. You thought you understood
them, but you did not. He had at last given up trying to understand them and took things as a matter of course. He had known
Frances for twenty-five years. He had seen more of her during that
time than any other woman, because she was with him in his
work, and yet even now he did not profess to understand her.
Tweed had ruined her life.[13] . . .

11 January

As he arrived at breakfast, I started to read a cable but he said:
'No, don't read it out. It is much more fun for me to read it myself.'
It was from Dame Margaret and Megan and it read: 'Arrive 8 a.m.
Thursday. Get us. Love.' L.G. said he thought 'get' should be
'meet'. I checked it three times and it was still 'get'. He said he
could not give up two whole days to meeting them. That would
mean 10,000 words to him and the breaking of the theme. 'I might
meet them for lunch at Shaw Park, which would be half-way,' he
said, 'and you can meet them at Kingston.'

Tonight, before dinner, L.G. was in exceptionally good form.
He said that he had been thinking out a novel for a long time – not
seriously, I suspect. It was about the rise of the Blacks. He thought
the Blacks would one day dominate the world. What an unhappy
thought for Americans, he said. Look, for instance, at Manley,[14]
the barrister of Jamaica: he had a fine face and, in his judgement,
was one of the finest advocates in the British Empire. Then there
was the American Black[15] who had won all before him for America
last year in the Olympics.

13 January

L.G. looked a lonely figure tonight. He said that Christ had liked
kind people better than honest ones. He talked bitterly of Herbert
Samuel, whom he loathed. Doubtless Samuel was honest in the
sense that he would account for every stamp used in his office,

13. It would be interesting to know on what basis Lloyd George made
this assertion!

14. Norman Manley (1893–1969). Founder-President of the People's
National Party, Jamaica, 1938, Chief Minister 1955–9, Premier 1959–62,
Leader of the Opposition 1962–9.

15. Jesse Owens, the runner, who scored a string of triumphs at the
1936 Berlin Olympic Games.

but he was a sneak. He talked of how he [L.G.] had made 'insolent' speeches during the Boer War. 'I was a martyr to that cause,' said L.G. 'I lost all my practice. People threw stones at my office windows in London. I was jeered at in any restaurant I entered. I told my wife to go back to Wales and take the kids. She said she was prepared to live in a garret on thirty bob a week. She is a most courageous woman.' Then he said: 'That is the trouble with Winston. He has never been a martyr.'

14 January

I accompanied L.G. to Port Royal to meet Dame Margaret and Megan.

When we were alone, L.G. said to me that Dame Margaret and Megan had raised an objection to their bedroom because the bath and lavatory were in the same room. 'By Jove,' he said, 'I nearly said it was good enough for Frances, but just stopped myself in time; otherwise the fat would have been in the fire.' Referring to Dame Margaret, he continued: 'She has never helped me in my work. In the early days she did not even help me in the constituency, as she does now. She was always at Criccieth and I was in London.' He said there were two kinds of wives: those who give up everything to their children, and those who give up everything to their husbands. 'My wife belongs to the former. All the same, she is the best of the bunch and when we were on the point of having a frightful row she stepped in and said: "I will have none of it", and I always remember that.'

17 January

L.G.'s seventy-fourth anniversary. He was at work at 5 a.m. I presented him with half a dozen golf-balls, on behalf of my wife and myself, wishing him many happy flights, not only on the golf-course but on the course of life.

21 January

L.G. gave a dinner-party tonight. Present: L.G., Dame Margaret, Megan, Mr and Mrs Harvey Clark, Mr and Mrs Lockwood, Mr and Mrs Charles Lloyd, and Captain F. R. M. Johnson and Commander A. J. Wavish from H.M.S. *Dragon*. I had arranged a native band to play old Jamaican tunes and sing.

L.G. told how in his early parliamentary days he went abroad. Before his return, he had his moustache shaved off. When he went to the House of Commons, few people knew him, he was such a different-looking man. Even the Speaker did not know him. Old Mark Lockwood (uncle of our guest Mr Lockwood) said he had always wondered where he got his insolence from and now he could see his upper lip he knew. (If he had studied L.G.'s lower lip, which is big, thick and hanging down, he might have dwelt upon some more intimate traits in L.G.'s character.) Dame Margaret told me afterwards that she hardly recognised him without his moustache. He had a terribly ugly upper lip. 'I hated him without his moustache,' she said.

25 January

I went with Dame Margaret and Megan this morning to the Baptist church, at which Mrs Hazlett, the evangelist, preached. Two weeks ago the Rev. Knight had prayed for Dame Margaret and Megan on their journey here, and we had sung 'For those in peril on the sea', about which L.G. made such fun when he saw Frances singing it, to think that she should sing it for Dame Margaret and Megan. I do not care for that kind of mockery.

Lloyd George and his family begin their journey home.

1 February

It was a truly sad moment to leave Montego Bay, where I have seen L.G. happier than in any other place, ever. I said so, and L.G. agreed.

6 February

L.G. has been most restless ever since he came aboard. He says he hates the sea and must work in order to occupy his mind. He cannot stand losing at games. When he lost at deck quoits today he became so upset and peevish and behaved like a huge baby. Yet he can play very well. In a better mood, he recalled an old Welsh preacher who was very fond of his meals. When he was asked to say grace, he looked at the scraggy piece of meat before him and said: 'O Lord, for the least of thy mercies, we thank thee.' But when he found a twenty-pound piece of beef in front of him he said: 'O Lord, we thank thee for thy bounteous blessing, and particularly for this lump of beef.' ...

12 February

Today Megan told L.G. that one of her difficulties was that when she read her speeches over before delivery they seemed so poor. L.G. said: 'My dear, it may sound an extraordinary thing to say, but I have also felt the same thing beforehand with the very speeches which have been acclaimed by the public and the Press to be my best, and which are now certainly the best known. Take Limehouse.[16] Immediately after I had delivered that speech, I thought it was a failure.'

11 February

L.G. handed me a sketch of Poincaré, which he has written today, and asked me to read it.[17] It is definitely an attack. Before I had finished reading it, he took it away and, handing it back, said, 'I have added this: "A fellow who cultivates honesty becomes tricky."' Wilson had once said to him: 'Poincaré is a cheat and a liar.' Laughing heartily, L.G. said that one day during the peace conference Clemenceau came in late, in a towering rage, because he had been summoned to see Poincaré (the President), who was evidently bothering the old man a great deal. Clemenceau whispered in L.G.'s ear: 'Can't you lend me George V for a short time?'

16 February

At 7 p.m. I was in his sitting-room for whiskey. L.G. had just arrived. Dame Margaret came in a moment later. At 7.25 p.m. Megan arrived and, raising her glass, said: 'Well, Tada, thank you very much for a most delightful holiday.' Dame Margaret drank to that toast, and so did I. L.G. said nothing. Megan went out. As soon as she had disappeared, he showed his great disapproval of her lateness. When Megan returned, he opened fire on her. 'If you intended to drink my health,' he said, 'and thank me for your holiday, you might at least have been here at seven o'clock, instead of being twenty-five minutes late. You have never thought me of sufficient importance to be on time.' Then, working himself up into a fit of anger, his face red and his blue-grey eyes flashing, he said: 'You have never once been up to have breakfast with me, either in Jamaica or on the boat, still less to walk with me before breakfast, which you know I like to do.' Then he added, with real venom: 'But your mother has always been there. That is what I would have expected of her. But then *she* is a lady and you are not.'

Megan's face went white with rage, and her eyes filled with tears. She stammered out that she was sorry if she had done anything wrong. 'Anything wrong?' snapped L.G. 'I said I apologised. I cannot do more than that,' said Megan. 'That is the first time you have ever apologised to me,' snapped L.G. and, jumping up,

16. Lloyd George's vituperative attack on the peerage at Limehouse in 1909 which attracted enormous attention.

17. Raymond Poincaré (1860–1934). Premier of France 1912–13, President of the Republic 1913–20 and Premier again 1922–4.

he left the room, put on his fur-lined overcoat and, followed by me, went on to the deck. It was a very cold night. I remarked: 'I have never heard you talk like that to Megan before.' He said: 'It's about time.' I returned to the sitting-room to find Megan in floods of tears. 'My God,' she said to me, 'it will be a long time before I forgive him for that.'

17 February

Immediately on landing, photographs were taken and films were made of L.G. and Dame Margaret and Megan, who appeared with very swollen eyes, as she had been awake all night crying.

We reached London and, as soon as I arrived at the office, I phoned my wife and was relieved to find that her health had somewhat improved.

My old friend Sir Henry Fildes asked me to have a quick lunch with him. He told me of a whispering campaign against L.G. in his constituency about his immoral life. That he had taken Miss Stevenson with him on this trip and that there was a child.

Chapter 9

'The British Empire is losing its nerve'

1937

19 February

Tonight L.G. came up for the Speaker's levee. When he and I were alone, I told him that enemies in the Boroughs[1] were carrying out a whispering campaign about his moral character. I have never seen him snort so much. His face went red; he spoke not a word but, seated in an easy chair in his levee dress, with his sword dangling by his side, he snorted and grunted until I thought he would have a fit. Suddenly he got up to go and snapped out: '*She* told you this.' (He was referring to Marian Williams,[2] who was in an adjoining room.) I said: 'No, it was your old friend Sir Henry Fildes, together with his partner.'[3] He said he would see them both and off he went.

23 February

At lunchtime I was suddenly summoned to Churt. It was 6.30 p.m. and whiskey time when I arrived. L.G. received me warmly and I helped both of us to an appropriate dose. As I was going to see Sir Henry Fildes and Sir William Letts tomorrow, L.G. said he wanted me to know what was in his mind so that I could talk to them frankly. First of all he assumed a very pious attitude. All his life he had been accused of this, and then, warming up, he declared that he intended to fight it with all his strength. He would send private detectives down to the Boroughs to find out who it was who was spreading these slanderous statements and he would take criminal proceedings against them. After all, he could not have done his book without Frances. She was the only person who had been

1. Caernarvonshire Boroughs, Lloyd George's constituency.
2. Daughter of Williams the ironmonger of Criccieth. See note to p. 108.
3. This was Sir William Letts, who lived at Llandudno and so was a constituent of Lloyd George. See note on him, p. 97.

there the whole time. To bring a charge of this kind against an old fellow who had had a serious operation six years ago, which has taken away some of his vitals, was a preposterous and ridiculous thing. The suggestion was that he was the father of Frances's child. Beside there was the Statute of Limitations,[4] and he said: 'I have a letter from Tweed saying that he is responsible for the child.[5] I will spend £100,000 in showing up the whole bloody lot, including Baldwin and the other persons in the Ministry. I have had, as you know, a tremendous number of letters asking me to start a campaign in favour of the ex-king, but I have said that I will have nothing to do with it. But nothing would suit me better than to have a damn good fight at the end of my days, about degrading politics to the level of American politics and calumny and slander, and they may depend upon it that the National Party will lose in the end. They have driven the King off the throne and now, by a campaign of slander and calumny, they want to drive another man out who has rendered good services to the country which nobody denies – an old fellow of seventy-four who has had a very serious operation.'

I said it did me good to see him in this fighting mood.

Continuing, he said: 'I am going to fight. A few moments ago some Conservatives were here to make arrangements for the coronation celebrations in Churt, and I promised to return here immediately after the abbey ceremony in order to speak to the children. I am loyal to the throne. I have nothing against this little man[6] – absolutely nothing. I am getting no end of letters asking me to start a campaign and saying that they have been

4. It is a legal principle that, normally, a man can be identified as the father of an illegitimate child only during the first three years of the child's life.

5. It must be presumed that no such letter now exists, if it ever did. Various explanations are possible of Lloyd George's statement, made in what could have proved to be a tight corner. It is plainly and in considerable detail within Sylvester's recollection (1974) that Lloyd George was proud of the child at the time of her birth in 1929. As shown in the diary, Lloyd George was devoted to the child, and continued to be. However, he would have faced political ruin had his private life come out and it is easy to understand him wishing to repudiate paternity. Sylvester (1974) stands absolutely by his shorthand note, as he made it at the time, but for present purposes he is not prepared to offer an interpretation. The child was born at a clinic in Welbeck Street, London W1, and in registering her birth, as mother, Miss Stevenson inverted her own forenames, so that they became 'Louise Frances'. Presumably this was an attempt at concealment. Miss Stevenson legally adopted the child in 1938: this is a common procedure in such cases.

6. King George VI.

awaiting my return to do so, but I have refused. I am quite fit
now and prepared to fight any bloody thing.'

Reiterating his former words, he said : 'I shall send detectives to
the Boroughs to see what they are saying. I shall pick upon my
man. I shall prosecute him for criminal libel against a privy
councillor and he will appear before a jury in that district. I will
meet anybody in the Caernarvon Boroughs. I will guarantee they
won't kick me out there. The old girl[7] will stand by me. Then I
shall fight here, publishing the libels here myself. I shall ask who
are they to tamper with the King on these grounds. What business
had they to do it? I have a dossier of the lot. I will make such a
stink that the coronation won't count very much because the
world will be more interested in this business. I have no party
now. Somewhat similar allegations were made against me some
years ago when I was in the Ministry, and I had a libel action and
was paid £1000 with which I built the institute at Llanystumdwy –
out of aspersions made on my moral character.'[8] Amidst loud laughter he added : 'I made him pay £1000 for suggesting that I was
capable of anything of the kind, and now I am seventy-four. If
they say anything about Frances, you can exaggerate. Tell them she
is a graduate of London University with honours and that she is
very able. Between ourselves there is no comparison between her
and ——.[9] Look at the difficulties ——[9] has landed me in. Frances
was there at the time. J.T. [Davies] was there. Now he is a
director of the Suez Canal and Ford Motors. As long as I am
writing these books, Frances is absolutely essential to me.[10] She
knows French. She knew Foch, Briand, Clemenceau, Bonar and all
the ministers – Smuts, Henry Wilson, Curzon, Austen Chamberlain,
Winston, in fact all the members of the Cabinet. I am not the sort
of fellow to wait to be attacked. Amongst the letters I have received,
the largest number are from Conservatives who are very unhappy
about the treatment of the ex-King. Anybody who has rendered
service to this country but does not support the National Govern-

7. His wife, Dame Margaret Lloyd George.
8. Here Lloyd George refers to a libel action he brought against the
People newspaper in 1909. The *People* had implied that he was about
to be cited as co-respondent in a divorce case. He went into the witness
box and denied the allegation on oath, whereupon the *People* ceased to
contest the case, apologised and paid £1000 damages. His wife contributed
greatly towards this result by accompanying him to court.
9. The name omitted here is of a former member of Lloyd George's
staff.
10. Sylvester writes (1974): He said not a word about me, although
I was the fellow who kept all the state and cabinet papers and later
made an index of his own papers, and without which nobody could
have found a single paper. I was not mentioned in this conversation !

ment has a campaign of calumny started against him. When they say that Edward has no friends, that is not so. They all say that the only reason why there was no expression of opinion was because they were frightened by the Archbishop and the rest. Moses's second tablet will be broken, because I am fighting not only my own battle, but the battle of my late King. I will mix both these things up so that there will be such a stink at the coronation that it will go right through the world, and *they* will be responsible. I was not going to do anything, but if this is going on I will do. If they do it, I will be like Samson. I will pull down the pillars to kill the Philistines, even if I am overwhelmed.'

I said to L.G.: 'I have made careful notes and I will be sure to put them over at my interview with Fildes and Letts tomorrow.'[11]

24 February

Sir Henry Fildes and Sir William Letts dined with me in a private room at the House of Commons. After we had filled the 'inner man', I asked Sir William Letts what the position was in north Wales. He made it clear that a lot of L.G.'s friends in the Boroughs disagreed with him profoundly in his attitude to Windsor.

'But what about the whispering campaign concerning L.G.'s moral character?' I asked. Sir William waved his hand and said he was not going to be embroiled in that. I replied that I had met five different people from the Boroughs in the last few days. They had all told me about this whispering campaign. Then I got off my chest the observations which L.G. had made. I knew that Sir William knew much more than he cared to admit. When we parted, I had left nothing to the imagination of either. As Sir William said good night, he added: 'I don't know what L.G. pays you, but judging by the way you have argued tonight he ought to pay you £10,000 a year.' I replied, 'Will you tell *him* that?'

2 March

At 4.30, L.G. asked me to telephone to Dame Margaret at Criccieth that he wanted to arrange for films of his farm and of Jamaica to be shown at Criccieth during Easter. He asked why I had not taken more pictures of Dame Margaret.[12] He is going to Criccieth to be with Dame Margaret at Easter, and these pictures are to show what a loving family they are.

11. In his original diary, Sylvester abbreviated this statement of Lloyd George, although keeping in all the salient points. For the purpose of this book, he has gone back to his original shorthand note, made while Lloyd George was speaking, and given a complete transcription.

12. Sylvester had taken a movie film, in colour, of both Miss Stevenson and Dame Margaret with Lloyd George in Jamaica.

8 March

Sir Thomas Jaffrey, who at one time wanted to marry Frances, had invited her to lunch at the Savoy.[13] L.G. decided that he, too, wanted to lunch at the Savoy, and asked me to arrange it. Accompanied by Muriel Stevenson, Finney and myself, we went to the grill. Frances and Sir Thomas, seated alone, sat on the other side of the grill, Frances facing L.G., and Sir Thomas with his back towards us. L.G. fixed his eyes on Frances and kept toasting her. Sir Thomas was much upset.

27 March

I accompanied L.G. from Euston to north Wales. As he took up a lamb cutlet and started to bite off the meat, he recalled many years ago going through Battersea with John Burns, who had been a sort of engineer at Price's candle factory. As they passed the factory, Burns had remarked: 'Ah, those were the happiest days of my life, which I spent there. I used to finish my work at night, and nothing ever bothered me, then.' L.G. said: 'The happiest times of my life have been since I gave up all responsibility for the Liberal Party. I enjoyed the first part of my premiership during the war, because there was a big job of work to do and then the peace conference. Afterwards there were a large number of smaller things to do, which I found tedious.'

After dinner at Brynawelon, L.G., Gwilym, Thorpey and I adjourned to the drawing-room. L.G. compared Eden with his predecessors as Foreign Secretary. He had been looking at Eden's head the other day. It was not a good head.

L.G. talked of Balfour as First Lord of the Admiralty in the war. He had been no administrator. He would arrive at the Cabinet at 11 a.m., not having first of all been to the Admiralty because he did not get up until 10.30. Well, said L.G., you could not run a fighting service in the war by getting up at 10.30. 'Balfour would then see his First Sea Lord (Jackson)[14] for the first time at the Cabinet meeting, who would proceed to read out the sinking of ships. ' "We have had a bad day", he would say. "We have lost six ships." ' Then L.G. imitated Balfour by throwing back his head, adjusting his glasses and looking over the top, and said in truly Balfourian style: 'How tiresome.' . . .

13. Sylvester's recollection (1973) is that Sir Thomas Jaffrey proposed marriage to Miss Stevenson 1931. He was then aged seventy and his first wife had died the previous year. He remarried 1932.

14. Sir Henry Jackson (1855–1929). First Sea Lord 1915–16.

In 1936–8 there were widespread disorders among the Arab community in Palestine, directed against the greatly increased flow of Zionist immigration (due to anti-Semitism in Germany and Poland) and against the continuance of the British mandate. The British Government appointed a royal commission under the chairmanship of Earl Peel to investigate the situation. In the autumn of 1937 it recommended the partition of Palestine into a small Jewish state and an Arab state, with the British keeping control of the Jerusalem area. Lloyd George, who had played a large part in starting the recognised Jewish 'national home' in Palestine, goes to give evidence.

16 April

I accompanied L.G. this morning to the Treasury, where he appeared before the Palestine Commission and gave evidence as to how he had understood the mandate when it had first been planned. He was brilliant. It was remarkable to see L.G., the radical, beseeching men like the Tory diehard Peel to keep their words and not run away from the honourable word of Britain. I have rarely seen him deliver so many flips in so short a time. Some of the most interesting were:

'They (the Jews) kept their word and the only question now seems to be whether we are going to honour ours.'

'There are two people I would not quarrel with, if I were running a state. They are both international forces. One is the Jews and the other is the Roman Catholic Church, and Hitler is quarrelling with both.'

'We ought never to have started on the job or we ought to go through with it. It looks to me as if the British Empire is losing its nerve. It clearly has, and this is not the only case, and I do not like it. As an old Briton, who belongs to the most ancient race in these islands, I do not like it. I hope you will not run away.'

'I would claim Transjordania with a lot of cash.[15] As Birrell used to say: "You must make these propositions swim in butter." '[16]

Sylvester and his wife are staying at Churt.

18 April

Breakfast was at nine o'clock and we had it in L.G.'s bedroom. Half-dressed, he lay in bed, with a specially constructed table to

15. The meaning of this is not plain. Perhaps Lloyd George meant 'conciliate' rather than 'claim'.

16. Augustine Birrell (1850–1933). Liberal M.P. 1889–1900 and 1906–18. He was one of the Liberal organisers at the time of the 1906 landslide victory and in charge of Irish affairs 1905–16.

hold his meal. He was in a merry mood. It made one feel refreshed
and exhilarated to watch him and hear him speak.

He never talks long without turning to politics. He asked Gwilym
what he thought were the chances of Neville including Winston in
the Cabinet. Gwilym thought they were favourable, at the moment.
L.G. said he had noticed that, when Winston and he went to see
Neville the other day, when Winston was talking Neville had his
eyes on him, L.G.'. . .

A. P. Herbert, his wife and brother came to tea. L.G. said that
hardly anybody would receive William Hearst in England at one
time, but he had received him as Chancellor of the Exchequer,
since when they had always been good friends. He added: 'Moreover, when I went out of office, not a single person asked me
whether I had a bob in my pocket except one man, and that was
Max Beaverbrook, and he offered to buy me war bonds. That is
why I always have a special feeling towards him. Hearst was the
chief client in the concern that took my articles by contract.'

*As part of the coronation celebrations, the King and Queen were
to visit north Wales in July 1937. They were to open an extension
of the National Library of Wales at Aberystwyth and to make a
ceremonial visit to Caernarvon Castle. Lloyd George was much
involved in the arrangements; apart from anything else, he was
Constable of Caernarvon Castle.*

25 April

L.G. phoned me from Churt to say that the musical programme
for the Caernarvon Castle ceremony was altogether too gloomy and
he could not possibly accept that kind of thing. It was Edwardian.
He wanted something which was challenging. He asked me to get
Sir Henry Morris-Jones and suggest that Sir Walford Davies, the
Master of the King's Musick, should be asked to meet them at lunch
on Tuesday to give his advice.

27 April

I accompanied L.G. to the Savoy Hotel, where I had fixed a private
luncheon to talk about music in Caernarvon Castle on 15 July.
Present: L.G., Sir Walford Davies, Sir Henry Morris-Jones, Megan,
Bob Richards[17] and myself.

L.G. said he was not pleased with the programme. He thought
'Y Cariad Cyntaf' was feeble. It was not up to the dignity of the

17. Robert Richards (1884–1954) was a Labour M.P. 1922–4, 1929–31
and 1932–54.

occasion. He preferred a tune like 'Caerllyngoed'; that was a majestic invocation. It was delightful to see L.G. singing, and as he gave more volume to his voice his arms worked in unison. Walford Davies took up a Methodist hymnal. L.G. said: 'I would burn this in the public square, this wretched Methodist hymn book.' L.G.'s knowledge of hymn tunes is amazing. ' "Cwm Rhondda" ', he said, 'is not so hackneyed as "Aberystwyth".' Another he liked was 'Caer Salem'. Sir Walford was commanded by L.G. to play this over on the piano, which, at L.G.'s request, I had had placed in the room where we lunched. ' "Caer Salem" ', said L.G., 'could be played as their majesties left the Castle.'

Then there was 'Llanfair'. He said it was one of the oldest hallelujah songs and one of the most joyous. L.G. sang it, Sir Walford playing, his face all puckered up, then brightening into a wider expression. He sang with an enthusiasm fit to burst, his arms swinging over the table as his voice roared up to the ceiling.

L.G. rarely goes far, even in music, before talking of politics, and soon he was discussing Neville Chamberlain. 'Neville is all right', said L.G., 'as long as he has a plan, as long as he is in blinkers. I am doubtful whether he will stay the course, because of his health. I have studied phrenology. That is a good gauge. Neville has not an organiser's head.'

Then back to hymn tunes. 'Shall I make private inquiries', asked Walford Davies, 'to see what their majesties would like?' 'No,' said L.G., 'they don't know the difference between the "Hallelujah Chorus" and "Tommy make room for your uncle". Edward's favourite music was "Hitchy-Koo".'

30 April

I accompanied L.G. to lunch with Olwen and Megan in the House of Commons. He suddenly darted out of the room and, like a shot out of a gun, disappeared up the stone staircase to committee room 13 for his committee meeting about the Caernarvon Castle arrangements. Megan and I were left standing, until we raced after him. Megan cried out: 'Tada.' He shouted back: 'Come on.' It was the funniest spectable imaginable to see him racing up those steps, two at a time, in a light-blue suit, his hair waving in the breeze which he created by the speed at which he travelled, leaving trails of cigar smoke behind him. Megan cried out: 'I am coming, but I cannot come faster.'

Sir Watkin Williams-Wynn[18] was in the chair and Sir Walford Davies was present, at L.G.'s special invitation. L.G. said: 'I am

18. Sir (Herbert Lloyd) Watkin Williams-Wynn (1860–1944) seventh baronet and member of one of Wales's oldest families of landed magnates.

appalled at the music programme which I received from Sir Henry
Morris-Jones. Music is a thing of our own. There will be people
present from all over the world and they will look for something
which is quite distinctive. One thing will be the great castle itself,
the finest in Europe. The next will be our music. I am not speaking
as a musician but as a person who appreciates music and who knows
what Welsh music really means. "Llanfair" comes down from the
Catholic times. A tune that survives in a nation for centuries represents its soul.'

Sir Watkin ventured to interpolate how much would it cost.
L.G. retorted: 'It does not cost any more to sing "Llanfair" than
"Aberystwyth", not a penny. There is no choir which sings so
badly when the music is bad as a Welsh choir, but when the music
is good there is no choir which sings as well.'...

Later in the day, Sir Walford Davies, Mr Matthews Williams
and the Mayor of Caernarvon assembled at 2 Addison Road for a
further discussion. Matthews Williams played over all the tunes
they had previously discussed, and L.G. sang them with great gusto.
Suddenly he cried out to Matthews Williams: 'Stop. Play that
much slower. Otherwise you will have the Queen walking down
the castle steps like a milkmaid.'

At tea, L.G. talked of Winston. He said that Winston had a con-
suming ambition to be Prime Minister but he had no following and
few loyalties. 'If he were in a cabinet of mine now, I should know
he would turn round on me when it suited him, though, to do him
full credit, he would come to me beforehand and tell me he was
going to do it. He has no convictions and no loyalties to a cause
and no interest in a particular cause. He fights for himself.'

*On 12 May Lloyd George (and also Sylvester) attended the corona-
tion of King George VI.*

13 *May*
L.G. invited a number to lunch at Thames House. Present: L.G.,
Frances, Nanny, Jennifer, Tweed, Finney and myself. Speaking of
the coronation, he said: 'It was all mumbo-jumbo with the Priest
Zadock.'[19] The thing that had impressed him most was old Queen
Mary trying to look dignified. Here he sat very erect, by way of
imitating Queen Mary. When L.G. was served with a piece of
Gruyère cheese, he said to Jennifer: 'I am afraid I shall not be able

19. The anthem 'Zadock the Priest' is sung at a British coronation
while the monarch is being anointed with oil.

to eat all these holes.' Jennifer replied: 'Then, Taid, you must leave them on your plate.'

21 *May*
L.G., accompanied by Megan and myself, left Euston on the 1.30 to Bangor. We picnicked on the train. When he awoke after his sleep, he said: 'Now we will have a rehearsal and Sylvester will be the adjudicator.'

L.G. and Megan then sang a translation of 'Caer Salem' which he himself had translated, but which he did not want anyone to know he had done. He said it was pitched too low, so they sang it again in a higher key. It was very good, and the words were beautiful and translated from the Welsh by L.G.:

> 'As we part, O Heavenly Father,
> Grant thy blessing from above.
> May our tongues exalt thy glories
> And our hearts extol thy love.
>
> Peace from heaven
> Give us now and ever more.'

Dame Margaret met us at Bangor, and as we passed through Caernarvon L.G. unexpectedly dropped in to hear a rehearsal of a choir of 150 practising for the castle ceremony. How they sang! It was the first time L.G. had ever been in the Conservative Club at Caernarvon.

8 *June*
Coles is the new farm manager, the fourth at Churt in a very few years. None last too long. Coles has done good work, and the whole place is different. When L.G. returned from Jamaica, Coles informed him that he wanted to leave: he did not like the moral atmosphere of the place. He also told L.G. that nobody could make the place pay so long as he, L.G., continually interfered with the manager's arrangements. This was a hobby and not a business. This greatly upset L.G.

At tea, I got him talking about his early days at Llanystumdwy and how he had acquired the Welsh language. He said he was born in Manchester and his mother tongue was English. His brother William, who was born two years afterwards at Llanystumdwy, had Welsh as his mother tongue. His mother and his uncle had fostered him in English. Thus he had grown up on English and William on Welsh, and for some time they had not been able to understand one another.

L.G. said he had talked to George Lansbury in the House about Lansbury's recent visit to Hitler, and Lansbury had entirely agreed that Hitler wanted peace and to be friends with this country. 'Lansbury talked to me very frankly. He said he was in despair in regard to his own party.' L.G. also remarked: 'I always said I would smash Ramsay for his attacks on me, but look at him now. I feel I cannot kick a carcase.' Talking of Herbert Morrison's speech in the House yesterday, L.G. said: 'He has got that narrow face and not the head of a good organiser. He would have made a good Presbyterian minister.'

20 June

Referring to Sir Eric Geddes's death, L.G. said to me: 'So Eric has gone. When I think of all these fellows who have recently passed away, I feel like a man walking through the valley of shadows.'

We talked about the position in France, where Blum has ceased to be Prime Minister while remaining second-in-command. L.G. said that Blum was in a similar position to what he had wanted in the war. He had wanted Bonar to accept the premiership. It would have been very much better. A prime minister had an enormous number of things to look after. Bonar could have done that, and L.G. would have been left free to have conducted the war in his own way, which Bonar would have allowed him to do. Instead L.G. as Prime Minister had had all sorts of ministerial questions to attend to, but Bonar would never make up his mind on anything. Once a question had been decided, Bonar would stick to it and fight for it to a finish, but he would never help in the taking of a decision.

Lloyd George followed with keen interest the progress of the civil war in Spain. The position now was that the nationalists, under Franco, had won control of the greater part of Spain but that the republicans were training a new 'workers' army' and that until this had been tested in action the outcome of the war remained in doubt. Britain had taken the lead in the 'non-intervention' agreements by which twenty-seven countries had pledged themselves to assist neither side. In fact, Germany was giving some and Italy considerable assistance to the nationalists. The republicans had some assistance from the Soviet Union and Mexico. On 25 June Lloyd George strongly attacked the British Government in the Commons for the failure of non-intervention. He said the British should get together with the French and the Russians and 'brutally' tell the Germans and Italians to leave Spain alone. Alternatively, Britain should withdraw into normal neutrality and sell arms to the republicans.

25 June

It was Liberal day in the House, with a debate on foreign affairs. L.G. arrived primed to the teeth with information on which I had worked for days. During his speech he said : 'The Prime Minister says we must keep cool heads, yes, but we must not only have cool heads but stout hearts. Any fish can have a cool head. . . . These dictators are very clever men, very daring men, very astute men, in fact very exceptional men. . . . They are taking at the present moment a rather low view of the intelligence of our government, very low.'

15 July

Today their majesties visited Caernarvon Castle, in connection with which L.G. has worked so hard. It was a marvellous setting, full of colour, and from the ruined walls of the old castle there came volumes of music as a result of L.G.'s vision and endeavour. L.G. wore the levee dress of a privy councillor and seemed in his element. Everything went without a hitch.

Afterwards, I went to L.G.'s bedroom at Brynawelon and found him lying on his bed, wearing his levee-dress trousers, minus his coat, sipping his Irish whiskey. I asked him how today's ceremony had compared with the investiture.[20] He replied that both the music and the colour had been better today. I said that an honour should have been conferred upon the Mayor. He, laughingly, said : 'They ought to have knighted me.' And he kicked up his legs and had another swig at his whiskey and water.

3 August

I attended Berea Chapel, Criccieth, with L.G. and Dame Margaret, where Dr J. D. Jones preached.

At lunch L.G., who sat on Dame Margaret's right, explained to Dr Jones that since he had been turned out of his position at the head of the table he always had that particular place. Dame Margaret explained that why he had been turned out was because he could not carve. He had once tried to carve a goose and had made such a mess of it that, since, she had always been the carver.

J. D. Jones said he could not take the view about war taken by pacifists. Neither could he understand the attitude of the Welsh Nationalists. L.G. said they were a lot of second-rate cranks. There was not a man of first-rate intellect amongst them. The present Welsh nationalism was an aggressive nationalism, which was not making any contribution. There was a religious issue. A number

20. The investiture of the Prince of Wales in 1911, in which Lloyd George had played a prominent part.

of their leaders had definite sympathies with Roman Catholicism. The time would come when that would have to be pointed out.

17 October
We left Chester on the 9.32 a.m. train. During the journey, L.G. said that one of the things that had influenced him more than anything else in favour of women's suffrage had been Ibsen's play entitled *The Doll's House*. Prior to that, he had simply thought of women as performing their normal functions in the home. But after he had seen that play he could not help feeling that they had a bigger mission in the world and he made up his mind to fight for women's suffrage.

21 October
At 6.30 p.m. Ellen Wilkinson[21] brought Mr Simon to see L.G. He is a confidant of Negrin the Spanish Prime Minister.[22]

When L.G. was about to leave for Churt, he said to me: 'Are you ready to go to Barcelona.' I said: 'Yes.' He said: 'You may be shot, you know. I have just received an invitation from the representative of the Spanish Prime Minister. He says that nothing would hearten them so much as a visit from me.'

10 November
The adjournment of the House was to be moved in order to pay tribute to Ramsay MacDonald.[23] The Prime Minister, Attlee and Sinclair were to speak, and I was asked to inquire whether L.G. would speak as Father of the House. I had to make an excuse. He disliked Ramsay MacDonald intensely.

21. Ellen Wilkinson (1891–1947). A Labour M.P. 1924–31 and 1935–47, a junior minister 1940–5 and in the Cabinet 1945–7. She was known as 'Red Ellen' both for the colour of her hair and her political views.
22. Juan Negrin (1889–1956). Prime Minister of Spain 1937–9. In 1939–46 he headed the Spanish republican government-in-exile.
23. Who had just died.

Chapter 10

'That little swine Beneš'

1938

At the start of the year Lloyd George is at Antibes, finishing his book The Truth about the Peace Treaties. *Miss Stevenson is with him. Later, as had become customary during these winter sojourns abroad, she was due to go home and Dame Margaret and other members of the family would come out to join Lloyd George. This year Dame Margaret's arrival was to be of more than usual interest. In Antibes she and Lloyd George were to celebrate the golden anniversary of their wedding, an event which attracted attention on an international scale. The diary for the year starts with Sylvester still in London.*

11 *January*
I accompanied Dame Margaret and Megan from Victoria this morning for Antibes. I went only as far as Paris. . . .

12 *January*
I returned to London on the *Golden Arrow*. It was a filthy crossing. As we arrived at Folkestone, I ran into Frances. She had left Antibes as Dame Margaret and Megan left London. We agreed that we should not let L.G. know that we had even met, because he is absolutely mad if Frances is even seen speaking to anyone else. He is mental on matters of sex, and therefore has no understanding. A man and a woman could not possibly in his view be friends without sexual intercourse. He judges everyone by his own standards.

She told me that Vansittart had come to lunch at Antibes.[1] L.G. had thought that Vansittart would talk more freely if Frances were not present. He had said that she and Finney had better go out to lunch. Frances had reminded L.G. that the suggestion was his and had said she would go on the understanding that he made no accusations against her afterwards.

1. Robert Vansittart (1881–1957) was kicked upstairs 1 January 1938 to become 'Chief Diplomatic Adviser to the Foreign Secretary'. He was Permanent Under-Secretary at the Foreign Office 1930–8.

That night Finney was in the salon with L.G. and Frances, and presently L.G. went to bed. At the same time Finney wished him good-night and made his exit. In a few moments, however, Finney came back into the room. L.G. had gone into his bedroom, which adjoined. Finney in a very confidential tone asked Frances to ascertain whether it was advisable for him to return home. He did not want to outstay his welcome. When Frances went into L.G.'s bedroom, she opened the door suddenly and found him with his ear to the door trying to listen. The fact that Finney had spoken very softly only aroused L.G.'s deepest suspicions. There was a hell of a row. Frances said that either she or Finney would go home next day. Finney went. Finney had apparently been trying to bludgeon L.G. into taking a more active part in the Council of Action, and in insisting that its success depended upon L.G.

L.G. has an idea of starting a weekly or monthly paper, price twopence. He has an idea that Cummings might run it, in addition to his ordinary work on the *News Chronicle*. He is prepared to lose £100,000 a year for three years on this paper alone, presumably to get rid of his Fund. Finney does not realise that this paper is instead of the Council of Action.

The one thing that is exercising L.G.'s entire mind at the moment is how he is to get rid of his family from Antibes after the celebration of the fiftieth anniversary of his wedding on 24 January. Finney told me all about this in a letter, and now Frances confirmed it. . . .

15 *January*
The *Weekly Illustrated* has a very fine series of pictures of Dame Margaret and L.G. at various stages of their lives. It is very well done.

17 *January*
Today is L.G.'s seventy-fifth birthday.

19 *January*
John Carvel of the *Star* asked me: 'Have you bought the coronet?' He then explained that he had it on good authority that the office of the herald was busy designing L.G.'s coat of arms and that he was going to the Lords. I said at once that it was a cock and bull story. I phoned to L.G. at Antibes and spoke to him personally. He said: 'It's damn-fool nonsense.' L.G. was anxious to know whether any photographs had appeared of him playing golf on his birthday. I told him they had appeared yesterday evening and this morning and that I had sent him copies.

21 January

At eleven o'clock this morning, the following members of L.G.'s family left Victoria for Antibes: Dick and June, Gwilym and Edna, Olwen and Margaret, together with myself. We had rather a rough crossing.

22 January

On the stroke of 10.4 this morning, we arrived at Antibes. There was no L.G. to meet us. He was on his way but late, and we had to wait for him for some minutes. Reason: our train was on time. He had banked on it being late. The hotel was delightfully situated. L.G. was in a happy mood. He said he was glad to see me. 'The Press has nearly worn me down,' he said. . . .

A shower of telegrams arrived. L.G. said that he found the same delight in opening telegrams as he had as a boy. That explains a lot. He opened one from Sarah[2] in Welsh, which much pleased him. 'Ah,' he said, 'the thing that has touched me most is the overwhelming number of messages from the man in the street.' That I took as my main message in interviewing the Press.

At dinner . . . Dick asked L.G. what he thought of Eden. He replied: 'Eden is a nice fellow, but he is not a big man. If he had told "those others" to go to Hell, he would have been a big man, but because he did not he is not, for that reason.'

23 January

Went to see L.G. in his bedroom at nine o'clock. He had already had his breakfast and lay in bed wearing his bedjacket and reading the Paris edition of the *Daily Mail*, smoking a cigar.

Last night L.G. had suggested that the whole of the family should take a motor trip to the Corniche and Monte Carlo. He wanted to get rid of them. This morning Megan stated that Mami was not going. Everybody suspected that this was one of Megan's whims. L.G. went to inquire for himself and returned from Dame Margaret's room quite satisfied that she really did herself prefer to remain quiet today, in view of the morrow.

Last night L.G. had read a statement in a French newspaper to the effect that the Archbishop of Canterbury claimed that there were 26,550,000 members of the Church of England. L.G. had said that this was a monstrous statement. He now said, referring to 'His Grace', 'I will bust him.' He said: 'If a businessman put that in his prospectus, he would be sent to gaol like Kylsant.'. . .[3]

2. Sarah Jones, the family housekeeper.
3. Lord Kylsant (1863–1937), a shipping magnate, was sentenced to a year's imprisonment in 1931 for issuing a false company prospectus.

When the family had left, he talked with me alone. He said he wanted to be rid of them and stressed that he wanted to get on with his book on the treaties of peace, and he could not work while they were there. 'I do not want the old lady left behind,' he said. . . .

Neither Dame Margaret nor Megan went on the motor trip today, so we three lunched together in the hotel. I asked Dame Margaret what had happened at their silver wedding. 'Nothing,' she replied. Caernarvon Boroughs had intended to stage something, but it had not matured. That had been in 1913. 'I wonder who found out about our golden wedding?' she inquired. 'The Press,' I replied. 'Well, I would never have said anything about it and I am sure my husband would never have remembered it,' she said.

L.G. is very much affected these days when anyone of his own age passes away. He is now much upset at Dr Dinsdale Young's passing. In his quiet moments, he is no doubt thinking of his own passing. He has got a dirty lane to go down some time, when he is called to give an account of his actions. What he dreads most is the thought that he may partially lose his faculties. Stretched out on the settee, he said: 'Old Henry Norman,[4] who is eighty, agrees with me that it is better to put an end to it by taking Veronal. I saw Joe Chamberlain when he had had a stroke.' L.G. impersonated him. 'I also saw President Wilson when he had had a stroke. It is not worth while.'

24 January

This is the anniversary of L.G.'s and Dame Margaret's golden wedding. I was busy with the Press, cables and telegrams long before 8 a.m. I did not get even a cup of tea until 10.30 a.m., to say nothing of breakfast. I went to see L.G. in his bedroom at 8.45 and congratulated him. I jocularly said that, today being his golden wedding, we were giving him instructions for a change and he was not to go into his sitting-room until we gave the word. He meekly concurred. As Hannah[5] squeezed the juice of two oranges on to a plate and fed him with a spoon with the juice and the fibre, I remarked what a difference there was between him and a man like Ramsay, especially seeing what L.G. had been through. 'Yes, or Baldwin either,' said L.G. 'He went out at seventy.'

How he likes to be fussed – by a woman. He does not like men around him. He was like a young bird with an ever-open mouth, waiting for the parent bird to drop something into it. His bed was strewn with papers of every description.

4. Henry Norman (1858–1939). Journalist. Liberal M.P. 1900–23.
5. Hannah Sharp, housekeeper at Churt. She was young, buxom and capable and later married a butcher. A.J.S.

He then went into Dame Margaret's bedroom, which was some distance away, and kissed her. She is a dear, but has a great faculty for mixing up what she wants to say. 'Tada (as she calls L.G.), do you know that fifty years ago today I had not even met you?' she said.

At about ten o'clock, L.G. and Dame Margaret, having had the signal, came into the sitting-room, where the rest of the family was assembled and where I had laid out all the presentations on a table. As they entered, L.G., looking at the gifts, said: 'By Jove.' Then he took each one up and examined it with great delight, while Dame Margaret looked on. They were both very much touched.

There was no gift from L.G. to Dame Margaret and none from her to him. That seemed a little funny, but he is paying for the whole family to assemble here – or the Fund is. L.G. and Dame Margaret kissed each other and then they each kissed all the members of their family in turn. Cables poured in in shoals. The telephone never stopped ringing. Press representatives filled the hotel. I interviewed them all and showed them the presentations and gave them a story. The family gave L.G. and Dame Margaret a silver-gilt loving-cup, which was unique in its wording.

On one side there appeared:

January 24th

D.Ll.G.   1888–1938   M.Ll.G.

I Tada a Mami
oddiwrth eu plant

Dick–June	Olwen–Tom
Valerie	Margaret
Owen	Eluned
	Robin
	Bengy

'Bo'r heulwen ar eu hwyliau'[6]

And on the other side:

(Welsh dragon)

Gwilym–Edna	Megan
David	
William	

6. In English the inscription reads: To Father and Mother from their children. 'May the sun shine on their sails.' The final line is in strict metre (cynghanedd) and should be taken poetically.

. . . At 1.30 they all went to lunch with Mr and Mrs Winston
Churchill at the Carlton Hotel, Cannes. Winston made a little
informal speech saying that L.G. would figure great in the history
of the world and congratulated them both. L.G. replied that there
was no one with whom he would sooner have spent part of his time
on this occasion than Winston and his wife. Winston afterwards
told Dick and Gwilym that he was so pleased with these remarks,
because he knew they were sincere. In talking about this later in
the evening, L.G. said it was a remarkable friendship. In fact it was
a record. They first met in 1890,[7] and throughout all the vicissitudes
and quarrels between them their friendship had survived all these
forty-eight years. . . .

The room in which dinner was served resembled a flower show.
Lord Derby's tremendous basket of orchids was there and a mass
of flowers from Miss Maxine Elliot.

The table plan was as follows :

Lady Carey Evans

Edna	Dick
L.G.	Dame Margaret
June	Gwilym
Margaret[8]	Megan

A.J.S.

L.G. and Dame Margaret were in great form. When we reached
the champagne, Dick filled the cup presented by the family. L.G.
insisted that the oldest traditions should be observed, whereby it
should be passed round the table, the next one standing up to receive
it. Dick started by standing up, but did not drink. He merely
passed it to his mother, who took the first drink and passed it to
Gwilym. After Megan, I indicated that I should pass it to Margaret,
because I was not a member of the family, but L.G. insisted that
the circle should not be broken and Megan therefore passed it to me.
It went its round, L.G. standing up to receive it, drinking the precious
liquid and passing it on to Edna. Dick finished the circle.

Then L.G. and Dame Margaret clicked their glasses together, and
we then all clicked ours together. Before the party left the table,
Dame Margaret toasted L.G. on her own. Raising her glass, she said,

7. This was the year Lloyd George first entered Parliament. Churchill
was then a sixteen-year-old schoolboy. It is possible but unlikely that
they met as early as this. Their real friendship was formed in the 1900s.
8. Elder daughter of Sir Thomas and Lady Carey Evans.

laughingly, 'Good health, sir', and then she added : 'Perhaps I should
have said "good health, my lord".'

'You might have done very much worse than that,' replied L.G.
'Many a husband has been worn out by his wife after a hard day's
work.' He then jocularly added : 'Tonight I will recall the virtues
of you all, and forget your shortcomings.'

After a firework display in the grounds, we reassembled in L.G.'s
sitting-room, where Olwen and Gwilym kept us in roars. I have
never laughed so much in my life. Olwen dressed up in a pair of
L.G.'s grey trousers, his brown smoking-jacket, collar and blue and
white tie, with his walking-stick. She is a consummate actress.
Gwilym was adorned in one of his mother's grey evening-dresses
and one of her hats, with his face made up, including an abundance
of rouge on the lips. He was marvellous. Those two would jam any
theatre and bring down the house. Every movement made one
burst into laughter. Then they both disappeared, only to return with
Gwilym dressed up as Princess Juliana, the very-much-expectant
mother, and Olwen dressed up as her attendant nurse. Then he ran
about in only his shirt, socks and evening waistcoat. L.G. said he
had never laughed so much in all his life, and Dame Margaret said
the same. . . .

This has been a most interesting day. The world has paid tribute
to L.G. and Dame Margaret on their golden-wedding day. What
would it think if it knew that for the greater part of every year L.G.
lives with another woman?

25 January

Before dinner tonight, a telegram arrived in Spanish from Juan
Negrin, the Prime Minister of the Spanish Government. Dick translated this as follows: 'Barcelona; 25.1.38. In your family fiesta
I take the liberty of felicitating you myself personally and as chief
of the government the great friend of Spain who figures as one of
the most eminent contemporary statesmen. Juan Negrin, Presi-
dente Consejo Ministros Republica Española.'

To this L.G. dictated the following reply : 'Deeply moved that
amidst your terrible anxieties you should find time and thought to
send a kindly message to my wife and myself on the fiftieth anniversary of our wedding. From our hearts we both wish that victory
may crown your glorious efforts to establish democracy, liberty and
social justice in Spain. Lloyd George.'

26 January

Before he went to golf, L.G. told me that Megan was making difficulties about returning. After all, he was the only member of the

family who worked, and worked hard. He had written an article only yesterday to help to keep her. She liked her fun, but she would not let him have his. He said that it was necessary for him to have Frances to help him with his book. He added: 'J.T. [Davies] and Frances are the only people who know the papers', which is absolute balls. Frances only knows the papers when they are asked for by him and then they are only there because they were sent there by me from London. I said nothing, but thought a lot.

27 January

When L.G. returned from golf, he trapped his second and third fingers on the left hand in the car door. How he yelled. The fingers were placed in hot water and bathed, and when I went down later he showed them to me. They were in a bad mess. His nails were black in the middle, and the fingers were black with bruises at the back. As each member of the family trooped in for cocktails, there was another inspection. L.G. was indeed very sorry for himself. Dame Margaret said: 'You remember how Ernest Brown got his fingers trapped at Criccieth.' 'Yes,' said L.G., 'but he was a much younger man.'

He dined alone in the sitting-room, having only cold ham. When we returned from dinner, L.G. was in grand form. Talking about royalty and titles, L.G. said: 'Although I created duchesses and made the titles for them, I never understood which was which. I did that very badly when I was Prime Minister.' L.G. said the Duke of Clarence[9] died of german measles. 'A damned good thing he died, too,' said L.G., 'because George was a decent fellow.' L.G. thought that the present Queen[10] was very good. She was the real live half. He[11] was a nitwit. If she ever became regent for the little Princess Elizabeth, she would be good.

'That woman,' said L.G., referring to Queen Mary, 'whom I very much dislike, is the root of all the present trouble. She was always against the little fellow [the Duke of Windsor]. She would not allow him to marry that Ednam girl with whom he was very much in love. The old King, George V, told me he never showed her his papers and never consulted her.'

He told me tonight that he was passionately interested in the sinking of the well at Churt. They had got 1500 gallons an hour, but he wanted 5000 and they were now in sight of that at 145 feet.

9. Elder brother of King George V.
10. Now Queen Elizabeth, the Queen Mother.
11. King George VI.

G

31 January
. . . I had a tremendously busy day, paying bills, packing and getting ready for departure. We left in a whirlwind. When L.G. said good-bye to his family, he was much touched and almost wept. Yet I knew he was only waiting to get rid of them all and to welcome Frances tomorrow. What can one make of him?

In February 1938 Anthony Eden, Foreign Secretary, resigned over a minor dispute with Neville Chamberlain, the Prime Minister, about relations with Italy. The event attracted the most widespread interest and was of great long-term advantage for Eden in his career.

11 February
During my private note of today to L.G., I warned him that Eden and Neville were again at loggerheads. There were rumours that Eden might actually resign.

12 February
Immediately after a conversation with Jack Broadbent[12] at 7.30 a.m., I telephoned to L.G. at Antibes. I told him I had warned him last night in a note of difficulties between the P.M. and Eden, but the situation might develop quickly. I explained the exact position.

Shortly afterwards Frances phoned me from Antibes with a message from L.G. that I was to try to get to Eden. It was as follows: 'Tell Eden that the country is on the look-out for a young man with ideals, brains and courage, that Eden has the first two, but he has not yet shown he has got courage; and that if he takes a firm stand now, on the question of Italy, even if he has to resign, he will be the biggest man in the country in two or three years time. If he takes a strong line, he is made.'

That message was delivered to Eden tonight.

Much attention was being focused on a by-election in Ipswich, where the Tories, in a straight fight with Labour, were defending the majority of 7250 they had won in 1935. The Labour candidate, R. R. Stokes,[13] was a man of individualistic views, and foreign policy was a prominent issue. Stokes made much of the fact that

12. J. Wilson Broadbent was political and diplomatic correspondent of the *Daily Mail*.
13. R. R. Stokes (1897–1957). Labour M.P. 1938–57, a minister 1950–1.

in 1936 he had offered to manufacture shells for the Government on a cost basis, with no profit for the company of which he was chairman, and that this offer had not been taken up. This was significant in that Stokes was showing that the Labour Party and opposition to rearmament were no longer necessarily synonymous. This was all against the background of Abyssinia, the Spanish Civil War and the first moves towards the amalgamation of Germany and Austria which Hitler was triumphantly to bring off the following month. Stokes also made proposals for land taxes in his campaign.

17 February
Stokes, Labour, was in with a majority of 3161 for Ipswich. I immediately telephoned L.G. He was so delighted, he could not take in the fact. I had to repeat it three times and then give him the figures. . . .

19 February
As a result of secret information, I telephoned L.G. at 7.45 this morning, informing him that Eden had resigned and urged him to return to London at once. This is very hush-hush. At lunchtime Hannah phoned from Antibes to say L.G. was leaving tonight. Frances asked me to make arrangements this end, and to have dinner ready for them at Churt. Nurse and Jennifer were also to be present.

20 February
The Sunday papers are full of news about the possibility of Eden's resignation. I met my friend under the shadow of the Foreign Office at 4.30 p.m. The position was still exactly the same. Eden is resolute in his determination to go. I met L.G. at Victoria. Tweed was unexpectedly there too. Tweed told L.G. that Eden would definitely not resign. I accompanied L.G. and Frances as far as Putney, when I confirmed my secret information that Eden had already resigned. At 7.30 p.m. my telephone bell rang and my friend's voice rang out: 'He's gone.' I immediately telephoned this to Churt.

At 11.3 p.m. there was a broadcast message to the effect that it was officially announced that the Prime Minister had accepted the resignations of Mr Anthony Eden and Lord Cranborne[14] and that

14. Lord Cranborne, Foreign Under-Secretary, resigned in company with his chief. He was Robert Gascoyne-Cecil, Viscount Cranborne (1893–1972), who became 5th Marquess of Salisbury 1947.

Eden would make a statement in the House of Commons tomorrow.

Bravo, Jack.[15]

21 February

L.G. came to the House to hear the statement by Eden on his resignation. L.G. was in a bad mood; he had wanted Jennifer to stay up for supper last night, but it was too late and she had been sent home. Dinner at the House. Present: L.G., Gwilym, Megan, Aneurin Bevan and myself. L.G., who had lunched with Winston, said Winston had described Neville as 'that provincial undertaker who is taking an interest in foreign affairs'. Then L.G. said he knew that Eden had many excellent qualities, but until today he doubted whether he had the guts to resign. 'Clearly, I underestimated his bowels,' said L.G. 'His resignation may alter the whole orientation of politics. Eden has today paid a big cheque into the bank on which he can draw in future.'

A foreign-affairs debate in the Commons followed Eden's resignation. Churchill, in a moderate speech, deprecated a decision by the Government to initiate conversations with Italy with a view to restoring normal relations. (It was the Chamberlain government's long-term aim to detach Italy from Germany.) Lloyd George followed the same line as Churchill but much more militantly. He said Chamberlain's political innocence did 'not fit him to deal with some of the Machiavellian dictators of Europe; he is only fit for a stained-glass window'. He got the worst of a direct verbal duel with Chamberlain: he virtually accused Chamberlain of dishonesty in not having shown a particular document to Eden but failed to make the charge stand up.

22 February

L.G. took part in the Labour motion of censure on the Government. Afterwards he came to his room at the House to change and have a whiskey and water. Then he asked me to find out the reactions to his speech. He had had a row on the floor of the House with the P.M. I personally did not think it had been his happiest effort, and I do not think he thought so himself, though he did not say so. For the first time in my experience, he made many lapses of the tongue, which the House had to correct. Thus when talking about having read up the peace-conference papers he meant to say he had done this 'carefully' but he said 'successfully'.

15. J. Wilson Broadbent.

At 7.30 he asked me to get a party for dinner – rather a late hour to start this. At 8 o'clock the following assembled in a private room: L.G., Commander and Mrs Fletcher,[16] Megan, Olwen, A. V. Alexander,[17] Finney, Gwilym and myself. L.G. said that Mosley was one of the worst tragedies he knew. If Mosley had stuck it, he was just the type that was needed at the moment. He was just the sort of fellow who could talk to this crowd. You needed a fellow today like Mosley, who could have cheeked them. Then L.G. caused much amusement by handing round a newspaper cutting, which in leaded type in French said: 'Mr Churchill, the old Minister of Marine', but instead of giving a picture of Winston there was one of a mother exhibiting her triplets. L.G. said he had shown it to Winston, but 'he was *not* amused', and L.G. roared with laughter.

24 February

I had dinner in the House with L.G., Gwilym, Edna, Megan and Marian Powell Williams. L.G. said Maisky, whom he had seen today, had summed up Neville very well when he had said that the Prime Minister was playing with one card, on which he had put all his money. 'If this dinner party were a prayer meeting,' said L.G., 'I would pray that Neville Chamberlain may be left as Prime Minister for some time.' When he was reminded of his duel with Neville, L.G. said: 'When I came into the House tonight I felt just like a man, who has had a row in a pub, going back to be thrown out.'

Suddenly L.G.'s face glistened. I had mentioned his well at Churt. 'That well', said L.G. 'is producing 300,000 gallons a day.' (Actually, the figure is 12,000 gallons an hour, but L.G. always thinks big and 300,000 gallons a day sounds so much bigger.) The well was found by an old Scotswoman water-diviner, who lives in a caravan and discovers water through the medium of twigs.

25 February

On arrival by train at Bangor at 4 p.m., L.G. and I motored to Criccieth. . . .

26 February

I telephoned Churt to find out the latest amount of water produced from the well. It was 14,000 gallons of water an hour.

16. R. T. H. Fletcher (1885–1961). Liberal M.P. 1923–4, Labour M.P. 1935–42 and created Baron Winster 1942.
17. A. V. Alexander (1885–1965) was a Baptist lay preacher who was a Co-op Labour M.P. 1922–31 and 1935–50. He was a junior minister 1924 and in the Cabinet (or of cabinet rank) 1929–31, 1940–51.

The Mayor of Conway, Councillor Jones, the Deputy Mayor, Alderman Smith, and the Town Clerk, Mr Arthur L. Ralphes, arrived, after an accident in which all were badly shaken, to talk about the position of the fishermen at Conway. Dame Margaret was congratulated by Alderman Smith on her recent broadcast talk on castles. They at Conway had benefited from her advice, and had now had a large amount of the ivy around the castle walls taken away. He had been shown an extraordinary thing. A small ivy root had started to grow under a huge wall, how during the years it had steadily increased in size and strength, until it had actually displaced a huge stone. L.G. observed: 'That's life coming up amidst a dead thing.'

As they left, Alderman Smith talked to Dame Margaret about 'the village'. She much dislikes Criccieth being called a village, and she corrected him, emphasising that it was a town. L.G. said that whenever friends came who were strangers to Criccieth he always told them to call it a village, in order that he could enjoy Dame Margaret's reaction.

After dinner, L.G. talked over his cigar. He said the present situation reminded him very much of the time when Gladstone was hitting out right and left during the Midlothian campaign. Everybody said: 'The old man is at it again, he just cannot help it', and L.G. added: 'Just the things they are saying about me.' All the same it was the beginning of the end for the Government. . . .

Megan talked of Winston's speech and of his new system of notes. He now has his speech written out on large sheets. L.G. thought it had been a brilliant speech. 'Winston', said L.G., 'is like me. He is happiest when he is at work. Sylvester is the same. What troubles me is what I shall do when I am not able to work – what I shall do then I shudder to think. I should not have been happy in the south of France if I had not had plenty of work to do.' . . .

Lloyd George prepares for what was, in the circumstances, a considerable ordeal: the ceremony at Cardiff for the presentation of gold plate to him and Dame Margaret, purchased by public subscription in Wales, as a gift for their golden wedding anniversary; the ceremony was to be on 1 March, St David's Day.

27 February

After lunch, in response to a request by L.G. that he must be made fit to go amongst respectable people, Dame Margaret brought in a basin of hot water, placed it by his side and then, out of a wallet, produced implements with which to file his fingernails. Meantime he smoked his cigar and talked to Megan and me of politics. Dame Margaret filed away with her 'knitting face', as Megan calls it. Suddenly she filed too much and L.G. cried out, 'Maggie-bach, do keep on the nail, if you don't mind.' We shrieked with laughter, especially at the remark: 'If you don't mind.' It was a most plaintive voice. . . .

During supper there was a hue and cry from L.G. for a Welsh dictionary. Three or four of us got up from the table to search for one. When it was found, he wanted a quotation for his Cardiff speech. He said 'verdant and full of sap' in the Welsh version was so much better than 'fat and flourishing' in the English version.

1 March

As L.G. read his newspaper in the library after breakfast, I noticed he had dropped half his egg down his trousers. Sarah arrived with a wet cloth. Meantime he had lost his notes for his speech. He was most blasphemous and ran all over the place hot and bothered, until I discovered he had put them in his little bag.

We caught the 11.30 a.m. train from Shrewsbury. With a board placed across the seats, and using a suitcase to sit on, I typed out his speech, which he dictated to me. He was very nervy about his speech. He said that if I had a moustache and a wig I could deliver it for him. As we steamed into Cardiff station, he said: 'I never felt so much funk before a speech as today.'

He was met by representatives of the Lord Mayor and the police and driven to the Capitol Theatre. Six and seven deep lined the roads and gave L.G. and Dame Margaret a marvellous reception. The theatre holds 3500; today it was to take 5000. But the Lord Mayor's secretary told me that 20,000 letters applying for tickets had not even been opened. . . .

L.G.'s telegraphic address ought to be 'Audacity', especially in the light of his reply to the presentation by the Lord Mayor to Dame Margaret.

With a quiver in his voice, he said, 'I am not everybody's favourite', and the audience laughed loudly. 'I disagree with a great many people and they manage to disagree with me, but nothing has impressed us and nothing has reached our hearts more than the messages we have received in France from men and women of all parties and those above party, such as the King and Queen.' (Loud applause.) 'Marriage is the greatest and oldest partnership in the world. It is the best and truest friendship in the world. It carries one through the troubles, bothers and worries of the world and it is one of the very few institutions which enable people whose dispositions and temperaments are exactly the opposite to live in perfect harmony for fifty years. I need hardly say that my wife and I are of different temperaments. One is contentious, combative, and stormy.' (Laughter.) 'That is my wife,' said L.G., and he turned with a broad smile towards Dame Margaret, but she showed she entirely disagreed with him. (Loud laughter.) Continuing, he said: 'Then there is the other partner, placid, calm, peaceful and patient. That is me.' (Loud laughter.) 'But in spite of the fundamental differences in our dispositions, we have lived in perfect harmony for fifty years. Now that is a great tribute to the institution of marriage.' After the meeting, I sought a room and helped L.G. change. He was wet through with perspiration. . . .

10 *March*

L.G. received a deputation consisting of the Mayor of Conway and others in regard to the new road at Conway, and then gave them lunch at the House. He struck good form. Talking about his land at Churt, he said he had recently reclaimed twenty acres which were all sand. 'It had never been cultivated since the days of Adam,' he said, 'and he was too busy in Mesopotamia to be bothered with it.' He intended growing potatoes on this reclaimed land because it was the only suitable crop. But the trouble was that if you grew more potatoes than formerly you were subject to a fine of five pounds per acre. That, he said, was the kind of encouragement that was given you to improve your land. 'All the same, I am going to grow more potatoes and be damned to them.'

They talked of Conway bridge. L.G. said: 'Conway bridge was the first big deal carried out by the late Sir Robert Perks.[18] He was chief clerk in his firm. He went to the managing director and asked for a partnership. The answer was "No". "Would it make a difference," asked Sir Robert, "if I were to marry the daughter of so-and-so?" "Ah yes, it would," was the reply. Sir Robert then went to see the father of the lady in question and asked for the hand of the daughter. "No," was the answer, "you are only the chief clerk." "Would it make any difference if I were a partner?" Sir Robert inquired. "Yes, it would," was the reply. He won the heart and hand of the lady. He got the partnership, and he got the contract for the building of the Conway bridge,' said L.G. Then he remarked, amidst loud laughter: 'Nobody but a Methodist could have made a bargain of that kind.'

18. Robert Perks (1849–1934) was an engineering contractor connected with many projects, including the Inner Circle line in London, the docks at Buenos Aires and a railway across the Andes. He was a prominent Methodist.

On 12 March 1938 Hitler, by threat of force, overthrew the Austrian
Government and the following day he declared the union of Germany and Austria. The British Government protested but quickly
recognised the union, which was obviously popular with the majority
of Austrian public opinion.

13 March
I telephoned L.G. this morning to get his reactions on the present
situation. He said that Hitler's move into Austria was a natural
sequence of events.

Lloyd George arranges to go to Paris for talks with French leaders
on the international situation, particularly the plight of the Spanish
republicans.

14 March
Personally, I believe L.G. is fast on the downhill grade. He is the
picture of health, but he is different. He acts the part of a virile,
strong man when he is in the House. He walks quickly on purpose
to create an impression. But put him at a difficulty, face him with
an important situation and a speech: he funks it. He is full to the
brim with an inferiority complex. Many a time he has told me that
people do not credit him with being shy. I was told that L.G.
would decide definitely at 5 p.m. tonight whether he would leave
on Wednesday for Paris. The answer came at seven o'clock, when
all the offices were closed, saying that Frances and Jennifer were
going on Wednesday, instead of Tuesday, and L.G. on Thursday
instead of Wednesday. I started the arrangements all over again.

Tweed told me the other day that he had been talking about
the general political situation with L.G. and the possibility of L.G.
taking office in a Labour government. L.G. had said that he would
never take office again. 'Fancy having to be in town every day,
running a department, or in the House – it would kill me.' That is
the first time he has made an admission of that kind. L.G. had added
that he would not mind helping in an advisory capacity. 'They
could always come to see me at Churt.'

16 March
Goronwy Owen came to see L.G. in the House. He, J.T. [Davies]
and I went in to see L.G. together. Speaking of the general international situation, L.G. said: 'You can roll up the map of Europe

for twenty years. These men were born without guts.' By 'these men' he meant the Government.

J.T. told me that he had spoken to L.G. about a cheque for £6000,[19] and that when J.T. had asked Gwilym to sign it he had telephoned his father at Churt. J.T. had been ill and had said that he would send particulars as to why that cheque had been drawn. It included £2000 for the test ballot of Chamberlain versus Eden for four constituencies, and the rest was almost entirely for paying L.G.'s own bills in connection with the sinking of the well, the building of new cottages and expenses abroad. Did L.G. want Gwilym to know that his own expenses came out of the Fund? L.G. did not want this known by Gwilym, although Gwilym was a trustee.

L.G., Gwilym, Megan and I dined in the Harcourt Room. Talking about the foreign situation, L.G. said: 'I am not certain that they have not buggered the whole thing up irretrievably.'

17 March

I left Victoria with L.G. this morning for France. He and I had a picnic lunch, prepared by Hannah, in his cabin. He said he had warned Winston that if he went into this cabinet he would not be able to achieve anything. When he, L.G., had tried to get things done in the Asquith government, he had been baulked by McKenna and Runciman and others, who had gone behind his back to Asquith. L.G. said that if he had had a guillotine in 1909 it would not have been the Lords upon whom he would have used it. They had not been the real obstructionists. He would have used it upon members of his own party, and he chuckled when he speculated on the names of the men who would have fallen under his guillotine.

The difficulty in making a cabinet, he said, 'is that one is always fettered by the names of people who have always been faithful to the Party or to their leader and who thus considered that they had "strong claims" to preferment. Thank God', said L.G., 'that when I formed my ministry in 1916 I had no difficulties because all the old fogies went with Asquith, and I was able to appoint men like Geddes, Maclay and other first-rate business people.'

L.G. talked of Hitler. He said: 'Hitler is a man to whom race is a religion. He is ascetic, very simple, and is a very remarkable man with none of the vanities of Mussolini. Mussolini is a schemer.'

Talking of the period immediately preceding the war, L.G. said that on the Friday, the week before the outbreak of war on Bank Holiday 4 August, a sudden notice had been issued, asking cabinet

19. On the Lloyd George Political Fund.

ministers to meet in the Prime Minister's room behind the Speaker's
chair. For an hour there had been a discussion as to whether
certain parishes in Ireland should go to northern Ireland or the
south. Right at the very end of the discussion, Sir Edward Grey
had said he would like to mention one matter, and that was that the
European situation was not as good as he would like to report,
but he had sent a note or a letter and he hoped he would be able
to report an improvement on the following Monday. The whole
discussion under this head had not taken more than a quarter of an
hour. Yet within a week we had been at war with Germany.

Lloyd George in Paris.

18 *March*
I was at work at 7.30 a.m. I went to see L.G. soon afterwards. He
was reclining in bed, his face lathered, and shaving himself with
his Rolls razor whilst Hannah held the mirror. We discussed
arrangements for the day. Ellen Wilkinson came for breakfast. At
9.45 a.m. he went to lay a wreath at the Invalides. He asked me to
go in advance to arrange for Frances and Jennifer. The wreath
which he laid on Foch's tomb was the most beautiful and largest
I have ever seen. Afterwards he went hand in hand with Jennifer
to see Napoleon's tomb. I thought this was a most unwise procedure for there were many photographers and cinema people
always photographing him. He showed her Napoleon's death mask.
L.G. said he thought it was a kindly face. Curiously remote from
Napoleonic interest and history, we waited at the Invalides for a
telephone message. It was to let us know whether Clemenceau's
old house was open, but, getting no reply, we proceeded there.

We arrived at the house at the Rue Franklin to find that it
could not be open until later. We were kept waiting for some
time whilst the caretaker put on his collar and then he specially
took L.G. round. Hand in hand with Jennifer, he took her from
room to room. A very enterprising French photographer asked me
the name of 'the little girl' but I avoided an answer. Frances looked
on with evident satisfaction. The result may be a sad page for
L.G., especially when the family see it. Whilst waiting, L.G. had
talked of Sir William Robertson. He said that when Robertson
knew that a certain plan originated from the French side the
French declared that they knew beforehand that the answer would
be 'No'.

Clemenceau's house was tremendously interesting. In the hall, in a glass case, was Clemenceau's peculiar-shaped hat which he always wore at home. There was the room where he worked, containing a large table, almost three-quarters of a circle, so that he had plenty of space all around him. Jennifer sat in the old man's chair at this desk. L.G. said it was here that he had come to see Clemenceau on several occasions. . . .

L.G. did not wish to go upstairs, but deferred to Jennifer's wishes that she insisted upon going. There we saw the heavy overcoat, the hat, the walking-stick, gloves, boots and leggings worn by Clemenceau when he went to the Front. Clemenceau always wore gloves, even in his office and at meetings. He suffered from some form of eczema, which necessitated his hands being kept in oil, hence the gloves.

At 11.30 L.G. went to see M. Paul-Boncour,[20] the Minister of Foreign Affairs.

Speaking of the Spanish situation, Boncour said that France was ready to do whatever was necessary, if the British Government was ready to support them.

L.G.: 'You won't get the British Government saying to you "Open your frontiers." But if you were to open your frontiers and pour your stuff in nothing would be said. The British Government would not intervene. They would allow it to be done. The British Government is a government of the right. Several of the more intelligent members of the Party, like Winston Churchill, were pro-Franco at first. But he now begins to see the danger, and is anti-Mussolini now. In my opinion they would be rather glad if it were done by France without her saying a word. All the intelligent men on the government side are coming round to that way of thinking.'

Boncour: 'For some time past, the frontier has been practically open. Nevertheless, the situation is now so critical that everything that can be done is not enough, and nothing is, short of real intervention.'

L.G. asked France to intervene to the same extent as Italy and Germany. He wrote on a piece of paper the urgent requirements of the Spanish Government – aeroplanes, heavy artillery, ammunition, staff officers. M. Boncour said the situation was so critical that nothing but French intervention, pure and simple, would save the Spanish Government. He said the military authorities in France were very anxious and did not want to go in too quickly. Everything would be possible if England and France acted together. France would be in a very dangerous position if she acted by

20. Joseph Paul-Boncour (1873–1972). Prominent among the French moderate socialists. Prime Minister 1932–3 and Foreign Minister on four occasions between 1933 and 1938.

herself. L.G. said the British Government lacked decision, but that if France got into trouble there would be no question of the attitude of England. 'You will have the advantage that all men of the left will rally to France, even if it were war.' At this point Boncour indicated that I should cease to take notes.

The Spanish Ambassador came to see L.G. at 6 p.m.

For dinner there were L.G., Frances, Pertinax[21] and his wife (M. and Madame Géraud) and myself. Talking of Neville Chamberlain, L.G. said he was narrow, with a certain amount of courage, but had an inability to see a new view.

When Neville had been at the Ministry of National Service, during the war, he had insisted on having as his chief adviser the town clerk of Birmingham, without whom Neville would do nothing. It had been a great mistake. Whenever there was a difficulty, Neville would explain that Mr So-and-so, his town clerk from Birmingham, where Neville had been Lord Mayor, said that everything was all right, and if he said it was all right, then it was all right. 'I cleared them both right out,' said L.G.

Of the Spanish situation, L.G. said to Pertinax: 'Make no mistake, if the French take the plunge[22] England and especially the workmen will be behind France. But don't wait for the British to take the initiative. Now is the time. Ten days hence may be too late.'

19 March
L.G. left with Frances and Jennifer for Versailles. L.G. was due with Prime Minister Blum[23] at the Matignon Hotel at twelve. At 11.55, I was just going out of the Crillon Hotel, thinking he had gone straight to his appointment, when L.G. rushed in like a madman. He went upstairs without speaking a word. He had sweated and his underclothes were wet. He changed and arrived for his appointment with M. Blum a quarter of an hour late, at a time when Blum had only just formed his ministry and was very pressed. He was late through buggering about with Jennifer at Versailles. I thought this distinctly bad taste.

Pictures of Lloyd George in Paris with Jennifer were published in various newspapers. One referred to her as his granddaughter and

21. André Géraud, prominent French journalist with pseudonym 'Pertinax'.
22. To assist the Spanish Republicans.
23. Blum started to form his second ministry on 10 March and was to resign on 8 April.

in another she was his 'small friend'. (Lloyd George and Sylvester are now back in England.)

25 March
Megan is bloody annoyed about the Paris visit, and so are the rest of the family. Only Dame Margaret is decent to me.

Difficulties come over the Lloyd George Political Fund owing to the almost simultaneous deaths of Lord St Davids and Sir John Davies, two of the three trustees. (Gwilym Lloyd George was the third.)

29 March
Cabled L.G. early this morning that Lord St Davids died last night.

31 March
When I returned to my room[24] just before three o'clock there was a telephone message from the office that Sir John Davies passed away at 1 p.m. I was stunned with shock. L.G. was so upset he could not talk. He could just say nothing. I talked with Sir John only yesterday. He told me a story and said he was off to Paris for a most important meeting on the Suez Canal.

11 April
A message has come from Frances to Tweed that L.G. talked of putting Tweed on a retainer, and he intended to effect this by bringing over to Thames House the staff of the Council of Action.[25] Thus Tweed's room would be required. Tweed was very angry. He said he would be damned if he would let the family get away with a quarter of a million of money.

14 April
L.G. is definitely very worried. He is confronted with two positions: (a) To have the Fund in his own name, or his nominees, arranged in such a way as he could do what he liked with it. In this case he would have to pay death duties and, besides, he is not quite certain of the attitude of some of the family at the moment, particularly Gwilym, whom L.G. thinks has got a swelled head.

24. At the House of Commons.
25. The Council of Action offices were in Abbey House, Victoria Street. Putting Tweed on a retainer would, in effect, be to dismiss him but to continue to pay him a salary.

L.G. thinks Gwilym will go to the right and Megan to the left, eventually. He wants his money spent on the left. (b) He could have a proper trust, but the difficulty then would be that he could not do as he liked with the money. L.G. wants to keep his cake and eat it.

Following the Anschluss of Germany and Austria, Czechoslovakia was now in a position of extreme difficulty. The German minority of Czechoslovakia, especially the Sudetenlanders, inflamed by Nazi propaganda, was in uproar. In April 1938 the Chamberlain government made an agreement with Italy which recognised the latter's conquest of Ethiopia. The aim of it was to detach Italy from Germany. On 2 May Lloyd George attacked this agreement in the Commons, saying that he had no doubt that Hitler and Mussolini had complete mutual understanding. If Mussolini had accepted the Austrian coup 'why should he boggle over Czechoslovakia?' Lloyd George's general line was, and continued to be, that there should be an alliance of Britain, France and the Soviet Union to deter German expansion in central and eastern Europe. He held that without Soviet participation Britain and France were almost powerless in this area. He was frequently in touch with Maisky, the Soviet Ambassador in London, as were Churchill and leading figures in the Labour Party. However, the Prime Minister, Neville Chamberlain, detested the idea of Anglo-Soviet co-operation.

2 May

L.G. listened to Neville opening the debate. L.G. spoke for forty-five minutes. Not only did he do well, but, what was more important today, he did well in his own estimation. Since the row with the Prime Minister in the House, he had lost confidence in himself. Coming out of the Chamber, he met Winston. 'A magnificent speech,' said Winston. Neville passed at that moment. Winston said: 'You are having a quiet time.' 'Yes,' said Neville, looking at L.G., 'I did have until just now.' The Prime Minister does not like L.G.: it is mutual.

After his speech we had dinner in the strangers' room. Present: L.G., Gwilym and Edna, Megan, little David[26] and myself. L.G. told a story of two old Welsh preachers, one of whom was a considerable poet. One was named Rees. One liked a glass of whisky as a nightcap. The other liked a good old soak, and his nose showed it. One

26. Son of Gwilym and Edna.

weekend these two found themselves staying with a family renowned in the locality for their total abstention. The hostess made an apology that there was no whisky available. The hostess, however, was a kindly and thoughtful soul. Later on, she went into the kitchen and asked the maid to go to the Red Li-on and get a bottle of whis-ky, tell Mr Jones the proprietor that Mr Rees was unwell. Meantime the host and hostess retired for the night. The maid returned, knocked at the door and found the two ministers on their hands and knees praying – praying that the Almighty might answer their supplications and send them some whis-ky. When the maid entered, the weather-eye of the hard-drinking parson caught sight of the bottle. 'Keep on praying hard,' he remarked to his brother-minister. 'The good Lord in his infinite mercy has already answered my prayer and he will soon be answering yours.'

At dinner L.G. congratulated Edna on her hat, which was covered with fur in Russian style. 'I made it myself,' she said. L.G. replied: 'It does credit to the creator, which is more than we can always say – of Him.'

20 May

On the invitation of L.G., I went to Churt for the inauguration by Dame Margaret of the irrigation scheme. I went with Dame Margaret and Olwen. We went off to the field 'to make it rain'. I had arranged for a grand lot of representatives of the Press to be present and all the film companies, illustrated papers, photographic agencies and the farming, fruit and market-gardening journals, to see how L.G. had produced rain in a veritable Sahara.

L.G. wanted to give the impression that *he* had arranged everything. He started by taking the car up the wrong road. Four cars following had to back. In the middle of Old Barn Lane, he got out and, like a shot from a gun, hatless, his white hair flowing out in the breeze, his Tyrolean cloak flying out in all directions, he made his way through the dust caused by the drought to where the crowd had assembled, leaving Dame Margaret and the rest of us half a field behind.

Dame Margaret turned on the wheel and the appliances started to work. It was truly remarkable. An inch of rain could be produced in eight hours. Four crops could be grown where one doubtful one is now raised. 300,000 gallons a day, a fine record. What he did not say was how much it had cost. It was more than £3000. He'll want to grow a few crops to pay for that.

Then the old showman demonstrated that he was a past master at advertising himself. With outstretched hand and up-raised stick, he pointed to the distant effect of rain, saying: 'Maggie, is not that just like the mountain mists in Wales.' As they stood side by side, photographed and filmed, one might have thought that throughout the years they had been the happiest and most united of couples. Instead he had cleared out Frances just before Dame Margaret arrived, and now he was only hurrying through this ceremony so that he could get rid of his family and have another demonstration for Jennifer.

Then L.G. walked up the hill at a terrific pace. I brought up Dame Margaret miles behind. Here we saw the pump over the well, which was 230 feet deep. Mrs Wyllie, the old Highland woman, was requested to give a demonstration of her water-divining faculty. She possessed herself of a new hazel twig. Then L.G. marched her to a particular spot. Here he fairly stormed and stamped because someone had removed a stone which he had put in the road to mark the spot where the twig and the hands were to start to work.

Then he had the water turned on from the well. It came out with a terrific rush – 300,000 gallons a day – pure water which, he said, had been subjected to a most careful analysis. He told the story of how Mrs Wyllie had divined the water. It was a marvellous story for the press representatives and photographers.

But there was another one, which has not been told. The 'rain' they saw came from the urban district council's waterworks and not L.G.'s well. They had not had time to connect it. After lunch, L.G. hastened off to Avalon, where Frances and Jennifer awaited him. He had arranged to have another demonstration for their benefit. This was the second story which the journalists and photographers did not get. Jennifer turned on the plant, and he presented her with a little bracelet in memory of the occasion.

24 May

A storm broke out at Churt this morning and extended very rapidly to me. Frances phoned to say that L.G. was very angry about a statement in the *Evening Standard* of last night and the *Daily Telegraph* of this morning which contained information which must have been the result of someone seeing his secret minutes.

The story is that Beneš had told L.G. that, at the time of the peace treaty, there were only one and a half million Germans in the area proposed for the state of Czechoslovakia, and that the facts today proved there were three and a half millions. This had not become apparent until after the treaty was signed. (L.G. maintains that the German minority has been ill-treated for years.)

Frances implored me to get some explanation. L.G. was saying that the journalists who wrote those paragraphs must have seen his minutes and he was accusing everyone at Churt, and me also.

'He is so horrible,' she said. I hunted high and low for an explanation. I found it. The statement originally appeared in the New York *Tribune*, published in Paris, and was based on the diary of an American secretary named Miller.

Lloyd George prepares to address an open-air meeting in support of the Labour candidate in the Stafford by-election.

2 June
When I got home tonight at 9.30 p.m., there was a message for me to telephone L.G. He told me he wanted a huge map prepared. Something which 5000 people could see easily. As he conversed, his imagination worked, and by the time he had finished he wanted something four or five times the size, so that it could be seen by 20,000 people. I told him he wanted a billposter. *That* struck his Celtic imagination. 'Yes, a *billposter*, something that can be seen.' And he wants it for this weekend, Whitsuntide.

3 June
I was at Stanford's this morning, discussing with them the layout of the huge map. They were able and willing to do it and the work was at once put into hand. The map will be about twenty-eight feet long and about twenty feet deep. It is the biggest they have ever made. It shows the encirclement of France by the Fascist powers, especially through the overrunning of Spain.

Yesterday Frances told me that L.G. had been most difficult with her, that when he informed her that he was not going to Criccieth for Whitsun she seemed disappointed, and said she had thought she could just last out until then. This had brought him to reason a little, but not for long. He was now always going round his orchard, counting thousands of small apples forming on the trees and making a computation of his crop. The truth is that he was after two girls on the estate.

4 June
Finney and I went to see the map. It is a monumental work and will be as large as one side of Brynawelon.

6 June
We left Euston on the 10.40 a.m. train and arrived at Stafford at 12.59. L.G. was full of talk of the map, which is his baby at the moment.

It was a marvellous meeting – my estimate was that there were 30,000 people present. On arrival there was no sign of the map; L.G. was very disappointed. It was said that the wind was too strong to put it up. With the help of a number of volunteers, we took this enormous map up the side of an adjoining hill. On arrival at the top, we unrolled it, and Tweed and I, along with a number of boys, sat around the edges to prevent it being blown away. It was so large that it could be seen perfectly from the top of the other hill, on which L.G. was speaking. . . .

8 June

L.G. was very angry this morning at an article in the *Evening Standard* of last night giving dimensions of the map, that I had sat on it to keep it from being blown away and saying that there were 300 present. I assured him it was only a typographical error, but he would not hear of it. He gave me phrases to give to Finney to be used in a letter from him to the Editor, complaining about misrepresentation. This was on his mind during the whole of the day.

10 June

We left Shrewsbury on the 4.35 train, after a committee meeting of the B.B.C.[27] Just before it ended, I handed him the result of the Stafford by-election, which showed a bigger majority than ever for the Tory candidate and fewer votes for Labour.[28] As we got into the compartment, he said : 'Give me my Wild West story to help me to forget about Stafford.'

22 June

L.G. was in the office at 10 a.m. and had interviews with bankers and lawyers. Things are difficult in regard to the Fund. L.G. twists about so much that he does not know himself where he is or what he wants. What he is really after is to get personal possession of the whole Fund and blue as much as possible of it in his life-time. That I gathered from a remark at lunch yesterday, apparently said in fun.

He has had an interview with his dentist. Let us hope he now has a decent set of teeth. The others would only stop up with a thick paste of Correga, which I always carry and give him before he makes a speech. He always dreads that his teeth might shoot out of his mouth in public.

27. The B.B.C. Welsh Religious Advisory Committee.
28. The Tory majority went up to 4408 as against 3661 in the 1935 general election : both were straight Tory–Labour fights.

L.G., Frances, my wife and I dined with L.G. at the Savoy Grill. He talked of his visit to Winston's house on Saturday. Winston had turned on his water, which had come rushing down. L.G. had remarked upon the large flow, but Winston had said he had been saving it up for weeks. L.G. had asked him how many gallons an hour he could produce. The reply had been 'Fifteen'. L.G. roared with laughter and said he could produce 20,000 gallons an hour.

26 June
L.G. took the chair at the annual Castle Street flower service and spoke upon : 'This is not the age of faith.'

4 July
L.G. came up from Churt alone – he had quarrelled with Frances and Tweed. I lunched with him in his room, after he had had an interview with Evan Davies, the solicitor acting in connection with J.T.'s estate.

L.G. said there was a lot to be said for smoking, especially after a meal. It prevented you getting up immediately afterwards and rushing off. He said he had been tremendously impressed with two sermons he had recently heard. One had been by John Williams, who had a lovely voice and could produce the *hwyl*. This could only be obtained by a man with a big, powerful voice. The first time he had ever experienced the *hwyl* had, oddly enough, not been in Wales but in a speech by John Redmond.[29] He talked about logic. He said he was guided not so much by logic as by instinct. He talked about agriculture and about Germany. He said : 'I would rather have a wild boar like Göring, than a lot of swine like Hoare and Neville.'

8 July
I doubt if anyone knows the exact position in regard to the Fund, but the following is a summary as I have gleaned it from L.G., Gwilym, Frances, Tweed and Miss Pitt.

St David's executors and those of J.T. [Davies] have satisfied the authorities that the monies and shares standing in their names, regarding the Fund, are not part of their private estate. That is all right. To whom they do belong is another matter. L.G. comes forward and says, 'They are mine.' Proof of this is not easy. If he claims them as his own, then he has to face the music as to why he has not paid tax on the income. If he says, 'They belong to my trust', then he may be asked, 'Where is your trust deed?' Answer:

29. John Redmond (1851–1918). Leader of the Irish Nationalist Party 1900–18.

'There is not one.' He has always wanted to keep his cake and eat it. Now I think he would be willing to pay super-tax, or anything else, as long as he could make sure that he was somehow or other going to get the Fund. That is his present anxiety – and a gigantic anxiety it is, too. The documents have been looked up and there seems to be no document which gives precise information on the point of exact ownership. It is a question which in former days was always burked.

Meantime, the executors of St Davids's estate have copies of letters sent by J.T. to Lord St Davids saying that £5000 was required for a holiday in Jamaica for L.G., or for building or something of the kind at Churt, making it clear that he was using this money for his own purposes. No wonder L.G. said to me the other day that in future he would be content with a modest $2\frac{1}{2}$ per cent interest. It is thought by some in the know that, instead of L.G. personally claiming the Fund as his own, he would be in a stronger position if he said that Gwilym had been a member of the committee since 1924 and that the money belonged to the committee, whatever it was.

There is no doubt that L.G. made the present Fund through his sale of the *Daily Chronicle*. But where did he get the original money from with which to buy the *Daily Chronicle*? Was it L.G.'s, and where lies the proof?

11 July
L.G. came up from Churt alone. He came into my room with a face like a yard of pump-water. I learn from Churt that he has been terrible there during the weekend. He has properly got the jitters about the Fund and about the meeting at the Public Trustee's office which he was attending at 4.30 tonight, when, besides Gwilym and himself, there were present representatives of St Davids's and J.T.'s executors and counsel for the Public Trustee.

26 July
L.G. received this morning a written decision from the Public Trustee saying that the Fund was his property.

Frances, Tweed, Finney and I accompanied L.G. to lunch in his room. When I reported that Morgan Jones, in today's foreign-affairs debate, intended to speak on Spain, central Europe and China, he scoffed at the idea. He said: 'I learned from Gladstone that to be effective in attack you must confine yourself to one subject on a narrow front. When Asquith used to attack me on a wide front, I knew I was well away, and just sat back and waited my time. Later, I picked out what subjects suited me, dealt with them at great length and apologised for not dealing with the rest because of lack of time.'

As he lay down on his settee and I pulled a light rug over him and got him a novel, for him to read himself off to sleep with, he said : 'I am greatly relieved this business is settled.' He was so pleased and relieved that I thought he would never stop talking about it. Of Radcliffe,[30] his K.C., he said : 'What a difference a big man makes.'

Radcliffe had come straight to the point. He had said to J.T.'s solicitors : 'Do you claim this money?' They had answered : 'No.' Then he had asked Lord St Davids's solicitors : 'Do you claim this money?' They had answered : 'No.' Radcliffe had said : 'In that case there is no doubt that it belongs to Mr Lloyd George, and I do not see what the trouble is about and why Mr Lloyd George has been troubled.' L.G. repeated : 'Radcliffe is a big man.' Radcliffe had gone on to talk about leases. 'That is a practical question,' he had said. 'Let us deal with that.'

27 August

I accompanied L.G. on the 11.5 train to Bangor. Pointing to a book, which he had placed on the opposite seat of our reserved carriage, L.G. said to me : 'That is the greatest book in the Welsh language.' It was the life of John Jones of Talsarn, written by the late Dr Owen Thomas of Liverpool. L.G. opened it at the title-page where there was a photograph of John Jones. Handing it to me, he said : 'Is not that a fine face?' L.G. was on his way to Wales to preside at the centenary meeting of Christmas Evans, one of the greatest preachers Wales has produced.

L.G. related how at the end of this book there was an example of Christmas Evans's style. L.G. said : 'Christmas Evans lived at the time when there was a great controversy between the Law and the Gospel. He was an allegorical preacher. He cited the case of a poor prisoner in the dock. The counsel pleaded for leniency, but the Judge said : "I am here to administer the Law. The Law must be kept. The prisoner must be condemned." Then a fair lady appeared. She informed the Judge that her name was "Mercy". She also pleaded that mercy should be shown to the prisoner. But the Judge was unable to reverse his decision. Downcast "Mercy" left the court and presently returned with a handsome young man on her arm. His head bore the marks of a crown of thorns and his hands the holes of the nails of crucifixion. On entering the court, this young man cried aloud : "In the name of justice, I demand pardon for the

30. C. J. Radcliffe (b.1899) became a K.C. 1935 and was a Lord of Appeal in Ordinary 1949–64.

condemned man." The Judge said that this was a plea he could not resist and he would therefore set the prisoner free.'

L.G. told of the governor of a gaol who visited a condemned man to inquire if there were anything he could do to help him by way of comfort. 'It is not comfort I want, but pardon,' said the condemned man.

L.G. told me that he had heard Spurgeon several times. What had struck him most was his earnestness, but there had been no dramatic appeal. The same had been true of John Clifford. Silvester Horne[31] had been a more dramatic preacher. There was, however, no one to compare with the old Welsh preachers.

L.G. took with him to Criccieth large supplies of fruit and vegetables. He insisted on having all this exhibited in the drawing-room. The place resembled a fruit-and-vegetable show. This was done to impress A. V. Alexander, who is to preach at Berea Chapel to-morrow.

28 August

We all went to Berea Chapel to hear A. V. Alexander preach on the text: 'The common people heard him gladly.' Afterwards L.G. congratulated him on 'a very powerful communist sermon'. Afterwards we all drove to Llanystumdwy to see the cottage where L.G. was brought up; his old uncle's cobbler's shop; the school which he attended; the house where Squire Nanney lived, whom he defeated as the member for Caernarvon Boroughs. L.G. is indeed a most remarkable man. Today he has been the devout nonconformist. At Berea this morning he and his family walked up to the front seat, which had been reserved. During the singing, he turned round and faced the audience. It was a sight to see L.G., who at heart is a true pagan if there ever were one, singing loudly and apparently feelingly. He is indeed a man of many parts.

29 August

Mr and Mrs Attlee and their four children came over to Criccieth, in response to an invitation from L.G. to join him in a picnic in the mountains. Today with the Alexanders, L.G., Dame Margaret, Megan, Lady Carey Evans and her four children, we motored

31. C. H. Spurgeon (1834–1892) was ordained a Baptist minister 1852 and rapidly became one of the most famous preachers of his day.

John Clifford (1836–1923) was minister of Praed Street and Westbourne Park Baptist Church, London for fifty-seven years.

Silvester Horne (1865–1914), ordained a Congregational minister 1889, chairman of the Congregational Union of England and Wales 1910–11, Liberal M.P. 1910–14.

through Blaenau Ffestiniog on the road to Dolwyddelen, where, in the mountains under the shadow of Snowdon, we had our lunch. It was very successful. In a conversation with Attlee and Alexander, L.G. said he would make a prediction. It was that Hitler would get all he wanted in Czechoslovakia without war, and that neither the French nor ourselves would fight.

At night Sir Arthur Salter[32] and Rowse,[33] a Labour candidate, called and stayed for dinner. Talk was, of course, political. Of Ramsay MacDonald, L.G. said: 'He had sufficient conscience to bother him, but not sufficient to keep him straight.'

The Czechoslovak crisis was now nearing its peak, with the Sudeten Germans rising in open revolt. On the basis of information obtained by Sylvester for him from the Soviet Embassy,[34] Lloyd George on 11 September published in the Sunday Express *an article advocating that Hitler should be warned that if he attacked Czechoslovakia he would have to face both the Soviet and French armies.*

13 *September*
L.G. talked with me alone. Strolling up and down his room, with his hands tucked in the top of his trousers, which is a favourite mannerism, he told me that Archie Sinclair had invited him to attend a meeting of the Liberal shadow cabinet. I said it was a national scandal that Neville had not called him into consultation in this national emergency. L.G. intervened to say that as the man who had organised this country for war, in all its aspects, he thought it would have been worth while for the Government to have consulted him. 'After all, there is only one man in this cabinet who held office during the war, and he was a complete failure – that is the Prime Minister himself.'[35]

32. Arthur Salter (b.1881) was a civil servant 1904–22, on the staff of the League of Nations 1919–20 and 1922–3, and Professor of Political Theory, Oxford, 1934–44. He was an Independent M.P. 1937–50 and was a junior minister and holder of other official posts 1939–45 and a Tory M.P. and minister 1951–3. Made a baron 1953.

33. A. L. Rowse (b.1903), the historian, stood as Labour candidate for Penryn and Falmouth 1935.

34. Sylvester's memo to Lloyd George on this occasion is among the Lloyd George papers in the Beaverbrook Memorial Library.

35. Lloyd George is referring to Neville Chamberlain's dismissal from the post of Director of National Service in 1917 on the ground of incompetence.

On 15 September 1938 Chamberlain flew to see Hitler at Berchtes-gaden and agreed in principle that Germany should have the Sudetenland area of Czechoslovakia.

19 September

Everybody is asking what L.G. is thinking about the Czechoslovakian situation. He has not been consulted by the Government, and is sick about this, but he is thinking far more about appointing a new farm manager at Churt than about the international situation.

War now seemed almost inevitable, owing to Hitler's determination to march into Czechoslovakia, despite the concessions he had been offered.

28 September

I lunch with L.G. in his room. Gwilym was there also – the first time they have seen one another for some weeks, because Gwilym has been in L.G.'s bad books through asking for financial assistance to get him out of a difficulty, caused by speculation I believe. Megan and Tweed were also present.

Tweed does not like Hitler. He remarked that Hitler was quite willing to commit many millions of men to slaughter. 'Ah,' said L.G., 'all the same, he is a brave man. He went through 1914. We felt then that we were committing others to something we ourselves had not been through. But Hitler has been through it all himself.'

L.G. talked of Czechoslovakia and what might have been if the promises made at the peace conference had been kept. 'We have committed ourselves to defend Czechoslovakia, which strategically is very difficult to defend. It is not such a good strategical position as Belgium was in in 1914. Supposing the Germans attack the Czechs from Hungary and attack that country around the waist, get the territory which contained the minorities and then ceased further aggression: are we still going to fight?' Both Gwilym and Megan asked L.G. what he would do. His reply was not very clear, and I think was not intended to be so. He said it was like someone asking a question of a dying man. He could only reply, 'I told you so', and then one would be criticised for harking back.

In the Commons, Chamberlain made a gloomy speech. Then towards the end of it a note was passed to him. It contained the message that Hitler, on the mediation of Mussolini, had agreed to a conference of Britain, France, Germany and Italy at Munich to settle the Czechoslovak crisis. The Tory side of the House of Commons rose in frantic cheering and Labour rose to cheer Attlee when he wished the Prime Minister's mission well. It was one of the most extraordinary scenes in the history of the Commons, with enormous emotional tension. Sylvester was there.

I shall never forget the demonstration that followed, unexampled in my experience or in that of anyone else I have met. Every government supporter rose and waved handkerchiefs and order papers, and cheered and cheered and cheered to the echo for several minutes. I stood on my tip-toes under the gallery to see whether L.G. was on his feet. He was not. I thought L.G. made a mistake.

30 September
I telephoned L.G. this morning and told him the latest story about Dame Margaret. Lady Carey Evans telephoned to her mother at Criccieth and said : 'Things are much better this morning.' 'Why?' inquired Dame Margaret. 'Have you been ill?' 'No, no,' said Lady Carey Evans. 'I mean in the international situation.' 'Phew . . . that thing,' said Dame Margaret, as much as to say that we in *Criccieth* have much more important things to think about than the international situation. When I had finished relating it to L.G., he roared with laughter and said : 'I think it is worth recording.' Little does he think this has already been done.

On 30 September an agreement was signed at Munich by which Czechoslovakia lost the Sudetenland to Germany. The Beneš government in Prague collapsed and this in effect was the end, for some years, of Czech nationalism. The unitary Czechoslovak state broke up and the country became Czecho-Slovakia, with substantial autonomy for Slovakia.

3 October
The P.M. opened the two-day debate on the Czecho-Slovak situation, giving an account of his visit to Munich.
We had dinner downstairs in the House. Present : L.G., Gwilym,

Edna, Megan and myself, and later Oliver Baldwin.[36] L.G. alluded
to Chamberlain's return from Munich on Friday, when there was
an immense crowd, when all cars were jammed, when the King and
Queen and Neville Chamberlain and his wife had come out on the
balcony of the Palace. But what had he got except this small piece
of paper which Hitler had signed, and just what did it mean?
'Neville came back with only a promise,' said L.G., 'but when
I returned, I brought back an added population of 100 million to
the British Empire, and the King came to greet me at Victoria
Station.[37]

The great question at the moment is whether L.G. will speak in
the debate. Tweed and Finney, during the whole of lunch, tried hard
to get him to promise to do so, but L.G. fobbed them off and said
his family were against it – all of them.

Presently Tweed and Finney left. L.G. put away his half-smoked
cigar, and I tucked him up with his rug. At the same time I handed
him his Wild West novel, entitled *The Fighting Tenderfoot*. I am
sure L.G. does not intend to speak. He left the House early and
returned to Churt, promising to come up tomorrow. It is terribly
difficult for me. Everybody in the lobby asks why L.G. has not
spoken. Letters are pouring into the office asking why he is silent
and for a lead from him.

5 October

L.G. decided not to come up at all, not even to hear Winston. My
summing-up of L.G.'s feelings these days is one of helplessness. He
knows more than anybody else about this question; he has been
ignored. He knows that Beneš, whom he hates, has brought this misfortune on his own people through not carrying out the conditions
of the treaty to give the minorities their rights, and to this extent
he is in favour of the Sudetens. That is not a position which can
easily be explained in public. L.G. said to me yesterday at lunch :
'You remember how that little swine behaved at the peace conference and again at Genoa? He would not take my advice.'

*Lloyd George attended the Commons on 6 October and, in company
with his family group of Gwilym, Megan and Goronwy Owen,
together with the Labour and Liberal parties, voted against the
Munich agreement. However, apart from interjecting a question on*

36. Oliver Baldwin (1899–1958) was son and heir of Stanley Baldwin
and an active socialist. He was a Labour M.P. 1929–31 and 1945–7.
37. When Lloyd George returned from signing the Treaty of Versailles
in 1919.

a technical point he made no speech. Churchill had spoken strongly against the agreement but merely abstained in the vote.

23 October

There is discontent in L.G.'s constituency because he has not addressed a political meeting there since the general election. His chairman wrote inviting L.G. to address a public political meeting. This letter arrived dated 22 September. I acknowledged it on 23 September, saying it would be brought to L.G.'s notice. On 10 October, E. P. Evans[38] at my instigation sent another letter to L.G. saying: 'There is a deep and genuine desire on the part of the members of the Association to meet you once more – both on personal grounds and because of the terribly difficult times we are passing through.' On 13 October, L.G. wrote personally: '. . . I am opposed to a big political demonstration. It does not lend itself to the calm and judicial – as well as the judicious – statement of the whole of the facts. In making a speech on this topic, I shall be suffering from an embarrassment from which most of the prominent controversialists are completely free, i.e., that I know the whole of the facts from the foundation of the Czecho-Slovak Republic to its practical failure.'

Lloyd George broke his silence on the Munich agreement on 26 October when, accompanied by Dame Margaret, he addressed the London Free Church Federation Ministers' Club on the theme 'The Free Churches and the World Situation'. In passage of his speech, which was strongly anti-Munich, he actually predicted that the ultimate outcome would be Britain 'without friends' at war with Germany. From this time onwards his imagination and intuition seemed to be foreseeing the disasters that were to come to Britain in the spring and summer of 1940: this sense of foreboding is, perhaps, the key to his attitudes which, from now onwards, were diverging from the conventional liberal–leftish line.

26 October

L.G. spoke at the City Temple, which was broadcast to America. Wickham Steed was in the chair.[39] L.G. made a very critical speech and hit right and left, especially when he said: 'Having urged the Czechoslovakian Government to make concessions, having succeeded

38. Chairman of Lloyd George's constituency party.
39. H. Wickham Steed (1871–1957). Editor of *The Times* 1919–22.

in doing so, we handed over a little democratic state in central Europe, the land of John Huss, wrapped in the union jack and the tricolour, to a ruthless dictator, who will deny freedom to Czechs and Germans alike. We were not ready even to defend ourselves, let alone rescue others. That is our only excuse for not standing up to the dictators, and history will ask but one question over that episode : "Is incompetence a justification for bad faith?" '

11 November
L.G. talked of setting aside a room at Thames House for Winston and Eden, so that they could make use of our records for their speeches.[40]

17 November
L.G. phoned me this morning to say he had decided to go to Criccieth to see Dame Margaret, who has been unwell for two weeks. Today he has suddenly developed a conscience. He is afraid of people talking.

Evelyn and I dined at 8 Victoria Road, with L.G., Frances, Tweed and Muriel. . . .

L.G. said that Hankey was a man with no humour. He had once offered to help L.G. to draft a speech. L.G. had replied that he already had everything except the peroration. Hankey drafted a peroration. L.G. roared with laughter and said that Hankey's peroration had been composed of contradictory similes, something like the ship of state going up a mountain. 'I wish I had kept it,' said L.G. L.G. said he had had an invitation to go to Buckingham Palace, but he had got out of it because he would not meet an immoral king – King Carol.[41]

21 November
I informed L.G. that the Sunday Dispatch had intended publishing a very unfriendly article about his Fund. An influential friend connected with the paper, to whom this article had been referred, had advised that it should be suppressed, and this had been done. Lately L.G. has been giving himself airs about his Fund, and I have not been satisfied about his attitude towards the office, so I was glad of

40. This was a cock-eyed idea and most unpractical. It came to nothing. Winston once asked me in the House to see one of L.G.'s secret papers. When I asked L.G.'s permission, he said NO. I could not see these two looking through those secret files ! A.J.S.
41. Carol II (1893–1953), King of Romania 1930–40. He had a notorious liaison with Magda Lupescu which caused much scandal and political upset.

this opportunity to let him know that there is such a thing as the public and the Press.

At lunch he flared right up when he thought of Herbert Samuel, whom he described as the politician he hated most. The meanest thing he had ever done had been, some years ago, to take as his own idea L.G.'s proposal to get together the economists, artists and writers who were Liberals. . . .

Finney said he had just reread the article L.G. wrote in the *Strand Magazine.* 'That is the one you wrote in Jamaica,' I added. 'Yes,' said L.G. 'I claim that the writing of that article was a feat of concentration. I wrote that article whilst sitting on my balcony, beneath which there were numerous half-naked beauties bathing in the pool below. So concentrated was I on my job that the result was that article. I give myself a 100 per cent for concentration.'

God forgive the thoughts that ran through my mind. I happened to be there. He took days to write that article and no fresh belle went into that pool without his noticing her.

22 November

Tonight Frances telephoned to me. From her manner I knew that L.G. was standing over her, telling her what to say. My story about the *Sunday Dispatch* had sunk in. She said: 'Would you tell your friend to tell his friend that the Chief does not mind at all if the article is published. Let them publish it, and he will retaliate. If they do anything about his Fund, he has got ample evidence about the Conservative Party, and he knows the names of people who have actually paid cheques for their honours. He has a complete dossier and he will proceed to retaliate, not only against the Conservatives but against the Simonites. He has plenty of evidence. If they like to publish, they can; he will do the same.' I smiled, and passed the information on to my friend, who told me that the thing was dead, at any rate for the time being.

8 December

I saw the balance sheet for Churt for this year, up to November. It disclosed a remarkable state of affairs on the farm. It showed expenditure at £11,534, income at £6030, and a deficit of £5504.

15 December

I discovered a note in L.G.'s handwriting in his case which was a draft will leaving me £1000, if still in his service, as a token of faithful and devoted service. When he came back from the chamber, he immediately went to his bag, looked for the envelope containing this note, looked at it and replaced it.

Chapter 11

'I want to stop this war'

1939

This was a bad year in European history. Britain was rearming with the determination to resist any further German expansion. In March the now enfeebled Czecho-Slovakian state collapsed. Hitler declared a German protectorate over the Czech part of it (Bohemia and Moravia); Slovakia became independent, with bits nipped off it by Poland and Hungary. Chamberlain felt personally affronted. On 31 March he gave unconditional British guarantees to Poland and Romania and, grudgingly, began to work towards an Anglo–Soviet alliance. The Soviets decided that the British were so lukewarm as not to be trusted and they settled for an agreement with Germany instead, by which they partitioned Poland and other areas of eastern Europe between them. Germany could then safely attack Poland and, as a consequence, Britain and France declared war. Lloyd George was appalled at what he regarded as incompetence on Chamberlain's part.

1 *January*
Tonight L.G. went to Wales on the midnight train with Valerie.[1] He intended to appear at Brynawelon in the morning disguised with a beard, in order to give a complete surprise to Dame Margaret. As he approached the drive, however, Olwen saw him coming before he had adjusted his disguise. Cannot make out why he has left Frances and Jennifer.

10 *January*
The Rev. Watkin Davies, a native of Criccieth and now of Birmingham, has written a life of L.G.[2] He has been assisted by William George.[3] He says this is the first volume. It just stops short of the war. L.G. took exception to three references: that his mother was a domestic servant, that he sacrifices his friends in favour of his

1. Daughter of Richard Lloyd George.
2. W. Watkin Davies, *Lloyd George: 1863–1914* (1939).
3. Lloyd George's brother.

enemies and that Charles Masterman[4] played a dominant part in
National Health Insurance. L.G. told me to tell Frances, who has
been dealing with the matter, that it was a most extraordinary
biography. Several aspects of his career were completely distorted. It
was Wee Free tittle-tattle which was spiteful. . . .

L.G. remarked at lunch : 'I have always said that Sylvester is "the
Card" in Arnold Bennett's story.'[5]

20 *January*
Returned to London with L.G.

31 *January*
Tweed, Finney, Frances and I accompanied L.G. at lunch in his
room at the office. There was a first-class debate on the foreign
situation in the House, in which there is no doubt L.G. should have
spoken. At lunch he went into a long explanation to show why it
was useless speaking in the House when there was such a big
majority against one. Gladstone and Joe Chamberlain had realised
that in such circumstances it was useless, and they had spoken in
the country.

*The following passage is possibly the most significant in the whole
of Sylvester's diary. It gives the first full account of his meeting, on
Lloyd George's behalf, with Maisky, the Soviet Ambassador, on the
day of the British unconditional guarantee to Poland, which was one
of the immediate causes of British involvement in war.*

31 *March*
L.G. telephoned me early this morning to seek an interview with
the Soviet Ambassador, M. Maisky, before the statement by the
P.M. in the House of Commons today. L.G. was coming up and he
wanted to know what was the precise information from the Soviet
side before the statement was made.

M. Maisky told me : 'I do not know what the statement is likely
to contain. I heard in a roundabout way that something is in
preparation. As far as we are concerned, we were not consulted
about it and we were not a party to this agreement.' He understood
that the agreement was between Great Britain and France on the
one side and Poland and Romania on the other. Britain and France
pledged themselves to come to the aid of the other two countries

4. Charles Masterman (1873–1927) was a junior minister 1908–15 and
a prominent Liberal M.P. and writer.
5. Arnold Bennett's *The Card* (1911), about a young man on the
make.

in case of aggression. Mr Maisky added: 'We were not consulted about it and have not been informed. I heard something about it, but not officially.'

On L.G.'s arrival at the House, I told him the gist of the above. He was amazed.

I lunched with L.G. at the House and he was in his place at 3 p.m. when the P.M. made a statement, after which I saw David Margesson[6] throw an envelope across the floor of the House, which L.G. picked up. It was a private letter from Neville Chamberlain to L.G. to say he would be glad to see him in his room at the adjournment.

After meeting the P.M., L.G. told me the P.M. had said that the German Army would not fight on two fronts. L.G. had asked: 'What is there on the other front?' The P.M. had replied: 'The Polish Army.' L.G. had pointed out that the Poles were very inadequately equipped and they had not got an air force. Neither had the French and ourselves a force equal to facing the Germans with the help of the Italians. Therefore he thought that Russian aid was indispensable. The Prime Minister's view had been that Russia would come in ultimately. L.G. said that this was a very reckless gamble. The Prime Minister had been fairly confident that Hitler would recoil when he realised that he was being confronted with a war on two fronts and had a feeling that Mussolini would not fight.

I carried this information to M. Maisky from L.G. this evening. M. Maisky told me that he had been summoned to see Lord Halifax[7] at the Foreign Office at 1 p.m. Lord Halifax had read out to him the statement which the P.M. was to give the House this afternoon and had asked M. Maisky's opinion on it. M. Maisky had replied that certainly this was a very considerable advance on previous statements on foreign affairs but it seemed to him that this state-ment was not quite clear, because the crucial point was the phrase to the effect that the British Government 'would feel themselves bound at once to lend the Polish Government all support in their power'. This might be interpreted in different ways. Lord Halifax had said that it was intended to include military support. Lord Halifax had further pointed out that this was in a way an emergency statement and that his government had not abandoned the idea of coming to a more general and permanent agreement with other peaceful powers to prevent further aggression taking place.

6. H. D. R. Margesson (1890–1965) was currently Government Chief Whip.
7. Edward Wood, Viscount Halifax (1881–1959), was currently Foreign Secretary.

H

Lord Halifax had then asked His Excellency whether the P.M. might state in the House of Commons that the declaration, which Lord Halifax had just read out, was approved by the Soviet Government. M. Maisky had said that he could not approve the declaration because the Soviet Government had not been consulted when it was drafted. He had never seen it until this moment. M. Maisky had said: 'I cannot see my way to agree to the P.M. saying anything like that in the House.'

M. Maisky explained to me that, as a consequence, that statement which was read out in the House of Commons by the P.M. was different to the one read out to him by Lord Halifax. M. Maisky referred me to a particular passage read out by the P.M.: 'The Foreign Secretary saw the Soviet Ambassador this morning and had a very full discussion with him on the subject, and I have no doubt that the principles upon which we are acting are fully understood and appreciated by the Soviet Government.' M. Maisky laughed the laugh of disgust. He agreed with L.G. in saying that this was a reckless gamble on the part of the P.M. to believe that he could really stop Hitler by combining Great Britain, France and Poland.

On 3 April in a foreign-affairs debate Lloyd George strongly attacked the Government. He warned that, without Soviet participation, the guarantee to Poland was 'walking into a trap' and would lead to war of a 'kind that would just suit Hitler'.

5 April
On L.G.'s instructions I went to see M. Maisky at 3.15 today to ascertain what was the precise position.[8] He told me that he had not been invited by the Foreign Office and was simply waiting. He was very pleased with L.G.'s speech; he said it had been a very telling speech and had said what ought to be done if the British Government were in earnest. The Soviet Union was quite prepared to wait, if it were necessary, but if it were all a colossal piece of bluff the less they were connected with that bluff the better.

6 April
The House adjourned today. L.G. came up. The P.M. made a statement on the international situation. When he said, in answer to a supplementary question about Russia, that the Government were in close touch with the Soviet Government, L.G., although primed to

8. Over Anglo-Soviet negotiations.

the teeth through my interviews, said not a word but merely shook
his head. I felt as sick as mud. What has happened to his rapier
which at one time he would have run right through his adversary?

In the car L.G. talked to me about Winston. This morning, he
said, Winston had talked to him in private conversation about our
'smashing through' in case of war. L.G. had asked him: 'With
what?' L.G. said they had been talking alone, but Winston had been
talking so loudly that others had come up to ascertain their views
on the P.M.'s statement. L.G. had been so annoyed with Winston's
views that he had walked away.

*On 27 April Chamberlain announced in the Commons that the
Government would bring in legislation to empower it to call up
men of twenty and twenty-one for six months' military training.
This was the first ever peacetime conscription in Britain. A debate
followed.*

27 April

L.G. came up from Churt for the debate on conscription. He had
made elaborate preparations for his speech, and I arranged with the
Speaker's secretary that he should speak at about seven o'clock.

The Prime Minister, in the first few minutes of his speech,
opened point-blank fire on L.G., who sat opposite, when he said:
'It is a fixed part of the practice of the Right Honourable Gentleman
to belittle or pour contempt on everything that this Government
does. The further in time the Government gets from the period when
he himself was Prime Minister, the worse it gets in his estimation.
I do not know whether he is going to speak in this debate. If so, it
will be interesting to know whether he is in favour of a larger
measure of conscription, or against conscription altogether. I am
sure that he is agin the Government whatever they propose.'

In face of the Prime Minister's attack, I expected L.G. to intervene
at once. But he just sat. Attlee followed the P.M., then Sinclair and
then Winston. L.G. sat through the lot. When Winston sat down,
L.G. left the chamber and I followed him to his room. There I
found him trying to bite a Genasprin in two. On his table were
various bottles from brandy to whiskey and whiskey to medicine.
He said he had an attack of neuralgia. 'It is across my eyes and
round my neck and I am taking Genasprin to try to cure it.' He
took one and a half Genasprin, then paced round the room, rubbing
his forehead and his neck with his hand. I asked L.G. when he was
going to speak. 'I cannot speak with an attack of neuralgia if you

paid me 500 guineas,' he replied. I was thunderstruck. I had just told everybody in the lobby that he was speaking at once.

L.G. gave a long dissertation on the bad effects of neuralgia. Then a letter arrived from Dame Margaret, who was in the ladies' gallery. 'Ah,' said L.G., 'the old gel would like to come to dinner.' Everything was fixed up, and eventually L.G., Dame Margaret, Megan, Mr and Mrs Thorpe, Olwen and Carey, Gwilym, D. O. Evans[9] and I sat down to dinner. From eight o'clock until eleven, L.G. never stopped talking. He stayed until 11 p.m. and voted with the Government.

At about 10.30 p.m., when the ladies of the party had gone, Eden, with Jim Thomas and Charles Peake[10] of the Foreign Office, joined L.G.'s party and had liqueurs and a cigar. L.G. asked Eden what he thought of Hitler and Mussolini. Eden replied that, having met both personally, he believed that Hitler is sincere but the other fellow – Mussolini – is just a gangster. L.G. thought we had most to fear from Mussolini because of the Mediterranean. Eden said that we ought to have an agreement between Great Britain, France and Russia. L.G. agreed.

On 8 May Lloyd George made one of his most bitter and telling attacks on the foreign policy of the Chamberlain government. It was on the second reading of the bill to introduce conscription. He said he would vote for the bill but that it was inadequate in view of the commitments the Government had entered into. He said that three years before the start of war in 1914 there had been detailed preparations, with roles worked out for the French, Russians and British. Now there was no such thing. France faced possible war on three fronts – from Germany, Italy and Franco Spain – instead of just one. There was no agreement with Russia and without this the Government guarantee to Poland was 'madness'. He said that British guarantees to Poland, Romania and Greece were 'the most reckless pledges that any country had ever entered into' and that they were 'demented pledges'. The official Liberal line on the conscription bill was abstention from voting, but the Lloyd George family group all voted in favour.

9. D. O. Evans (1874–1948). Liberal M.P. 1932–48 and a leading figure in Welsh cultural life.

10. J. P. L. Thomas (1903–60). Tory M.P. 1931–55, a government whip 1940–3, a junior minister 1943–5, a minister 1951–5 and created Viscount Cilcennin 1955.

Charles Peake (1897–1958) was currently head of the Foreign Office News Department.

8 May

L.G. came up from Churt to deliver his much-promised speech, upon which he had been working for days.

When he returned from lunching with M. Maisky at the Embassy, he told me that M. Maisky was very depressed and feared that his country might return to a policy of isolation.

L.G. spoke for fifty-five minutes. Afterwards, Dame Margaret, Frances and others sent him notes of congratulation. He was sick because he had not received one from Megan, though she had sent one and it did not arrive. After every speech he always likes these notes and gets frightfully sick if he does not get them, as well as verbal messages from everybody. If you don't congratulate him, you are quickly informed that you have sinned against the light.

Afterwards he dined in a private room in the House, accompanied by Dame Margaret, Megan, Macmillan and myself. Dick Law[11] came in later. Talking about Bonar Law, L.G. said that every morning[12] he used to breakfast early and then went into No. 11[13] to see Bonar to discuss the prospects for the day. Bonar's invariable remark was: 'We have lots of trouble.' L.G. would inquire, 'What is your trouble?' and Bonar would tell him all about his difficulties in the House. Then L.G. would tell Bonar all his troubles in the international sphere. 'He always acted on me. . . .' Macmillan interrupted: 'Like soda water to a brandy.' L.G. said: 'Exactly. It kept me down, for my qualities in certain circumstances might become my defects.'

Dick Law asked what was Eden's future. After a pause, L.G. remarked that if he was not brought into the Government the British Empire would suffer one of the biggest disasters in its history. L.G. suggested to Macmillan that he and his friends ought to table a resolution to the effect that as the country was in great danger there should be a change of premiership.

L.G. spoke more about Bonar Law. He said that he and Bonar were at Cannes and were motoring over to play golf at Cagnes. 'I told Bonar that, on the previous evening, I had been to a Mozart concert and the music was wonderful. Bonar casually and languidly remarked: "I don't care for music." As we motored along, there was the Mediterranean blue sea on one side and the rolling snow-capped Alpes Maritimes on the other. This inspired me to exclaim: "Look,

11. Richard Law (b.1901), son of Bonar Law. Tory M.P. 1931–54, a junior minister 1940–3, a minister 1943–5.
12. That is, when Lloyd George was Prime Minister and Bonar Law was Tory leader serving under him.
13. 11 Downing Street.

Bonar, what a wonderful scene that is." "I don't care for scenery," remarked Bonar. Presently we came to a bridge.' Here, addressing Dame Margaret, he laughingly said: 'You must not listen to this.' He went on: 'I said to Bonar: "Look, Bonar, aren't those handsome women?" "I don't care for women," remarked Bonar very drily. "Then what the hell do you care for?" I asked. Then in his very soft voice, and quieter still, Bonar replied: "I like bridge."'

15 June

There is a hell of a row in Caernarvonshire and in Anglesey because L.G., Goronwy Owen and Megan voted in favour of conscription. This trouble has been increased by a number of pacifist ministers of the gospel. These, and a number of others, quite decent ministers, are upset because of the desire of the Air Ministry to have Sunday bombing and air-fire practice in the Lleyn peninsula.

L.G. and I talked of Horatio Bottomley. L.G. told how Bottomley called one day upon Lord Cholmondley. When the butler answered the door, Bottomley said: 'Is Lord Chol-mond-ley in?' 'Lord *Chum-ley*,' corrected the butler. 'All right, tell him that Mr *Bummerly* would like to see him' was the answer.

25 June

L.G. presided at the annual flower service at Castle Street Chapel. This is his forty-ninth appearance.

Afterwards Evelyn[14] and I went to tea with L.G. and Dame Margaret at 8 Victoria Road.[15] L.G. said he could just remember his first general election; it was in 1868 when he was five years old. The Liberal candidate was a man named Parry. He had learned his Welsh, such as it was, in the kitchen. He was addressing a meeting one day in the local chapel in south Caernarvonshire when he suddenly turned round to his chairman, Mr Rowlands, and in an aside which was audible asked: 'What the devil is "religion" in Welsh?'

28 June

L.G. has turned peculiar with Finney. He has developed a very weird idea that when Finney accompanies Tweed home from Churt by car late at night Tweed drops him at the bottom of the road and then Finney walks back to L.G.'s house and sleeps with Frances. That is why for many nights L.G. has several times peeped into

14. Mrs A. J. Sylvester.
15. Lloyd George's London home from the end of 1937.

Frances's room in the dead of night to see if anybody is with her. On sex matters, L.G. is absolutely mental.[16]

At a by-election in north Cornwall, the Liberals were defending the seat in a straight fight against the Tories.

7 July

When L.G. is to make a speech, he gets wildly excited. Ever since he decided to go to the North Cornwall by-election I have been continually on the telephone to North Cornwall finding out how the election is progressing and making arrangements for the trip. Tonight he came up to Victoria Road in readiness for the journey to North Cornwall in the morning. He telephoned me this morning to dine with him tonight, and later asked Tweed. . . .

He said he had been reading Dumas. 'He is damned good,' remarked L.G. 'I was brought up on Macaulay, Carlyle, Dumas and, later, Ruskin.' He said he liked Wild West stories for relaxation, but if he wanted mental stimulation, then he would read Froude's essays. Simply as a distraction, however, a Wild West novel gave you all the description and all the thrill and you knew it would come out right in the end; but you did not know how, and so there was always an element of surprise.

Dame Margaret, who had been speaking at a Liberal fête at Liverpool, telephoned for Megan. L.G. tried – very inadequately – to speak with a woman's voice.

L.G. said how Dame Margaret loved attending meetings. 'Personally I hate them,' he said. 'Dr Smith is a wise old fellow,' said L.G. 'He advised me not to talk too much before and after my speech. I had not thought about that before, but Smith said it took up more energy than actually making a speech. By Jove, he is right. Disraeli found that out and in the end he made up his mind never to talk when he went out to dinner. That is why I cut out all social events. Talking for two hours an evening in order merely to entertain needs a lot of energy. Gladstone did much the same; he would not attend dinners.'

'It's a bloody world,' he remarked as he prepared to go to bed. 'It is the first time in my life that I have not been able to formulate a clear idea of my own as to what should be done.'

16. There was, of course, not the slightest substance in L.G.'s suspicions. I recorded them to throw light on L.G., not on Finney or Miss Stevenson. A.J.S.

8 July

I met L.G. at Victoria Road and accompanied him to Paddington
where we left on the 10.30 a.m. train for Newquay, Cornwall.
Tweed nearly missed the train. L.G. alternately slept and worked
on his speech, and we had a picnic lunch of chicken and ham. He
is about the dirtiest eater I have ever met. He had a collection of
butter, bacon fat and orange juice all down his coat and trousers.

L.G. started to speak at 8 p.m. and almost immediately it started
to rain. But the vast crowd assembled in the open and, numbering
8000, remained unperturbed. It was the biggest crowd ever assembled
in Newquay.

14 July

The Soviet Ambassador lunched at the House with L.G. During
lunch I got the result of the Newquay by-election and ran post-
haste to L.G. to tell him that the Liberal was in.[17] He was delighted.
He had said in the car that if we lost he would have a glass of wine
to cheer him up, but if we won he would have two.

18 July

Evelyn and I went to the inauguration dinner of the London Welsh
Regiment, of which L.G. is President, at the Park Lane Hotel. L.G.
was in the chair and Hore-Belisha, Secretary of State for War, was
the chief guest. It was a grand affair and L.G. made a fine speech.
I was amused by a passage in it in which he said that memory was
composed of the things that we wanted to remember.

31 July

On Saturday L.G. told me that he would come up for today's
debate on foreign affairs. He did not come, however. Instead, he
was busy playing with Jennifer in a caravan in one of the fields,
where he remained all day.

*The Government proposed to adjourn Parliament for the summer
recess from 4 August to 3 October, with provision for it to be
recalled early in the event of a crisis. In view of the state of foreign
affairs and the possibility of war, many M.P.s objected to this.
However, the Government carried the day.*

2 August

Today was very important in the House, where the Prime Minister
introduced a motion for the adjournment of Parliament. It was

17. The Liberal held the seat, with an increased majority.

violently opposed by the Opposition, also by some of the Tories, including Winston, Cartland[18] and Sandys. Cartland's speech was the most terrific onslaught I have heard on the Prime Minister for a long time. Of course, L.G., who had promised all sorts of people that he would be present, did not come to the House at all. Again, he was playing with Jennifer in the caravan. I reported to him on the telephone as usual what took place. But he is a most unappreciative fellow. When you have given him everything you know, all he can do is to ask : 'Have you any news?'

4 August

L.G., Winston and Bracken lunched together. L.G. told me afterwards that he had advised Winston not to go in with Neville's government. They would only sit on his head. If he went in now and there were an election, Neville would claim that it had been *his* victory. Bracken had told L.G. that he was absolutely right and that he had been telling Winston this for weeks. Winston was passionately fond of office, yet, said L.G., 'He has made all his reputation out of office. Joe Chamberlain was the same. Bright and Cobden did likewise. Charles James Fox was the same.' L.G. himself had no hankering for office, he said.

L.G. said: 'Sometimes when I am on my own, I shriek with laughter. One might think it was the result of old age. It is nothing of the kind. I am just recalling one or two amusing incidents which never fail to amuse me.'

8 August

Colonel Davies, of the newly formed London Welsh Regiment, came to lunch at Brynawelon with his son. L.G. related the story of John Elias giving an address on elocution and the importance of emphasis. Noting that old Sir Watkin of Wynnstay was asleep on the platform, John Elias said, speaking very softly: 'Were I to say "Sir Watkin Williams Wynn Wynnstay is on fire", it would have no effect. But if I were to say, speaking in a loud voice, with great emphasis: "Sir Watkin Williams Wynn Wynnstay, is on F-I-R-E", it would have a different effect.' In an instant, old Sir Watkin was aroused and he shouted out whilst still half asleep: 'Fetch the buckets.'

On 21 August it was announced in Berlin that Germany and the Soviet Union had concluded a non-aggression pact. This was a

18. Ronald Cartland (1907–40) was a Tory M.P. 1935–40. He died in action in May 1940: it was reckoned that he had much political promise.

thunderbolt, not least to the British Government. A German attack on Poland was now almost inevitable.

24 August

Yesterday morning received wire from L.G. asking me to return from holiday; left at once and motored as far as Devizes, and arrived in London this morning.

I met L.G. in the office; he received me kindly. He was most depressed and pessimistic. Walking round his room in his customary fashion when he is thinking hard or worried, he said that three times in the past he had pointed out that our guarantee to Poland was madness and insane and he had not altered his view. He was exceedingly apprehensive lest Neville Chamberlain had not landed us in a trap. I have not seen L.G. so pessimistic, ever.

On 1 September German troops crossed the Polish border. The British Government gave the Germans an ultimatum that unless they withdrew by 11 a.m. on 3 September Britain would commence war against Germany.

3 September

I waited in my room at the House of Commons and listened to Big Ben, sitting right above my head, boom out eleven o'clock on this Sunday morning. L.G. arrived at about 11.30 and immediately afterwards there was an air-raid warning. He asked me to get hold of Frances and take her to the refuge. He went off to it himself, carrying his gas mask. It was stiflingly hot in the refuge. Everybody was very calm and good-humoured. If Hitler could have seen these representatives of democracy in an A.R.P. refuge within half an hour of the Prime Minister's declaration of war, how he would have chortled. Very soon the 'all-clear' signal was given, and L.G. came up to his room very bucked, saying it was well worth while coming up to have had this experience of an air-raid warning; he was a little annoyed that I suggested that it might have been a dud warning for he wanted to believe that he had been in a real one.

He regaled himself with whiskey and went into the House, arriving in time for prayers. I watched him through the door kneeling down. I wondered what was going through his mind. It is a long time since he has said his prayers anyhow. L.G. made a short speech in which he generally supported the action of the Government. Referring to the Great War, he said: 'The nation closed its ranks then. By that means, we went through right to the end, and after four and a half years, terrible years, we won a victory for right. We will do it again.'

L.G. invited Frances and me to lunch with him in the strangers' room. First of all Bob Boothby[19] joined us, then Sir John Anderson[20] and then Sinclair. L.G. remarked that Labour were right in not joining the Government, and when Sinclair arrived L.G. said he hoped he would not do so. He said he had already told Winston the same thing.[21] Archie said that he thought Winston was in a different position. Boothby said: 'You have only to show Winston a red box and he would fall for office. But he would stand out from the rest.' L.G. retorted: 'Yes, but let him make sure that he does stand out all right.' L.G. said that Neville Chamberlain was not the man to wage a war. 'Look at his head. The worst thing Neville Chamberlain ever did was to meet Hitler and let Hitler see him. Who else is there?' Answering his own question, L.G. quickly added: 'Well, there is always the pale young curate', by which he meant Halifax.

'What would you do?' asked Boothby. L.G. replied: 'They always ask you that question when they are in a mess. Look at that discussion on Poland. I could not believe it when I heard that declaration.'

'Can anyone tell me how we can help Poland?' L.G. asked. 'And when are we going to start?'

Colin Coote[22] of The Times came up and was very optimistic. He said the Poles were splendid fellows and fighting well. 'What can we do?' asked L.G. 'Attack the Siegfried Line,' replied Coote. 'At any rate that is Gamelin's[23] idea.' Coote thought he could do it, but it would be very costly. Coote thought the Poles were brilliantly led. L.G. said he hoped he was right.

19. Robert Boothby (b.1900). Tory M.P. 1924–58, junior minister 1940–1, made a life peer 1958.

20. John Anderson (1882–1958) was a civil servant 1903–32, Governor of Bengal 1932–7, a National M.P. 1937–50, in the Cabinet 1938–45 and created Viscount Waverley 1952.

21. Churchill disregarded this advice and accepted office the same day as First Lord of the Admiralty.

22. Colin Coote (b.1893) was a Coalition Liberal M.P. 1917–22, became parliamentary sketch-writer of The Times and was managing editor of the Daily Telegraph 1950–64.

23. Maurice Gamelin (1872–1958) was Allied Commander-in-Chief in France 1939–40.

In the Sunday Express of 10 September Lloyd George wrote an
article deriding Italian fighting power and saying that it represented
no real threat to Britain. The Government, which wanted to keep
on good terms with Italy, was embarrassed. Churchill, presumably
at Chamberlain's behest, wrote to Lloyd George to complain.

12 September

L.G. sent a snorter of a reply to Winston, saying that the Cabinet
had no understanding of the tragic mess into which they have
plunged this country. In his article he had not been sneering at
Italian bravery but pointing out that no peasant army will fight if
its heart is not in its cause. Since war was declared, he had refrained
from saying publicly what he thought of the crass ineptitude by
which we had allowed ourselves to be manœuvred into a terrible
conflict under the most hopeless conditions. His article had been
an attempt to gather as many elements of hope as were still left
for us in a terrible situation. He wished Winston good luck in his
difficult task.

By now the Polish forces had almost been annihilated by the
Germans. On 12 September Soviet troops entered Poland from the
east to occupy the areas allotted to them by a secret clause in the
Soviet–German pact.

18 September

L.G. telephoned me at 8.30 this morning, asking me to see the
Soviet Ambassador and the Ukrainian representative in London for
information on the following: What is the nature of the population
of White Russia, which is the territory which the Russians are now
invading? What is their language? Are they Poles by race,
language or religion? He also wanted to know whether the Russians
intended to leave any Poland at all, or to divide it between themselves and Germany.

I was received by the Soviet Ambassador at 3 p.m. I like M.
Maisky; he has always been kind to me. I got all the information
I wanted about race, language and religion, but what interested me
most was his personal view of the intentions of his government and
of the Germans. His understanding was that the Soviet intended to
create a Polish national state more or less within Polish ethnographical boundaries. The parts which were now being invaded were
outside that ethnographical boundary and, laughingly, he added:

'Even beyond the Curzon Line.'[24] They only wanted returned to them what had belonged to Russia twenty years ago and which had been torn off by Poland with the help of the Allies. Then he added significantly: 'Otherwise we would have left it to Germany to occupy.' As I bade him adieu, he said very deliberately: 'Things may not turn out so bad as they now appear.' Later I had an interview with Dr Kisilewsky, who represents the Ukrainians in this country.

20 September
When L.G. arrived this morning, I suggested to him that he should demand a secret session in the House. At 11.30 a number of M.P.s came to see him. This is the nucleus of the parliamentary action group, which included Miss Rathbone,[25] Harold Nicolson, Bob Boothby, Graham White[26] and several others. Boothby said they must get rid of Neville Chamberlain. L.G. suggested to these people that there ought to be a secret session. This group met again in the evening and L.G., who had returned to Churt, asked me to phone him the result. Wilfrid Roberts[27] told me that the Tories had been very enthusiastic. They wanted L.G. to address them and they were also very keen on a secret session.

27 September
At twelve noon, I attended the parliamentary action group with L.G., who was invited to address them. He preferred to answer questions and did so in brilliant fashion. It was a thoroughly representative group of twenty-three of all parties.

3 October
Several persons asked me in the lobby last night whether L.G.'s article in the Sunday Express meant that he was in favour of peace now. This morning Jack Broadbent telephoned me that L.G. ought to be bloody well locked up, that it was understood he was out for peace at almost any price and that he ought to make a statement in the House if this were not the case.

When I got to the office, there was one letter among many which congratulated L.G. upon insisting on peace. I kept it to show him.

24. The Curzon Line was a suggested frontier for eastern Poland drawn up in 1920 by Lord Curzon, the British Foreign Secretary of the time. In fact, as a result of the Soviet–Polish war of 1919–21, the Poles won considerable territory to the east of this line.
25. Eleanor Rathbone (1872–1946), Independent M.P. 1929–46.
26. H. Graham White (1880–1965), Liberal M.P. 1929–45, junior minister 1931–2.
27. Wilfrid Roberts (b.1900), Liberal M.P. 1935–50.

When he arrived at the office, I told him of my experience. He walked towards the window overlooking the Thames and I walked with him. I said to him bluntly: 'Are you in favour of peace *now*?' His answer was: 'I am in favour of fighting if these fellows won't settle on reasonable terms. The question is whether you are prepared to meet and discuss terms.' Those were his words, taken down at the time. From his demeanour as much as from his answer, I read that he did want peace now. It was a shock for me.

Presently I had further evidence. Tweed and Finney were sent for, and in my hearing L.G. said: 'We are going to lose this war.' In the afternoon, I accompanied him to the House. In the car, he said: 'I want to stop this war, otherwise it will mean the break-up of the Empire.' Then he added: 'And Liddell Hart agrees with me. All the points are directed against us.' . . .

In the House, the P.M. made his statement and made it clear that we intended to fight on. So did Attlee and so did Sinclair. L.G. immediately followed. He made a most remarkable speech, not because of what he said but because of what he did not say. He created, by his personality, the impression that we had damned well lost and that we should come to terms. But he damned well did not say so. L.G. has that great gift. In private he is doing it every day of his life on some poor devil, but I have never before seen him do it in public with such success. In my opinion, Duff Cooper[28] was nearer to the truth than most people imagine when he said: 'The Right Honourable Gentleman's words will go out to the world, with his name at the head of them, as a suggestion of surrender.' During the whole of Duff Cooper's speech, Winston was applauding him. When L.G. protested, his voice showed very clearly that he felt the sting. I could read more into that speech than most people, for I know his mind, which is far in advance of what he said. When he came up to his room, he had regained some of his perkiness and was quite ready to receive adulation for his speech from Frances – she had left him a note, as usual. For the first time in my life, I said not a word of congratulation.

4 October

I was exceptionally busy collecting opinions of L.G.'s speech. There is no doubt that opinion is growing in his favour, but I am very perplexed whether M.P.s realise what he really means. I do not believe that they realise he is a defeatist. They think he only wants to make sure that the peace proposals receive very careful consideration.

28. A. Duff Cooper (1890–1954) had resigned over the Munich agreement.

9 *October*

The post which L.G. is receiving as a result of his speech in the House is the greatest I have ever known. It comes in large batches by every post and he has received thousands. All these I send to Churt. I notice that they all cry out for *peace*, but none of them say on what conditions. And for the life of me I have no clear idea of what conditions L.G. would impose, if any.

10 *October*

L.G. is jubilant about the number of letters he has received and talks of nothing else. He told me on the telephone this morning that he had received a wire from Rothermere saying: 'Warm congratulations. Go on. You will win hands down.'

12 *October*

L.G. came up from Churt accompanied by Frances. I lunched with them, though I was delayed because Captain Liddell Hart telephoned me from Totnes his private views on the situation for L.G. Liddell Hart takes very much the same line as L.G., though he does face up to the difficulty: how can you have a peace conference without admitting defeat? Since Liddell Hart doubts we can win, his way out would be to arrange a suspension of hostilities, while continuing a state of non-intercourse. At worst, this would allow time for our strength to grow. Better still, he said, it would give the necessary opportunity for Russia and Germany to rub against each other.

It is my belief that these bags of letters have literally turned L.G.'s head. It is a terrible thing if it is true. Every day he is crazy about the letters – not what is in them but 'How many are there?' If I am right in my surmise, a very bad knock is awaiting him.

A police officer entered our Council of Action meeting this morning. He said he had been sent by his superior officer. When he was informed it was a private meeting, he withdrew. L.G. was rather affected by this incident when he learned of it afterwards. The idea that the Father of the House, the man who won the last war, should be watched, upset him. I am afraid there will be more of this. Speakers for the Peace Pledge Union and for Mosley are being carefully watched. The Government is considering whether to take action against all such speakers. I shall look out at our meeting at Caernarvon on Saturday.

Lloyd George prepares to make a speech in his constituency on his policy towards the war.

The general situation was that, with the conquest of Poland accomplished, the combatant countries were in a state of what an

American journalist termed 'phoney war'. The British and the French, although they had initiated war in the west, stood largely on the defensive.

18 October
Belcher phoned tonight from Caernarvon, where at my suggestion he has gone to look at the situation arising out of L.G.'s recent speech in the House and his articles in the *Sunday Express*, and to superintend the arrangements for Saturday's meeting.

He said: 'As far as I can gather, there is great curiosity to know what L.G. is going to say. There is a hope he won't attack Chamberlain. There is a general feeling that the man at the wheel should receive united support. They cannot understand his altered attitude. He was all for fighting for Spain and Czechoslovakia. They are bewildered to know about his change of front. They also feel that criticism of the Government will encourage Hitler at this moment. I saw one of the Press men, and he thinks the meeting is a big mistake at this moment. There is a good deal of cross-current of feeling. Only the parsons and pacifists would support a peace conference at any price.' I dictated this to Churt.

19 October
I met M. Maisky at Euston this morning and conducted him to L.G.'s compartment, where they had a long talk before the train started.

Frances got off at Colwyn Bay and Dame Margaret and Margaret Carey Evans met us at 5.30 at Bangor. At the Liberal Club, Caernarvon, where L.G. talked to E. P. Evans, Jarrett,[29] Belcher and, presently, W. G. Williams of the *Caernarvon Herald*.

L.G. said to Jarrett: 'What is your opinion, Jarrett?' 'Well, Mr George,' replied Jarrett, 'I would have preferred that you did not have a meeting at all.' L.G.: 'Do you think we shall get a meeting?' Jarrett: 'Oh, yes.' L.G.: 'Do you think we shall have a good meeting?' Jarrett: 'I dare say. We want to know what you are going to say.' This brought forth the observation from L.G.: 'I would like to meet one man who could tell me how you can put it through now. I shall not be able to say that tomorrow.' (By 'it' he meant the war.)

L.G. then explained how he had had a long talk this morning in the train with M. Maisky. Even now we could have Russia on our side if we played up to her. He thought this was vital. He then spoke of the importance of making clear our war aims. He had come to Caernarvon in 1916 to deliver his first speech as Prime Minister.

29. Mr Jarrett was one of Lloyd George's oldest constituency supporters. A.J.S.

Immediately previous to this, he had summoned an allied conference in London to settle what our war aims were, before intensifying our effort. We had to make it absolutely clear for the benefit of our own population, and for the neutrals as well, what we were fighting for. That had brought in Wilson.[30] Germany had refused to state her war aims. Now Hitler was playing the other game. He wanted to put us in the wrong position. It was a very clever move on his part.

'If you are going to win,' said L.G., 'you will have to capture not merely forts of the enemy, but, above all, allies for our side. Asquith got Italy. I got America. Were it not for those two allies, which we got after the war had begun, we should have been beaten, quite frankly. It is no use slamming doors in the face of a man, when it is really playing his game to do so. Hitler is now able to say: "I talk peace, and what did they do? They simply say: 'You are a liar, a thief and a cheat; and we will not answer you.'" But you are not talking to Hitler. You are talking to the whole world. Toward the end of the Great War, you had practically no neutrals. Now you have both Russia and Italy. Russia and Italy would make all the difference in the world. And there is America outside, too.'

20 October
L.G. dictated his speech for Caernarvon to Miss Russell. She, in turn, dictated it to me on the typewriter, to expedite it. At tea-time he asked Megan, whom he had asked to read his speech, what she thought of it. 'There are some passages which I do not like,' she said. He retorted: 'Yes, but what do you think of the general line?' She said: 'Well, the general line is affected by those passages which give a defeatist attitude.' She cited a passage about German aggression against a Poland which was itself a result of aggression. Discussing the line of his speech with me this afternoon, L.G. said it was odd that Gwilym was in favour of it and Megan was not. 'Do not say anything about that,' he said, 'otherwise it might injure Gwilym's position in the Government.'[31]

21 October
I was up at Brynawelon early this morning and found L.G. at breakfast in bed, enveloped in a big Cambridge-blue dressing-jacket. He had just read the offer of the Nordic kings,[32] as announced in

30. i.e., President Wilson of the United States.
31. Gwilym Lloyd George had become Parliamentary Secretary to the Board of Trade on 6 September 1939.
32. The kings of Denmark, Norway and Sweden and the President of Finland had just met at Stockholm and afterwards issued a statement affirming their neutrality and offering mediation.

The Times. Lighting his cigar, he said: 'The more I think of it, the more I am convinced that they will all look damned silly. There ain't going to be any war.' Miss Russell and I worked hard all morning and produced twenty-five copies of the speech. Seated in the drawing-room over what L.G. called 'Our last drink', in which I joined him, he remarked: 'We have muddled ourselves into such a position, from which we cannot extricate ourselves.'

It was a truly remarkable meeting. I was amazed at the numbers present. I estimated there were over 6000 present, but L.G. promptly corrected me to 8000 or 9000. Bearing in mind wartime conditions of transport, it was an astonishing number. Most people there were very perplexed as to where he stood. Some people, it was said, had gone there to make trouble, but you would hardly have thought that if you had seen that great concourse of people rise and give L.G. a welcome as he entered.

Jarrett came into the wings when L.G. had been on his feet for ten minutes and said: 'He has got them in his hands.' And so he had. You could have heard a pin drop. The only noise was the tumultuous applause which punctuated his discourse. Speaking first in English and then in Welsh, he departed no end from his typescript.

On Thursday night, L.G. had given personal instructions to E. P. Evans, Chairman of his Association, to see that the Pavilion was partitioned. At two o'clock today the number of persons was so great that the partition had to be removed. The seating accommodation on the ground floor, which covered half the area, was packed, with hundreds standing behind. The galleries down each side and at the back were packed to suffocation, and the huge stage at the back of L.G. was also full.

I stood in the wings and watched his play-acting to these masses of people. It was superb. One moment he was playing up to the blue-blooded Tories – and many were present – talking about our superb air force and about the greatest navy in the world; you could feel them puff with pride. Next he was playing up to the peacemongers, by advocating a conference and peace. Next he was giving a recital of intimate facts, not before stated, regarding our relations with Russia. The burden of his speech was really to influence the Government to bring in Russia on our side, and to send a highly placed minister to see Stalin. Thus he carried everybody off their feet, and there was not even a single heckle or question. He had them so that he could make them laugh or cry at his will and pleasure.

I spent the evening telephoning around the constituency getting impressions and reactions of the meeting, whilst L.G. sat with his feet before the fire, receiving adulatory messages. He sipped his Irish whiskey and water, and Dame Margaret rubbed his forehead and around his eyes with her fingers.

23 October

L.G. wanted me to telephone around for more impressions of the meeting. He wanted more adulation, so again I had to go through the performance of supplying his needs. In between times we played bagatelle – L.G., Dame Margaret, Olwen and Margaret Carey Evans.

23 October

L.G. said he intended asking Lord Dawson to give me an overhaul. I have not been looking well for some time. I thanked him. All the same, I know that the only thing I want is rest and a bit of peace. I am a different being when I am away from him and from that office. With him it is all tension. He just sucks the life out of one. He derives his strength and his vitality by feeding on others. He hates to see anyone else enjoying himself. He is a sadist. When you are slogging at it, he is happy. He goes short of absolutely nothing, and his wants are colossal.

26 October

This morning I went with Dr Roberts to see Lord Dawson at 10.30 a.m. Lord Dawson is a remarkable man. For the first few minutes he talked to Dr Roberts. Suddenly he talked to me about the situation and about L.G. All the time he talked, I knew that his quick brown eyes were watching my every movement and reaction, even to the vigour of my observations. Talking of L.G., he was particularly interesting. He asked me: 'Is L.G.'s mind as good as it was?' I replied: 'Confidentially, no, it is not.' He said: 'I know it is not.' He said when he last saw L.G. he urged him not to undertake too much. When he undertook too much, he became tired. L.G. would deal with some one big question very well. He would bring a first-rate quality of mind to its consideration, and the decision would be right. But when he attempted too much, the other questions would not have the same quality of mind applied to them and there would not be the same balance or the same poise. I said that that was absolutely true.

We then proceeded to his examination room, where I almost stripped and he went over me. He said I was organically absolutely sound but very much overworked. . . . He then said that in normal times he would have ordered me two months' rest, but we were at war. I said a week. He smiled and said he would recommend a fortnight. I reported to L.G. at once. He did not relish Lord Dawson reporting that I was overworked.

9 November

Recommenced at the office after ten days' rest. L.G. is as artful as a cartload of monkeys. He greeted me warmly and, as he entered the room, he walked straight to the window so that he could see me with the light on my face. 'Ah,' he said, 'I can see you are better. I could see that also from your handwriting.' He prides himself on judging character on handwriting and heads.

Tweed told me that L.G. had actually talked to him about the advisability of sending a congratulatory message to Hitler on his having escaped from the bomb explosion in Munich the other day. . . .

24 November

My fiftieth birthday today. God help me and mine. In looking back across half a century, help me, God, to see the mistakes and my follies, and in the future help me to trust in Thee more and give me health and strength, wisdom and determination to achieve something worth while for my fellow men, as well as for myself and to Thy honour. Help me to be effective.

13 December

First secret session of the House of Commons today. L.G. present. He went in at 3.50 and did not come out again until nearly seven. L.G. told me that he had spoken for nearly an hour. My information is that he did well. He told me that he thought the Government had not thought out at all how the war was likely to develop. When we went down in the lift tonight, I asked L.G. why he was wearing a black tie. 'For Princess Louise,'[33] he said. I was amused because he has never shown the slightest respect for royalty. He then said: 'She was the only one whose name I could ever remember.'

14 December

L.G. lunched with Winston at 1.45 and did not return until four o'clock. When he did return, he said he had thought Winston would never let him leave; he had wanted to show L.G. everything.[34] I asked him if he were satisfied with the position, as explained. He said: 'As far as he goes.'

33. Princess Louise, Duchess of Argyll (1848–1939), sixth child of Queen Victoria.
34. At the Admiralty.

Chapter 12

'I shall wait until Winston is bust'

1940

The final possibility of Lloyd George returning to office came in the year 1940, during which Britain was involved in defeat and the possibility actually arose of a German military occupation. He was past the peak of his powers but, at seventy-seven, he was still an active man with an imaginative mind: his store of political experience was unparalleled. He was, in fact, the same age as Churchill was when he became peacetime Prime Minister in 1951.

4 January

I have been waiting for any sign of what happened between Winston and L.G. when they lunched together at Winston's invitation recently. Tweed has it from Frances that nothing definite was said but that 'It is all right', meaning that Winston intends to get L.G. into the Government when the chance arrives. I shall believe that when I see it actually happen.

The major political sensation of the 'phoney-war' period was the abrupt dismissal by Chamberlain of the energetic, publicity-conscious Leslie Hore-Belisha from the office of Secretary of State for War. All kinds of speculation existed as to the reason. In fact Hore-Belisha had quarrelled with the generals, and Chamberlain had sided with them.

5 January

A chance telephone call to William Alison[1] of the Evening Standard tonight about golf tomorrow gave me news of first-class political importance: that Hore-Belisha had gone from the War Office, that

1. William Alison (1884–1973). Political correspondent of the Evening Standard 1921–53.

he had refused to take the Board of Trade, that Oliver Stanley had been made Secretary of State for War. I flashed this to L.G. at Churt. He could not believe it.

6 January

L.G. said to me on the telephone: 'I think they have treated Hore-Belisha scurvily. There is certainly a sense of rivalry between Winston and Hore-Belisha, and Winston wanted him out of the way. It is a fatal thing to give in to generals. I had this. History shows every time they are wrong. I had to fight generals who had already got a considerable public record behind them. Robertson was supposed to be a very great general. Then, on the other hand, Haig had a great reputation too. He also had a great public behind him. Yet I knew he was ruining the Army and I fought him right and left. But these [i.e., the 1940] generals have done nothing. They are only bringing the British Army to ridicule. They have only had about three casualties and have done nothing. To sack a Secretary of State because he did not agree with his generals, with no reputation at all, is a scandal. I am very glad Hore-Belisha refused the other chance. He would have been completely broken if he had taken the other offer. I think he would be very much stronger as an independent and I think Winston will find that.'

I said that my information was that there had been such a row between Winston and Hore-Belisha about the Canadian Army in this country that they had almost come to physical blows. L.G. replied that Winston would have had the worst of it. He asked me if it was realised that Winston was concerned in this business, and I said that it was. 'My sympathies are with Hore-Belisha,' said L.G.

19 January

The *Daily Sketch* contains an article bitterly attacking L.G., entitled 'THE JITTERS OF LLOYD GEORGE'. When I telephoned Churt this morning, L.G. came on personally. He was as surly as a bear. I learned later from Frances that he had been reading the *Daily Sketch*. He did not like it. Was considering replying to it.

I 'extracted' two decisions from him. Marvellous !

When I got a copy of L.G.'s American article for this week, I was very concerned about the following sentence, referring to Hore-Belisha's resignation.

'It is not approximately true that there were no differences of an important character between the War Minister and the generals in charge of the campaign. One of these disagreements must ultimately be revealed should the Germans launch an attack on Holland and Belgium. If that occurs it is not the reputation of the late War

Minister which will suffer when it comes to be known how his recommendations were repelled.[2]

Tweed telephoned to L.G. when I had shown him this: he thought it was treacherous to give information to the enemy. Tweed told me that L.G. was all of a dither when he told him this and asked what he could do, as it had gone off. Anyhow it was amended; Frances telephoned urgently the correction to those concerned. After the word 'revealed', the following words were substituted: 'as the campaign develops'.

23 January

Sir John Simon, Chancellor of the Exchequer, made an important announcement increasing old-age pensions in needy circumstances. When I telephoned a summary to Churt, I was in the middle of speaking when I suddenly heard music. 'Damn and blast you and your music,' I said. 'Get off the telephone. I am on serious business. Get off the bloody telephone.' That music ceased at once. Miss Russell told me later that they had not stopped laughing since, because it was L.G., who listened in from the library with his wireless on. He got an earful.

25 January

L.G. invited me to join him at dinner, together with Megan, Sir Thomas and Lady Carey Evans and Colonel Proctor.[3] When L.G. came to his room at 7 p.m. he said he would have a whiskey, even though it meant breaking his self-imposed resolution not to take anything. This vow he took a fortnight ago, but only because Frances had started. Damn silly I call it. I left the dinner table to find Carey Evans and Proctor and returned a quarter of an hour later to find that L.G. had had oysters – after whiskey! L.G. asked each of us how long we thought the war would last. Colonel Proctor said between eighteen months and two years. Tom Carey Evans said until September next, 1940. I said five years from the commencement. L.G. said if it did not come to an end in two years it will go on for a very long time. L.G. said: 'When both sides realise it may go on for years, and it is not in the interests of either, that makes a difference. It depends on what "giving in" means. If "giving in"

2. In fact, the major cause of Hore-Belisha's quarrel with the generals was that he believed that the British forces on the Franco-Belgian border had put up inadequate defences. Sylvester's diary records that Hore-Belisha visited Lloyd George after his resignation but Sylvester was not present at the conversation.

3. H. A. Proctor (1879–1950), a friend of Sir Thomas Carey Evans. He reached a high position in the Indian Medical Service.

means Hitler must give up Czechoslovakia, to which he has no right, gives up the real Poland – the Poles are thieves: they stole bits of Lithuania and Czechoslovakia. They have stolen about three million White Russians and nobody wants us to continue the war to get those back. Once it is realised that Danzig must not go back [to Poland], nor the Corridor, Hitler and the Germans will not go on saying "No", but it is too early for that.' L.G. thought everybody will shrink from attacking the civil population. The Germans were shrinking from it. Likewise the French and ourselves. With all this terrific bombing, Helsinki had lost very few civilians.[4] It was the big guns that mattered, not bombs and aeroplanes.

L.G. said: 'Great statesmen never lie. They have people to do that for them.' . . .

6 February

L.G. came straight up to the House from Churt with Frances. He spoke for one hour. The high point of his speech was: 'You cannot dig for victory with a pair of Treasury scissors.' It really was a great success. Afterwards I stayed with L.G. at the Hyde Park Hotel.

11 February

Tommy, Evelyn and I motored around Churt and lunched at the Royal Huts Hotel, Hindhead. L.G. has erected a lot of buildings with cottages and glasshouses. Little Jennifer has now got an orchard! Churt becomes a bigger mystery to me every day. Nobody knows what are the true facts about the financial aspect. The agricultural aspect is absolutely mucked up, and discontent is rife amongst all the staff. It is an unhappy place and is a cemetery to many an innocent and enthusiastic person.

Lloyd George was speaking quite frequently in the House on agriculture. He had a great success on 14 February on the Agriculture (Miscellaneous War Provisions) Bill. He said that the Government's measures to increase food output were of 'piffling inadequacy'. Food was Britain's 'weakest plank'. If food ran short the people's strength for war would sap.

14 February

L.G. came direct to the House with Frances from Churt. He said at first that he would speak about 6.15 p.m. He sat on the front

4. The Soviet–Finnish war of 1939–40 was in progress.

opposition bench, seemingly making lots of notes, but in truth he was merely putting in additional points to the speech which he had already very carefully prepared. These days he can never make up his mind. He was dithering not only as to *when* he should speak, but *whether* he should speak. At 6.30, after a division, he came to his room and I primed him with a dram of whiskey. He disappeared, saying, 'I will speak now, I think.' M. Maisky asked me when he was going to speak and I told him almost at once. I had arranged a table for him for dinner, to which he had invited me. At eight o'clock he came through the lobby and ran into Mrs Tate.[5] I thought they would have embraced one another. He complimented her [on her speech in the debate] simply because he is mad on her. He then said: 'I want to get something out of Boothby' – that was a broad hint that he did not want me to eat with him. At a few minutes before nine o'clock I informed him that Tom Williams[6] had just risen and that it was time for him to go into the chamber. He went and then I sat down to have my meal. I was bloody wild. When I had eaten my meal, I went to listen to L.G. He started at 9.2 p.m. and finished at 9.32.

Afterwards he was absolutely full of himself. He came up to his room expecting to see Frances, but she had gone and he was very annoyed when he realised she had not heard his speech. He had spoken exceptionally well and afterwards told me that everybody had come up to congratulate him. They had said it was the best of the three speeches he had made in the last few weeks on agriculture. I think that is true.

You can tell a man once or twice how wonderfully well he has done, but it is difficult to keep on telling him. Yet L.G. goes on talking about himself and his performance until the whole business is threadbare. 'How did I speak?' 'Did I speak with energy?' 'Could they hear me?' 'I threw away the notes that I had prepared.' He said that the remark about Shylock was absolutely spontaneous. But he had thought it out very carefully beforehand. . . .

I am always amused as he walks down the corridors. He just flies. That is all stage-managed to make people say what remarkable energy he has. Take him some papers upon which to get a decision ! Watch his energy then. He will use up six times as much energy in dodging me as it would take him to say 'Yes' or 'No' to questions that have been all thrashed out by me.

He kindly brought me from Churt a pound of butter, for which I was thankful, and two pounds for Lady Carey Evans.

5. Mavis Tate (1893–1947). Tory M.P. 1931–45.
6. Labour spokesman on agriculture.

15 *February*

I went to him at 7.30 this morning with what papers I could get, as they are now all rationed. Considering he spoke so late, he had a good Press. But Mrs Tate had got the scoop. The *Express* had a picture of her on the front page and a leaded headline that she had led a Tory revolt.

He has broken his pledge about not drinking whiskey; he had some in the office this morning with Tweed and Finney.

In the car I got him talking about the arrangements for the celebration of his fiftieth anniversary as member for Caernarvon Boroughs. A week or so ago I had put up a proposal to him that there should be an album signed by all the electors. He had turned this down, saying that he preferred to have only the signatures of those who had voted for him in 1890! I have telephoned Belcher, and E. P. Evans, the Chairman, and put words into the mouth of the latter, and built up an overwhelming case showing how impossible this is; that whilst the 1890s could have a separate section it was necessary to link up this great parliamentary record with the present-day electors, to arouse their enthusiasm for the next election, whenever it comes. This morning he agreed to this. . . .

27 *February*

Tweed was taken seriously ill at home in the early hours of this morning.

Britain was drifting towards the absurdity of going to war with the Soviet Union over Finland as well as being at war with Germany. Lloyd George tries to stop the drift.

28 *February*

L.G. addressed a record gathering at a luncheon under the auspices of the International Defence Public Interest Committee, with Nathan as chairman. Had thirty more than the P.M., there being 480 present.

L.G. spoke for fifty-five minutes in brilliant style. He made a great impression, all the more remarkable because his audience was comprised of ambassadors, ministers, big businessmen and magnates, who would certainly know the difference between a turnip and a mangel-wurzel. Some of the high spots of his speech were: 'Better a long war than a mean get-out.' 'The great advantage and superiority which a democracy has over an authoritarian state is that during war it permits fair, constructive criticism.' 'The last war was won by criticism.' 'I would not allow reckless or inconsiderate steering on icy roads to skid us into war with Russia.'

29 February

I took the newspapers into L.G. this morning at 7.15. They were very good. It is true that L.G. does not read reports of his speech: he simply devours everything said about him and his speech. When I went into him this morning, he was already reading a Wild West novel. Immediately he had read the newspapers, he started to go through his draft article for the American Press. Propped up in bed, wearing a blue bed-jacket, with a huge yellow pencil resembling a hedge stake, he made copious alterations. He makes his alterations without any thought of someone else having to read his writing. He never by any chance uses a hard backing-sheet, the only support to these thin pages being the palm of his left hand. The result is a Chinese puzzle.

Having had his bath, which I prepared for him, he said, 'The reports of the Press are very good.' Then, in the next breath, he said, 'By Jove, I have not shaved.' He had completely forgotten to do so. Whilst he lathered himself in the bathroom, in his blue trousers and shirt and wearing his slippers lined with lamb's wool, meantime dipping his shaving-brush alternately in his little bowl of Evan Williams shaving-soap, which he favours, and hot water, I talked to him.

Tom Jones had asked me to inquire whether during the Great War, when he was Prime Minister, he had read Burke on the present-day discontent and Gibbon on the Roman Empire. The former he did not remember reading, but the latter, given him by Lord Chalmers,[7] he said he often read and reread. I then asked him if he had had any terms of reference when he had formed his War Cabinet. Leaving off his shaving, he said: 'No, none. We did what we thought was necessary, and like Providence had no terms of reference.'

He had several appointments in the office, and then Frances and I went into his room and we both joined him in a whiskey to celebrate his success. He was in a very happy mood; he wondered whether they had got the real meaning of some of his phrases. He said he was very suspicious that Neville might try to get a patched-up peace. Then, after sipping his whiskey and breaking a biscuit, he suddenly said: 'And Frances must keep me free. I have a great part to play in this war yet.' He referred to the statement in his speech that he did not get depressed. 'I do not get depressed,' he remarked. 'I get worried mostly about little things.' I should think

7. Robert Chalmers (1858–1938). Permanent Secretary to the Treasury 1911–13, Governor of Ceylon 1913–16, Joint Permanent Secretary to the Treasury 1916–19 and created a baron 1919.

he does, too. Not only does he get depressed, but he certainly gets damn bad-tempered, which lasts for days on end. . . .

4 *March*
Frances went to Colwyn Bay on Friday to see Jennifer and returned today.[8] L.G. was suspicious that she was going to see Tweed.[9] She went, but he did not find out.

In February 1940 Sumner Welles, American Under-Secretary of State, set off on a month's fact-finding tour in Europe as President Franklin D. Roosevelt's special representative. He visited Rome, Berlin, Paris and London, in that order, and spoke with heads of governments and foreign ministers in each capital. In London he also called on Lloyd George at Thames House.

13 *March*
This morning Sumner Welles, President Roosevelt's special emissary, called upon L.G. He was accompanied by the American Ambassador, Mr Joseph Kennedy.[10] He arrived at 11.30 a.m. I met them in the hall and brought them up in the lift and introduced them to L.G. Sumner Welles is very tall, with a military moustache. He might have been a Guards officer. His sentences were short and snappy and he gave the impression of being unbending. But he unbent all right when L.G. talked to him.

When L.G. rang for me it was to arrange for the photographers to take pictures. These were taken on the balcony. Afterwards the three stood talking in L.G.'s room. L.G. said to Sumner Welles: 'Did you know President Wilson?' 'Very well,' was the reply, 'but no one knew him as well as you did.' L.G. said: 'Clemenceau did not like him. At any rate, not at first. I remember at the beginning of the peace conference Wilson was not well. Clemenceau came up to me one morning, rubbing his hands with evident satisfaction, and remarked: "He is not well today." ' Then, reflecting quickly, L.G. added: 'That was at the beginning, but in fairness I must tell you this. At the end of the peace conference I said to Clemenceau: "Well, I like Wilson." "So do I" was the instant response of Clemenceau.'

8. Jennifer was at school at Colwyn Bay.
9. Whose illness was continuing.
10. Joseph P. Kennedy (1888–1969). Multi-millionaire who was American Ambassador in London 1938–40 and whose son J. F. Kennedy became President of the United States.

I was in the room whilst L.G. narrated this, and then accompanied them in the lift. While descending, I remarked to the Ambassador: 'I hope this long interview has not unduly upset your other plans.' He replied: 'Our schedule has completely gone bust. But I could listen to that fellow for hours.' 'So could I,' added Sumner Welles.

When I returned to L.G.'s room, I related this to him and he was obviously very delighted. I remarked to L.G. that Sumner Welles seemed unbending. L.G. said: 'After I had been talking for about twenty minutes, he unbent, for he interrupted me to say: "After what I have been through during the last forty-eight hours, listening to you is like a breath of fresh air."' (During the past forty-eight hours he has been talking with our P.M. and Foreign Secretary.) Frances and I then lunched with him; he was immensely pleased with himself.

20 *March*
Along with Bill Edge,[11] I had a most important and instructive talk with Willie Henderson. On the first or second wave of dissatisfaction with this government, he envisaged the possibility of Labour coming into the Government under L.G. as Prime Minister; they would never take office under Neville and he doubted even under Winston. He thought L.G. was too pro-Russian, and he was aware of the many mistakes he had made, but he had courage, vision and experience, and he had a great reputation, which would produce a psychological effect. He had been pushing this view inside his own party for some months. If L.G. would not play, then he would turn to some other plan. Frances told me, on my asking her, that he was much interested. He had just given her my memorandum. Personally, he has not said one word to me.

Lloyd George goes to Wales.

23 *March*
Frances telephoned me this morning to say L.G. left at 9 a.m. with Miss Parry, whom he would drop at Bangor. He had arrived home last night very tired and had said if he did not feel fitter he would not go to Wales in the morning. Clearly he did not want to go. This morning Jennifer went to him to say good-bye. He made some remark to the effect that he knew he was not wanted, and off he went, taking with him a pantechnicon of food, in order, as Frances said, to make himself welcome at Criccieth.

11. Sir William Edge (1880–1948) was a Liberal M.P. 1916–23 and 1927–45.

29 March
Frances told me from Churt that it was in L.G.'s mind to cut
salaries and to get rid of the Council of Action staff. She said she had
had german measles. L.G. used to go to see her wearing his gas
mask. It would be laughable if *he* got german measles!

31 March
L.G. motored back from Criccieth to Churt.

9 April
On the eight o'clock news this morning, there was a dramatic
announcement that Germany had occupied Copenhagen and Oslo
during the night. I telephoned L.G. as soon as I got further informa-
tion. He was terribly excited. 'The war at last has started,' he said.
Later he was very sniffy because in the messages I was sending him,
and I was sending them hourly, I did not say definitely whether
Copenhagen had been occupied. I gave him a snorter when I told
him that, although I had inquired of Winston's secretary at the
Admiralty, Lord Halifax's secretary at the Foreign Office and the
Danish Legation, not one of them could confirm this statement.
Later, not even the P.M. in his statement to the House of Commons,
which I at once telephoned to Churt, could make a definite statement. He could only say: 'It is reported that Copenhagen has been
occupied.' When L.G. gets in that mood he is impossible.

There was great tension in the House when it met and considerable
astonishment that the Germans had been able to occupy so many
important parts of Norway. My private information is that an
elaborate trap has been laid for the Germans and that they have
fallen into it. Great feeling of expectancy in the House.

17 April
L.G. and I travelled to Llandudno junction on the train leaving
Euston at 1.30 p.m. We had a picnic lunch on the train. . . .
    . . . We talked of Winston. L.G. said he always remembered
Winston saying that he (L.G.) understood politics better than he
did, because he had been brought up a soldier. 'My mind', said
L.G., 'goes back to the time when Winston was Home Secretary.
I was called in by Asquith to settle a railway strike. I settled it.
Afterwards I went to the Home Office to see Winston. He was
very angry with the result. There he stood before a huge map
showing police stations all over the country, and all the available
forces ready to take action wherever necessary. His mind was on a
fight. Charles Masterman, his Parliamentary Secretary [i.e., Under-

Secretary of State], was sitting there drinking whiskey and chipping and making fun of him.'

L.G. thinks Winston ought to have waited before going into the Government. His chances would have come later on. It was a mistake for him to have gone into a department. Milner went into a department and that finished him, although he had a first-class mind. He discussed the relative ages of persons in key positions today with those of 1916. L.G. said he was fifty-three when he became Prime Minister. He certainly would not be able to do now what he had done then, and he was sure that Neville could not exercise the necessary drive at seventy-one, especially as his chief lieutenants, Sam Hoare, Simon, Kingsley Wood and Halifax were sixty-five-ish. . . .

Lloyd George is in his constituency, ready for a meeting that was to celebrate the fiftieth anniversary of his election to Parliament. His speech on the occasion is to be broadcast.

19 April

Last night L.G. turned peculiar. Although I had spoken to him a week before to get his consent to his speech being broadcast, he now made out that he had not been consulted, that he had had no knowledge that it was to be broadcast, and that it had altered the whole tone of his speech, which he wanted to be of a conversational kind and not a speech at all. I just took no notice of him.

I had conceived the idea that the broadcast ceremony should open with the singing of the Welsh hymn 'Marchog Iesu yn Llwyddianus'. The public will then get the atmosphere of the meeting and hear the tumultuous cheering which was bound to greet L.G. on his rising to speak. L.G. was pleased with my suggestion. He called for a hymnal and sang the verse. Suddenly, he had a brain-wave. He said he would have the first half of the last verse sung twice over, but continue with the ordinary tune. So impressed was he with the words which, he said, so aptly described the present situation. They were to the effect: 'Ride Jesus triumphantly with Thy sword by Thy side.' It was a great battle-song, L.G. said. Then the verse continued: 'I seem to hear today the sound of songs from afar; a multitude singing for their deliverance and for a greater freedom.'

L.G. is so suspicious that someone will want to take his time on the broadcast that I have hammered home to them [the organisers of the meeting] the necessity of his starting exactly at 3.30 and ending at 4.10, which is the official time allowed. I also had to

arrange the exact time of L.G.'s arrival, for he did not want to be
kept waiting. 'I am like a racehorse, stamping and scraping his feet
before the starting of a race,' he said. 'I am such a nervous fellow
that I do not want to have to sit there for three-quarters of an hour
before I speak.'

20 April

This is the day of celebration of the fiftieth anniversary of L.G.
becoming a Member of Parliament. The stage had been well and
truly set. The size of the audience surprised me, the Pavilion, holding some 9000, being full. He spoke for an hour. I was frightfully
annoyed at the way in which he delivered his speech; it looked to
me as if he were just fooling. He turned violently to the left now,
and then violently to the right, but never straight in front of the
microphone. His voice was thin and without punch. People com-
plained to me bitterly that they could not hear. So I sent him a note
to speak up. He then put volume into his voice.

21 April

I left Criccieth with L.G. by car at 8.45 a.m. in pouring rain.
Because he was returning to Churt, he was in a much better mood,
which, fortunately, continued for the whole journey. Periodically
he took out his watch and consulted the map and said: 'Now we
have done one eighth of our journey', 'Now one fourth' and so on.

He talked a lot about politics. The most interesting thing, he said,
was who was to be Neville's successor. I said I did not think Labour
would take office under Eden, Simon or Sam Hoare, and I was
doubtful about Winston, but I knew they would come in under
L.G. They intended to wait for a wave of dissatisfaction which
would result from some calamity. Then L.G. would have his chance.

'Ah,' he said, 'but it would have to be made perfectly clear that
I could not bring about a decisive victory, as I did last time. We
have made so many mistakes, that we are not in nearly so good a
position.'

The country looked lovely. L.G. remarked: 'Whatever happens,
whether we win or lose this war, nothing will alter this countryside.'

24 April

Tonight the Liberal parliamentary party entertained L.G. to dinner
in a private room at the House of Commons. The only person present
who was not a member was myself. In response to a toast proposed
by the Chairman, Sir Archibald Sinclair, L.G. said: [12]

12. The original diary contains a verbatim report of the whole speech;
the present version gives extracts only.

'I have had many invitations in connection with my fiftieth anniversary, but I have accepted only two. One was in my own constituency, and the other is this one. I limited my acceptance to these two, because they were more or less family gatherings.

'I am told that mine is not a record because it was broken by Villiers who represented Wolverhampton for sixty-three years. He was one of the silent members: not like me. It is my boast that for the first four years of my membership of the House of Commons Gladstone was my leader. I hope that the real life of Gladstone will be written one day. Gladstone's reputation has suffered because all the vitality had gone out of Morley when he wrote his life. He was devitalised physically when he wrote it. Gladstone was the greatest and most vital figure which ever appeared in British politics, and Gladstone's memory ought not to be allowed to suffer. I am sure there will be a glorious resurrection for the memory, character, and the achievement and inspiration of that old man. We are suffering today largely from the complete neglect of the doctrines to which he devoted his life – the doctrines of peace. . . .

'The House has changed very much since then. They could then be very rude, very rude indeed. When I now see that there has been a scene in the House, I say: "What was it?" Then I see that the Speaker has suspended a member. Ph . . . h. . . .

'When I came to the House it was largely a House of country squires, representing plutocracy. Democracy was represented almost exclusively by the Irish members. There were in addition a few mining members, that is about all. There has been a very great change in that respect. It is very extraordinary that whilst the average social status of the House has gone down, its manners have improved. In those days a thing happened which one rarely sees now. When a member got up, the rest of the members carried on a conversation with each other during the whole of the time, and it was a loud conversation, too. It was not regarded as rude at all. It was the usual thing. Now, when you get that sort of thing, there is a cry of "Order, order".

'In those days, members were constantly shouted down by cries " 'Vide, 'vide". I got it several times, especially during the Boer War. That has quite disappeared now. To a certain extent, perhaps, the Labour members were responsible for this. They are men who in the main have been trained to meet their opponents around the same table to discuss very vital questions: the conditions, hours of work, etc., but always around a table, where there is perfect courtesy.

'The other thing is that there are no great divisions of principle. Just before I started politics, in the rural areas it was not Liberal and Conservative but Whigs and Tories. This disappeared more than

I

fifty years ago. There on a Liberal platform you had a Welsh word
egwuddor, which means 'principles'. But the fight for principles has
gone. The last was the fight for home rule for Ireland and perhaps
disestablishment in Wales. You have not a great dividing principle
at the moment. Whatever principles the Labour Party have, they are
not putting them forward as a great challenge. They say they
are socialists. When do you ever hear socialism discussed? Debates
at the moment are on the means test and an extra sixpence.
The greatest fights in the world have been upon the question
of principles. There is nothing like a ferocious Christian for
fighting.

'The result I think on the whole has affected our administration.
A government like this could not live in those days. They would
have been regarded as inadequate champions. All this cheap sort of
talk by the Prime Minister that he is ten times as sure of victory is
nonsense. Asquith and I never talked like that. There is no guidance in that sort of talk.

'All the things that Gladstone stood for are things that will
triumph in the end, whatever happens in this war. It does not
depend on victory or defeat in this war. The other thing lasts. If
there is triumph on the other side, it will be such a terrible thing
for Europe, and to all this great, intelligent people. Allow me to say :
Keep on repeating these doctrines. You will sow here and there on
stony ground, and often amongst brambles, but you will get good
ground, too, and it will spread and bring forth its hundredfold in
the end.'

Everybody felt that it had been a most inspiring evening. L.G.
was at his best in this conversational style and in reminiscing mood.
I succeeded in making notes of L.G.'s speech on a number of menus,
without L.G., Megan or Gwilym detecting my doing so; not a very
easy matter. I do not want them to think I am Boswellising.

30 *April*
Tweed passed away.

2 *May*
Neville Chamberlain announced that we had withdrawn from
Norway. I strongly disliked his manner, which was full of cock-
sureness. He might have been announcing a great victory rather
than a defeat.[13]

13. British forces which had been sent to Norway to resist the German
occupation were withdrawn from central Norway on 2 and 3 May,
but held on in Narvik until 28 May.

3 May

Today the [Tweed's] cremation ceremony was to take place at Golders Green. I received a very unusual call from Lady Carey Evans first thing this morning that Sir Thomas and she would be glad if I would reserve two seats on the left-hand side of the chapel for them. I remembered that L.G. had always said that if he ever went to that place again, after visiting Sir Vincent Evans's funeral, he would not sit on the right-hand side because you could see the fire. (At least his Celtic imagination saw it.) This message made me suspicious. L.G. had said he would not attend and had told everybody accordingly.

I went to the funeral with Finney, Miss Smithers and Miss Dann. There I met Frances and Muriel in deep mourning. They were obviously terribly upset. No sooner had we taken our seats than L.G. entered, with Lady Carey Evans; they took their seats on the left-hand side. *Never* have I seen him attend a funeral service thus. He is always most particular about his attire on all occasions. Today must have been a studied insult to the dead, and intended to persecute the living in the person of Frances. He wore a blue suit, a blue overcoat, a blue hat, with a dark tie that was not even black. His face was white – knowing him, he was het up. He sat in the front seat, well towards the left. As he looked towards the pulpit on the right, he could see Frances in the second row and watch her every movement and reaction. . . .

What was the motive for this extraordinary behaviour? Jealousy. He is eaten up with it.

Afterwards, on the telephone, Frances told me that he was literally persecuting her to death. He had twitted her about being upset. He wondered whether she would be upset when *he* died. He criticised her deep mourning. In the end, and unwisely as I think, she said she had confessed to L.G. that she had been very fond of Tweed, that Mrs Tweed had been very kind to her and had taken her home, where they had had a frank talk.

On 7 and 8 May came the great debate in the Commons which led to the fall of Neville Chamberlain as Prime Minister. Lloyd George, in his last important contribution in the Commons, made a slashing attack on Chamberlain. This, coming from the war leader of 1916–18, was undoubtedly impressive and may well have swung votes. Lloyd George spoke on the second day and said of Chamberlain: 'He has appealed for sacrifice. . . . The nation is prepared for every sacrifice, so long as it has leadership. . . . I say solemnly that the Prime Minister should give an example of sacrifice, because there is nothing more that can contribute to victory in this war than that he should sacrifice the seals of office.' When Churchill interrupted in defence of the Government, Lloyd George remarked, 'The Right Honourable Gentleman must not allow himself to be converted into an air-raid shelter to keep the splinters from hitting his colleagues.' The normal government majority was around 240. At the end of this debate it fell to 81, with 43 Tories having actually voted against the Government. Chamberlain resigned, and on 10 May Churchill became Prime Minister and formed an all-party coalition government.

8 May

At lunch today, while talking of the political situation, L.G. said that we were fighting a fellow outside the House, named Hitler, who did not take David Margesson's Whip. He used a similar remark in his speech. Frances did not come up yesterday. L.G. had told her he would not speak. I felt certain he would and advised her to come to town. He was most difficult. He could not decide what he would do, but finally he spoke, and a great speech it was too.

Chamberlain resigned as Prime Minister on 10 May and Churchill succeeded him the same day.

The same morning the Germans launched their 'lightning-war' offensive in the west, racing over Belgium and the Netherlands and into France.

10 May

Before seven o'clock this morning, I telephoned to L.G. to say that in the early hours of the morning the Germans had invaded Belgium, Holland and Luxembourg. I predicted that Neville would resign and that by the evening Winston would be Prime Minister. In the afternoon I had to warn L.G. that I was not quite so sure, as Neville seemed to be hanging on. All the same, my prediction became true.

11 May

I told L.G. on the telephone that Neville might become Leader of the House, in which case he would have the whips and the machine. L.G. said he was glad to be out of it. 'It would be like the old horse in the pantomime, with the front legs of a race horse and the hind legs of a mule.'. . .

12 *May*

Lord Dawson called on L.G. at Churt. There was a good deal of speculation amongst us as to the motive. Was it to see exactly what was L.G.'s mental and physical fitness for office?

In a talk on the telephone, L.G. said to me: 'I do not think Winston will approach me. I think it will be the old coalition – a coalition of parties, and their nominees. In that I would not have a place. That suits me to the ground at the present moment. This is not the end by any means. I would simply be there fretting and fuming, and having no real authority, and that would do me no good. I would be responsible. I would not be able to say anything in public. It would not be a real national government with me, under present conditions. Neville would have infinitely more authority than I would have, and he would oppose everything I proposed. I think it would be far better for me to go on with the food-production part of it. I would have a better chance of pushing it now than I would with Neville. I would get Winston to listen to me.'

Frances told me later that Winston wanted L.G. to lunch with him on Thursday next. 'That looks extraordinary to me,' she said, 'because I think all the appointments will be made by then. I think it is a hint that he is not going to get anything, but he still thinks he is. He will be absolutely broken if he does not. He still thinks Winston will offer him something to do with food. There is no doubt he was very much upset when he realised that the War Cabinet was fixed – and he had an idea he would be a member. Since then he has fortified himself with the idea that he will be given Agriculture or Food. Food production is what he wants. Dawson came to see him today and said he was quite able to take that sort of job, but not a routine job in a department, where he had to go every morning, but only to preside over a council of that kind, and L.G. still thinks he will get it.'...

13 *May*

House was specially summoned today, and Winston took his seat for the first time as Prime Minister. I was very disappointed, for the cheers given to Neville Chamberlain, architect of our disasters, were greater than those given to Winston, who now has the responsibility of getting us out of all this mess. Winston's speech was grim. Only a few weeks ago Neville made a speech in which he said he was ten times sure of victory. Today, Winston, the new P.M., said all he had to offer was blood, sweat and tears. I was glad L.G. supported Winston and did it very well, paying him a very good tribute. Winston's eyes filled with tears; he buried his face quickly in his left hand and wiped his face. He admitted afterwards that L.G.'s words had caused him to break down. L.G. told Winston privately in the lobby that if he could not fight Neville Chamberlain how could he hope successfully to tackle Hitler?

15 *May*

Frances told me on the telephone that she had had a very straight talk with L.G., who had been talking of nothing but peace. 'If you were in the Government, you would not be talking peace,' she had said to him. She continued to me: 'He talks about giving in without fighting because he thinks we are beaten. The whole point is that he hates Neville and the Government so much he would like to see them beaten, and he would like to see the English beaten. I said to him: "Don't you make any mistake; if you are beaten, Wales will be beaten also." I think Max[14] has got something up his sleeve. L.G. says he is not going to be buggered about like he was last time.'

16 *May*

L.G. lunched with the P.M. at Admiralty House. He returned to the office looking very grim; shook his head when I asked him a question, which he did not answer. Then he said: 'Things are very bad.' At tea today he said he was glad to be out of this War Cabinet. He would definitely not serve with Neville Chamberlain, and he would certainly not accept the Ministry of Agriculture requiring his daily attendance in a department. I am a little doubtful personally whether this is sour grapes, because he has not been asked again.

On 20 May German armour reached the English Channel at Abbeville. Preliminary planning started to evacuate the British Expeditionary Force and northern French armies to Britain via Dunkirk. Between 26 May and 4 June 338,000 men were evacuated to Britain via Dunkirk, mostly without their equipment.

21 *May*

In discussing his arrangements for tomorrow to meet Esmond Harmsworth[15] and Max, L.G. said on the telephone to me this morning:

14. Beaverbrook.
15. Esmond Harmsworth (b.1898). Tory M.P. 1919–29 and successor to his father as head of the *Daily Mail*. He succeeded as second Viscount Rothermere 1940.

'I begged them – the Government – not to come into it – the war. I knew we were unprepared. I said definitely that without Russia on our side you will be smashed. How angry they were with me. That is one of the things that makes me hesitate whether to go into anything in which Neville Chamberlain is concerned. He would be tricky, he would worry me and not help me. You cannot do anything unless you have supreme authority. I am not going in merely to cajole and persuade, and certainly not to wrangle. He is a cantankerous fellow. I am getting more and more doubtful about it. Besides, the situation is a very, very serious one.'

22 May

L.G. saw Esmond Harmsworth and then lunched with Beaverbrook. Beaverbrook is urging L.G. to go into the War Cabinet. He is absolutely right.

Rhys Davies,[16] Stokes, Sir Ernest Bennett and Culverwell,[17] representing a committee which is mostly composed of pacifist Labour men, came to see L.G. on the general situation. He told them : The idea that we could sign a humiliating peace was ridiculous. We could not even consider a negotiated peace : that would also be ridiculous. There were, however, the mandated territories, which formerly belonged to Germany. L.G. said he was always in favour of giving those back. If there were a general agreement on disarmament, there might be an understanding about the Navy in order to get world peace. Otherwise we should fight to the bitter end.

28 May

Leopold, King of the Belgians, this morning capitulated, without any concerted action with his allies, Great Britain and France. Winston made a statement in the House. L.G. came up from Churt accompanied by Frances. There was a row because she went out. Immediately after his statement the P.M. sent for L.G., who went to Winston's room. The P.M. then offered him a position in the War Cabinet, subject to the approval of Neville Chamberlain.[18] L.G. told me this when he returned. Gwilym and Megan agreed that he should not accept under such conditions.

16. Rhys J. Davies (1877–1954). Labour M.P. 1921–51.
17. Ernest Bennett (1880–1947). Liberal M.P. 1906–10, joined Labour Party 1916, Labour M.P. 1929–45 (from 1931 as National Labour).
C. T. Culverwell (1895–1963). Tory M.P. 1928–45.
18. Chamberlain retained considerable power. He was still leader of the Tory Party, the majority of which had wanted him to continue as Prime Minister.

29 May

Last night at 10 p.m., L.G. telephoned me from Churt to get Gwilym, Megan, Ernie Evans[19] and Lady Carey Evans at the office this morning at 11.30. All were present except Olwen [Carey Evans], who was fixed to go to Liverpool. Frances did not come up with him. They were in private conclave for a long time. He then handed me a draft of a letter which was absolutely mutilated, which he wanted me to type personally. Nobody else was either to see it or to know about it. I first of all went through it with him, but even he could not make out his own writing. Then I locked myself in my room and typed it.

Secret and Personal
My dear Winston:

You were good enough yesterday to ask me if I would be prepared to enter the War Cabinet if you secured the adhesion of Mr Chamberlain to the proposal. It is the first time you have approached me personally on the subject, and I can well understand the reason for your hesitancy, for, in the course of our interview, you made it quite clear that if Chamberlain interposed his veto on the ground of personal resentment over past differences you could not proceed with the offer. This is not a firm offer. Until it is definite I cannot consider it.

I am sure you will be just enough to realise that the experience I have already had in this war justifies my reply to your conditional inquiry. Since the war began I have in public thrice offered to help the Government in any capacity, however humble. No notice has been taken of my tenders. I have never been consulted. I have never been invited even to sit on a Committee. Since you became Prime Minister I offered to do my best to help in organising the Food Supplies of this country. I have acquired considerable knowledge and experience both in peace as well as in war in this line. At the request of your personal friends I put forward alternative proposals for the intensive production of food in this country, and I suggested the part I might play in directing this essential branch of national service. Nothing came of that scheme. I have not even been informed of the reason for its rejection. I say this in order to show that it was due to no unwillingness on my part that you found it impossible to utilise my services. I apprehend that party and personal considerations frustrated your wishes. I cannot be put in that position again. I am no office seeker. I am genuinely anxious to help

19. Ernest Evans (1885–1965) was a barrister who was a private secretary to Lloyd George 1918–20 and a Liberal M.P. 1921–3. (I do not know why he was involved on this occasion – he was no longer close to Lloyd George.) A.J.S.

to extricate my country from the most terrible disaster into which it has ever been plunged by the ineptitude of her rulers. Several of the architects of this catastrophe are still leading members of your Government, and two of them[20] are in the Cabinet which directs this war.

Like millions of my fellow-countrymen I say to you that, if in any way you think I can help, I am at your call. But if that call is tentative and qualified, I shall not know what answer to give.

> Believe me,
> Ever sincerely,
> D.L.G.

I typed this letter several times before it was finally approved. When L.G. left at five o'clock for Churt, I delivered the letter personally into the hands of Seal,[21] the P.M.'s secretary at No 10. As originally drafted, the letter contained the following:

'After reflection I have come to the conclusion that I will be more useful to you outside rather than inside the War Cabinet as it is at present constructed.

'The policy pursued by two members of your Cabinet is directly responsible for the terrible mess in which we have been landed. One of them is politically a most powerful member of your Government and is officially leader of by far the largest section of your supporters. In fact, he is so indispensable to you that you cannot invite to your counsels a man who had the greatest and most successful experience in the conduct of the last war without first of all obtaining his doubtful assent. Hitherto every step Mr Neville Chamberlain and Lord Halifax have taken in policy – or in war preparation – or lack of war preparation – has led straight to disaster. The nation has every reason for distrusting the judgment of both in the momentous decisions which you will have to take in the course of the next few weeks or even days. . . .

'Had you and I been brought into consultation even as late as twelve months ago the country would not have been brought into the terrible situation into which we have been muddled by the ineptitude and lack of vision of some of your colleagues.'

30 May
This morning a letter arrived from the Prime Minister, addressed to L.G. personally. I rang up L.G. at once for instructions. He asked me to open it and give him the gist over the telephone, which I did. He was so impatient to know at once that he could not wait

20. That is, Chamberlain and Halifax.
21. Sir Eric Seal (b.1898), career civil servant who was Churchill's private secretary 1938–41.

until I had even opened it. I told him at once it was indeterminate.
I then dictated it to Frances Stevenson and later sent the original
to him by bag. The letter, which was undated, read:

                                              10 Downing Street,
                                              S.W.1.
My dear L.G.

I have just received your letter of today. I am sorry that the same
difficulties in regard to persons which you mentioned to me are also
only too present elsewhere. I cannot complain in any way of what
you say in your letter. The Government I have formed is founded
upon the leaders of the three parties, and like you I have no party
of my own. I have received a great deal of help from Chamberlain;
his kindness and courtesy to me in our new relation have touched
me. I have joined hands with him, and must act with perfect loyalty.
As you say the inquiry I made of you yesterday could only be
indeterminate, and I could not ask you to go further than you have
done in your letter.

With regard to the organisation of food supplies of this country,
of which my personal friends had some talk with you, I can assure
you that no personal or party differences have frustrated its consideration. The Ministry of Agriculture was discussed and my
friends made representations to you. It was only after you had
taken the decision that you did not at that time contemplate sharing
the responsibilities involved in joining the administration, that
I made another selection, without making any stipulations with the
new Minister. The alternative project of organisation of food supplies
could well be taken up on another occasion. I have simply been so
over-pressed by terrible events that I have not had life or strength
to address myself to it.

Thank you very much for what you say in your last paragraph
and I trust that we shall keep in personal contact, so that I may
acquaint you with the situation as it deepens. I always have the
warmest feelings of regard and respect for you.

                              Yours ever,
                              WINSTON S. CHURCHILL

4 June

This morning Mrs Hill, Winston's private secretary, telephoned me
asking whether L.G. could see the P.M. at No. 10 at six o'clock.
It was a matter of importance and urgency, she said. I replied that
he was not in town but I would get him.

It was arranged that I should be waiting outside Thames House
to accompany L.G. to No. 10. I was there before 5.40. He was due

at 5.45. He actually arrived at eight minutes to six and said he would change. He was wearing a light-grey summer-suit, but I had with me a new blue suit and that was the one he wanted. He really had not sufficient time. Consequently he got terribly het up in the middle of his changing, and doubly so when it was found that Frances had not got the tie which he said he had specially chosen before he left Churt. I tore down in the lift, only to find him following me in the next for he was already some minutes late. I found his special tie in the car and as we proceeded to No. 10 along Millbank I took off his grey and put on his new blue tie to match his suit. As we approached No. 10, L.G. said: 'I won't go in with Neville.' As the car drew up to the door, I moved to help him out, but he would not let me get out. 'No, you stay there,' he said. He did not want me to be photographed with him; he wanted all the show.

I waited one and a quarter hours. Then he appeared at the door of No. 10 smoking a cigar. On our way back he told me that Winston had made him a firm offer this time to go in. He had never had such a delightful talk with Winston, and he had never known him more friendly. L.G. said the P.M. gave instructions that someone else should be kept waiting for half an hour to enable them to finish their talk. L.G. had told Winston that he must give him time to think it over. L.G. said: 'I told Winston if you cannot stand up to Neville Chamberlain and Margesson how can you stand up to Hitler?'

7 June
Beaverbrook is pressing L.G. hard to go into the War Cabinet.

On 10 June Italy declared war on Britain and France.

14 June
Fall of Paris. Shades of Clemenceau and Foch! Harold Macmillan lunched with L.G. in the office. He has been very active lately with Harold Macmillan, Boothby, Amery and Beaverbrook.

The other day L.G. received a firm and definite offer to go into the Cabinet from Winston, Neville Chamberlain having concurred in the suggestion. I was against L.G. going in at the time he wrote to Winston, but now the situation has deteriorated so much that it is vital that L.G. should be inside. He has such a vision, and I have such faith in him still. Beaverbrook has been trying to induce L.G.

to accept. Frances and I have both impressed upon him the importance of his accepting. But he now sticks his toes in and says:
'I won't go in with this crowd', which means with Neville.

*On 22 June the French Government, under Marshal Philippe Pétain,
dropped out of the war, having signed an armistice which, among
other things, entitled the Germans to occupy northern France in
order to prosecute the war against Britain. Although still well
defended by her air force and navy, Britain had virtually no army
fit to engage in major combat and so stood in danger of further
defeat and German occupation.*

25 June

Winston spoke [in the House], and I telephoned a full summary to
L.G. I was personally perplexed as to the meaning of it.[22] L.G. telephoned me later that he considered it a very mysterious statement
by Winston. What did it mean? I repeated that I was bewildered. 'If
we are going to fight,' he said, 'what is there to consider about the
best methods of fighting? I said to someone the other day: "Can
you think of any blunder that could have been committed by the
Government, during the last two or three years, including the
present one, which they have not committed?" ' L.G. continued:
'This is not a leader's speech at all. There is nothing new, except
with regard to Italy, and everyone knew that the French would
have to sign with Italy. It is deplorable. That is one of the evils of
having a cabinet which is not a cabinet at all. Winston has brains
but the others have none, for an emergency. When I had a cabinet
I had men of wisdom, courage and experience, pulling their weight.
If I had a situation, I had four or five men, each of whom could
contribute something to the discussion. Therefore I was not alone.
No man in a situation of this kind ought to have to decide an issue
himself. The greatest general in the world has to get a council of
war. It is no use getting a council of war of duds and mutts. It is
damnable, perfectly damnable. Winston is an able man, but he is
not a leader. He does not want men around him with understanding
minds. He would rather not have them. He is intolerant of them.
That is bad leadership.'. . .

22. This was one of Churchill's less inspiring statements. It dealt
largely with the position of the French navy. On 3 July the British were
to sink units of the French navy at Oran, to keep them from German and
Italian hands. This was not something to announce in advance.

26 *June*

I agree with Jack B.[23] This country has the biggest chance in its history of rising to the greatest heights. He is sure, however, that Winstone is bust. He told that to Randolph[24] same days ago, and he was terribly annoyed. If he went, he said, that unfortunately would mean L.G. He was inclined to think that would be a sign that the end was near, unless L.G. underwent some queer change.

Frances told me that she had had a row with L.G. last night. She had told him categorically that he had done absolutely nothing to help his country in this war. She said that he had been very annoyed with her and had said it was a damned lie.

L.G. had the following to lunch in the office today: Horrabin,[25] Gwilym, Megan, Goronwy[26] and Hore-Belisha. Horrabin has grown in my estimation. We had a talk before he went in to lunch, at which I was not present. I found his information compared with mine. What I am afraid of is that it will be thought that L.G. is waiting to play the part of Laval or Pétain, and I am genuinely alarmed about it. As Horrabin felt as I did, I suggested that in talking to L.G. he should be blunt and, without any fringe or mucking about, he should hit right out and say what were his fears. He told me afterwards that he had done so and that L.G. had been very annoyed. It was well that he should have this from some source other than me. I am satisfied that it has been well rubbed down his neck.

27 *June*

Lately L.G. has been giving close attention to the Welsh parliamentary party. He came up specially the other day to attend a meeting. They drafted a memorandum to the Government on the importance of the Welsh members having the right and the necessary power to investigate defences in their own constituencies. L.G. has done well on this, but I have good reason to believe that he also has an ulterior motive. It gives him a very good excuse for clearing off to his constituency at the first serious threat of invasion, without being accused of being a funk, which he truly is.

Bombing has started in the Churt area. At first L.G. was afraid of coming up to London. Now he is wondering whether London is safer than Churt. He is frightened to death of air raids. He is terribly anti-English. Talks about 'these damned English' and how they have run away to hide in Wales against bombs and invasion.

23. J. Wilson Broadbent.
24. Randolph Churchill.
25. J. H. Horrabin (1884–1962), artist, journalist, Labour M.P. 1929–31.
26. Goronwy Owen.

Frances told me that when she told him she did not want to go to Wales if we were invaded he said he would dig himself or barricade himself in. She had said she did not want to be on the Welsh side, and would remain on the English side. Then he had twitted her by saying that she would soon change her mind if Jennifer were on his side. For a man of L.G.'s distinction and eminence, I have never seen such a funk. One thing, however, is still true, and that is that L.G. still has *vision*. His imagination is bloody annoying ofttimes, but I realise that L.G. can be so very big on big things and damned small on small things. In today's national emergency, I think he could make a superb contribution. As L.G. and I sat talking alone, I made up my mind to draw him. I said that I had formerly taken the line that it would be a mistake for L.G. to go into the War Cabinet with Neville. The situation now, however, had become so serious that I thought L.G. ought to be in, whether Neville was in or not. 'Never would I go in with Neville' was his firm reply. 'If Winston disagreed with me, it would mean that I would have everybody in the Cabinet against me and I would be overruled.'

He so hates Neville that he would almost rather see the country go to the dogs, so that he could point his finger at Neville and say: 'That is the fellow who is responsible.' This is the view of Frances. He sought consolation in impressing upon me that Wales held out centuries ago, even when England was invaded. Wales even then held out against the Teutons, and she could hold out again today, if she were properly defended. Strolling up and down the room, he said: 'If I am to go through a war which I never wanted, and was always against, I will make myself as comfortable as possible.' He then told me that he was going to have a special air-raid shelter constructed, where if necessary he could sleep.

2 July

Willie Henderson lunched with me in my room. Willie is very keen that L.G. should come into the Cabinet and is pressing that L.G. should make a 'comeback' speech to encourage and help his friends.

5 July

For the first time since our trip with him to Jamaica, Evelyn and I were invited to spend the weekend at Churt. The real reason was because Frances had gone to Wales to see Jennifer at school, and it was very doubtful whether Gwilym or Edna could come down tonight and he wanted to be certain that he would not be alone. We arrived about 6.30 p.m., when L.G. took us to inspect his old dug-out and the new one, which has just been started. This new dug-out was to be about thirty-six feet long and about fifteen feet wide. It is now about five feet deep. We sat on the veranda with L.G. and Miss Parry. Gwilym had telephoned that he and Edna would be there for dinner, so we refreshed ourselves according to our tastes from the variety of drinks brought by Molly, the maid.

I have been scrupulously careful not to let L.G. know that I recently won a cup for golf. He is no sportsman. He would not appreciate that I could properly do my work – even though I worked, as I do, a regular fourteen to sixteen hours a day for seven days a week – if he knew that I played an occasional game of golf, still less won a cup. But I got him talking golf. He said that he had got down to a handicap of thirteen at one time. He said he could never hit a long ball, 'but, unlike what might be imagined', he said, he was always straight.

Sylvester and his wife are staying at Churt.

6 July

Here we are staying in the house which I have known since before the foundations were laid and have watched it rise to its present state. When the roof was only partly done, I came down with L.G. when he was Prime Minister and with Frances, and we spent the night pigging it and eating in one of the bedrooms. Since those days it has been altered out of all recognition. The garage has been turned into the dining-room, where the furniture is made out of wood from his own estate. The oak panelling was presented to him by Philip Sassoon. The finest room in the house is the library, which is some thirty-six feet long and twenty-seven feet wide, built very high with a domed ceiling. At one end of the room, painted on the walls, is a picture in colour by John Churchill[27] of the Gulf of Tigullio, with his wife in the foreground. The fireplace is big and wide, built of red brick in the old-fashioned style, with an open hearth capable of burning huge logs of wood. . . .

On the right of the fireplace is L.G.'s high, comfortable chair, where he sits. It is the chair of a conversationalist, I was once informed, because it has side wings. In this case, as I have good reason to know, it is also the chair of a worker, for a great part of his *War Memoirs* were written by L.G. sitting in that chair – holding his notebook in his left hand and pawing away with his right,

27. John Churchill (b.1909), nephew of Winston Churchill; painter, sculptor and composer.

making those abominable higgledy-piggledy characters, so undecipherable that he himself was many a time unable to read them. At his feet and before the fire was an enormous pouffe, which I bought with him in Morocco. He used to sit in his easy chair and sprawl his legs on this pouffe.

On the right-hand side of this chair is a small table, which is crammed with things. There is a telephone, the bell of which always rings whenever anyone telephones to the house, so that you can take up this receiver and hear the conversations. L.G., being highly suspicious, takes full advantage of this. I can tell immediately when he listens in and many are the times when I have got over some pretty hot criticisms of him in this way. . . .

Beside the telephone there is a pile of letters which have accumulated and upon which no action has ever been taken. For many years, now, L.G. has himself opened all the letters going to Churt, whether they were for him or for anybody else, and particularly those for anybody else. I could never understand this until one day he let the cat out of the bag by a casual remark to me that it gave him a kind of boyish delight 'to see what was in them'.

On this small table there is also a notebook, beside which is a big yellow pencil, about a foot long and as far round as my big fingernail. He uses these enormous pencils, like miniature hedge-stakes, because he cannot so easily lose them, and because they are easier to hold, especially with his terribly shaky hand. Whenever L.G. has a brain-wave, he immediately flies to his notebook and writes it down. Sometimes this is on the international situation, sometimes about the farm, sometimes about an individual with whom he is on bad terms. . . .

Today being Saturday, Miss Parry put something else on this small table, a Welsh hymnal, with all the hymns marked and flagged on the top in red for the Welsh broadcast service at 11.30 tomorrow, Sunday, morning. A note is attached on which is written : 'Welsh Service from Wesleyan Church, Liverpool, Rev. M. Roger Jones.'

Opposite L.G.'s chair is a large grand piano, the top of which has been turned into a veritable gallery of photographs of old colleagues. There is one of his mother, which he recently took from the office. One of Clemenceau himself; F. E. Smith (Lord Birkenhead); the Rt Hon. G. N. Barnes;[28] Lord Lee of Fareham; General Smuts, with an inscription 'To a Great Man from his Friend J. C. Smuts'; President Wilson, inscribed 'Hon. D. Lloyd George with the best wishes of his friend, Woodrow Wilson'; Foch, inscribed 'à M. Lloyd George un Premier Ministre qui chasse les nuages d'un ciel, fort cordialement,

28. G. N. Barnes (1859–1940). Trade union leader; became Labour M.P.; broke with Labour Party to remain in the Lloyd George coalition 1918.

F. Foch, 11.10.18'; there is a painting of M. Venezelos;[29] Asquith and L.G. with Princess Bibesco,[30] with a little girl standing between them – it is signed 'H. H. Asquith to D. Lloyd George', and underneath Asquith has written 'A little child shall lead them, Is.xi.6.' On a small table near the piano there is a small oil-painting of old Robert Owen, a photograph of Baldwin of Bewdley, one of Captain B. H. Liddell Hart, one of L.G. talking to Edward, Prince of Wales, at Caernarvon Castle, and in a little alcove an unframed photograph of my old friend J.T. (Sir John Davies). There is also a bronze bust of L.G., which is a very good one, by a little Austrian Jew named Weiss.

On an occasional table there is a beautiful cigar-box made of many different kinds of wood. I had a hand in the design and presentation of that. Inscribed on a silver plate on the top of the lid is: 'To our Chief as a token of our affection on the 70th anniversary of his birth, January 17, 1933.'. . .

Then there is a magnificent wireless set, presented to him by Sir John Reith, when he was Director-General of the B.B.C. At first L.G. and he did not get on, but Reith learned quickly how to make the right approach to L.G. Whenever L.G. went to Shrewsbury to attend the Advisory Committee on Welsh Religious Services, formed in deference to L.G.'s wishes, Reith always went out of his way to accompany him. Consequently they learned to appreciate each other very much.

Nearby is another interesting cabinet, though not so large. Lift the handle of this cabinet and up comes a bottle of whiskey, accompanied by a syphon of soda and three or four glasses. The thirst slaked, the body regaled, press the button and it just as readily disappears.

In the oak shelves are many valuable and interesting books. One of these is of elephantine dimensions. It is a newspaper record of L.G.'s doings in Canada and America in 1923. I have only to look at that book to bring back showers of memories of that wonderful visit. There is, however, one set of books on L.G.'s shelves which especially interests me. First of all, their subject matter is all-absorbing. They contain everything that is interesting about our foremost British statesmen. There are over a hundred volumes. They include volumes on Bradlaugh, Beaconsfield, Macaulay, Peel, Pitt,

29. Eleutherios Venezelos (1864–1936) started his career as leader of Crete nationalism against the Turks, which resulted in Crete uniting with Greece. He was Prime Minister of Greece 1910–15, 1916, 1917–20, 1924, 1928–32 and 1933. In 1917 he deposed the pro-German King Constantine I and brought Greece into the war on the Allied side.
30. Daughter of Asquith.

Cobden, Cromwell, and many others. (I just took these names at random from the shelves.) The second reason they fascinate me is the beautiful binding. They are covered in red calf, with green silk inside the cover. Their titles are inscribed in gold. They are all bound in the same colour in the same way. They cost £3 10s 0d *each.* They therefore cost something like £350. The third reason I am so interested in them is because they were presented to L.G. by my old friend Sir Henry Fildes. You will find no plate on which there is any inscription signifying who was the donor, or that there was any donor at all. It is just my memory which recalls that these books were sent by Sir Henry in a box addressed to The Rt Hon. D. Lloyd George at 18 Abingdon Street in the year 1922, when L.G. resigned from the premiership and when I was still at 10 Downing Street, with Bonar Law as Prime Minister. Those books arrived quite safely, and not only did they not have an inscription placed inside them, but the donor did not even get so much as a single sheet of paper in acknowledgement of safe receipt, let alone a word of thanks in the fair hand of the receiver. Harry [Sir Henry Fildes] has often talked to me about that incident, and many is the time he has 'bequeathed' them to me at L.G.'s death, with the laughing remark, 'If you can get them.'

Over there is a silver cup which L.G. won three times outright for his blackcurrants. This was presented by the National Farmers' Union Kent Branch Fruit and Vegetable Committee. Nearby is a small silver shell, with wings, presented to him when he was Minister of Munitions. Until recently this has been L.G.'s mascot on his various Rolls cars through the years. The first Rolls-Royce which it adorned was the one L.G. acquired from Kitchener. Throughout the war and L.G.'s premiership it was specially protected. It is still owned by L.G. and is pensioned off in a London garage with a great sentimental value but a commercial value which is precisely nil. . . .

No room has the least interest for L.G. unless it has an outlook. For years L.G. had only two ordinary windows before this room assumed its present form. In 1936 L.G. went to Berchtesgaden and there met Hitler in his Bavarian retreat. I shall never forget Hitler's window. It was the biggest I have ever seen. It was enormous. I shall never forget that outlook over the Bavarian Alps, with the ravine on the right and Salzburg beyond. It made a deep impression on me; it must have made a still deeper one on L.G., because when he returned he, too, had a huge window made in this room, and he made himself an outlook, too, and a very beautiful one. Beyond the window L.G. has had a number of trees removed so that the eye looks down the hill, which is a profusion of roses and arum lilies.

At the bottom is one of the three large ponds, abounding with trout and fed by a spring which is eternal. Beyond stretch the acres of L.G.'s own hungry land, much of it reclaimed from scrub by L.G. himself and, almost against all known rules, is made to produce heavy crops of fruit. Behind and beyond the eye sees across forty miles or more into Surrey and Sussex on the one hand and Hampshire on the other. It is a wonderful view. It is an inspiration. . . .

L.G. strolled into this room this afternoon, after his nap, and went up to the picture of Clemenceau on the piano and remarked: 'I wonder what he would have thought of this situation.' Then, looking at the picture of Foch, he said: 'At any rate, he will dissolve his partnership with Weygand, when they meet.'

L.G.'s bedroom always interests me. There is a big, low bed, by the side of which is a low mahogany table, over which hangs a specially constructed light. He reads himself off to sleep every night and it burns right through the night. Many a time I have had breakfast with L.G. in this room while he has been in bed. Many a time have I, with him and others, retired to that room for a swig of whiskey before we went to dinner with life-long abstainers. . . .

7 July

L.G. talks of nothing else but bombs and invasion. He is very jumpy. He is talking now of coming to live in London. Beaverbrook told him on the telephone this morning that it was the safest place, and that he thought Hitler had given up the idea of invading this country and was going east. Beaverbrook is still pressing L.G. to join the Cabinet.

Commander King-Hall, M.P.,[31] and his wife came to tea. There was a long discussion as to whether Hitler would invade this country. L.G. said that 'the realm of conjecture is infinite', but that we must do something to break the invincibility of Hitler's army. That was the first necessity.

At dinner, Colonel and Mrs Proctor were present. There was a general discussion about the war. L.G. said: 'Hitler is a prodigious genius.'

8 July

This morning L.G. handed me a letter, saying: 'Look what I have just received.' It was a letter written in Bob Boothby's own hand and the purport of it was: 'Winston feels the need of you.' L.G. was obviously delighted. I helped him pull up a bench and he, Evelyn[32]

31. Stephen King-Hall (1893–1966). Independent M.P. 1939–44, founded the King-Hall News-Letter 1936, knighted 1954, made a life peer 1966.
32. Mrs A. J. Sylvester.

and I sat upon it in the gorgeous sunshine and gossiped. He was as happy as could be. It was a joy to be with him. My own belief is that if he got office half his own difficulties and doubts about the war would disappear. . . .

9 July

L.G. saw Garvin at 11.30 a.m. He is most anxious to have L.G. in the War Cabinet and is doing everything he can. L.G. saw Maisky at twelve and lunched with Beaverbrook at 1.30 at Stornoway House, where I accompanied him. Max[33] told him he thought Halifax[34] ought to go. L.G. told us that at one time Harold Spender had a cockatoo brought up by a sailor. His sister was very religious. One day she had a lot of religious workers coming to a meeting at his house. Suddenly this cockatoo shrieked out: 'What a bloody row.'

11 July

Dr Negrin, ex-Prime Minister of Spain and Mr Ascarate, ex-Spanish Ambassador in London, lunched with L.G. today. Megan and I accompanied him. Dr Negrin thought that Mussolini had personally conceived every new idea which had been carried out in Italy, whereas Hitler, who was more or less a lunatic, depended upon others. L.G. immediately developed a terrific defence of Hitler, saying that he was a genius and had all the understanding of a genius. For instance, everybody laughed at Göring's apparent childishness in wearing so many medals, but behind that vanity Hitler had been quick to realise there was a mass of outstanding ability. Take, for example, the Norway expedition from Germany. Winston had told him that it had been a tremendously clever plan and brilliantly executed. It might be said that Hitler did not plan that personally, but he had at any rate chosen the man who could do it.

Negrin said that L.G. was definitely wrong about Hitler. L.G. replied at once: 'Do you think Germany would be in the position in which she is today if Hitler had not been there?' He said he had met Hitler. He [Hitler] was a fanatic in many ways, and there was a very thin margin between a fanatic and a lunatic. It was Hitler himself who conceived the ideas. Hitler's speeches might seem fanatical, but if you read Cromwell's speeches today they seemed equally fanatical.

The impression left on my mind was that Negrin was not convinced. Personally, I doubt the wisdom of L.G. waxing so warmly in favour of Hitler in conversation with a man who had put up such a great fight for liberty against Germany. When Negrin thanked

33. Beaverbrook.
34. Foreign Secretary.

L.G. for all he had done for his country, L.G. said not a word. At lunch, we all drank whiskey. I noticed that L.G. helped himself from the bottle before offering it to Negrin. He is singularly ungentlemanly in many of his manners.

12 July

As L.G. strolled up and down his room at Thames House, with the fingers of both hands tucked in his trousers, we talked of Winston's position. He wanted to know what people were saying of Winston. I said he had the confidence of the country but so far he had given no brilliant display. Many thinking people were getting apprehensive. We wanted something else besides brilliant retreats. L.G. said: 'The future will decide not only the future of Winston but the future of this country. It will decide whether we shall be a democracy or otherwise. Winston is not a real democrat. His real interest is in the governing classes. He does not want a strong proletarian party. I know him very well. He would rather be at the head of a kind of plutocratic state and would govern them exactly the same as is done in Italy.'

26 July

Tweed's Will appears in the evening papers. In the *Evening News* there is a photograph of Frances and Tweed side by side. The Press started to ring up Frances and she deemed it necessary to inform L.G. He was so angry that he went to his bedroom. *Evening News* says, '£2000 for L.G.'s Woman Secretary in partial repayment of a loss incurred on an investment taken on my advice.'[35]

5 August

I have not yet got the real reactions of L.G. on Tweed's Will, but judging by the fact that Miss Smithers[36] can get no instructions because things at Churt are so difficult it does not look too good.

14 August

The War Office have requisitioned Thames House. This is a godsend to L.G. for he has wanted to get out for a long time. The office is to be at Victoria Road.[37]

35. In addition to the £2000 for Miss Stevenson, Tweed bequeathed a life interest in £1000 to her sister, Miss Muriel Stevenson, and £500 to Jennifer.
36. Private secretary of Sylvester.
37. 8 Victoria Road, Kensington, Lloyd George's London house.

22 *August*
L.G. went to Wales by car. Whenever he goes to Wales it is to be
with Dame Margaret. He deposited Frances at Ruthin.

*On 15 September came the peak of the German daylight air attacks
in the 'Battle of Britain'.*

17 *September*
We motored off to Churt. On arrival L.G. and I enjoyed an Irish
whiskey and water and Megan had sherry. L.G. at once wanted
to know whether there had been any air activity and, leaving his
drink, he insisted that I should accompany him to the air-raid
shelter to decide where we should sleep. He led the way to a most
luxurious underground apartment which, when I last saw it, was
merely being dug out of the ground. There were a number of beds.
There was a reading-lamp by the side of each, an electric fire, with
furniture made of non-flammable material. The cupboard contained
everything that one might require: drinks, eatables, fruit, cigars.
I saw, I listened, I wondered, I wondered exceedingly whether he
would in this state ever take office again, and, if he did, how he
would function. I felt unhappy.
    As we left, he suddenly stopped, and holding up his finger, to
emphasise the point he was about to make, he said: 'Do you know
the Prime Minister and his family sleep in an air-raid shelter at 10
Downing Street every night? Winston told me that himself.'
    Megan told me that Dame Margaret had had a terrible time with
L.G. in Wales. That he thought of nothing but air raids, that he
had got them completely on his mind, and that they were afraid
he would make himself really ill.

21 *September*
L.G. returned to Criccieth by car, accompanied by Megan. He had
travelled 270-odd miles to come to the House and had never been
nearer than forty miles of the place.

23 *September*
I spoke to Frances on the telephone. Talking of L.G. she said: 'I
am awfully sad about L.G., too. I have tried my best to persuade him
to believe that the chances are that one does not get hit, and that
if he takes a proper job of work he would not have the time to
think about it. But you cannot budge him. He is more terrified than
a child. He is shaking. He was not so bad when he came back here,
but two or three nights here have reduced him to a doddering old

man. He does not want to go. He was almost in tears when he went. It was pathetic. He said: "I cannot help it; you must forgive me for being like this. If I stay here it will just kill me." And, of course, it would. Whenever there was a suggestion of a German plane over, his face would get red and blotchy and he could not control himself. The only thing for him to do is to go to Wales. On the other hand, if he does not do anything, he is finished.'

Talking of future possibilities, Frances said: 'L.G. has some idea he is coming in on the peace settlement, that he will be able to make peace where Winston won't. But when you see him in the state in which he is you wonder whether he would be capable.'

A cable arrived today from William Randolph Hearst from California: '. . . Unless England should win an overwhelming victory, she might never make a better peace than now. . . .' L.G. replied by cable: 'I am in complete sympathy with your desire that an offer should be made to bring this horrible struggle to a peaceful conclusion but I am strongly of the opinion that this moment is inopportune for appeal while a grim battle now pending has not reached issue. When German plan for invasion definitely checked and both sides faced with prospect of prolonged and exhausting war then appeal for peace conference might succeed. Premature intervention would prejudice chances.'

25 September
L.G. writes to Sir Leo Chiozza Money: 'Your letter seems to me to take a much too one-sided view of the merits of the dispute between the authoritarian States and the democratic countries. . . . As you are aware I have been an unsparing critic of the policy of the British Government when I have found it lacking in thought and wisdom, but that does not prevent me seeing the peril to liberty which is involved in Fascist and Nazi aggression.'

30 September
Yesterday I finished reading a book on Clemenceau by his secretary, Martet. There was a conversation recorded in that book with Clemenceau which inspired me. I decided to write a *magnum opus* to L.G. and I did so today. It is the most audacious memorandum I have ever sent him, but as he has got a sort of complex or feeling of terror or whatever it is about air raids something only a little less than dynamite will shift him.

The memorandum was calculated to give him a picture of the position. I asked him: 'Whether Neville does or does not go and you get another chance to enter the Cabinet, will you reconsider? Your taking office would create a new psychology not only in this country but abroad – in Russia, in Turkey, in America, and last, but by no means least, in Germany itself. I am sure that Hitler is frightened of you because you would always keep him guessing as to what you were going to do.

'What a contribution you could make to your country if you could induce Russia to join us. If anyone could do this, you could.

'Won't you try?

'I know you don't like some of the present crowd in office and you may even feel that the position cannot be retrieved. If you do take that view, then let me try to console you with the thought that another great man as long ago as 1917 thought then somewhat as you do now.'

Then follows the quotation: it is terrific. I quote the most striking passage. Martet said to Clemenceau: 'I am sure that Poincaré is only waiting for a sign from you in order to appeal for your co-operation. For the love of God, make that sign!'

'No,' answered Clemenceau, 'I shan't make that sign – you can do what you like. I shan't do it for this reason: that, far from seeking power like all these worthy people, I am afraid of it. I am terribly afraid of it. I would give anything to escape from it. You have merely to look at me and see clearly that I am a gonner; seventy-six years old, rotten with diabetes. . . . How do you expect me to pull it off? Secondly, I am not at all sure that we could pull it off in the pass to which we have come.'

Then I proceed to point out that shortly after that interview, at seventy-six, Clemenceau became Prime Minister of France and achieved the greatest of all his great triumphs. Office gave him a new lease of life. I pointed out that a somewhat similar effect had been produced on Beaverbrook and I held him up as a fine case of courage overcoming disability to perform a national duty.[38] I ended up with the following:

'The country is crying out for the old patriot who rescued it from destruction in the Great War. The country has faith in you. Will you show your faith in your country and lend a hand now whilst you may.

'Tomorrow it may be too late.'

3 October

Last night I went to the Ministry of Agriculture. There I ran into big news: Neville's impending resignation.[39] Having failed to get

38. Beaverbrook, aged sixty-one, was performing prodigiously as Minister of Aircraft Production. He suffered from asthma.

39. Neville Chamberlain was mortally ill with cancer. He died on 9 November 1940.

L.G. on the telephone last night I spoke to him early this morning at Criccieth, warned him of these cabinet changes and asked whether he had been approached. He had had no approach and he was very interested.

Then I said: 'Did you receive a special memorandum from me.' 'Yes,' he replied. 'What do you think about it?' I asked. 'Yes, very important. What are the air raids like in London. Is the bombing getting better?' 'They are just as heavy,' I replied.

I felt too sad for words. I knew from those remarks that he meant to do nothing. When I pressed him further he said: 'Anyhow, it is a different situation now to what it was then; Clemenceau had power; I shall wait until Winston is bust.'

29 October

L.G. asked for a copy of Boccaccio's *Decameron* to be sent to Churt. This I obtained from Hugh Rees. For some reason the account was sent to Megan at Criccieth! If L.G. gave his mind to thinking out how he could best help his country, instead of thinking cunt and women, he would be a better man.

10 November

L.G.'s deep air-raid shelter at Churt, sixty feet below the earth's surface, is like a Piccadilly underground station. It has certainly not cost less than £6000 and it is the talk of the place. Everybody is talking about L.G. and asking whether he is frightened. Frances told me on the telephone that if you argue with him about it he just gets annoyed. 'He feels that when the crash comes he will have to come in and make peace.'

26 November

Dame Margaret had a fall today at Mrs William George's house. She slipped on the parquet floor; an X-ray has revealed a cracked hip.

12 December

This afternoon, while the House was in session at Church House, I got news that Lord Lothian[40] had died. I immediately put through a priority telephone call to L.G. and spoke to him personally at Criccieth. He was flabbergasted. He said: 'I feel as if a shell had fallen at my feet and numbed me. I am glad I saw him. I do not think I noted anything particular about him: he had not quite the vitality which he had. You know how vital he was.'

I said: 'You know that already your name is being mentioned as

40. British Ambassador in Washington. Lloyd George had lunched with him in London the previous month. See note to p. 123.

his successor.' 'Ah,' he said, 'that would involve a great physical strain.'

I am completely tired of L.G.'s mucking about. The man is doing nothing for his country, and he is just living amongst the clouds, quarrelling with everybody. He has just quarrelled with Willie[41] the gardener at Brynawelon. Willie just went into the kitchen and wrote out his resignation, and sent it upstairs to Dame Margaret. When she asked him to reconsider his decision, he refused. It all arose out of the heating-pipes not been sufficiently warm, according to L.G. Dyer[42] told me that he cursed Willie in Welsh. Workmen were working downstairs in the air-raid shelter and heard it. They were chapel people and had no idea that L.G. could swear and were very shocked. That has gone the round of Criccieth. L.G.'s stock has gone down since he has been living here. . . .

14 December

Frances phoned me that L.G. was motoring to Churt tomorrow, Sunday, and that she was meeting him at Oxford. Gwilym had phoned to say that the P.M. wanted to see L.G. and that I could attach what importance I liked to this. It was obviously about America. L.G. wanted to see Dawson and Maisky, and I was asked to arrange this. I did.

16 December

Lord Dawson arrived at 8 Victoria Road this morning before his time. He said he wanted to have a talk with me. I gave him the low-down about L.G.'s behaviour and his fear of bombs. He said he was against his going to America. Later he had a long talk with L.G. Dr Smith had already vetted him at Churt and was against his going to America. After he had seen L.G., Lord Dawson read out to me the draft of a letter which he was going to send to L.G. at No. 10, where he was lunching at 1.30 with the Prime Minister. It pointed out that L.G. was not an ambassador and had not much patience with people who 'dig deeply into the surface' – a phrase which amused and pleased L.G. immensely; in other words, L.G. would not stand having to listen to a lot of damn fools talking and having to show some interest in them. This letter was produced by L.G. to Winston as documentary evidence why he could not accept. Before L.G. left for No. 10 he told me that if Winston offered him the ambassadorship at Washington he would not accept. He laughed loudly as he left for No. 10.[43]

41. William Evans.
42. George Dyer, L.G.'s very capable chauffeur. A.J.S.
43. Lloyd George declined, on grounds of health.

Chapter 13

'I do not see how we are going to win'

1941

15 January
Last night L.G. phoned, asking me to go to Churt today for lunch and to bring Evelyn with me.

Some weeks ago Dame Margaret fell and injured her hip whilst at tea in William George's house; she slipped on the polished floor. Early this morning I received a telephone message from Miss Brady at Criccieth. Dr Prytherch, Dame Margaret's local doctor, had asked Miss Brady to let me know urgently that he was much concerned about Dame Margaret. She had been vomiting rather violently for three days and he was afraid of the effect this would have on the heart. Neither Olwen nor Megan had wanted to worry their father, but the doctor had thought L.G. ought to be informed and wanted me to do it. I did not wait to get to Churt but telephoned at once to L.G. He said that obviously we must get a specialist. . . .

Evelyn and I motored down in a snow storm. L.G. said, after welcoming us very kindly in the library: 'I don't know which is the bloodier, this war or this weather.' He was obviously much preoccupied about the news concerning Dame Margaret.

Seated in his wing chair by the side of the fire, sipping his Irish whiskey, he fixed his eye on me and said: 'One thing I will not do. I am definitely not coming into this government under present conditions.' Pointing to the telephone, he said: 'Winston himself telephoned me at Christmas and asked me to join him, but I said "No".'

He then compared the strength of the German armies and those of the Great War. He said that in the Great War the Allies had outnumbered the enemy, but this time the enemy outnumbered us. He excused himself more than once because, he said, the news of Dame Margaret had prevented him having the talk with me that he had wanted to have. His mind was not on it.

'How is it all going to end?' he said he had asked himself. 'I have asked many others but nobody can tell me,' he said. 'I do not know.'

I said : 'If you joined the Government, you would do more than anyone else to bring in Russia, or at any rate make her more friendly with us.' 'You see, I am already in close touch with Maisky' was his answer, which was no real answer.

'If I went in, Winston's friends would be opposing me; so would Labour. At our last luncheon, I had a particularly good talk with Winston. Winston was in a mood to listen. On a previous occasion, when I tried to talk to him, he started his bellowing tactics. "Here," I said, "don't try that one on me." ' It was a good illustration of what Winston did with other people. To bully a fellow into what you wanted was no policy. (It amused me much to hear L.G. saying this.)

18 January

At 4.30 p.m. Carey telephoned me that Dr Prytherch of Criccieth had telephoned him that Dame Margaret was worse, her pulse was faster, though her temperature was about ninety-nine. But she was very drowsy. Prytherch was very apprehensive. I informed L.G. at once. He was annoyed because Prytherch had telephoned to Carey instead of direct to him. He asked me to arrange for Lord Dawson to go to Criccieth, which I did.

19 January

I travelled with Lord Dawson on the 10.15 a.m. train from Euston to Bangor. Most interesting conversation. Lord Dawson said that L.G. had plenty of moral but no physical courage. That was why he was frightened of bombs. I told him that both Frances and I had done our very best to get him to take office but he had refused. Dawson was definitely of the opinion that L.G. should not go into the Government. It might kill him. If he entered the Government and died at his post, that would be a great ending, but the danger was that he might, through lack of physical courage, become a failure and that would ruin his reputation.

He had suspected for some time that Dame Margaret was suffering with her heart. L.G.'s treatment of her and his carryings-on had no doubt worried her and this would undoubtedly aggravate the trouble and speed the end.

When we arrived an hour late at Bangor, the snow lay thick and it was freezing very hard. To my astonishment, there was no car to meet us. I quickly telephoned to Criccieth, only to learn that there was a deep snowdrift which made it impossible for any car to get through. We came for the night to the Castle Hotel,

where we found Sir Thomas Carey Evans. The latest news from
Prytherch was not good. Lord Dawson retired at midnight, very
worried.

L.G. left Churt early this morning with Miss Parry. He ran into
a snowdrift at Bridgnorth and had to be dug out. At Cerrig-y-
Druidion, when it was almost dark and the lights of the car were
on, he ran into another – everything suddenly became perfectly
dark through the car being buried. A local garage proprietor and
his friends dug him out and took him to what was formerly a
coaching inn, the White Lion. There he is staying the night, having
been much shaken.

20 January

Dr Prytherch telephoned me that Dame Margaret died at 10.20 a.m.
Lord Dawson spoke on the telephone to L.G. as soon as possible
afterwards. I was beside him when he spoke. He passed the time of
day with him and asked him about his journey. Then Lord Dawson
said: 'Your wife died at twenty minutes past ten this morning.'
There was a slight pause, and Lord Dawson said: 'You were prepared for it?' – evidently repeating L.G.'s words. Then L.G. asked
to speak to me. It was most pathetic. L.G. was broken and he
sobbed at the other end of the telephone. I expressed my deep grief
for him. He sobbed: 'She was a great old pal.' I said: 'You are
very brave,' but he said: 'No, I am not.' He then said: 'Don't take
any risks but come through to me here as soon as you can. I want
your companionship.'

There has been another blizzard. Last night I tried to get an
aeroplane, but there was nowhere to take off. A horse was impossible,
because there is a complete block. My business obviously was to
look after L.G. but I could not get to him.

21 January

All roads from Bangor to Criccieth and to Cerrig-y-Druidion were
still blocked. At breakfast I had a brain-wave. Tom[1] and I decided
to make a dash for Corwen on the 9.30 via Chester. Meantime, a
gang of men had cut a road through many miles of snow from
Cerrig-y-Druidion to Corwen. There we met the London train
bringing the family.

I shall never forget L.G.'s face when he drew up in the Rolls-
Royce, driven by Dyer. I have never seen anyone looking so near
death. His face was an awful colour. For the first time in my life
I saw him wearing a woollen scarf.

1. Sir Thomas Carey Evans.

At the Glyndwr Arms Hotel we had a private room, a roaring fire and hot milk, to which Tom added a pick-me-up. After about an hour, L.G. revived and smoked a cigar and chatted. He told me how a gang of forty men had turned out to cut a way through the deep snowdrift, so that he might get to Corwen. L.G. was deeply touched by the fact that in this gang were all classes of men from that mountain village, including the Wesleyan minister, the school-master, the local garage proprietor, named Bob Roberts, and many of the Home Guard. L.G. said that although Cerrig-y-Druidion was only a very small place no place he could imagine could have shown him more kindness.

When the London train arrived, it brought Gwilym and Edna, Dick and June. L.G. fell into Dick's arms and sobbed. Supported on the arms of his family, he boarded the train and went to sleep. After his sleep, L.G. said he was hungry and had a very good meal of cold goose, some cold beef, cheese and hot milk and whiskey, which had been prepared by the Glyndwr Arms Hotel. Then he smoked a cigar and seemed considerably cheered.

Outside Canada and America, I have never seen such snow. The Great Western Railway had been very enterprising and had had snow ploughs at work. Glad was I to reach Criccieth.

Carey and I went to see Dame Margaret in her coffin. She looked very peaceful. L.G. did not see her. I do not think he has ever seen death. I learn that he did not even see Mair.[2] Neither did Dick nor Gwilym see her. When I met Megan on arrival in the hall at Brynawelon, she just fell into my arms. The scenes I witnessed between members of the family were most pathetic.

24 January

The funeral service was private and was held at Brynawelon at 2 p.m. The Rev. J. W. Jones and the Rev. J. Lloyd Jones conducted the service. L.G. was overcome with grief and in floods of tears. The coffin was borne on a lorry, and pulled by sixty-five Home Guards-men, each carrying a wreath. The sun came out in all its glory. Fields on the mountain side showed green patches, around which there were deep snowdrifts. There were no women mourners. Mair's grave had been turned into a vault. I watched the coffin being lowered into the vault. L.G., standing between Dick and Gwilym, trembled and sobbed.

25 January

As he smoked his cigar after breakfast, which is the one he most

2. Lloyd George's eldest daughter, who died in 1907, to his passionate grief.

enjoys, he talked of the select committee on Bob Boothby.[3] He said that if he were in the House next week he would vote against the Government and for Bob Boothby, whom he thought had been badly treated, because they had been after his papers for two months and not even Winston had broached Boothby on the subject. It was clear from L.G.'s demeanour that he is friendly to, but critical of, Winston. . . .

L.G. told Megan this morning that he could not continue any allowance to enable her to keep up Brynawelon,[4] such as he had allowed her mother. Yet he is spending a fortune in having all sorts of people around him who do not earn a fraction of their salaries.

L.G. told me he did not see how we could get successfully through this war. When he had been a practising solicitor and a client consulted him, he always asked himself not only whether the client had right on his side but also whether he had a strong enough case to be sure to win in court. 'It is clear that that damn fool Neville never gave a thought to that question – whether we would win – when he declared war. I am not against war, but I am against war when we have no chance of winning.'

26 January

L.G. stays in bed for the greater part of each day. Every morning, immediately after breakfast at nine o'clock he goes to sleep until eleven. We are still in Wales, held up by the snow. This morning, when I went to see him, he talked of Megan and how she prayed. 'Just like my old uncle,' he said. 'He would suddenly flop down on his knees when faced with a difficult situation. There is none of the mystic in me that there was in my old uncle, or even in Megan. I feel I have no contact.' He laughed. 'I do not know which way to look to get hold of Him. I am more of a pagan. Yet I would rather listen to a good sermon than go to a good play or a good concert. Beaverbrook, on the contrary, is very religious. He does not go to church very often, perhaps; all the same he is a very religious person.'

Since Dame Margaret's death, telegrams, letters and cables have come in sheaves, including messages from the King and Queen, Queen Mary, President Roosevelt, General Smuts, Mackenzie King,[5]

3. Boothby had acted imprudently in a business matter relating to Czechoslovakia. The resulting fuss (scandal would be too strong a word) enforced his resignation from office as Parliamentary Secretary to the Ministry of Food, although he remained an M.P.
4. Dame Margaret had bequeathed Brynawelon, which was her property, to Megan.
5. W. L. Mackenzie King (1874–1950), Prime Minister of Canada 1921–30, 1935–48.

the Archbishop of Canterbury, the Speaker, the Archbishop of Wales, the Princess Royal and from an endless stream of the humblest homes, including old-age pensioners and ex-servicemen. But the one message which I knew L.G. was looking forward to was one from Winston. As it had not come, I telephoned to his secretary, Seal.

Today the letter arrived, in Winston's own hand. I took it up to L.G. and he read it in bed. After reading it to me, he said, handing the letter to me: 'Now, isn't that a wonderful letter. Winston always says so much in so little.' He was very delighted and I had to take it to show Megan and the rest of the family. It read:

> 10 Downing Street,
> Whitehall.

My dear David,

I learned with great sorrow of the death of your wife – that great woman, who embodied all that is most strong and true in the British race. I offer you my deep sympathy in the severance of a wonderful tie that has lasted through the storms and vicissitudes of two generations. I know how vain are words at these solemn milestones in our journey. But pray, believe me how much Clemmie and I feel for you and your children in their sad hour.

> Yours always,
> **W.**

L.G. said: 'Winston is the only one of my friends who calls me David.'

From the time of Dame Margaret's death, L.G.'s health steadily degenerated. The following entry in my diary reflects an early symptom. A.J.S.

29 January

Dr Prytherch came to my bedroom and stayed until nearly midnight, talking about L.G. He told me he had had a letter from Dawson and that he suspected that these stoppages in L.G.'s bowel movements were due to a growth which would not be apparent for some time. Prytherch said L.G.'s blood pressure had been up to 240, and was now about 190. He might go off at any time or he might live a number of years. I said I had made up my mind that he would never again take office and was not fit for it. Prytherch agreed.

9 *February*

I never was so glad to get back home and to the House of Commons after being at Criccieth. A week has rolled on since then. L.G. has done absolutely nothing, and I am satisfied that it is best for him to stay away from the House. He can do less harm at Churt.

The fight is now *on*, not only with Germany, but between Frances and the family. Frances said to me: 'Things are different now. I have had a lot to put up with for years.' Last Thursday Lord Dawson asked me to dine with him at the Dorchester Hotel and we had a long talk about L.G.'s intimate position and prospects. He does not think it would be wise for L.G. to marry Miss Frances Stevenson. I can only suspect that that is what she is after. Frances now stays at Bron-y-de even when Megan and Olwen are there.

13 *March*

When L.G. arrived in his room in the House, he looked many years older. It was his first appearance in Parliament for three months. At lunch the other day, Megan told me 'just between ourselves' that Dame Margaret had been convinced that L.G. would never take office again. Dame Margaret was a wise and far-seeing woman. She made the same observation to me, privately. I received a message from Peck, the Prime Minister's secretary, asking whether L.G. would lunch with Winston today at 1.30. L.G. said: 'An invitation from the Prime Minister is like a command from the King.' So he lunched with Winston at No. 10 and remained there until about three o'clock.

24 *April*

There is a terrific row in progress between L.G. and Megan. Since Dame Margaret's death, Frances remains at Bron-y-de during the weekend. Megan saw her there the other day and, as a consequence, just ignored her father and refused to speak to him. Megan was very bitter in talking to me. 'He is fussing and bothering about little things which he ought not to bother about. To think of all that brilliance, all those talents, all those gifts just going to seed, because that is what they will do, with a lot of women around him, fussing him, making an old man of him.'

This was, for Britain, one of the gloomiest periods of the Second World War. The disasters of the summer of 1940 had, at least, brought a certain tense excitement. Now British cities had endured a winter of relatively heavy German night-bombing. There were food shortages and rationing, owing to German submarine warfare.

K

In April 1941 *the German Afrika Korps recaptured Cyrenia and reached the approaches to Egypt. In the same month the British attempted to assist Greece by landing 62,000 troops to help her against German invasion: they had to be withdrawn again almost at once with severe losses of men and equipment.*

On 6 and 7 May the Government called for a vote of confidence from the House of Commons and obtained it by 477 votes to three. This was the last occasion on which Lloyd George made a full-blown speech in the Commons. He opened the second day of the debate, from the opposition front bench. He called for a more thorough prosecution of the war and talked of the need to obtain allies. (The British Empire was still, at this stage, fighting alone.) He criticised the building up of the Army to a strength of five million men. It was 'fatuous' to suppose that Britain could ever invade mainland Europe. It was more important to have manpower in agriculture than in the Army. He called for a War Cabinet of non-departmental ministers which would take collective responsibility for the conduct of the war and subject Churchill's ideas to thorough review.

7 May

L.G. arrived at 11.45 a.m. and proceeded to the lavatory. Whilst I was under the gallery, two of the government whips asked if I could hurry L.G. into the chamber. I rushed up to his room and yelled at him in the lavatory, and he entered the chamber only just in time. He nearly missed his chance. He spoke well, but the speech was too long, one and a quarter hours. It wanted tightening up. There was no talk of peace. There was a note struck wanting more effort. That was refreshing to me.

L.G. waited, as he was obliged to do, for Winston's speech. Winston criticised L.G. most strongly when he said : 'I must say that I did not think the speech of my Rt Hon. Friend, the Member for Caernarvon Boroughs, was particularly helpful. . . . It was the sort of speech with which I imagine the illustrious and venerable Marshal Pétain might well have enlivened the closing days of M. Reynaud's cabinet.'[6]

It was the unanimous opinion of members and the lobby that this was unjustified. But perhaps it would be better understood if it were realised that L.G. has been talking defeatist stuff to a good many members. Possibly Winston knew all about L.G.'s attitude

6. According to *The Times's* report, this remark of Churchill's was greeted with laughter. Thus it would seem that Churchill was delivering a quip rather than a serious attack.

in private talk. L.G. abstained from voting. Immediately the P.M. sat down after winding up, L.G. shot out of the chamber. When I arrived upstairs he had got his hat and coat on, ready to go, and shot out of the House and its precincts like a shot out of a gun.

8 May

The extraordinary thing is that there is not one word of criticism in the Press about L.G.'s speech. Frances told me on the telephone that he very much felt Winston's likening him to Pétain. There is no doubt it went right home. I think one of the reasons L.G. flew off was because he was a little ashamed to be put in the Pétain category.

16 May

Received a telephone message early this morning from Frances saying that L.G. thought the situation was serious and would like to discuss things with me and would I go down to Churt. Nancy Astor was going for lunch. I combed London for a dressed crab, which I had been asked to take. Miss Smithers telephoned around London. Wigg went to Scott's in Piccadilly, then by taxi to Putney. That crab cost 25 shillings, plus 1s, plus 1s 9d, plus 4s 6d – total 32s 3d.

L.G. greeted me and suggested we should have a drink before Nancy Astor arrived.[7] I helped with a dose of whiskey and he started to talk about Winston. 'Winston ought not to have said that about Pétain. There is nothing in my record in the Great War to justify it.' When we were in the middle of our drink, Lady Astor arrived, with her son David,[8] and we had to leave it.

She told L.G. at lunch that she had come to insist that he must go in the Cabinet to save the country and she would not leave this palace of his until he had promised to do so. He must not wait for Winston. He must go to tell Winston that he wanted to join him. She is a very lively character and a remarkable personality. How L.G. shrieked with loud laughter. She said he would not have to sit in an office all day. Three hours in the morning would be sufficient. He could supply the guidance, the inspiration and the direction.

She said Winston had been to the air-raid damage at Plymouth, where her husband is Lord Mayor. He came there and wept and said, 'God bless you.' She said : 'God damn you.'

She never let L.G. alone on the subject of his going into the

7. Lady Astor was a teetotaller.
8. David Astor (b.1912) was at this time in the Royal Marines; he has edited the *Observer* since 1948.

Cabinet. 'I shall get hold of Winston and Max[9] personally,' she said after lunch as she sat on the settee at the window in the brilliant sunshine. 'I shall get hold of *The Times* and the *Observer*,[10] and I shall insist that you are taken into the Cabinet. You go in. Make Tom Jones work for you and (pointing to her son) him. These two billynapes will help you.' David, of whom I formed an excellent impression, said Hitler had used propaganda in politics, just like a business firm. We had no effective answer to that yet. We should have.

When Lady Astor and David had gone, L.G. lay down on the settee to read his book. He said: 'I am not going in with this gang.' I said the only thing that mattered was that he kept his health.

On 22 June Germany invaded the Soviet Union and so Britain no longer lacked an ally. At this stage, however, it was very far from certain that the Soviet Union would be able to resist successfully, and initially the Germans made vast territorial gains.

24 June

Today Eden, Foreign Secretary, made a very important statement upon the German invasion of Russia. Last night I phoned L.G. at Churt. He said he was not coming up. He was definite about this. This morning I telephoned Frances early and suggested she should press him to come. She did, but it was only under very strong pressure that he came and then very unwillingly. Fancy a man who has all along insisted that we should try to get Russia in is not even wanting to be in his place in the House.

26 June

I lunched with L.G. in the members' dining-room. Clem Davies, Wilfrid Roberts and Gwilym were also present. Gwilym recalled a story of how, during L.G.'s premiership, when L.G. was trying to get a better understanding with Russia, Winston was asked whether he was now prepared to shake the hairy hand of the baboon. Like a flash Winston had replied: 'A baboon in the forest makes an interesting sight. A baboon in the zoo is not a pleasant sight. But a baboon in bed with your wife or daughter is very annoying.'

Gwilym told a story about L.G., Birkenhead and Winston travelling to Wales. Presently they came in sight of the Welsh mountains.

9. Beaverbrook.

10. Members of the Astor family owned both these newspapers.

How would they cross them? Birkenhead replied: 'Through them.'
Winston said: 'Over them.' L.G. said: 'Round them.'

1 August

Today I went to see Sir James Grigg,[11] Permanent Under-Secretary
of State for War, at the War Office by appointment. He is seeing
L.G. tomorrow night. He agrees with me entirely about the intensifi-
cation of the war effort. He said that Winston was impulsive in
small things, but in big things he was hesitating. He said this in
answer to a point, which I had made, that Winston wanted someone to sit on his head. I went through the whole story about L.G.
and said it was my conviction that he could make the greatest
contribution of all, if only he could be got inside. He would create
an entirely new psychology in Russia, America and this country,
and also in Germany, where he would have Hitler guessing.

4 August

Frances telephoned me to say that L.G. had had a very interesting
talk with Sir James Grigg. Grigg had been anxious that L.G. should
join the Government. He had taken the line that we could win the
war if certain things were done, and we had the men who could
do them. L.G. tried to prove that we could not win this war. Therefore there would be no use in his going in. Until there were another
disaster, Winston would not do what he, L.G., wanted Winston to
do. Grigg had pointed out that when that disaster occurred it would
be too late. She said that Grigg had told her: 'I think I am going
away more depressed than when I came.'

8 August

Captain and Mrs Liddell Hart arrived tonight. He has just been
married again. He told me Russia had done better than he expected,
but not so well as he had hoped. Last night Megan and I failed to
get the German wireless news and L.G. was angry. He has now
arranged with Frances to have Miss Russell to take down the
10.30 p.m. German news[12] at Churt and then dictate it to me on
the telephone.

9 August

After a talk with L.G. tonight, Liddell Hart made it plain to me
that he had talked straight to L.G., who had played the part of a

11. Sir James Grigg (1890–1964) was a career civil servant who became
Permanent Under-Secretary of War 1939–42 and then Secretary of State
for War 1942–5 and a National M.P.
12. That is, the English-language news and commentary broadcast
from Germany, to which L.G. regularly listened.

super-pessimist, with which Liddell Hart did not agree. Liddell Hart told me that up to the time the Russians came into the war he had thought that a negotiated peace would be better than a possible defeat. When the Russians had come in, he hoped that they would alter the position in our favour. But he said L.G. had taken an absolutely negative attitude.

9 September

L.G. came up with Frances from Churt for the statement by the P.M. in the House. The P.M. spoke for an hour, then he invited L.G. to lunch with him at 10 Downing Street at 1.30 and L.G. remained there until 4.30. 'He wants me to stay with him on Sunday night at Chequers, when he will have some of his experts present to discuss Russia with me,' L.G. said to me on his return. I thought L.G. looked terribly old today. He has lost all his bloom. When he talks, he repeats himself and hums and haws over the smallest question. As I took him down in the lift on his way to lunch with Winston, Megan asked him what he thought about Russia. His reply was 'Despair'.

Frances told me today on the telephone that L.G. still listened intently to the German wireless news. She told me that the other day she went over with L.G. to see Max,[13] and they almost came to blows. L.G. had said that the Government was not doing anything. Max had said that they were. Max had said that they were all out to win. He said that he had been as much against war as L.G., at one time. But once we were in it, for our own self-preservation, we all ought to be doing our best. Frances told me that L.G. had not agreed with that and had been still on the possibility of a negotiated peace. . . .

11 November

At lunch at the House, Vyvyan Adams[14] told L.G. that he was the greatest man in the world. This caused L.G. to say nothing but create an atmosphere of appreciation by his facial expression and his gestures. Adams asked: 'When you were Prime Minister, had you ever any doubt as to whether you would win the war?' 'No,' replied L.G. 'Once, at one stage only, in March 1918, when Russia had gone out, when the Americans had not come in, when the French had had some hard knocks and we were in retreat.'

Megan showed me her bracelet, given to her by her mother, made with diamonds and sapphires. She said that on the morning of Armistice Day, 11 November, 1918, a parcel had arrived, addressed

13. Beaverbrook.
14. Vyvyan Adams (1900–51). Tory M.P. 1931–45, 1947–50.

to Dame Margaret. Inside was this lovely bracelet with a note: 'To the Wife of the man who won the War'. There had been no name or address, and to this day they did not know who had sent it.

12 November

L.G. came up from Churt today to listen to the P.M.'s speech. Afterwards he went on a Welsh Parliamentary Party deputation to Arthur Greenwood,[15] on the subject of reconstruction in Wales after the war. At the deputation he pointed out that while Wales had no Secretary of State it had a language of its own and a literature of its own. Scotland had a Secretary of State, its own government, yet it had no language and literature of its own. All it had was an accent.

Lloyd George gives an interview to a prominent American writer. At this stage, of course, the United States was not yet at war, although it was affording considerable assistance to Britain.

26 November

Yesterday Lord Greenwood[16] telephoned me to say that John Gunther,[17] the American writer, was over here; he was a great admirer of L.G. and would like to see him. I telephoned L.G. He did not want to see him at first but agreed to see him this morning at 11.30. I met Mr Gunther in the central lobby. He is a blond man of big stature, with a very pleasing personality. He told me that he owed it to L.G. that he had become a writer. In 1923 he had done a special write-up on L.G. for his paper, the Chicago *Daily News*, and they had been so pleased that they had sent him to Europe to do more work. L.G. said he had been rereading Gunther's sketch of Stalin in his book *Inside Europe*. The mistake we, the British, had made was not to accept that view of Stalin and of Stalin's Russia, but our government had then been reactionary. It had taken the view that Russia was a shambles. Stalin's speeches were always very frank and extremely able – but frank. Stalin was a very remarkable man. We could easily have had Stalin with us in the struggle over

15. Currently Minister without Portfolio and a member of the War Cabinet.
16. The former Hamar Greenwood (1870–1948) who was the last Chief Secretary of Ireland.
17. John Gunther (1901–70). Journalist and best-selling author on current affairs. His most famous book was *Inside Europe* (1936).

Czechoslovakia because he had given his word. We had never called him in. Then L.G. asked Gunther: 'Where does America stand?'

Gunther replied that America stood in very much the same division of spirit as England had five years ago. She could not awaken to the realisation of her own danger. L.G. interpolated that she was 3000 miles away. He said it was very difficult to realise the possibility of the Stuka forces of Hitler crossing the Atlantic and attacking American cities.

Gunther pointed out that that was why the Americans asked why they wanted so many aeroplanes and tanks.[18] Then he added: 'If Hitler won the war, Lindbergh[19] would probably become President of the U.S.A. There would be a moral reaction against Roosevelt.' L.G. said that Roosevelt was not a big enough man. 'I only met him once. He did not strike me as a very brilliant man.' Gunther said that Roosevelt drew the crowds but his influence was diminishing. We were getting closer to war every day.

L.G. asked: 'What about the Middle West?' Gunther replied that it was of no great importance, as it used to be. Isolationism was not geographical. For instance, as a general rule the Roman Catholics were isolationist. So were the extremely rich, partly on account of Russia. On the whole, fascism would protect them against bolshevism. Finally, many American youth, just out of college, were indifferent to this war and were sceptical of it and did not believe in it. They said no war was worth fighting. They were much like our fellows were some years ago at Oxford University.

L.G. said: 'Quite frankly, I think Hitler will win. I do not say that Hitler will be able to invade this country. It is a very difficult channel to cross. Lots of people have tried it, including Napoleon.' L.G. then asked: 'Can you tell me the material factors on our side?' Then, as usual, he answered his own question. 'Take Russia, France and the British Empire, with a very small army, which is gradually growing. All those factors were in favour of time. Italy is against us. Japan, I should say, is probably against us. Now France is semi-hostile. Russia we have got. But then Russia has been so battered in the last few months; 3,600,000 of her soldiers have been taken prisoner. Unless we can count on America coming in, definitely, I do not see how we are going to win. You cannot count on the

18. This refers to Americans who objected to Roosevelt's rearmament programme.

19. Charles Lindbergh (1902–74) won fame 1927 by making the first solo trans-Atlantic flight and was thereafter prominent in the development of United States commercial aviation. In 1940–1 he ran a campaign in favour of American neutrality in the war.

dominions giving full measure; they have drawn the line at conscription. Maisky said the other day: "You must defeat Germany." I cannot see our winning, certainly not unless you, America, come in with conscription. That means an army of millions. I cannot see the United States doing that.' Gunther said: 'Certainly not, for a long time.' L.G. said: 'Two-thirds of the manufacturing resources in Russia have fallen into German hands. It will take years to build up their army.' Gunther said that all this made a very difficult problem for Roosevelt. 'If you tell us you cannot win without us, the people in America will be tempted to say: "We do not want to enter a war that is lost." ' L.G.: 'That is why I have not said it. I have ceased to write. You have to take public opinion into account. I do not see how you have a ghost of a chance. And then America must actually declare war and put herself in a war, just as in 1917.' Gunther: 'This raises a very perplexing problem for statesmanship. If Hitler knocks out Russia, and America does not come in, and Hitler calls for peace, a considerable public could be persuaded to accept a *status quo* peace.'

L.G.: 'You would have Stalin organising Asia, but it would not be effective for about a couple of years. I do not suppose Germany would bother about that. All they want is the Ukraine. I do not know whether they want the Caucasus.' Gunther: 'Have you met Stalin?' L.G.: 'I never met Stalin. I am told he is a very great man. I always used to read his speeches.' Gunther: 'What kind of England do you envisage after the war?' L.G.: 'First of all, it depends what the war will be like.' Gunther: 'Presupposing it is an English victory.' L.G.: 'I think you would have a reaction.' Gunther: 'Don't you think there would be some social revolutionary forces?' L.G.: 'I do not see anybody rising among them. You have no Lenins or Stalins or Trotskys. Do you see any?' Gunther: 'I do not. I feel people, after going through pain and difficulties, will want some reward.' L.G.: 'There will not be unemployment because of our bombed cities. So everybody would have a job. You won't get any millionaires. Whilst you will lower the standard of the upper, I do not think you will lower the standard of the mass of the people.' Gunther: 'You have practically abolished starvation.' L.G.: 'I practically did away with starvation and sickness. As long as you do not lower the standard, I do not see a revolution. The temper is not right.'

Here I was called away. On my return Gunther said to L.G.: 'Would you join this government?' L.G.: 'If Winston had a small war cabinet. I ran my government as a council of war. I had all the experienced men, who gave me ideas which never occurred to me. But, as Beaverbrook said to me, "Winston is strategy of war." It is

no use talking of Dill,[20] or Admiral Pound,[21] or anybody else:
Winston himself decides. That is all very well provided you have a
council which comes to conclusions.'

Gunther: 'At this moment, there is a point in broad strategy
which is vitally important. It is understood that the British offensive
in north Africa may produce a *coup d'état* in French north Africa.
I have talked to several people, but that idea had never occurred
to them'. L.G.: 'Whilst we are fighting in Libya, we will liberate
a desert. The Germans, meanwhile, are acquiring fertile lands,
getting the greatest oilfields in the world. They do not mind our
fighting in the sandhills and the desert. We could be of great help
in the Caucasus.'

Gunther: 'Perhaps Churchill has a broad idea of the war, that if
Hitler takes western Africa America will come into the war.' L.G.:
'If the Caucasus goes, it will be bad.' Gunther: 'Americans react
badly to bad news.' L.G.: 'I think the Caucasus is the crux of the
present situation. If the Germans got the Caucasus, they have got
every conceivable commodity. They are perfectly self-contained and
self-sufficient. They may then declare a peace, not a negotiated
peace. They have never declared a war. They may declare a peace.
Then what would we do?' Gunther: 'I do not know. Do you think
that in the case of such a declared peace England would accept
such a peace, if it were completely impossible to win? What is the
duty of statesmanship in such an event?'

L.G.: 'What could we do? We could bomb their cities in Europe,
but there is a limit to that. The Germans are taking their manufac-
tures farther away from us. They have gigantic manufacturing
centres which would be almost out of reach of our aeroplanes. In
the first place, I would not have gone to war without having Russia
on our side. It was an idiotic thing to do.'

Gunther thanked L.G. for receiving him. He told me, as I saw him
out of the House of Commons, that his talk with L.G. had been the
most interesting he had had during the whole of his time in England.
'He is a wonderful man,' he said.

---

*On 6 December Japan opened a campaign to attack British,
American and Dutch possessions in the Far East and in the following
months achieved considerable successes, including the conquest of
Malaya, Singapore, the Philippines and the Dutch East Indies (now
Indonesia). In sympathy with Japan, Germany and Italy declared
war upon the United States on 11 December. Thus the war became
truly a world war.*

20. Sir John Dill (1881–1944). Chief of the Imperial General Staff.
21. Sir Dudley Pound (1877–1943). First Sea Lord 1939–43.

Chapter 14

'Catch wider visions'

1942

22 January

I talked to Richard Stokes, M.P. On Wednesday last he went to Churt. Mentally, he said, L.G. was as good as ever. But physically, he thought, L.G. would never be fit enough to become head of a government. 'Did he say whether he would serve with Winston?' I asked. 'He said he would not go in with Winston' was the reply. 'Did he say whom he *would* go in with?' I inquired. 'Yes,' said Stokes. 'He said he would serve with Eden as Prime Minister.' I heard from Churt that Stokes stayed during the afternoon and until 6.30 p.m. As a result, L.G. was completely exhausted and, as a consequence, stayed in bed most of the following day.

27 January

L.G. came up from Churt with Frances for the P.M.'s speech which opened a two-day debate on the war situation. When L.G. arrived, he looked very old and grey. His face and neck have shrunken considerably lately.

'What do you think of Russia?' I asked him. 'They are doing wonderfully well' was his reply. Then he made a surprising remark: 'If the Russians beat the Germans, that would mean a Russian peace.' He said nothing more, but it was clear to me from his demeanour that that is not what he wanted to see. I had confirmation of this from Frances. She said that for some reason or another L.G. did not want to see the Russians in a position to dictate at the peace conference.

29 January

Great day today, when Winston asked for his vote of confidence. L.G. did not even come up from Churt. He advised Megan to abstain. It was a good show for Winston, but it did not represent the feeling of the members or their anxiety about the situation in the Far East.[1]

1. Churchill won his vote of confidence by 464 votes to 1. Megan Lloyd George did not vote.

On 15 February the supposedly impregnable fortress of Singapore surrendered, with a garrison of 60,000 troops, to Japanese forces of inferior numbers. This was perhaps the biggest single disaster suffered by Britain in the Second World War.

18 February

L.G. came to town, along with Frances, in order to hear Winston's statement on the appointment of Beaverbrook as the first Minister of Production. Afterwards Gwilym and I lunched with him at the House. L.G. said that Winston was wrong to have concentrated on Libya. Winston had once said that we had three-quarters of a million men on the Nile. Rommel had only 50,000 men. We had known that the Japs were giving close attention to China, Indo-China, Thailand, as well as Burma. Of this we had had ample warning. Yet, as far as L.G. could see, we had made no effective preparations to counter it. We should have concentrated in the Far East in preference to Libya.

15 February

On Friday night, I sent down to L.G. at Churt a memorandum warning him that Winston was in a sulky, defiant mood, and that he had discussed the possibility of a general election, even during the war. This could be carried out, so he had been told, by means of food ration cards or identity cards. (I know this to be true because Sir Henry Fildes told me that Hutch – General Lord Hutchison[2] – had spent an hour with the P.M. when the question was discussed.) I added that alternative names to Winston were being discussed, including Eden, John Anderson, Stafford Cripps and L.G. Then I said in my memo : 'Has not the time arrived when you should come forth and give a lead to the nation? You have given this government and Winston their chance. You are entitled to say so : you are fully entitled to say what you think ought to be done at once to stop the rot and save the State.'

17 February

L.G., Megan, Gwilym and I lunched at the House. Lord Hutchison came to talk to L.G. during lunch. 'You have to come into this government,' he said, 'otherwise we shall lose this war. Do you

2. Robert Hutchison (1873–1950) was a regular officer who was Director of Organisation at the War Office 1917–19 and then entered Liberal politics, becoming friendly with Lloyd George. He was an M.P. 1922–3 and 1924–32, and Chief Whip 1926–30. He followed the Liberal Nationals in 1931, becoming their treasurer, and was made a peer in 1932.

remember how we fought for Amiens and the Channel ports in the last war?' 'Yes,' replied L.G., 'and we not only fought, but held them *both*. But these fellows have lost Singapore.' Hutch repeated: 'You *must* come in.' L.G. replied: 'It is no use as long as Winston is in the mood not to reorganise his cabinet completely.'

18 February

Last night Eden was very persuasive with L.G. and wanted him to go to see Winston on his own initiative. This morning Frances informed me that L.G. had decided not to see Winston. He thought that Winston himself might go out. In any case, L.G. did not think he could take the initiative in trying to see Winston.

5 March

The other day I sent privately to Frances details of the procedure of a marriage in a Baptist chapel. L.G. and she are to be married – some time. He does not know that I have supplied the information. She said he had talked about the possibility of resigning his seat in the House. If he does not intend to do anything, perhaps that would be best. He might take a peerage. She said that L.G. would make provision for me; he had actually discussed this with her. Meantime, she said, he was again talking about a negotiated peace and the possibility of his being asked to form a government for that purpose.

4 March

Hankey phoned me this afternoon. He said he was resigning and that he would like L.G. to know. He said he had been on the brink of doing this for some time, but had not done so because he had not wanted to embarrass the P.M. when he was in a difficult position. When the P.M. had asked him to place his office at his disposal, Hankey had readily done so. But when he had been invited to continue to work in connection with radio-location [radar], which was very important, he had declined and had explained that he was dissatisfied with the management of affairs and he welcomed an opportunity of getting out.[3]

26 March

William Jones, who is in charge of the Ty Newydd farm,[4] and his wife, have been to Churt recently and returned to Criccieth with

3. Hankey, as Paymaster-General, was chairman of several War Cabinet committees. He published no resignation letter but on 26 March, in the Lords, he advocated a reconstruction of cabinet machinery.
4. Lloyd George's farm at Llanystumdwy, which he had bought in 1940.

instructions to get the place ready for Easter, as L.G. is going to stay there with someone else. These instructions have been spread around the town. If L.G. takes Frances and Jennifer to Ty Newydd, there will be an unholy row. Megan will regard it as an insult to the memory of her mother, and Megan tells me that even Gwilym would not tolerate that. But, happily, the place is not ready, so he cannot go. The situation is not an easy one for me personally. I have to make sure that I do not find myself between two fires – yet that is a position in which I daily live. . . .

L.G., Megan and I went to tea in the cafeteria in the House. Lord Davies,[5] Seymour Cocks[6] and Professor Balogh[7] came to talk. L.G. said he would send a big force to France, something like 1,000,000 men. That would compel Hitler to bring back 2,000,000 men from the Russian front, thus enabling the Russians to break through. L.G. said that, unless we made a great effort in 1942, there might not be a 1943 at all. Hitler was out to gamble; so must we.

6 May

Frances telephoned me and asked me to commit an indiscretion. Would I let it be known to Megan that the thing is contemplated (the marriage of L.G. to Frances). 'I think L.G. is frightened of Megan and her reactions,' said Frances. 'But I do not see how she could quarrel about it. I do not think she would like it, but I do not think she would break off relations.' She asked me to let it be known to Megan that no date had been fixed but that inquiries had been made about a licence and that sort of thing. 'He is so frightened of saying anything to her himself. I think I am justified in taking things into my own hands. Everyone in the neighbourhood is expecting it.' I acted immediately. I told Miss Smithers and Miss Brady what was in the air and asked the latter to tell Lady Carey Evans, but not to say where the information had come from.

7 May

Megan told me it had come to her knowledge that her father was thinking of being married and was going to live at Ty Newydd. Nancy Astor had even asked her in open committee if it were true. Then one day whilst she was at Criccieth a wagon had arrived, full of furniture for Ty Newydd. On another occasion, Clough Williams-

5. David, Baron Davies of Llandinam (1880–1944), was a Liberal M.P. 1906–22, Parliamentary Private Secretary to Lloyd George 1916–17, and received his peerage 1932.
6. F. Seymour Cocks (1882–1953). Labour M.P. 1929–53.
7. Thomas Balogh (b.1905), the economist.

Ellis[8] had shown her a plan of the reconditioned house and the various rooms. Was it any wonder, she asked me, that she was ill. She then told me that she had arranged to see Lord Dawson tomorrow. She was going to tell him what was on her mind. She intended to try to persuade him to have a talk with her father.

9 *June*
I have seen L.G. in many a wangle, but never one like this. He is playing a very deep game between Megan and Frances. One of them must be disappointed one day.

Lloyd George's last appearance at the Castle Street flower service.

28 *June*
Evelyn, Alice[9] and I went to the Castle Street flower service tonight, over which L.G. presided. On Friday I received a telephone message that at all costs I had to obtain a book on the life of William Carey.[10] I sent it down by Megan, who went to Churt on Friday night. This is the third time only she has been down since the death of her mother.

L.G.'s utterance was decidedly that of an old man. Most of his address was in Welsh. He started in a whisper. That is in accordance with the old Welsh preachers' habit to get people to listen. I think it is an insult to an intelligent audience.

He wound up in English, saying: 'Another world war has passed over us since the Napoleonic wars. That is not a generation ago, and now we are in the third. Are we at its beginning, or in its middle, or is it coming to an end? God alone knows, but we can only hope for the best and strive our best, and see that at any rate this strife shall not be in vain. There is one sentence of the great immortal missionary sermon of William Carey: ' "Get up," God said. "Find larger canvas, stouter and taller poles, stronger tent pegs. Catch wider visions: dare bolder programmes. Dwell in an ampler world." '

On 1 and 2 July the Commons debated a censure motion on the Government. This was the lowest point in the parliamentary fortunes

8. Clough Williams-Ellis (b.1883), the architect and town planning consultant. He acted for Lloyd George in redesigning Ty Newydd and he also designed Lloyd George's tomb at Llanystumdwy.
9. Miss Alice Parkes, a friend of the Sylvester family.
10. William Carey (1761–1834). A founder of the Baptist Missionary Society and a missionary in India from 1793.

of the Churchill government during the war in Europe. The fall of
Singapore had been followed by the loss of Tobruk in north Africa,
a strongpoint of considerable symbolic importance to the British.
Dissatisfaction was more widespread than was reflected in the vote
at the end of the debate, which was 475 for the Government and
25 against.

1 July

I spoke to L.G. on the telephone at 10.15 p.m. He was just about to
go to bed in his deep air-raid shelter, which he still patronises. I told
him that the Government had had a bad day in the House. He was
obviously pleased. 'Are you coming tomorrow?' I asked. 'I am just
wondering,' he replied. 'Because Winston is last speaker, I should
have ostentatiously to walk out of the House. I shall not vote for
the Government and I shall not vote for the motion either.' I said:
'You can abstain.' He said: 'Yes, but it is abstaining in the presence
of the whole House.'

14 July

Secret debate in the House. L.G. lunched with Winston. They went
to see the damage to the old chamber. After the session, L.G.
returned to his room. To give an impression of wonderful fitness,
L.G. deliberately walked at a hell of a rate down the corridor, that
all men and women might see his seemingly superb health and
vigour. When he reached the staircase, no lift for him; he bounded
upstairs two steps at a time. But once inside his room what a
miserable picture he made.

Frances told me today that, on his own initiative, L.G. had told
her that he meant to marry her. She wore a new ring made of a
big single diamond on her engagement finger.

1 October

L.G. came up from Churt. I am told by Miss Russell that last night,
whilst Hitler was on the wireless, L.G. paced from one room to
another listening to his speech, although he could not understand
a single word, because it was in German. L.G. was very het up and
excited. Hitler said: 'Stalingrad will be taken. You may be sure of
that.'

Gwilym opened the debate on coal and did exceedingly well. He
was very confident in his manner and made a good impression on
the House. At two o'clock, whilst L.G., Megan and I were at lunch,
Gwilym joined us. L.G. said to him: 'However worried you were, it
was nothing like what I felt.' I must say that L.G. looked the part,

too, as he sat on the front opposition-bench. With his eyes and mouth open, he was terribly het up all the time Gwilym was speaking. During the whole of the lunch an endless number of M.P.s came up to congratulate L.G. on Gwilym's speech and saying that he must feel a proud father. L.G. seemed really pleased.

23 October

Frances told me, referring to her marrying L.G.: 'He wants to wait two years, for the sake of appearances. After that I do not think L.G. will bother about Megan.'

17 November

Frances told me that L.G. has decided to ask Lord Dawson to see Megan and put it to her that his marrying Frances is necessary on medical grounds. He hoped to lunch with Dawson on Friday. Frances asked me to see Dawson and put the position to him and try to induce him to function. 'The trouble,' said Frances, 'is that L.G. is not quite frank.'

19 November

Today I talked to Lord Dawson during tea at the House of Lords. I told him what L.G. wanted to talk to him about. Lord Dawson was very pleased that I had given him a warning. I told him something that I have told no one, except Carey Evans: that L.G.'s bowels are peculiar. He has to take enough medicine to stock a chemist's shop to get any bowel movement; then he cannot hold it. But if he does not take all this dope, he gets something comparable to a stoppage and has to have an enema. Lord Dawson was immensely interested in this and thought there might be a growth. He would work round this point with L.G. and try to get him to have an X-ray. I said that would frighten him.

He thought that if L.G.'s health were in doubt that would strengthen the case for the marriage. He thought that Frances had a case and that she would marry him even on L.G.'s death bed. He asked me if Frances knew that there would be unfavourable reactions around Criccieth. I said she did. He thought Megan might just break off entirely from her father.

23 November

Late last night, Frances telephoned me at home. She was perturbed. She said L.G. had had a talk with Gwilym about his proposed marriage. L.G. had told Frances that Gwilym had not been very favourable. Gwilym had said that it would not be popular with the people of Criccieth and that Megan would not accept it either.

Frances told me that L.G. had said to her that the present circumstances were all right. They suited him all right, why alter
them? Frances told me she had reminded him of the chances she
had had to be married, which she had given up. 'That is all done
with,' L.G. had replied. 'Honourable people think you should do
it,' Frances had said. 'There are no honourable people,' L.G. had
said.

I said it looked to me as if L.G. were trying to get out of it; at
any rate, he had a game on. Frances agreed. She asked me to make
inquiries about ways and means, which I promised to do.

This morning, therefore, I went to the Faculty and to the Caxton
Hall Registry Office. I established that the £25 special licence, under
the law of the Church of England, was entirely different to the civil
law, observed by the registry office. Sent a memo to Frances.

25 November

L.G. attended a meeting of the Welsh Religious Advisory Committee
in his room at the House of Commons. He had told me that he
thought it would be over in half an hour. He kept them two hours.
He is making much of very little these days. I think he wants to
keep in the good books of the clergy, prior to his marriage with
Frances.

Prior to this committee meeting he lunched in the old strangers'
room in the House. Megan, Hore-Belisha and I joined him. L.G.
agreed with Hore-Belisha that Greece had been our cardinal error
in this war. He said that he had told Winston at the time to
persuade the Greeks to withdraw their 150,000 men from Albania
and come south. As it was, the Germans had come right round
behind them and cut them off. But what interested him most, he
said, was the Russian offensive. It looked as if Stalin had a gigantic
secret army. The loss of 15,000 men was nothing to Stalin. The
Russians could cut off the Germans in the Caucasus; it would be
a great stroke. He did not think they could get back the Ukraine.
In answer to Hore-Belisha, L.G. said he thought fighting would be
more bitter the nearer the Germans retreated to their old lines, and
certainly as they got nearer to Germany.

There was talk about moral right in war. L.G. said there was no
such thing. One thing only counted in war, and that was to keep
up the enthusiasm of your own side.

30 November

Tonight Frances phoned me after ten o'clock. She had told L.G.
that it was very humiliating for her to have to go out when Megan
came. She said L.G. had been awfully sweet but was concerned to

get over this weekend. She said John Morris, the solicitor, had told her that the line she ought to take was that her position was quite intolerable. She should go away and let L.G. make up his mind. 'I cannot take action,' said Frances. 'L.G. is an old man. I do not like to bring pressure on him.'

3 December

Today Megan had an interview with Lord Dawson, though nobody is supposed to know. The idea was that Lord Dawson was to communicate to her her father's intention to marry Frances.

Frances phoned me from Churt late tonight. She rang off quickly because there was an air-raid warning and she feared L.G. might come into her bedroom.

11 December

Frances telephoned me tonight after 10 p.m. She had had an interview with Lord Dawson this afternoon at 3 p.m. She said he had been very nice and kind. He had seen Megan again and he told Frances that she is irreconcilable. He said he had thought after his first interview he might be able to do something, but he now realised that nothing he said made any difference. She just went round and round and came back to this one thing – *her mother*.

Dawson had said that apart from Megan there was no reason why it should not go forward. There would be some criticism, including the reopening of the criticism of the treatment of the 'old girl'. But for the people who would criticise him there would be another lot who would say he was doing the right thing. Gwilym would not stand in the way.

Frances said you cannot talk to Megan like a normal being. She did not understand. She was not a normal woman. She had this mixture of sex and religion which created the most extraordinary obsession in her.

18 December

I met Lord Dawson at Sir Henry Fildes's flat at 3.15 p.m. by arrangement. Lord Dawson made it clear to me that L.G. would have to be prepared for possible hostility from Megan. Probably Gwilym would be all right. There would be criticism from people in north Wales, where they had loved Dame Margaret during her life and whose memory was sacred to them. He had promised to help by taking soundings. Lord Dawson said he had seen Megan, whose attitude was irreconcilably opposed to the idea: it would sully her mother's memory. If the event took place, it would mean a definite break between Megan and her father. Lord Dawson said he had seen

Gwilym, whose attitude was that his father was at liberty to do whatever he desired; provided nothing happened that was detrimental to the memory of his mother, he offered no opposition.

Lord Dawson said he had had a very frank talk with Miss Stevenson and the impression he had got had been a very favourable one. She was an extremely well-preserved woman, who would be acceptable in any place or circumstance. He had been astonished to find that she had been with L.G. for thirty years. That was a long time. He said he had learned that the question of L.G. marrying her had cropped up over and over again, and it had always been understood, even in Dame Margaret's lifetime, that if anything happened to his wife L.G. would marry Miss Stevenson. She had had a number of offers of marriage, all of which she had turned down because of her association with L.G. What she wanted was the name.

16 December

Frances phoned me tonight. She said L.G. was coming up tomorrow and lunching with the young lady [Megan]. He intended telling Megan that she could go to Churt, but that Frances would be there. After lunch he was going to have it out with her. He was going to give her a fat cheque for the orchard as a sort of bribe. I think there will be fireworks. I told Frances that I had reason to believe that her interview with Dawson had created a favourable impression. She asked if Jennifer had been mentioned. I said she had been, and that I understood there was no difficulty, as her status was not to be affected. Frances said that L.G. was devoted to Jennifer.

17 December

L.G. came up from Churt alone, Frances having come up earlier by train to meet Jennifer, who came home from school for the Christmas vacation.

There was a remarkable scene in the House today. The Foreign Secretary, Eden, in reply to Silverman,[11] Labour M.P. who is a Jew, made an important declaration, issued simultaneously in Washington and Moscow, protesting most strongly against the German slaughter of Jews in the occupied territories in Europe, and particularly in Poland. Jimmy de Rothschild, who is also a Jew, then rose to speak. Disregarding all the rules of procedure and, in a voice that was full of emotion, he made a speech thanking the Foreign Secretary. During the whole of this time, the House was as silent as the grave. The atmosphere was extraordinary. Although every word uttered by de Rothschild was out of order, not even the

11. Sydney Silverman (1895–1968), Labour M.P. 1935–68.

Speaker stopped him. Then a Labour M.P., Cluse,[12] interpolated a question: 'Is it possible, in your judgement, Mr Speaker, for Members of this House to rise in their places and stand in silence in support of this protest against disgusting barbarism?' Mr Speaker: 'That should be a spontaneous act by the House as a whole.' Members of the House then stood in silence.

At lunch I asked L.G. if he had ever seen anything similar to it. 'Never, in my experience,' he replied. He gave Megan lots of ideas for her broadcast on Saturday night, obviously wanting to humour her and make her feel how helpful he is. He said today's incident in the House was the most important thing that had happened in the whole week's business. Speaking of de Rothschild's speech, L.G. said it was really an intonement, such as you get in a synagogue.

L.G. ate a hearty meal of steak-and-kidney pudding, apple tart, cigar and coffee. Meantime, Sir Edward Grigg[13] talked to L.G. There was talk about the coloured population. A problem was quickly arising in those places where the Americans had ninety-nine-year leases for military purposes. L.G. spoke of the enormous number of half-castes and thought the future might lie with them. They were extremely intelligent. He cited the case of Manley, a lawyer in Jamaica, whom L.G. had been told was the equal of Simon.[14] We would have to face that question. 'Our friend Smuts has not quite done that in Africa,' he said.

25 December

Evelyn, Maureen and I spent a very peaceful Christmas and appreciated every moment. We are thankful for many blessings. After three and a half years of war, we still had our turkey, and we all took part in preparing and cooking and eating it. L.G. is at Churt. We sent him a Christmas card, but from him we have not even had his good wishes.

12. W. S. Cluse (1875–1955), Labour M.P. 1923–31, 1935–50.

13. Edward Grigg (1879–1955) was a private secretary to Lloyd George 1921–2, Liberal M.P. 1922–5, Governor of Kenya 1925–31, Tory M.P. 1933–45 and held various ministerial offices during the Second World War, after which he was created Lord Altrincham.

14. See above, p. 168.

Chapter 15

'We have hardly tackled Germany at all'

1943

12 January

Arrangements have been made for a number of distinguished writers to interview L.G. on his eightieth birthday. These include Hannen Swaffer,[1] of the *Daily Herald*, Boardman[2] of the *Manchester Guardian*, Beverley Baxter, M.P.,[3] and a number of photographers and film people. On L.G.'s instructions, they have all been informed that they are not to question him on his views on the war and that he will only talk about his farm and the last war. That is the definite condition on which he is seeing them.

15 January

Hannen Swaffer's interview appears in the *Daily Herald* today. It deals with pre-war days and other things. He ends up by saying: 'As to the war itself, his views on that are only for the private ears of his friends. Although over the conflict he has never been an optimist, he retains his faith in the British peoples and their mission. "We are an island race which in the past has done so much," he said. "Safe from invasion, in which I never believed, not even in 1940, we can yet give a lead to the world."'

Yesterday Lady Carey Evans phoned me for advice about going to Churt. I said that nothing and no one ought to stop her and Megan going to Churt on Sunday and greeting their father on his eightieth birthday, whether Frances Stevenson were there or not. If he should die in his sleep on Sunday night, and they had not been to see him, how great would be their remorse. Olwen later spoke to Lord Dawson, who gave similar advice.

1. Hannen Swaffer (1879–1962), one of the best-known journalists of his day.
2. Harry Boardman (1886–1958), the gifted *Manchester Guardian* writer.
3. Beverley Baxter (1891–1964) held various editorial positions on Beaverbrook's newspapers 1920–33. Tory M.P. 1935–64.

16 January

I sent Bartling to Farnham today by train with a silver tankard. On one side it contained an inscription: 'To the Rt Hon. D. Lloyd George, O.M., M.P., as a token of esteem and respect on the occasion of his 80th birthday, January 17, 1943.' On the other side were the autographed signatures of the following:

F. L. Stevenson

R. Bartling	Ann Parry
Eileen Brady	Audrey Pitt
M. D. Dann	Winifred Russell
Paula Holcke	F. E. Smithers

A. J. Sylvester[4]

(It was a most attractive and artistic tankard and, as L.G. said later, 'It has a handle I can get a grip on.')

Bartling took down about £15 worth of spring flowers to decorate L.G.'s rooms, which I had purchased for him. They contained yellow narcissi and anemones.

Boardman's interview appears in today's *Manchester Guardian*. He quotes L.G. as saying: 'Here we are in the fourth year of war and we have hardly tackled our main enemy, Germany, at all. In the fourth year of the last war we had been hammering her through three years, from 1914 to 1917, with the whole of our strength.'

17 January

I telephoned L.G. at Churt early this morning to greet him, on behalf of my family and myself, on his eightieth birthday. I said it was wonderful that he had been through so much and yet had lived to eighty and was still sound in eye, wind and limb. He said he was very pleased that I was to be present at the parliamentary luncheon on Tuesday next.

Everybody had been most generous to L.G. From the King and Queen, Queen Mary, the Prime Minister and Mrs Churchill, members of the War Cabinet and the Press, down to the humblest citizen, L.G. has received messages of congratulations. As previously

4. The signatures on the tankard were of the remaining members of L.G.'s staff. Robert Bartling was the highly efficient messenger; he later joined the staff of the House of Commons. Miss Brady and Miss Russell were shorthand typists. Miss Dann looked after the accounts. Miss Smithers was my private secretary. Miss Parry (see above, p. 26) was L.G.'s Welsh secretary. Miss Pitt was in charge of the L.G. Political Fund, and Miss Holcke was in charge of L.G.'s press-clippings collection. F. L. Stevenson was, of course, Miss Frances Stevenson and she was still, technically, a salaried secretary of L.G. A.J.S.

arranged, Megan, Sir Thomas and Lady Carey Evans and Bengy⁵ went to Churt for lunch today. It was on the strict understanding that Frances, also, would be present. Gwilym, Edna and their son William were already there.

19 January

When L.G. arrived [at the office], he surprised us by cordially shaking hands with Miss Smithers, Miss Brady, Bartling and myself and thanking us for the tankard, which he said he much liked.

The House reassembled after the Christmas recess. I had just heard that Anthony Eden was going to make a reference to L.G. as Father of the House on the occasion of his eightieth birthday. L.G. at once got panicky and het up and, ignoring my comment that I had warned him yesterday, he made off for the toilet to think out what he would say. Eden made a fine tribute. When L.G. rose to reply, I was very disappointed. His reply was of a very perfunctory nature. He hummed and hawed and repeated himself so much that he might have been 180 instead of 80. I regretted I had not offered him some whiskey beforehand. Frances was not pleased either.

I accompanied him to the luncheon at Brown's Hotel, given by the Parliamentary Liberal Party. L.G. spoke better and freer than I have heard him for a long time. When the carburettor of a motor car has an insufficiency of petrol the engine misses, and that is what happens to L.G. Generally, now, he splutters over some of his words and hums and haws. This time, however, he spoke after whiskey, so his carburettors worked well.

20 January

L.G. asked me yesterday to telephone Mrs Timothy Davies (an old flame) to invite her to lunch at Fortnum & Mason with him today, but she could not come. He said: 'Well, I have asked her.'

Captain E. A. FitzRoy, Speaker of the Commons, was mortally ill and died on 3 March. The name of Gwilym Lloyd George was being canvassed as his successor. Although Gwilym did attract substantial support, in the end D. Clifton Brown, hitherto Deputy Speaker, was elected without formal opposition.

1 March

The Speaker is very ill. Last Friday I went to see Gwilym at the Ministry of Food and ascertained from him that he was definitely

5. Nickname of David, younger son of Sir Thomas and Lady Carey Evans.

interested in the Speakership, and that if it were offered to him he
would certainly take it. I am doing a lot of propaganda on his behalf.

16 March
Belcher called to see me this morning. He is dealing with L.G.'s
income tax. The following are the amounts L.G. made out of articles,
etc. :

1937	£14,800
1938	£3600
1939	£11,500
1940	£7200
1941	£6600
1942	£100

17 March
When L.G. arrived with Frances from Churt, he looked better than
I have seen him for some time. The Welsh parliamentary party presented him with a casket and a cheque for £660 to mark his half-
century as an M.P. The casket has been beautifully carved and is
made out of timber which I had obtained from the old Commons
chamber destroyed by a bomb, the Free Trade Hall, Manchester,
and from L.G.'s farm house at Ty Newyyd, Llanystumdwy. Delegates from both north and south Wales were present. Dr Ivor Davies
presented the cheque and Mr R. T. Jones the casket. In the course
of his reply, L.G. said :
    'I have now been here fifty-three years. I feel I have been here
too long' (cries of 'no') 'and that I am keeping younger and more
energetic men from undertaking the tasks which fell to me earlier
on. But I am still hopeful that I may be able to contribute something to the settlement. If I do not contribute to the victory, I may
contribute to the settlement after the victory, which will require a
good deal of thought, a good deal of reflection and an uncommon
amount of wisdom. Otherwise, this second war may end in a greater
catastrophe than the first. We should benefit by the mistakes that
ensued after the First World War, both here at home and in the
settlement of the world. I hope I may be able to make some contribution in that respect.'. . .

18 March
Frances telephoned a message from L.G. at eleven o'clock saying that
he wanted me to put out a statement that he had a chill and on
medical advice would be confined to his room for several days. He
had no chill at all. He felt that it would be funny if he attended the
Speaker's funeral service this afternoon and was not present at the

election of the new Speaker tomorrow. She told me that L.G. was 'bitterly disappointed' at Gwilym not getting the Speakership.

22 April

Yesterday Mr J. E. Morris informed me that he had just discovered that L.G. had been paying Schedule A income tax on Victoria Road, and not deducting it from the rent paid to the Prudential; £600 or £700 has been paid to the Prudential in excess. That is how our ragtime organisation works.

He talked about the Fund. When anything happened to L.G., there might be difficulties. Some time ago he had heard there was £30,000 left (but I know there is over £75,000). There were certain shares, which had appreciated in value. He had hoped that by the time L.G. died the whole Fund would have disappeared, but he did not think that it would. All his papers had been blitzed. He said that Gwilym was in a very vulnerable position as a minister. Questions might be asked publicly as to what had happened to the Fund. Mr Morris said he had tackled L.G. about all this recently. L.G. had said that Wilfrid Greene,[6] before he had been made Master of the Rolls, had advised him that he had complete control of this Fund and that nobody could say a word about it. 'He seems to think that that is a complete answer,' said Mr Morris. I said that Wilfrid Greene was not an income-tax authority. L.G. had also been advised by counsel that, on the death of St Davids and Sir John Davies, their executors would be justified in making the funds standing in their names over to Gwilym.

4 May

L.G. met Eden at the Speaker's staircase, made some complimentary remark about Stalin, criticised the Poles and then, putting his hand on Eden's shoulder, he said : 'But they are all a lot of buggers.' I do not think Eden knew quite how to take it. Irish whiskey was responsible for this remark.

18 May

Last night I telephoned L.G. informing him that Attlee was today moving a resolution of high appreciation of the services of all ranks in the triumphant conclusion of the north African operations, and that this would be followed by speeches in support by Arthur Greenwood, Percy Harris and others. I said that, as Father of the House, it was important that he should also speak on this occasion.

6. Wilfrid Greene (1883–1952) became a K.C. 1922, was a Lord Justice of Appeal 1935–7, Master of the Rolls 1937–49, a Lord of Appeal in Ordinary 1949–50.

When he arrived this morning with Frances, I asked him whether he was going to speak. 'No' was his very emphatic reply, which came with almost a snarl from his lips and certainly a scowl from his face. His face was grey and wicked.

Yesterday I phoned to Churt to inform L.G. of the secret thanksgiving service at St Paul's Cathedral and asked whether he would be present, because they wanted to give him an honoured position as Father of the House. 'Certainly not' was the reply I received. 'They are making far too much of this. I should not have thought it necessary to have a resolution *and* a thanksgiving service. After all, we had nothing like that in the last war, not even after the battle of the Marne.'. . .

23 May

Carey Evans has been to Churt. He phoned me tonight. He said: 'I cannot get on with that old bugger. He is not my cup of tea. He is not a man's man, you know. What a ménage it is there. It makes me sick. I do not like his appearance at all. He rests a devil of a lot and does not get up until ten. He sleeps in the afternoon and goes to bed immediately after dinner.'

Later in the conversation, Carey Evans said: 'You cannot imagine such a being. He is the greatest power in this realm. Nobody could have created such a being. He is quite unique. We cannot judge him from normal standards. At one moment L.G. talked that he would resign, and another moment that he would go into the Lords. I think the Almighty will decide for him. That is my opinion, and that not very long ahead. He has got some heart trouble. When he gets very excited, he gets pale with strain.'

8 June

L.G. came up from Churt with Frances to hear the P.M.'s statement in the House on his return from north Africa and the U.S.A. After his statement, Winston crossed the floor of the House and greeted L.G. They walked out together. L.G. made some observation, which I did not catch, in reply to which Winston said: 'Well, that is a matter for the Americans.' At lunch L.G. explained that he had remarked to Winston that he wished he had said something about the Chinese and the Japs. The quotation above was Winston's reply. L.G. now remarked: 'That shows how he was beaten in America. It is not very satisfactory.' L.G. said he had noticed a difference in Winston's eyes. 'Do you think they were a little bulging?' I asked. 'Ah,' said L.G., 'the light has gone out of them.' Welsh imagination. . . .

At lunch, Lady Astor had a table next to ours. Talking of Win-

ston's statement, she said : 'Isn't Winston enjoying this war? I don't
know what he will do without it.'

24 September

I reported to L.G. that, in deference to Winston's wishes, private
talk had taken place between Archie Sinclair and Ernest Brown as to
the possibility of the reunion of the Liberal Party. There have been
a number of talks, with little result. I said much stronger cement
would be required to stick them together.

21 October

Reported to L.G. that in regard to Liberal reunion the attitude of
the Ernest Brown group was to put the whole question into cold
storage to see what arises at the general election, when it comes.
Sir Thomas Carey Evans told me that Olwen had been to Churt on
Monday. L.G. had told her that he intended to marry Frances, probably on Saturday. She had told Megan, who was terribly upset.
Carey's own attitude and that of Olwen was that it was a matter
for L.G. himself to decide.

22 October

Ann Parry phoned saying L.G. would be glad if I would go to Churt
and stay the night. I took down masses of flowers, which I had
ordered from Mosey Stevens, and left them in the registry office at
Guildford, at the same time satisfying myself that all arrangements
were satisfactory for tomorrow's ceremony, not a word about which
has leaked out.

When I arrived just before dark, L.G. greeted me warmly, saying :
'Frances has told you why I asked you to come tonight?' 'Yes,' said
I (though this could be taken to mean anything or nothing. L.G. is
always clever, for no subject was mentioned, certainly no mention
of the wedding.)

'Do you think that the Russians will be able to drive the Germans
to the Russian boundaries this winter?' he asked.

'I think so' was my reply. He then handed me a typed report of
tonight's German wireless news, which claimed that the Germans
had brought down 196 Russian aeroplanes on the Eastern Front. This,
he said, showed that the Germans were putting up a great fight. He
thought the reason why the Germans were sending so few aeroplanes
to attack this country was because they were mostly on the Russian
front. Later, he said it was strange that Hitler, who had done so
well at first, should have fallen into exactly the same mistake as
Napoleon when he had invaded Russia.

'I am sure we are adopting the go-slow policy in Italy,' he said.

'The Germans have only six divisions there, and they are holding us up. What has happened to the First Army? With the Americans, we must have millions of men available. There must be a million in the Middle East. What are we doing with them? Nothing, as far as I can see. All this at a time when Stalin is putting masses of men and material into the fight. Stalin told Winston that he (Winston) was afraid of losing British soldiers.' Here L.G. gave me a very old-fashioned look and nodded his head, as much as to say: 'Yes, he did.'. . .

After supper, we were all enjoying a general conversation about politicians and Parliament when a message was received from Megan, who wanted to speak to her father on the telephone. She threatened that if he did not come to the telephone she would come down to Churt tomorrow. He disappeared and was away for so long that Frances went to see if he was all right. Presently she returned to say that she was certain Megan would make her father ill. Would I go to help him.

When I reached the new drawing-room, I found him somewhat upset and exhausted. I heard him say: 'But Gwilym and Edna agree and Olwen agrees.'. . . 'Well, my dear, that shows you are thoroughly selfish.' That was the last word he spoke to her, because I tapped him on the shoulder and he handed me the telephone. I wanted to save him the pain and strain of having to round off the conversation. Megan was crying on the telephone and saying excitedly: 'It is an anticlimax to a great career.' Then I told her who was speaking. 'A.J.', she said, 'did father hear what I said?' My reply was: 'Yes, he heard.' She continued: 'People will laugh at him. I could not bear people to laugh at him, because it would be terrible.' She continued to sob. 'He says he will see me next week, but does not realise that he won't.' 'I will see that he does' was my reply. 'I have made up my mind', she cried, 'that he won't because I could not do it. He must do this knowing what he is doing. It would be terrible if he did it and then realised his mistake afterwards. It will absolutely break my heart if he does. He says Gwilym and Edna and Olwen are for it. They are not. I thought it was right to tell him. It is ridiculous.'

I felt sorry for her in many ways, but it is the old, old question. Rightly or wrongly, I did think there might have been a danger of his doing this some time ago without his telling any of them; and that would have been unfair. That did not happen. When I returned to the library, L.G. was a little upset, but presently he got over it completely and was quite composed. That would never have been the case some time ago, which is another proof of his own wishes.

Frances phoned Gwilym and Edna, who said they were coming to

the ceremony tomorrow, and that pleased L.G. They then both
retired to the dug-out.

23 *October*

While I was breakfasting in my room at 8.30, Gwilym phoned
asking me to tell his father that he would come down after the
ceremony. He said that Megan had been on the telephone with him
for a long time last night, and, after all, he had many things to
think of.

When I saw L.G. this morning, I remarked that he looked very
fit and sparkling. 'Yes,' he said, 'I am going to do it; so now you
know what you are down here for.' 'Yes, sir,' I said.

Dyer brought the car round to the front door; he had no idea
what it was for or where it was going. At 11.15 a.m., L.G., Frances,
Muriel⁷ and I left for Guildford.

We entered the Registry Office, which was a bower of flowers,
which L.G. much enjoyed. In this very pleasant room, we sat in
chairs before a large desk, Frances on L.G.'s left, Muriel on Frances's
left and I on L.G.'s right.

Mr Catt, the Registrar, emphasised that though this was not a
religious ceremony it was legally binding on both parties. L.G. then
repeated after the Registrar the oath that he took Frances Louise
Stevenson as his wife. L.G. spoke in very clear and definite tones,
likewise Frances. I produced the ring. L.G. signed the register with a
special pen we had brought. Then Frances, Muriel and I signed. It
was a very happy ceremony. L.G. and Frances expressed the wish
that all flowers should be sent to the local hospital.

And so the deed has been done, after many months of doubt.
Frances had shown me the wedding-ring in a little box some time
ago when she was in the House of Commons.

As we drove back to Bron-y-de, L.G. was immensely happy. We
returned via the Devil's Punchbowl. The autumn tints of brown and
red on the trees in the great bowl and beyond, and the rolling hills
up to the Hog's Back looked wonderful. And the sun shone through
a rather angry sky. It was a picture representative of L.G.'s life.
We called at the farm office, where L.G. informed Withers, the
manager.

Miss Parry and Miss Russell had decorated Bron-y-de with the
choicest flowers. It was a great show. L.G. had a pleasant surprise
to find Jennifer waiting for him. We tapped a bottle of champagne
and drank the health of the bride and groom.

The *Sunday Dispatch* was the first to ask if it were true. When

7. Miss Muriel Stevenson, sister of Miss Frances Stevenson.

I gave out a notice to the Press Association, the News Editor was so flabbergasted he asked me to repeat it. Frances practised her signature: 'Frances Lloyd George'. I spent the following hours dealing with the Press, sometimes answering as 'the Butler', as I then did not have to know too much.

I waited until the arrival of Gwilym and Edna. Gwilym said that Megan was much upset and he had had a very bad time with her. Then we went downstairs to tea. I noticed particularly that Gwilym merely shook hands with his father and did not congratulate him. They are a funny family.

When I left, L.G. gave me a box of apples, which is the first he has given me for many years.

24 October
Splendid press for L.G. and Frances on their wedding.

25 October
Further good press for the wedding.

Carey told me that, as a result of him and Olwen talking to Megan, the wedding was a closed door, and that she was going to stand on her own feet. I personally never thought she would do anything silly, such as doing away with herself, as she has sometimes indicated.

I feel that L.G. is an exceedingly lucky man. The gods are certainly with him to a most remarkable degree. In somewhat similar circumstances as Edward VIII was dethroned, L.G. is elevated. He has lived a life of duplicity. He has got clean away with it. . . .

11 November
Foreign Secretary Eden made a statement in the House on the Moscow conference. L.G. and Frances attended for the first time since marriage. I was very much concerned about getting her a ticket at such short notice, but the Deputy Sergeant of Arms (Kingdom) was extremely kind and gave her one in Mrs Speaker's gallery. 'What gallery is it for?' L.G. asked me, when he arrived. 'Mrs Speaker's,' I answered, and he beamed with evident satisfaction. During Eden's speech, L.G. sat in his place on the front opposition-bench and often beamed up to his newly wedded wife, seated in the gallery right in the front.

Megan was speaking at Cambridge. When I told him this last night on the phone that she would not be in the House, it was clear that it brought him relief. He last saw her some time before the wedding. She has not spoken to him since it.

L.G. said to Eden, as they walked out of the chamber together: 'A very good speech, considering you said nothing about Poland.'

As he walked down the corridor, he said to me: 'We went to war over Poland, and yet he said nothing about Poland.'...

1 *December*

Mosley debate. I phoned L.G. that the division showed 372 for the Government and 62 against. I received a message from L.G. by telephone this morning. He wanted to know when Herbert Morrison was to speak, when the vote was going to be taken and whether there was likely to be a close vote, because if it were likely to be against the Government he would like to come up to support Herbert Morrison.[8]

8. Herbert Morrison, Home Secretary, had released Sir Oswald Mosley from detention under the defence regulations on the ground that continued imprisonment would injure his health. This was being challenged in the Commons.

Chapter 16

'It will not be for very long'

1944-5

11 January

I attended Mrs Tweed's funeral at Golders Green crematorium: the most pitiful service I ever attended – only three present, including myself.

12 January

L.G. came up from Churt alone. I talked to him in his room in the House about the Russian–Polish situation.[1] I asked him what he thought of it. He replied: 'I am with Stalin in this. The policy of the Poles has been *this*', and he demonstrated with his hands grabbing in the air. 'Pilsudski started it. Under the Treaty of Riga all this territory was conceded to the Poles, and the Russians mean to have it back. I am damned glad. I said at the time that this would result in another war, and it has.'

L.G. said we not only ought to have captured the Balkans but we ought by now to have had Italy up to the Brenner. 'They have just been dawdling,' said L.G.

'Do you think they have done it deliberately?' I inquired.

'Certainly,' he replied. 'Just to put off starting the second front. They want the Russians to do all the fighting; then we shall come smashing in (he demonstrated with his arms) at the last moment to give the effect we have done it all.' L.G. said that Stalin was 'head and shoulders above the others'. He said: 'Here is Roosevelt with his ten million men, but what has he done with them? He is not even fighting the Japs as he ought.'

I then accompanied him to the Foreign Office to lunch with Eden in his private flat. I returned at 2.45 p.m. to fetch him. As he took my arm and descended the long staircase, he was trembling like an aspen leaf. Now and then he gave a vigorous pull at the stub of his cigar. In the car he burst out: 'My God, I gave it to them. They won't ask me again.'

1. This refers to the dispute between the Polish government-in-exile in London and Russia over the section of 1921–39 Poland, in the east, which the Russians had occupied in 1939. The Russians refused to restore it but Poland was compensated with German territory.

'How did Eden take it?' I asked. L.G. replied: 'He said he was
very much obliged to me. I told him that Winston was afraid of
having a second front.'[2]

17 January

L.G. is eighty-one today. Many messages of congratulation. Early
this morning I got a tip that Winston was back and was likely to
make a dramatic entrance to the chamber. I flashed this to L.G. at
Churt, but L.G. did not come.[3]

19 January

L.G. will not even look at the telegrams sent him on his birthday,
even the selected ones.

Amidst all his preoccupations, Winston sent L.G. a telegram
immediately on his return home, as follows: 'Many, many happy
returns of the day. I am so sorry I am a day late, but I only returned
yesterday. Winston.' L.G. did reply to this, as follows: 'It was
delightful of you to remember my birthday. Welcome back to these
shores. Had I known of your return I would have been in the House
to greet you. Lloyd George.'

20 January

Last night Megan informed me that she had been invited by the
Ministry of Information to go to America to address a convention
of women's clubs. I advised her to accept.

This morning she ostensibly discussed this again with me, in the
House. Presently, she said she would like me to tell her father of
this, because of his advanced age. Then she opened up the question
of their relations. 'I want to make one thing quite clear,' she said –
then, speaking with great vehemence, 'I will never have anything to
do with *her*. I made up my mind twenty years ago and I will never
change. Tell him that I cannot be bought.' She said there was unmistakable feeling in Wales against his marriage. In unmistakable
language, she dealt with this at length, and she said that in 1931
and 1935 it had been her mother who had won the elections in the
Caernarvon Boroughs.

2. An Anglo-American force eventually landed in France to start a
'second front' in June 1944.

3. Churchill had been away from London for two months, first at the
Tehran conference with Roosevelt and Stalin November–December 1943.
On his way home he had succumbed to pneumonia and he went to
Morocco to convalesce. He took M.P.s by surprise by appearing in the
Commons on 18 January.

I suggested it would really be better if she saw her father and discussed these points with him, but she did not wish to do this.

Yesterday I sent L.G. a memo saying that Megan's election to the chair of the Welsh parliamentary party would be quite formal, and that it would come only at the end of the meeting. This has been done deliberately to prevent her having to preside over this first meeting with her father present. They have not seen or spoken to each other since the marriage, and only a more or less formal letter has passed between them.

I knew L.G. would be wound up when he arrived at the House. I told him exactly what had happened between Megan and me and gave him her message. His lips curled and like a flash he fastened on to the phrase: 'I cannot be bought.' He and Frances had picnicked on the road to avoid having lunch in the House. He did not want to run into Megan.

I accompanied him to the meeting and then left. Afterwards he said it had gone off all right and he had congratulated Megan on taking the chair. I know it was a strain for him. They had discussed the Welsh burial grounds and the creation of a Secretary of State for Wales. . . .

21 January
Frances told me on the phone that L.G. had written to his brother, William George, in his own hand, saying that they were going to Ty Newydd in April or May. That is most significant, and especially as he wrote in his own handwriting. These days he won't even endorse a cheque.

Frances said that Megan thought that people down there were all on her side. Frances said: 'They are not.' They had had many very nice letters from people in Criccieth, including from David Williams, the Baptist. The head of the Women's Land Army wanted to entertain them when they went down. Frances said that L.G. thought of taking Jennifer with them in May but she (Frances) thought that would be a very great mistake on their first visit. . . .

1 February
Frances told me yesterday that she would like Dawson one day to drop in at Churt and see the Chief. L.G. was all right now, but he had been upset by Megan when he went to that Welsh party meeting and had suffered an emotional strain. She thought he wanted a little tonic. I saw Lord Dawson by appointment at the Athenaeum Club today at 2.15 p.m. and told him this. He said he would be glad to go to Churt. He was very interested to hear that the marriage

was turning out so well and that L.G. was happier. He thought
Frances had behaved altogether admirably.

9 February

L.G. sent a letter to Lord Winterton,[4] chairman of the select committee on the rebuilding of the House of Commons.[5] In it he said
that the new chamber ought not to conform to the old plan. There
had been accommodation for only about 400 out of 600 members.
Whenever there had been a big parliamentary occasion, there had
been members for whom there was no room. This had been un-
justifiable. Every member was entitled to a seat. He also thought the
shape of the old chamber was not suitable for the group system
which had recently developed and was rapidly growing. He said the
Germans had given us an opportunity to reconsider the shape and
convenience of the chamber and we should not be rushed into a
repetition of the old chamber.

1 March

L.G. came up, accompanied by Miss Parry. He arrived in the House
alone, having picnicked on the way up. It was a cold day. Damn
silly I call it. He says it is because the food in the House is not worth
eating. The real reason is because he funks meeting Megan. He
never takes Frances to feed in the House, in the strangers' room.
(On reflection, I think he might have taken Frances once or twice
at most in my experience; but not since his wedding, certainly.)

I talked to Sir Henry Fildes this morning. He was annoyed to
think I have to spend so much time and effort on L.G.'s family
quarrels. He told me that when Winston went to inspect bomb
damage at a block of flats in Chelsea and showed the 'V' sign,
saying it was like old times, he was booed.[6]

22 March

I received a letter asking whether L.G. would send a message for
the commencement of the campaign 'Salute the Soldier'. I got L.G.'s
answer: 'No.'

4. Edward Turnour, 6th Earl Winterton (1883–1962). Tory M.P.
1904–51 (his peerage was an Irish one, enabling him to be elected to the
Commons) and successor to Lloyd George as 'Father' of the Commons.

5. The House of Commons debating-chamber had been destroyed in an
air-raid, and the House had met subsequently in Church House, Westminster, and in the Lord's chamber. Rebuilding was completed in 1950,
with the new chamber based on almost precisely the same lines as the
old. Churchill was a warm advocate of this.

6. There had been a relatively light recurrence of German bombing
on London. Later in the year came the flying bombs and rockets.

2 May

L.G. and Frances came up, accompanied by Miss Parry. All had crowded into Frances's Sunbeam car, the Austin 18 having taken Jennifer, with her special bed,[7] to school at Oxford.

After the meeting of the Welsh parliamentary party, at which they discussed the points they would put to Lord Woolton regarding the Welsh Development Report, L.G. came to his room with Megan and Clem Davies. I think it is most generous of Frances that she never intrudes.

Frances told me that L.G. had nicely mentioned me in his will and that she therefore did not want to talk to him again about later provision for me. It had now been formally established that everyone who left had one month's salary for every year served. This had been confirmed in her own case on marriage. I hinted that I had interests in agriculture. She suggested that I might like to farm and hinted that £7000 would be sufficient capital.[8]

24 May

L.G. came up from Churt with Frances to hear the P.M.'s opening speech in the two-day debate on foreign affairs. When he arrived, L.G. looked like death warmed up. I have never seen him such a bad colour.

Frances went to the ladies' gallery, and L.G. and I went into the House, I to my seat under the gallery. L.G. was obviously nervous about his corner seat on the opposition front-bench, which is always crowded on these big occasions. I suggested that he should walk straight down and they would soon make room for him; and they did. As he walked down the floor, the whole House applauded him. That gave me entire satisfaction. Winston spoke for one and a half hours. L.G. sat with his mouth wide open at times, listening to the speech and occasionally looking up to Frances.

Afterwards, L.G. walked out of the chamber with Megan towards his room. She looked awful in a new black dress which did not suit her. She told him she had low blood pressure. He told her that Dawson had seen him and suggested he should have a change. He intended going to Ty Newydd, in which case he would call on her at Brynawelon. She said nothing – obviously she did not like it.

Behind the Speaker's chair, Winston and Harvie-Watt[9] overtook

7. Jennifer had a bad back, necessitating a special bed. A.J.S.
8. Frances Stevenson did, in fact, receive one month's salary for every year she had worked for L.G., on her marriage to him. I received this later, too, but nothing came of the idea of giving me £7000 as farming capital. I received £1000 from L.G.'s will. A.J.S.
9. G. Harvie-Watt (b.1903) was a Tory M.P. 1931–5 and 1937–9, and Churchill's Parliamentary Private Secretary 1941–5.

them. L.G. remarked that he had cancelled going to Wales because he had wanted to be present to hear the P.M.'s speech. They stood for some minutes, talking of communists and kings. Winston laughingly said that he would by choice sooner deal with kings. Then they talked of the position in Italy. L.G. said he did not understand it. At this point, Megan suddenly flounced off, saying, 'I should think you do not understand.' Then Frances arrived. Megan had spotted her coming. Winston received Frances graciously.

L.G. became very acrimonious by asking Winston why he had not started the second front yet. Winston had not yet answered L.G. when, very cleverly, Frances turned the conversation to another subject by congratulating Winston on his speech.

1 June

Tom Carey Evans lunched with me at the Reform. I told him about L.G.'s looseness of the bowels. He thought that L.G. must have a cancerous growth. He did not think it would last long. It would not be surprising if he suddenly passed off. He must have a terrific constitution and be a man of enormous creative power. He said he preferred to view L.G. through a telescope rather than a microscope.

Lord Davies is very seriously ill. His friends estimate that he has given two millions in money to benevolent causes in Wales, including a mobile X-ray unit. The story goes that Lord Davies was the first to be examined by his own apparatus. It was discovered that he had a malignant growth – cancer of the lung. L.G. was asked by the London editor of the *Western Mail* for a message for this dying peer. L.G. refused. They have been estranged for years. David Davies said he had told L.G. that the nearest way between two points was the straight one.

On 6 June the Anglo-American landings began in France. On 4 June the Allies had entered Rome.

6 June

Winston made a statement in the House. Questions were over earlier than had been expected, and the Speaker suggested that the House should wait for a few minutes until the P.M. arrived. Then the P.M. made a statement about our capturing Rome and that we had made a landing on the European continent. L.G. was present to hear Winston make his statement. What had determined him to come up was to hear the statement about the second front, because

Frances told me last night that he did not intend to come up to hear the one about Rome. . . .

Evelyn and I dined with Sir Henry Fildes at 2 Whitehall Court. He thought I should remain on with L.G. until he passed on, then I should have strong claims on grounds of loyalty.

25 June

I took Evelyn to Churt, where she had been invited by L.G. and Frances to stay for a rest.[10] They were both most kind. We picked cherries with Gwilym.

9 July

I went to Churt to see Evelyn. Talked with L.G. He looked very old. He is a pathetic figure. 'No use my coming up to the House,' he said. 'Certainly not,' I replied.

The other day there was a bomb dropped four miles away when he was shaving. He went half-shaved as quickly as possible to the air-raid shelter. It is caving in in places. The wood is rotting and the mice are eating his precious records, which I know so well and have cared for for so long. I made many, many of them. As I walked about the farm, I could not help thinking what might become of it when he passed on. Clearly, he has no grip on that huge undertaking. Everybody is quarrelling with everybody else on the place.

23 July

Maureen[11] and I went to Churt. We took L.G. a bottle of whiskey. I walked alone along a path and found L.G. and Frances sitting under a tree like a pair of turtle doves. He wore his Tyrolean cape and had his stick; she had a pile of dandelions for the rabbits. He asked what I thought of Evelyn now, and agreed that she looked much better. He talked of the attempt on Hitler's life[12] and agreed that it was the first definite crack in the German armour. We talked about the possibility of Hitler and others escaping by aeroplane, perhaps to the Argentine.

9 August

I went to Churt to fetch Evelyn home. I talked to L.G., who was sitting in his library. Frances sat in the large window, accompanied by Valerie and her baby. The white-and-black cat lay sprawled on

10. My wife had been unwell, largely as the result of bombing around and on our home in Putney. A.J.S
11. Daughter of Sylvester.
12. On 20 July.

the floor. L.G. gets visibly more tottering, but looks better and may live to be ninety, for he is marvellously looked after by Frances.

I gave him a memo which indicated that there were those in responsible positions who thought that the war might be over in two or three weeks and that Parliament would be recalled. I expressed the belief that they were altogether too optimistic. L.G.'s face lit up as I talked thus. L.G. agreed that Hitler had strengthened his position by his recent purge. He pointed out that we were nowhere near Paris yet, let alone on German soil. In 1918 our troops had actually been far beyond Paris. He said Hitler had never had his generals with him. 'Neither had I,' he added.

He then prepared for his evening walk. As he stood outside, I mentioned the possibility of a general election. He said he would have to make up his mind whether he would stand again. If there were to be another Tory parliament, well he did not know. He agreed with me that it would be a big decision.

24 *August*
Bells of St Paul's and Westminster Abbey ring joy-bells at the capture of Paris.

Lloyd George with Frances left Churt for Ty Newydd on 19 September for what was originally planned as a short visit. In fact, he never returned.

19 *September*
Evelyn and I left Paddington at 9.10 a.m. and had a most tedious journey to Criccieth. Captain Williams, who has been very ill, welcomed us at the Lion. So did Sir Thomas Carey Evans, who was in hiding to give us a surprise. (He is staying with Megan and did not want to advertise the fact that he had seen us.)

L.G. motored from Churt to Llanystumdwy today. This is the first time he has stayed at Ty Newydd, the small farm I was commissioned to buy for him in 1940. He has not been to north Wales for several years. He always used to stay at Brynawelon, one and a half miles away from Ty Newydd. Brynawelon was bequeathed to Megan by Dame Margaret. Now L.G. is nervous about his reception by the rest of the family.

21 *September*
Sir Thomas Carey Evans and I went to Ty Newydd. L.G. came to see us in his pyjamas and dressing-gown. He is just a shrunken old man,

looking very delicate and feeble. He said he wanted to see Megan.
He said he would either go to her at Brynawelon or, if she preferred,
he would send the car to fetch her to Ty Newydd. I telephoned at
once.

Megan was acid. 'I shall be delighted to see him, but he must come
alone,' she said. It was arranged that L.G. should go to Brynawelon.
He asked me to accompany him. He rang the bell and Megan came
dancing to see him. They were alone for some time. Then I helped
her find some whiskey, and presently they were arm in arm, walking around the garden.

In the meanwhile I had been talking to Sarah in the kitchen. She
was cutting up runner beans when Megan called her to see L.G.
'I will not go,' she said, putting down her knife. 'He stopped my
money.'[13] I advised her to go. She did not move. Later I repeated the
advice, saying that it would be difficult for Megan to receive her
father and she, Sarah, not to. She went. They shook hands. 'How
many years have you been with us?' L.G. asked. 'Forty-four,' replied
Sarah. There was a short talk in Welsh. She told me afterwards that
he had looked so different that she could not be other than civil.

In the course of a discussion Sir Thomas made a remark to me.
He said that he would not be surprised if L.G.'s instinct had not led
him to his old home to die, like an old dog returns to his lair.

British air army holds at Arnhem. Americans capture biggest
flying-bomb base near Luxembourg – 500 a day. Boulogne is in our
hands. British patrols on Reich soil.

22 *September*

I accompanied L.G. and Frances to Colwyn Bay. After lunch, L.G.
went to the conference on post-war development and I accompanied
him. L.G. spoke and did quite well. He suggested that a committee
of industrialists should be set up, which was adopted.

I had done my best to persuade him not to go to this conference.
I had thought it would be too much for him.

Here is an extract from the shorthand note I made of what L.G.
said at the conference.

'I came to the conference to listen and not to make recommendations. I was in the Great War, and I had the dealing with the situation immediately after the war was over. What happened to us then
is a lesson to us now. When we came to the end of 1918, it was the
first experience of the greatest war that this country had ever
endured. Therefore it was quite impossible to reckon the immediate

13. On Dame Margaret's death, Lloyd George stopped the allowance
he had made for Brynawelon.

consequences. For the first two years, there was plenty of employment. There were plenty of orders and there were plenty of exports, and it looked as if all would be well, and that gradually we would get back to our old position. Then the ice cracked and we fell into it. For fifteen years we had unemployment, and that was the position when this great war came.'

The following is a summary of matter related in considerable detail in the diary.

With the end of the war now in sight, there would obviously soon be a general election. (The existing parliament had sat since 1935.) The question therefore arose of whether Lloyd George would again contest Caernarvon Boroughs. His constituency-party chairman, E. P. Evans, informed Sylvester that he would support Lloyd George for as long as he chose to stand. However, as a result of the war, and the arrival of evacuated civil servants, there had been a substantial change in the nature of the electorate. If Lloyd George did stand, there was a possibility of his being defeated, the more especially as he was unfit to conduct any kind of campaign. This would have been a terrible end to his political career. Yet he wanted to retain a public platform as he believed he had a contribution to make to the peace conference, which he obviously envisaged happening on the same kind of lines as in Paris in 1919. Accordingly Sylvester went to London to smell out the reactions of the national Tory and Labour parties to the idea of Lloyd George being allowed an uncontested return. He had a sympathetic reception but was told that it was a matter for the local parties in the constituency. Neither of the local parties were prepared to co-operate. Accordingly Lloyd George accepted his earldom, which would give him a platform in the Lords. The question then arose of who should succeed him in the Boroughs. There was a distinct body of opinion in the Liberal association, including that of E. P. Evans, that it should be Sylvester, who had become well known in the locality for carrying out most of Lloyd George's work on behalf of constituents with individual problems and grievances, particularly during the war. The Lloyd George family itself favoured David Lloyd George (now the second Viscount Tenby), son of Gwilym Lloyd George. Sylvester refused to compete with David Lloyd George but, after the latter had fallen out of the race, did try for the nomination. His disability was that he was not a Welshman (although he did offer to learn Welsh) and, by a majority, the constituency association chose J. Seaborne Davies, a Reader in Law at London University. To complete the story, Davies won the by-election, in April 1945, but under the

conditions of the wartime electoral truce had no Tory or Labour
opposition and his only rival was a Welsh Nationalist. In the
general election of July 1945 Tory, Liberal and Labour were neck
and neck, with the Tory winning by a narrow margin. Caernarvon
Boroughs disappeared as a constituency in the redistribution of seats
of 1948.

1 October (Sunday)
L.G., despite his cold, and Frances went to his old chapel, Berea,
at Criccieth.

2 October
L.G. sits for hours and says nothing.

7 October
I gave L.G. a report on the very bad condition of the Ty Newydd
orchards. The crop was very poor, also the quality – more fit for
pigs than for humans. A few years ago I should have expected him
to have skinned somebody. Today he said nothing.

13 October
. . . Tonight a children's concert was organised in the village hall to
welcome Mr and Mrs Lloyd George to Llanystumdwy. It was well
done. The rector and schoolmaster were active in its organisation.
  L.G., replying, said : 'Every credit is due to Mr Pritchard for the
way in which he has trained the children. It was really a first-class
performance. I am not very much in favour of children's concerts and
singing, and I do not like it on the broadcast. But tonight I enjoyed
every item of singing. It has been a great gift of kindness to my wife
and myself that you should have given this concert to us. I hope to
dwell amongst you as long as providence permits me. I mean to
make my home at Llanystumdwy, which is always dear to me. I
came here after sixty-five years. I could not find much change,
because you had the river, the same old river, the same old floods.
I come down after rain in the night, and I say there will be a flood
in the river, and so there will be. The river makes the village. It
gives character to it. It gives its meaning to it, and I am delighted
to come to its sound once more. I thank the rector for the trouble
he must have taken to organise this concert in the course of a week.'

15 October
When I was alone with L.G. in the downstairs drawing-room I
said : 'When I go back to London, I am going to try to arrange a

walkover for you in the Caernarvon Boroughs.' I told him that I had friends in all parties and I thought I had a fine case.

He was sitting in one of his favourite places, on the settee, and he looked out over Cardigan Bay. He listened attentively and quietly and then said, rather pathetically : 'You can tell them it will not be for very long.'

22 October (Sunday)

L.G. and Frances have been going the round of the chapels. Today they went to Sion, to hear the Rev. W. R. Jones. This was Dame Margaret's chapel. There was criticism that Frances sat in Dame Margaret's seat. Not in years at Churt has he attended his chapel, only in Wales. They are obviously buying themselves in. This chapel has just received a donation of £20 towards some district fund.

23 October

Today is the first anniversary of L.G.'s wedding to Frances. We have bought large quantities of flowers, so that their upstairs drawing-room is a bower of flowers. As usual, we assembled there today at 12.45 p.m., after they had had their walk, and drank their health in whiskey. He sits in his winged chair with his feet up and gazes through the bow window out to sea, or across to the Merionethshire mountains, or towards Criccieth Castle. Often he will take out his binoculars, which were found in the H.Q. of the German Crown Prince in the last war, and look across to Harlech Castle. He talks very little these days, and sits for hours saying not a word. He never says a word about the war, and if he refers to politics it is in criticism of Winston, if not directly, then indirectly.

30 October

I came to Llanystumdwy originally for a fortnight, accompanied by my wife. I have now been here for five and a half weeks. It is getting very cold, and my wife and I are walking about in our very thin summer clothes. Besides, every week I stay here, I am living on capital.

Yesterday I intimated to L.G. that I was thinking of returning to London. Today Frances told me that L.G. was displeased because I was thinking of going back, and wanted me to stay. She appealed to me to stand loyally by him. She thought it would be to my advantage to do so. She wondered whether it was not my duty. I thought it was high time to give my views, which I did in no uncertain voice. I told her that I had willingly come up here to suit L.G.'s convenience to help him over the difficult first visit, but he had not been straightforward. He was now trying to twist me into staying here permanently. And for what? To run a thirty-seven acre farm.

Was I, I asked, to give up my contacts and my parliamentary and political position. No, I could not do so. If L.G. wanted me to stay permanently with him in Wales, why did he not be straightforward and say so. I was not going to allow myself to tricked into it. As to my loyalty and my duty, hell, my intimate friends had been telling me for years that I had been a damned fool to stand so closely by a man whose attitude to the war was doubtful and who had long since shown that he was ga-ga and politically finished.

Later there was another talk and I reiterated the above points. He could sack me if he liked. I would not stay in Wales. I offered a compromise, however. I would do a shuttle service between Llanystumdwy and London. Finally, this is what was agreed to. Frances assured me that things would be all right for me later.[14]

17 *November*
During my visit to London, I took careful soundings of friends of mine in the Conservative and Labour parties. I had a most sympathetic reception, with an unofficial promise that everything would be done to give L.G. a walkover in his constituency at the next general election. But as power was vested in the local associations no absolute guarantee could be given. I knew I could go no further. I know also that the opposition parties in the Caernarvon Boroughs have no intention of giving L.G. a walkover.

My next commission was to make a move in the most diplomatic manner somehow to bring to the notice of the Prime Minister that L.G. might be even willing to consider an earldom. It had to be a very delicate approach. Knowing the close personal relationship between Archie Sinclair and Winston, the Prime Minister, and that Archie was the leader of the Liberal Party, I visited his private office in Whitehall, where he is Secretary of State for Air. I was met by Mr Maudling,[15] his private secretary, and ushered into the room of the Secretary of State. Archie gave me a very warm and sympathetic hearing when I discussed with him the possibility of an earldom being offered to L.G. by the King, for political and health reasons. I explained that although there was no certainty that L.G. would accept it would in any case be a gracious act and would give him immense pleasure. Archie promised to speak to Winston. I reported fully to L.G. by memorandum and telephone.

14. She did nothing to keep this promise! A.J.S.
15. Reginald Maudling (b.1917), who later became a leading Tory M.P.

24 *November*
My birthday, God help me.

28 *November*
Frances phoned from Llanystumdwy, saying: 'I think that thing
would be accepted if offered.' (She meant the earldom.) But, she
said, 'Lady' must not be asked. I said I had already warned against
this. (By 'Lady' she meant Megan.)

12 *December*
At 10.15 a.m. L.G. entered the library at Ty Newydd, where I was
waiting for him. He does not walk now; it is a shuffle, and I noticed
that his limbs are wasting fast. It is a sad picture. He took up his
weekly return of sales of produce from Churt and casually looked
through them.

15 *December*
Frances told me that L.G. had written to Winston suggesting that in
view of my long services he should consider me for the honour of
knighthood. He has said not a word to me and I am supposed to
know nothing about it.[16]

18 *December*
A telegram arrived this morning, as follows: 'The Rt Hon. D.
Lloyd George, Ty Newydd. Marine courier arriving Criccieth station,
6.54 this evening with urgent message from the Prime Minister.
Could messenger be met at station. Secretary to the Prime Minister.'
   I met Marine Davidson and took him to Ty Newydd. L.G. was
sitting on the settee in the library, before a huge log-fire, dressed
in a Welsh grey tweed suit, and wore soft leather boots, lined with
lamb's wool. Frances accompanied him. 'Here is the courier,' I said.
The letter, addressed to L.G. with the Prime Minister's name in the
bottom left-hand corner, was handed to him by Marine Davidson.
L.G. opened it. I watched his face. The contents seemed to give him
pleasure. He said not a word, but his eyes showed that he was
reading it again. Then he handed it to Frances, with the remark:
'That is very nice.' Then, after a pause and addressing Davidson,
he said: 'The Prime Minister wants an answer by wire. Will it do
if I send it in the morning?' Davidson said he did not know anything about it. I said: 'I would sleep on it, if I were you.'
   Marine Davidson and I left and I took him to the Lion Hotel,
where I had reserved accommodation for him. There we had dinner
together and talked about Winston and No. 10.

   16. This was the last request L.G. ever made of Winston Churchill
and there was no reply to it. A.J.S.

19 December

Miss Parry showed me a telegram she was sending off from Llanystumdwy to the Prime Minister, in Frances's handwriting: 'Prime Minister, 10 Downing Street, London. Gratefully accept. Lloyd George.' ...

Evelyn and I had tea with Sir Goronwy and Lady Owen in their kitchen (she had no maid). When I gave them the news that L.G. had decided not to stand again,[17] they were both very upset, so much so that Gladwyn cried and completely forgot the mince pies which were in the oven to warm. They were baked up to a cinder. ...

Whilst I was at Ty Newydd this morning, I got in a private word with Frances. I said that I was delighted both for L.G.'s sake and for hers. She said she had made it clear to L.G. that *he* must decide, and that if he refused she would be perfectly happy. I said that our plan had worked very successfully. 'You have done it,' she said. 'It was your conception and my execution,' I said. 'You must have presented a very good case,' she said. 'You have been a very good friend to me and so has Evelyn.'

I asked her what title L.G. would take, and wondered whether it would be Lord Dwyfor – that had been Evelyn's suggestion, not mine. Frances said they had talked of that and had chosen 'Lloyd George of Dwyfor.' I did not care much for the sound of it but they wanted to preserve the name. L.G.'s whole world has shrunken. He has become inward, as Lord Dawson once predicted to me that he would. His thoughts are confined to Ty Newydd and to himself. He raps out his instructions about things of little importance, but with an air of authority as if he were still Prime Minister. Poor old fellow.

31 December

Jack Broadbent phoned me after lunch. He had an advance copy of the New Year Honours List and said that L.G. was in as an earl. I phoned Frances and confirmed with her the title L.G. proposed to take: The Earl Lloyd George of Dwyfor. I spent the rest of the day on the telephone with the Press, mostly over the spelling of Dwyfor.

1945

10 January

Early in January, a letter was received from the Garter King of Arms regarding the titles L.G. wished to take. L.G. said he was very

17. I did not mention the earldom. A.J.S.

anxious to preserve his own name and asked me to reply to the effect that he was putting the matter entirely in the hands of his private secretary, but first of all he had to consult his elder son, who was ill. As soon as he had done this, another letter would be sent. L.G. then said to me: 'You had better see Dick. Point out to him that Caernarvon is divided into three districts, Arfon, Lleyn and Eifionedd or Eifion. And I suggest that he should take the title Eifion. Other names have been mentioned, such as Ednyfed, but they are not suitable.'[18]

Today, accompanied by my wife, in a blinding snowstorm and driving a very indifferent hired car with defective lighting – the only vehicle available in the district – I set off over the mountains to the sanatorium at Denbigh.

Dick and I have been very good friends throughout many difficult L.G. family circumstances. Despite the fact that he has now had two deflated lungs, he was gay and cheerful and full of fun and humour. We had a most enjoyable and instructive time, for Dick is a most interesting personality.

Dick wished me to emphasise that he was entirely in the hands of his father, and said: 'If he wants me to call myself "Viscount Anything", I shall not mind.' He thought, however, that Gwynedd was a better name than Eifion. He gave good arguments. As Member for the Caernarvon Boroughs, his father had represented Arfon, Lleyn and Eifion. But Gwynedd was the old province of North Wales. Eifion was simply a small strip between Portmadoc and Pwllheli, and Criccieth was the only part of the constituency actually in Eifion. This left out places like Conway, Bangor, Caernarvon, Deganwy, Pwllheli and Nevin, which were all in Gwynedd, and all of which had played a very important part in L.G.'s political career.

L.G.'s bardic name was Llwyd O'Wynedd, which meant Lloyd of Gwynedd. The title of Gwynedd would please the Gorsedd of the Eisteddfod tremendously. It was a title full of meaning, because centuries ago Owen Gwynedd was a prince of Wales whose castle was at Deganwy in L.G.'s constituency. Dame Margaret's father, old Richard Owen, had been very proud that he had been descended from Owen Gwynedd. It was for that reason that he, Dick, had named his own son Owen.

Another reason, perhaps a minor one, was that an Englishman would insist on pronouncing Eifion with an *f* sound, and he disliked that intensely.

18. There had to be a title for Richard Lloyd George as eldest son of an earl.

I was very pleased with my talk with Dick, which was most informative, but very sad because of his condition and position.[19]

11 January

I told L.G. of my visit to Dick yesterday and handed him my report. He gave it to Frances and she read it aloud to him. I could see from his face that he had turned awkward, for he said : 'So Dick disagrees with Eifion.' It was quite clear that L.G. was not at all inclined to agree.

Later, Lady Carey Evans and Megan arrived. I had previously seen both, and fully informed them of Dick's view, with which they agreed. By arrangement with them I got them to raise the question of the title with L.G., saying that it was a much nicer name. L.G. then agreed . . . .

17 January

L.G.'s eighty-second birthday. I shook hands with him and congratulated him on behalf of Evelyn and myself. Gwilym and Megan telephoned from London this morning to congratulate him. As L.G. was going out with Frances, Robin and Bengy[20] arrived with a brass sundial from Olwen and a Welsh jug from Megan as birthday presents. Robin pinned a red carnation in L.G.'s lapel and handed L.G. a bundle of forced rhubarb, which he likes. He was in a good mood today. When I suggested that it was time I went to London about the procedure concerning his earldom, he indicated assent by not dissenting.

18 January

I have been searching for evidence which would show that L.G.'s surname is Lloyd George and not George. I went to see Pritchard the schoolmaster, but his evidence was the wrong way. I talked with David Williams, who showed me the registers of the baptisms of the little old chapel, Pen-y-Maes, Criccieth. There it is recorded 'David Lloyd-George, February 7, 1875'. It is recorded in Uncle Lloyd's own handwriting. L.G. was baptised by immersion by Uncle Lloyd in the little stream that runs by the chapel when he was twelve years old.

22 January

. . . In company with Windsor Herald, today I had an interview with Garter King of Arms. V-2s were coming over pretty fast but I, too,

19. Dick was in what amounted to a Poor Law institution. A.J.S.
20. Children of Sir Thomas and Lady Carey Evans.

had a rocket to fire. The Garter at once said that he could not accept the title Lloyd George of Dwyfor because his name was George and not Lloyd George, and a birth certificate was produced in proof.

I pointed out that there was such a thing as common usage, and that he was known the world over as Lloyd George. All his children, and his grandchildren, were named Lloyd George. When he received the Order of Merit it was as Lloyd George. When Dame Margaret received the G.B.E., she became Dame Margaret Lloyd George. Then I produced a letter, signed by the secretary of L.G.'s chapel, certifying that on the seventh day of February 1875 he was baptised by immersion by his old uncle at Pen-y-Maes Chapel. In the register, the entry had been recorded by his old uncle, Mr Richard Lloyd, in his own hand and read 'David Lloyd-George', hyphenated.

As, however, the Garter could not agree, I suggested he should place the matter before the Law Officers of the Crown for their opinion. I then pointed out that L.G. was a very difficult man. So far I had not informed him that there was any question about his title; otherwise, I feared he might summon a Press conference and make ridicule of the whole thing. Eventually, it was agreed that, although a *caveat* would be entered, the Garter would submit the title if I would consent to the name of Lloyd George being officially hyphenated. This I agreed to.

By the early part of February, a big change had taken place in L.G.'s condition. On the night of 9 February he had a very bad turn, and Dr Prytherch thought it was the end. But L.G. was to give us many shocks. Next day, after Lord Dawson had been consulted, Dr S. W. Patterson of Ruthin Castle attended him. A.J.S.

21 *February*

A bulletin appeared in the Press, signed by Dr R. Rees Prytherch and Dr S. W. Patterson, saying that the Earl Lloyd-George of Dwyfor was suffering from increasing physical weakness, and this at present must cause some anxiety to his family, his friends and the nation at large.

26 *February*

I typed a letter from Dr Prytherch to Lord Dawson:

Dear Lord Dawson:

   At the end of a heavy day I feel I cannot retire without dropping you a line regarding L.G.'s condition. There is really little to report. He started last Sunday and Monday with 48 hours of intermittent hiccoughing which shook him badly, and as the response to simpler remedies – C.o.2 – was only temporary, I injected morphia on Monday evening. On Tuesday morning, after 13 hours of sleep, he was at his best – better than he had been for many a day. During the remaining days he has had short periods up from two to three hours (when he rallies himself for the occasion). I have never known anyone with such remarkable recuperative powers. He rises to the occasion every time.

I have escorted Megan there twice this week (this still requires patience, diplomacy and time). Each time he has rallied. When I see him in the evenings he has often had difficulty in getting his words out, and at times he cannot do so, with the left-sided weakness becoming more pronounced. Pulse rate varies from 80 to 120; blood pressure systollic between 110 and 220. Though he is aware and worries about any change in the pulse rate or temperature (when he finds out!), he is entirely unaware of the abdominal tumour which any other man would have remarked on. I think he knows the truth, but so far he is unaware or refuses to recognise this condition. When cherry blossom at Churt coming out in a month was mentioned, he shook his head. . . . He is comfortable and placid and extremely well looked after. His wife is doing a grand job of work. She has done so for the last six months, and latterly, with his loss of control, this is no easy task, but she is doing it with all the devotion he deserves, and she is doing it unstintingly and extremely well, and he calls for her constant presence. One cannot say more than that he is one of the best cared for patients I have ever had.

Since the issue of the Bulletin, the Press have been inundating us, and though I told them for their own guidance on Thursday that when immediate danger was apparent I would issue a bulletin with the word 'critical' in, they are still here – about 20 of them. Beyond the bulletin I have said nothing to them, and I would be grateful of your guidance for the future on this point. How much should one eventually put out regarding his true condition and underlying illness? . . .

As to prognosis, I have never known a more difficult one. At one moment he is too weak to talk, and the next he is walking across the room and back, and even jokingly refers to going out. The last three weeks he has weakened considerably, and the last three days his features have shrunk, his nose becomes more prominent and the face more lined, and his appetite is decreasing. When Patterson saw him a fortnight ago he said that he would follow up the case in *The Times*. It may be a week, a month or more. Undoubtedly we are dealing with a remarkable mind, body and constitution – L.G. for

a short time after 1½ hours daily – and a very failing constitution
for the rest of the 24 hours, most of which he spends sleeping.

Yours sincerely,

R. REES PRYTHERCH

The Rt Hon. Viscount Dawson of Penn, G.C.V.O., K.C.B., K.C.M.G.,
149 Harley Street,
London, W.1.

*David Lloyd George died on 26 March 1945, at 8.35 p.m., with his
wife Frances holding his left hand and Megan his right. Also present
were Lady Olwen Carey Evans, Ann Parry, Jennifer, Mrs Bennett,
Sarah Jones, Dr Prytherch, Nurse Thomas and A. J. Sylvester.*

Postscript

I EXPRESS my grateful appreciation for the advice given to me long years ago by my old friends the late Sir Henry Fildes and the late Mr D. P. Oliver, who both urged me to keep a private record of all the daily happenings within my own experience.

I record in the warmest terms my thanks to Mr Colin Cross who, in editing my diaries, has performed a prodigious task. With sound judgement and a rare gift of selection, he has reduced 1,000,000 and many more words to a mere 100,000, the contents of this book, and at the same time preserved the picture throughout.

We started as diarist and editor: we have ended close friends; a rare and delightful partnership.

For the constant advice, help and encouragement given to me over many years by my late devoted wife Evelyn, and for that of my daughter Maureen and son-in-law Alun, I express my warmest thanks and everlasting gratitude and appreciation.

1974   A. J. SYLVESTER

Index

In general, names and titles are given in the form in which they existed at the time the diary was written. A reference in **bold** type indicates a page containing a biographical note.